Papua New Guinea
The Struggle for Development

Since independence, Papua New Guinea has been through a period of great change. In just three recent years, the country went from a phase of oil exploration to becoming a major exporter. At the same time three 'lost' or 'unknown' tribes were (re)discovered. *Papua New Guinea – The Struggle for Development* is the first book to explore the economic development of this socially complex, rapidly changing nation. It seeks to go beyond the dry bones of quantitative changes described in government reports, and to examine the social influences on economic development. Subjects discussed include:

- rapid economic growth and political conflict
- civil war on the island of Bougainville
- population growth and urbanisation
- mining: gold, oil and environmental conflicts
- forestry and sustainable development
- uneven development and social divisions

Carefully researched, this unique and comprehensive study will be invaluable to all students of the Asian or Pacific economies.

John Connell is Associate Professor at the University of Sydney. He has written several books and many journal articles.

The Growth Economies of Asia

Series Editors: David Drakakis-Smith, *University of Liverpool* and Chris Dixon, *Guildhall University*

Each book in this series provides a concise and up-to-date overview of one of the countries in the region. It examines its place in the world economy, its historical development and its resource endowment. The analysis of its growth to date is balanced by an account of its prospects for future development. The relationship between the different sectors of the economy are discussed, as is the role of multinational enterprises, the government and the financial markets.

The interaction of political and social forces and economic growth is given special consideration, and any special features of individual countries are highlighted.

Papua New Guinea

The Struggle for Development

John Connell

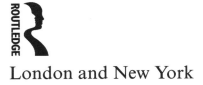

London and New York

First published 1997
by Routledge
11 New Fetter Lane, London EC4P 4EE

Simultaneously published in the USA and Canada
by Routledge
29 West 35th Street, New York, NY 10001

© 1997 John Connell

Typeset in Times by M Rules, London
Printed and bound in Great Britain by
TJ International Ltd., Padstow, Cornwall

British Library Cataloguing in Publication Data
A catalogue record for this book is available from the
British Library

Library of Congress Cataloging in Publication Data
A catalogue record for this book has been requested

ISBN 0–415–05401–X

To Bronte Surf Life Saving Club and the Spinal Unit of Prince Henry Hospital, Little Bay, Sydney, without which this book would never have existed – and for three wise Bougainvilleans, John Sune, Stephen Sukina and the late Anthony Anugu, who taught me more than they know about development in Melanesia.

Contents

Figures

Tables

Notes and abbreviations

The kina (divided into a hundred toea), the monetary unit introduced at independence in 1975, was then on par with the Australian dollar and valued at US$1.25. In 1980 it was valued at US$1.5, but by 1984 had fallen to US$1.1; between 1985 and September 1994, the time period mainly covered by this book, it was more or less on par with the American dollar, but after devaluation and its subsequent floating its value had fallen to US$0.8 at the start of 1996. In 1980 it was valued at A$1.3, but at the start of 1996 it was on par with the Australian dollar.

Words in *Tok Pisin* (Pidgin English or neo-Melanesian) are italicised.

The province and people in the central highlands are referred to as Simbu, but some quotations and references use the older form Chimbu.

ABBREVIATIONS

AFR	*Australian Financial Review*
AIDAB	Australian International Development Assistance Bureau
ANU	Australian National University
ASEAN	Association of South East Asian Nations
BCL	Bougainville Copper Limited
BHP	Broken Hill Proprietary Ltd
BRA	Bougainville Revolutionary Army
CRA	Conzinc Riotinto of Australia
CSIRO	Commonwealth Scientific and Industrial Research Organisation
EU	European Union
EEZ	Exclusive Economic Zone
FIFO	fly in – fly out
FMA	Forestry Management Agreement
GTP	Gogol Timber Project
IASER	Institute of Applied Social and Economic Research
IBRD	International Bank for Reconstruction and Development
IMF	International Monetary Fund
IMR	infant mortality rate
IRDP	integrated rural development project

JICA	Japanese International Cooperation Agency
KKB	Kainantu Komuniti Bisnis
MCH	Mother and Child Health (clinics)
MIM	Mt Isa Mines
MP	Member of Parliament
NCD	National Capital District
NCDS	National Centre for Development Studies
NCDs	non-communicable diseases
NFCAP	National Forestry and Conservation Action Programme
NFE	Non-Formal Education
NGO	non-governmental organisation
NHC	National Housing Commission
NIC	Newly Industrialising Country
NIDA	National Investment and Development Authority
NN	*Niugini Nius*
NPEP	National Public Expenditure Plan
OPM	Organisasi Papua Merdeka
OTML	Ok Tedi Mining Ltd
PC	*Post Courier*
PHC	primary health care
PJV	Porgera Joint Venture
PLA	Panguna Landowners Association
PMV	passenger motor vehicle
PNGDF	Papua New Guinea Defence Force
SMH	*Sydney Morning Herald*
STDs	sexually transmitted diseases
TFAP	Tropical Forest Action Plan
TFR	total fertility rate
TNC	transnational corporation
TPNG	Territory of Papua and New Guinea
TPNG	*Times of Papua New Guinea*
UNDP	United Nations Development Plan
Unitech	University of Technology (Lae)
UP	University Press
UPNG	University of Papua New Guinea

Preface

Our island world ceased to be. The world exploded and our island became a remote outpost . . . the last place in a country which has few centres and much remoteness.

(Caspar Luana, Buka: A Retrospect, *New Guinea*, 1969, p.15)

The principal focus of this book concerns the various facets of Papua New Guinea's social and economic development, in an attempt to develop a 'post-horticultural' geography that does justice to the sweeping changes that have followed the establishment of mining and two decades of independence. In just three years, from 1990 to 1993, the country went from a phase of oil exploration to one of being a major exporter, whilst at least three 'unknown' or 'lost' tribes were (re)discovered. It is a nation of unparalleled diversity, a fact that makes producing an overview of this kind particularly difficult. Moreover this book seeks to go beyond the dry bones of the quantitative changes described in government reports and statistical series, especially since statistical data are sometimes unreliable, are rarely disaggregated to provide indications of regional variation and are all too often simply absent. Social and economic changes are examined together since such 'modern' phenomena as commodity production, voting patterns or urban migration are thoroughly integrated into particular social contexts. It has been specifically intended to provide a qualitative account, partly via the local media and through Melanesian voices, of the perception and flavour of development rather than inevitably, elusive 'reality'. Such a task is fraught with problems. There have been dangers in producing more of a pastiche, than an independent analysis. Relatively few good studies of development issues have been undertaken since the mid-1980s, hence the best of these have probably unduly influenced this book. At almost every point caution is required in interpretation; many statements should include phrases such as 'reasonably typical' and vague adjectives like 'most' and 'many' occur all too frequently. Of course, generalisation could never be more than a flawed undertaking, especially in Papua New Guinea. All attempts to adumbrate a 'typical' Papua New Guinea or the 'essential' Melanesia are doomed to failure. The speed of certain elements of development has posed its own problems.

A number of people have been particularly helpful. Many Papua New Guineans, since my first arrival in the country in 1974, in good time to chart the unfolding of independence, have been invaluable. Many of these have been Bougainvilleans, a fact that may give this book a distinct flavour, and in villages rather than in government offices, where more recent visits have all too often ended up. At the other end of the process has been Alison Kirk at Routledge, whose patience and enthusiasm have been impressive. I have been particularly indebted to a number of people, who have transferred my scrawl – the lingering remnants of a pre-word-processor age – onto screens, disks and pieces of paper, not least Maree Pindar and particularly Sandra Donnelly, and those who have turned my pencilled graffiti into elegant maps, John Roberts and Peter Johnson. Others have been particularly generous with their time, in a university era where time (and money) are exceptionally scarce resources, in reading all or parts of this manuscript. Robert Aldrich, with purple pen, and Rebecca Reeves ploughed through the whole, whilst Bill Standish, John Lodewijks, Neil Maclean and George Curry waded through much of it. Michael Bourke (on Chapters 3 and 4), Glenn Banks (Chapter 6) and Mark Bray (Chapter 9) were particularly helpful. Any remaining defects are all my own.

John Connell
Department of Geography
University of Sydney

1 Introduction

Papua New Guinea in the international economy

> Until very recently indeed, as anthropologist Fredrik Barth has written, a man of the mountains could squat on his verandah, and see smoke rising in the forest three days' walk, 30 miles away, and know that no person he had ever met had visited such a place, or any place beyond it, or knew anything about the people lighting these fires.
>
> (Jackson 1982a:18)

No country in the world offers the stunning diversity and contrasts of Papua New Guinea (PNG), a country typified by the extent of social differentiation across even very small areas, with more than eight hundred languages, some spoken by fewer than a hundred individuals, and by such late and limited contact with global economy and society that cultural distinctions retain extraordinary vitality. PNG consists of the eastern half of the island of New Guinea plus many islands to the east, the largest of which are New Britain, New Ireland and Bougainville, with a total land area of about 465,000 square kilometres and a population of over 4 million. The 'last' parts of PNG were probably not 'contacted' until the 1970s – as the country became independent – in the final flurry of world exploration, yet it has become intrinsically part of a world economy. Whilst conventionally regarded as a South Pacific island state, it dwarfs other island states in every way. It shares a long land border with Indonesia (Irian Jaya), has observer status in the Association of South East Asian Nations (ASEAN) and diplomatic, aid and commercial ties of growing importance with Asia. As Australia's only former colony it maintains a 'special relationship' with its southern neighbour, though this relationship became more difficult and complex in the post-colonial era after 1975.

PNG belatedly and briefly experienced rapid economic growth during the 1990s. The real growth of the nation's gross national product (GNP) in 1993, at 16 per cent, was the highest in the nation's history and one of the highest in the world. This followed the first full year of oil production at the new Kutubu field, the increased value of log exports and slight growth in the agricultural sector; oil and gold dominated exports in a country still widely perceived as characterised by subsistence agriculture. Within PNG the mineral resources

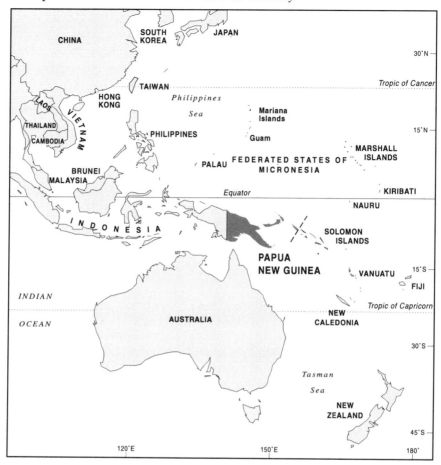

Figure 1.1 The Asia-Pacific region

sector is viewed as the critical engine of growth, and a means of reducing aid dependency. Consequently the agricultural sector has lagged, as the focus of change has moved from distribution to growth.

Global culture and society have arrived. Satellite dishes import Indonesian and Australian television channels; rugby league is the male national sport. Tee-shirts, jeans, sunglasses and digital watches are prominent in the towns, where university graduates distance themselves from rural folk, and are often perceived as *susokmen* (shoe and sock wearers), unlike barefooted or thong-wearing villagers. An elite choose to shield themselves behind the darkened windscreens of air-conditioned cars, sure targets for the gang *raskals* (criminals), envious of such isolation and conspicuous consumption. There is juxtaposition of corporate monoliths and plywood shacks, of affluence and poverty, of modernity and tradition. New lingua francas are crucial, and the principal one, Tok Pisin, accommodates such new constructs as *ekwiti* (equity) and *hansapim* (stick-up), different responses to economic change. In one glossary *sanguma* (sorcery, magic) is neatly juxtaposed with *sekonhan klos* (Tree 1996). On Bougainville, where the army seeks to overcome secessionist rebels, babies have been named Heli and Soe – the first born to a family forcibly relocated by helicopter (part of Australia's military aid), and the second born during a State of Emergency. In the capital, a migrant worker, Pepsi Cola Gabi, was jailed for murder in 1991 whilst in remote parts of the highlands, the last stone tools had only just been produced. A year later the Vanimo district court in West Sepik jailed two men for practising sorcery whilst national politicians began moves to establish the country's first stock-exchange.

Travelogues on PNG continue to emphasise such themes as 'unchanged over time' and 'Stone Age society'. In 1962 a *National Geographic* editorial informed its readers:

> At a time when astronauts have orbited the earth and scientists plan conquests of the planets, one corner of the world still competes with space for men's imagination. . . . Here, on an island flung across the tropical Pacific like a grotesque 1500-mile long bird, are mountain valleys and jungle pockets that await their first explorer. Here live people who never saw a wheel until it dropped to them from the skies on an airplane.

Seven years later, in an article entitled 'Journey into Stone Age New Guinea', the author recorded 'islands of Stone Age life still uneroded by currents of change' (Kirk 1969:568); although that phrase captioned a photograph of a Melanesian wearing shorts, and steel axes and airstrips were discussed, the principal themes were remoteness, traditional medicines and cannibalism. It was just six years before independence. A few years later Carleton Gajdusek received the Nobel Prize for research on the links between virus transmission, cannibalism and a fatal disease (*kuru*) in the Eastern Highlands. In such ways no country has been seen as more exotic: a place of exhibition, curiosity and spectacle, existing in supposed timelessness. The rapidity of change since the early 1970s has shown that there are other very different realities.

A HISTORY OF DIVERSITY

PNG has an extremely lengthy history of human occupancy, following the migration of Melanesians from the west. Radiocarbon dates have established settlement at more than 40,000 years ago. Permanent agriculture and water control techniques in highland valleys date back at least 10,000 years. Large areas of PNG were unknown to the world beyond until well after the Second World War. Not until the 1920s was exploration of the interior combined with the search for gold; in the 1930s, expeditions crossed into the highland valleys contacting large numbers of people whose presence had not even been suspected. In the post-war years administration patrols travelled into still uncontacted areas; administration reached some interior areas only in the late 1960s. During the 1980 census a handful of villages were enumerated for the first time, and others have since been 'discovered'.

The mainland is extremely rugged with mountain ranges reaching over 4,000 metres. Other islands are mountainous microcosms of New Guinea itself. Transport infrastructure is limited; no road links the capital, Port Moresby, and the second largest city, Lae. Many active volcanoes have caused deaths and forced population migration. North and south of the main dividing ranges are vast swampy areas around the Purari and Fly rivers in the south and the Sepik river to the north (see Figures 1.2 and 2.1). Within the massive central cordillera lie valley basins, all more than 1,000 metres above sea-level, that are the most densely populated part of the country.

Despite an enormous variety of cultures in PNG, almost all the indigenous population in pre-contact times was Melanesian, apart from the tiny Polynesian outlier populations on the northern atolls of Bougainville. Linguistic diversity has given rise to lingua francas: Motu in the Papuan region around Port Moresby and Tok Pisin (Pidgin English) throughout the rest of the country. English however is the language of education, government and commerce. The social systems of the various cultural groups differ; patrilineal descent systems predominate in large areas of the highlands and matrilineal systems in the eastern islands. Leadership, exchange systems, rituals and ideologies vary substantially. A massive difference exists between coastal areas, with more than a century of culture contact, and more isolated inland groups which have experienced minimal acculturation and have little concept of any national identity. Post-contact transformation has at certain times and in particular places been so rapid that structural changes which elsewhere evolved gradually over many generations have been telescoped into a few decades (Howlett 1980). PNG populations have retained many small-scale and distinctive social and economic systems, with limited division of labour (other than by gender). National unity is restricted by linguistic and cultural diversity, regional divisions, especially between the highlands and the Papuan coast, and the recency of colonisation and decolonisation.

Towards the end of the nineteenth century planters and missionaries from Germany, Britain and Australia had established mission settlements and plantations on the coasts and islands; traders and labour recruiters moved these frontiers inland but it was not until after the Second World War, and in parts of the more remote highland regions much later, that the social and economic institutions of colonialism – taxation, wage labour, cash cropping, missions, local government councils, health and education systems – were established throughout the country. Britain claimed Papua – the southern half of the mainland – in 1884, whilst Germany simultaneously established authority over parts of New Guinea. Following the First World War, Papua and New Guinea were administered by Australia (the latter under mandate from the League of Nations). After the Second World War, the two administrations were combined, and the country moved towards self-government in

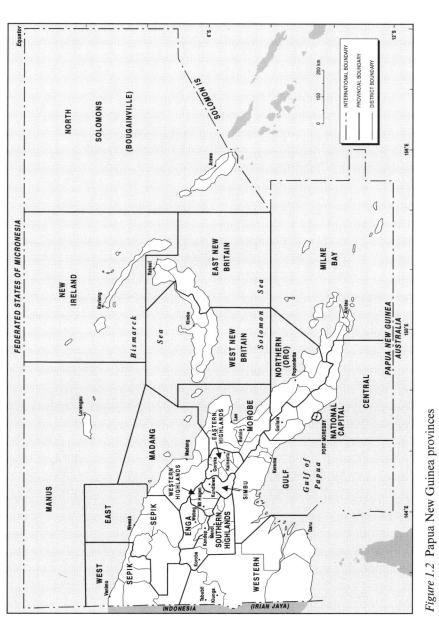

Figure 1.2 Papua New Guinea provinces

1973 and independence in September 1975. The possibility of decolonisation in PNG was an eventuality that Australian administrations were generally content to ignore until well into the 1960s. Indeed PNG was one of the last places in the world where white settler colonialism was advocated as colonial policy (Ward and Ballard 1976:440). Independence largely failed to generate a spirit of national development. Secessionist movements, especially on Bougainville, have posed grave and still unresolved problems about national unity. Australia played the most crucial role in the colony, a special relationship shaped by colonial economic structures (especially in commerce), new economic relationships in the mining industry, assimilationist assumptions in policy and administration, and in post-colonial times by investment and economic aid. All this was heightened by the proximity of the two countries. In the Torres Strait Australia and Papua New Guinea were barely a kilometre apart (Figure 1.3). Geography contributed to the maintenance of many colonial ties. The legacy of colonialism was the continued – and seemingly inescapable – significance of Australia for national development.

Although European contact has been extremely recent, the rapidity of change before or after contact was sometimes exceptional. Customs sometimes disappeared surprisingly quickly; the Fore of the Eastern Highlands gave up fighting when the first administration officer appeared, 'almost as if they had only been awaiting an excuse to give it up. . . . They looked to his arrival as the beginning of a new era' (Sorensen 1972:362). More generally the recognition that the new arrivals were to be a permanent feature of their lives often provoked a crisis (Rowley 1965). The veneer of colonialism was relatively light, but its impact was uneven, though the tentacles of overseas commerce reached out to every part of the country. In the two decades since independence, change in PNG has been extremely rapid as the economy has moved from its historic orientation to agriculture towards mineral production and export. For much of the 1970s and 1980s there was steady economic growth, as both sectors developed, but in the past few years there have been severe challenges to this. The most dramatic of these has been the closure of the Panguna gold and copper mine in Bougainville, and the isolation of Bougainville from PNG; this led to a sudden drop in gold and copper exports, a less precipitate but still significant loss of agricultural exports, civil war conditions, resulting in many deaths and much misery, the return of migrant workers from Bougainville to rural and urban areas where population was already growing rapidly, and a consequent disinvestment in the public sector. World commodity prices have largely continued their recent decline. The population has continued to grow extremely quickly, at an average rate of perhaps 2.3 per cent since the 1980s, increasing demands on inadequate services and leading to considerable population pressure on resources in localised areas. Urban facilities have been particularly strained, and squatter settlements, despite local hostility, have steadily grown as a result of immigration in response to growing perceptions of deprivation and uneven development. Urban unemployment is increasingly visible, hence the emergence of crime,

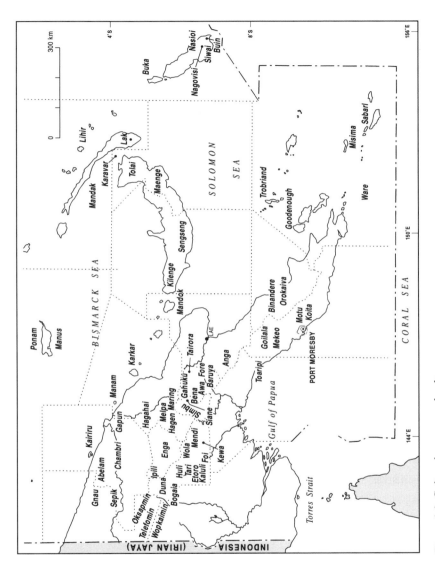

Figure 1.3 Cultural groups and culture areas

violence and *raskal* gangs. After two decades, the optimism that coincided with independence largely disappeared, whilst corruption in the chase for privileges, perks and power has emerged. The police and the army, divided amongst and between themselves, have been unable to challenge corruption, crime or the separatist tendencies of remote regions. With a relative and new-found abundance of natural resources (especially minerals), a low population density, and an independence date later than in most other parts of the world, PNG had opportunities for economic choice and change that were rarely present elsewhere. Yet, in the end, late development tended to reproduce colonial conditions rather than produce a distinctive economic and political structure.

The integration of economic growth and social development has been difficult, there has been little concern for environmental degradation and women have been excluded and marginalised by development trends. Despite fundamental problems, macro-economic management has been effective, the country remains a parliamentary democracy, though militarisation has increased and human rights have decreased. Tribal tensions have irregularly appeared, especially in the highlands, whilst on Bougainville a civil war has lasted more than six years. Early constraints to development – the lack of a unifying infrastructure, rugged terrain and a widely dispersed, poorly educated and culturally diverse population – have been compounded by administrative fragmentation, complexities of land tenure, global commodity price fluctuations, rising expectations and increasing populations. Parts of the country are without roads, telephones, electricity, adequate water supplies or access to health and education services. Until quite recently almost everybody in Papua New Guinea was more familiar with sorcery, spirits, reciprocal violence, gift exchange, subsistence agriculture and local languages than 'such bedrock institutions of the economically developed world . . . as money, buying and selling, employers and employees, wages, salaries, and the calendars and clocks used to measure time and organise labour' (M.F. Smith 1994). Not surprisingly, moving between such different worlds – physically and metaphorically – has posed problems, created tensions and made development elusive.

2 The constraints of late development

Petroleum may be regarded as the pearl shell of industrial civilisation. The avarice it evokes, the ruthlessness with which government bureaucrats and multinational corporations compete over it, and the political forces, rivalries and skulduggery that are called into play in the process are the modern versions of life in the Waga and Nembi Valleys [Southern Highlands] in the late 1930s. These corporate struggles carried on from lofty glass buildings, plotted with the aid of computers, organised through satellite links, and fought by warriors who arrive on executive-class flights – all take place beyond the peripheries of the people who inhabit the regions concerned. The direction of their future will be decided in deals struck between bureaucrats in Port Moresby and executives in London, Sydney and New York, by people they don't know about and will never see. It might as well be the spirit world.

(Schieffelin and Crittenden 1991:282)

THE ENVIRONMENTAL STAGE

More than a hundred populated and unpopulated islands make up PNG. These islands contain an extraordinary variety of landforms, ranging from massive cloud-shrouded mountains, vast lowland swamps, atolls and reefs that barely rise above sea-level and marine chasms of considerable depth. In the jungles the diversity of flora and fauna ranks with that of any other part of the world. Volcanoes regularly threaten life, in Rabaul and elsewhere. Though the climate is tropical, except at the very highest altitudes, extremes of drought and flood, and more rarely cyclones and tidal waves in coastal areas and landslides and frosts in the highlands, pose intermittent problems.

New Guinea, the world's largest island after Greenland, has a central cordillera that stretches 2,400 kilometres from the west of Irian Jaya to the Coral Sea and the archipelagoes of Milne Bay Province. Mt Wilhelm rises to nearly 4,500 metres; around this and other mountain peaks the barren landscape is clearly of glacial origin. On the outlying islands the pattern is similar but on a smaller scale. Landforms are steep and human settlement is extremely restricted. Massive peaks, deep gorges, turbulent rivers and enclosed valleys are specific to the island of New Guinea but the isolation and remoteness imposed by stark mountain ranges are now often little different from that of many of the smaller islands (Figure 2.1).

Sheer mountain ranges, vulcanicity and earthquakes characterise relatively recent land formation. The ranges are composed of igneous, sedimentary and metamorphic rocks, on which many soil types have evolved, that contain minerals, many of great commercial importance. The boundary of the Pacific has become the rim or 'ring of fire' that runs in a broad arc through New Guinea, and onwards to Vanuatu, Fiji and New Zealand. Contemporary geological and geomorphological activity is striking. Villages that lay on the Papuan coast in the nineteenth century are now several hundred metres inland (Mackay 1976:36). On the north coast there are raised coral platforms, indicating continuing spectacular rates of uplift of 3 mm per year. The steep-sided ridges and valleys that predominate in Melanesia severely restrict the area available for agriculture and settlement. Relatively few parts of PNG are below 300 metres, and extremely broken topography has meant that less than 20 per cent of the land is potentially arable. Especially in the central highlands agriculture is carried out on slopes of over 35 degrees. Soils formed on such steep slopes are limited in depth and development; this too inhibits agriculture.

Volcanic activity and earthquakes mark the unstable continental islands, especially in the area between eastern New Guinea and the Solomon Islands. Bougainville, for example, has three active volcanoes and earthquakes occur some forty times a year. Between 1990 and 1993 the country was hit by more than a hundred earthquakes with a magnitude of seven or greater on the Richter Scale, and a series of earthquakes over a one-month period created prolonged problems in Madang and Morobe. More than forty people were killed and numerous villages destroyed, followed by landslides and flooding. Although earthquakes are occasionally severe, low population density, limited urbanisation and the relative lack of permanent structures have minimised their human impact. Landslides characterise many mountainous areas, often in association with earthquakes, and have been responsible for loss of life, particularly in the highlands. Volcanic activity has occasionally had even more dramatic impacts. When Mt Lamington (Oro) last erupted in 1951, extensive destruction, loss of more than three thousand lives in a matter of minutes and much migration away from the devastated area followed. Less damaging in loss of life but much more costly in economic terms was the eruption of Vulcan and Tavurvur, on either side of Rabaul, in 1994. Rabaul, built within an active volcanic caldera, was devastated though only four lives were lost; it was officially declared the country's worst disaster. A state of emergency lasted for six months and more than ninety thousand people were displaced. Off the north coast of New Guinea, both Manam and Karkar occasionally shower ashes on surrounding areas and prompt flight to the mainland. Volcanic activity however has a beneficial effect on soil formation. On the fringes of volcanoes, away from the direct impact of lava flows and

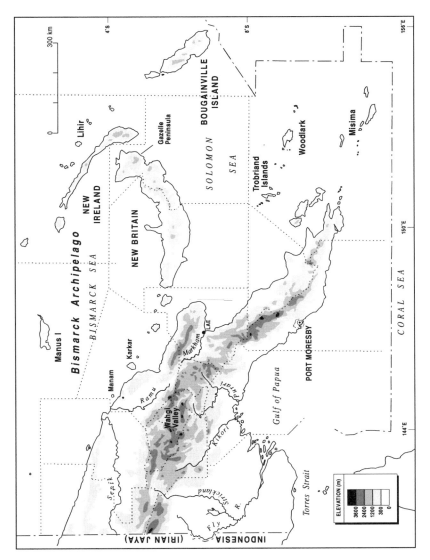

Figure 2.1 Physical geography

ash-falls, soils are often rich and particularly suited to intensive agricultural development. Many of the richest cocoa plantations have been developed on volcanic soils.

Other natural hazards affect coastal areas. Cyclones are unusual, though Cyclone Hanna in 1972 cut great swathes through forest on the north-east coast of New Guinea, and several people were killed in 1993 when Cyclone Adel swept through Milne Bay province. Most rivers, especially the Sepik, have flooded at one time or another, whilst the Southern Highlands was badly affected by floods and frost in 1994. Fires have been occasional problems in the dry coastal areas around Port Moresby. Coasts have been eroded where there has been significant human activity, such as the removal of mangroves or the construction of wharves. Beyond the larger islands are a scatter of coral atolls, characteristic of the South Pacific but relatively few and thinly populated in PNG. None rises more than a few metres above sea-level, and all have thin porous soils, on which few plant species can survive. The greenhouse effect may pose new and unpredictable threats to future atoll life. Already the Carteret Islands, north of Bougainville, have been affected by locally rising sea-levels, which destroyed the island agricultural economy and forced migration to Bougainville (Connell 1990). Throughout PNG, environmental change in the contemporary era has led to population migration and the abandonment of an environmentally hostile, and often economically difficult, periphery, whether of mountains, swamps, atolls or small islands.

There is considerable climatic diversity. Coastal areas have tropical climates of high temperature, humidity and rainfall but, around Port Moresby, the local topography has produced a rain shadow area, where evaporation exceeds rainfall; the capital is often dry and dusty, water is sometimes scarce, bushfires are not unusual and food production difficult. Droughts and floods can occur in both the highlands and the lowlands. In the highlands the tropical climate is substantially modified by altitude and, at the very highest altitudes, hailstorms and even snowfalls occasionally occur. Diurnal variations in temperature are much greater than on the coast, and frosts can be an occasional hazard. The upper altitudinal limit of sweet potato based agriculture occurs around 2,800 metres. Frosts often accompany drought, as in parts of Southern Highlands where deaths from starvation occurred in the 1930s (Sillitoe 1993a). A variety of climatic and other hazards have hindered communications and development throughout the highlands.

Heavy rainfall has meant that in much of PNG the natural vegetation was rainforest. The vegetation is amongst the richest in the world, with around 20,000 plant species (including 2,500 orchid species), about 700 bird species and 180 mammals (Paijmans 1976). New species, even such large animals as Scott's tree kangaroo, first captured by scientists in the West Sepik in 1991, continue to be discovered. Numerous birds of paradise, the world's largest lizard, the pitohui (a bird with toxic flesh, feathers and skin) and crocodiles have all contributed to the image of an exotic country. Both the fauna and flora are transitional between Asia and Australia, with important species from both regions.

Climatic diversity has contributed to a variety of vegetation regions, from lowland rainforests and mangrove swamps to open grasslands and patches of alpine moorlands. On the eve of independence 'forest and natural vegetation still covered about three quarters of New Guinea' (Robbins 1972:82). Population growth, the extension of agriculture and the rise of a rapacious timber industry have subsequently led to the clearing and depletion of rain-forest. More extensive and sophisticated hunting techniques have reduced rainforest fauna; some endemic species, such as varieties of the bird of par-adise, have become rare. Though agricultural techniques were adapted to occasional natural hazard and scarcity, no conservation ethic existed in most places (B.J. Allen 1983); the Goilala (Central Province) people, 'like us, treat the bounty of nature as inexhaustible, and squander their resources recklessly until brought up short by the realisation that they are nearly bankrupt' (Hallpike 1977:68–9). In the post-independence era the destruction of the natural landscape has accelerated. New scourges, such as introduced *salvinia* weeds and water hyacinths, have threatened the livelihoods of many of those living on the Sepik river banks. Nowhere else in the world does the natural landscape provide such a complex and diverse physical stage for its equally complex and diverse population. In few other parts of the world is the phys-ical landscape so influential in the structure of contemporary social and economic development.

FIRST SETTLEMENT

At least fifty thousand years ago, but probably long before that, the first set-tlers moved from Asia to the continent of Sahul, the single landmass that incorporated New Guinea, Australia and Tasmania. These early settlers reached most of the coasts, the outer islands and the highlands more than forty thousand years ago. The island of New Guinea was not formed until about eight thousand years ago when the Torres Strait finally separated it from Australia. There were already permanent agricultural systems in the inter-montane basins, more than 1,200 metres above sea-level. As evident at Kuk, near Mount Hagen, more than nine thousand years ago highlanders had a complex agricultural system. Sedentarism, forest clearance, stone tools, and elaborate water control techniques then existed in the highland valleys and coastal shells were being traded with the highlands. Root crops such as taro were cultivated fully thirty thousand years ago, the earliest cultivated crops in the world. The development of a sedentary agricultural system in the highlands was a local evolutionary process, rather than the result of transfer of techniques from Asia. The highlands of New Guinea was a core global area for the domestication of agriculture.

The present principal staple crop, sweet potato, is a relatively new intro-duction. It probably did not reach New Guinea until some time after its sixteenth-century introduction by Europeans into Indonesia and the Philippines. Sweet potato matures more quickly than other root crops and because equivalent labour inputs usually produce greater outputs than for other root crops, it may well have then been adopted extremely quickly. The crops that preceded it, notably taro, were largely displaced from the central highlands to lower altitudes. Two of the most significant agricultural changes had occurred before European contact.

Parts of Papua have extensive historic field systems which may prove to be even older than those in the highlands. Stone tools sealed beneath volcanic ash on the Huon peninsula have been dated to forty thousand years ago, perhaps the oldest date yet recorded for human occupancy in the whole of the Sahul region (J. Allen *et al.* 1989). This very long period of settlement, and some degree of isolation, enabled the evolution of distinctive physical types and skin colours, most obviously the black skins of Bougainvilleans (and other islanders of the western Solomon Islands). Human settlement is extremely ancient, therefore, and very substantial changes that occurred in prehistory have contributed to contemporary regional diversity.

THE ERA OF EXPLORATION

At the start of the twentieth century no country in the world was less well charted. PNG has been widely celebrated as the 'last unknown' (Souter 1963) and one of the only places where the experience of 'first contact' has been filmed, documented and analysed. Some parts of New Guinea, however, experienced tentative European contact more than 400 years earlier, during distant expeditions from the Spanish and Portuguese empires, and there was Asian contact before that. Spanish ships may also have reached the north coast of New Guinea in 1528, rather optimistically calling their landfall Isla del Oro (Island of Gold). The first certain European contact came in 1606 when the Spanish explorer Torres, sailing westwards from Vanuatu, received food and water on the south-east coast of Papua and fought a battle further westwards at Mailu Island. Other European explorers and traders, Dutch, English, German and French, later arrived and charted the coasts of New Guinea and the outlying islands, traded, demonstrated their superior military might but rarely remained long. New Guinea seemed a hostile physical and social environment, there was no visible evidence of significant wealth and there were many intervening opportunities for the profitable expansion of European empires.

The last three decades of the nineteenth century brought colonial contact in one form or another to virtually the whole coastline of PNG. Trade was more extensive, with pearlers operating from northern Queensland and whalers coming from more distant ports. Dried coconuts were widely available, and in the 1880s a goldrush brought miners flocking from Australia (Chapter 6). Missionaries, many of them Pacific Islanders, brought Christianity, and labour recruiters took coastal Melanesians to Samoa,

Queensland and beyond. The goods some coastal people obtained, their mastery of the emerging Tok Pisin, and coastal trade ensured that many coastal communities increased their wealth and power relative to inland people (Griffin *et al.* 1979:7). Small numbers of Melanesians in a scatter of places began to learn the ways of the outside world.

The colonial endeavour took on a more formal presence in 1884 when Britain reluctantly and belatedly claimed the new colony of Papua (British New Guinea), largely to protect the Australian colonies. In response to Britain's claim Germany made its own territorial claims to the north coast and the islands, leaving a highly indeterminate border through the centre of New Guinea, where no European had ventured. Germany rather than Britain saw prospects of economic gain from the new colony. The protectorate of British New Guinea was little more than a name on a large area of land that was quite unknown to the colonists. Port Moresby became the capital of the new colony in 1885; the location, on grass-covered hills, was chosen because it was thought to be healthier than other parts of a mainly low-lying coast, had a good harbour and was close to Australia (Griffin *et al.* 1979:11). The countryside remained unexplored at the turn of the century. The German colony to the north had a more established economic base, and was administered by the Deutsche Neu-Guinea Kompagnie, founded in Berlin with responsibility for colonial administration alongside its primary goal of promoting trade and plantation development. In the islands independent foreign traders and planters were also more successful; by the end of the century Rabaul was the most important town in the country. There was a scatter of plantations from Aitape, in the Sepik district, to Bougainville, but government control was confined to within 10 kilometres of the coast.

After the war the Territory of Papua remained much as in earlier years; though a thin scatter of plantations had produced localised economic opportunities, these were nowhere near as extensive as in New Guinea. External constraints, including low copra prices, bounties for agricultural activities in tropical Australia, and inadequate shipping services discouraged plantation development. Administrative control brought little benefit to the local population. Even relatively liberal observers, such as Sir Frank Fox, had jaundiced perceptions of the prospects for incorporating Melanesians in the development process:

> Papua has already a labour problem. All the necessities of native life, practically, are produced by Nature without assistance. As is the case in Australia, there are no deadly animals to threaten human life and to provide the pleasures of the chase. In his original state the native, owing his food to the unaided bounty of Nature, and not needing clothing, amused his leisure with tribal warfare. Head-hunting was the national sport, cannibalism the national pleasure. Civilised administration has abolished head-hunting and cannibalism, but has not managed to instil into the native a desire to substitute for them a habit of steady work. The Papuan,

like many other of the Oceanic savages, has an hereditary indisposition for regular labour, because during the course of all his past generations lavish Nature has given him his food free of the curse of Adam. 'Civilisation never flourishes where the banana grows,' says a philosopher. . . . It is difficult to convince the Papuan that with the banana, the yam, the taro available, he should set his energies to working for wages which he does not want. So, deprived of head-hunting as a sport, he lapses into ennui and habits of laziness which threaten his very existence as a people.

(Fox 1927:164–5)

There was minimal interest in extending education to Papuans, since it was widely believed that they had little ability to benefit. Colonial society was organised around the Australian assumption that Papuans were inferior.

In New Guinea, the First World War brought an abrupt end to the German colonial era, and from 1914 Australia took over the war-time administration of the colony, under mandate from the League of Nations. The plantation economy was not disturbed, labour recruiting continued but, in the war years, administrative influence receded rather than expanded. Though New Guinea effectively became an Australian colony it was administered separately from Papua. Australian policy aimed to make New Guinea financially self-reliant, and left economic development to private enterprise. Plantations were further developed in coastal areas, by the 1930s copra production was more than ten times that of Papua and there was a scatter of Chinese traders. Though the plantation economy made a small profit, it was the success of the gold-fields that made the New Guinea administration rich relative to that of Papua. More correctly, 'only the discovery of gold in the Wau-Bulolo region during the 1930s rescued the government of the mandated territory from penury as grim as Papua's' (Denoon 1985:121). Despite some Melanesians gaining employment, colonial economic and social policy was largely untroubled by local dissent or demands.

When Australia formally added New Guinea to Papua, there were few parts of the country, other than along some rivers, where Europeans had penetrated inland. Even the interiors of islands like New Britain and Bougainville had not been explored. However, the inter-war years proved to be a critical era of expansion; gold-miners moved into the Wau and Bulolo areas in 1926, and prospectors subsequently pushed into the highlands. Exploration was largely motivated by commercial imperatives. It was however not until Jim Taylor's fifteen-month Hagen-Sepik patrol in 1938–9 that exploration of the huge western highlands and upper Sepik areas completed a very crude geography of the whole country. Of all these great explorations that of Jack Hides and Jim O'Malley into the southern highlands in 1935 most captured public imagination; Hides believed he had discovered an unspoiled world beyond the peripheries of civilisation, exactly the world that western nostalgia dreamed of during the long years of the Depression (Schieffelin and Crittenden 1991:290). Romanticisation of European colonial expansion helped to legitimise the whole colonial enterprise and fostered dreams of new riches on this last colonial frontier.

THE POST-WAR YEARS

The Second World War brought an end to a period of colonial quiescence that the Depression had put in place. Though the great explorations into the highlands had put the country on the map, and provided a map of the country, the revenue of the colonial administration had barely increased and the economy was not generating profits. Papua and New Guinea were wholly unprepared for war; in 1941 there were few soldiers there, fewer defence facilities and no trained Melanesians. In January 1942 the Japanese bombed Rabaul, which quickly fell, but the commitment of Australian military resources to New Guinea enabled Australia to defend its northern flank. PNG became a country that was not merely exotic; the battlefields of the Kokoda Trail, Bougainville and elsewhere became household (and street) names in Australia, Papua New Guineans were seen both as 'fuzzy wuzzy angels' working as carriers and guides, and as individuals of strength, character and humanity (Griffin *et al.* 1979:89). The sense of debt led to more generous and enlightened colonial development policies in the post-war years. It also led many Papua New Guineans to question the necessity for European dominance and seek their own forms of development, some in cargo cults and others in attempts to construct new economic systems detached from, but modelled upon, those of the colonial 'masters'.

Until the war virtually the entire commercial economy was owned and controlled by colonists. The agricultural sector was dominated by plantations. Planters and traders obstructed Melanesians whose ventures into the cash economy might reduce their own profits, and opposed attempts by administration officials to encourage villagers to process their own coconuts (Griffin *et al.* 1979:107). In the islands, a number of Melanesians had planted their own cash crops, and earned small but regular incomes. In areas more remote from trade, participation in the cash economy was more intermittent, but substantial enough to suggest that Melanesians could participate directly in the cash economy (Connell 1978:50–6), despite a general administration perception that 'the native peoples, due to their disinclination to adopt new methods or ideas, are at present in a primitive stage of agricultural development' (Connell 1978:81). Nonetheless cocoa-growing was encouraged in East New Britain, sheep were introduced and rice – which was becoming a popular food – encouraged. Co-operatives were promoted as the mode of organisation and missions played an important role in stimulating economic development. The early post-war years brought an immediate increase in financial assistance, but war damage and a shortage of materials, shipping and skilled labour, all slowed the pace of development. The plantations survived and administration expenditure boosted the service sector. The main beneficiaries were such major international trading companies as Burns Philp and Steamships. Education and health services were extended. At the end of the war less than 5 per cent of Melanesians were literate and there were no secondary schools in the territory. Malaria and other diseases remained serious problems.

Well into the post-war period, economic development was minimal, political evolution virtually non-existent and contemporary social changes, such as literacy and education, in their infancy. The prospect of any rapid or significant change was slight. The colonial administration was poorly funded, centralised in Port Moresby (and Canberra) and absorbed with the task of remedying war damage and bringing much of the country under control. It was 'an outcrop of pre-war passivity and clerical procedurism, lacking experience in planning, and unaccustomed to thinking about economic change' (Denoon 1985:122). With inexperienced bureaucrats and minimal local participation, even attempts to co-ordinate basic services were fraught with problems. Despite the centralisation of power there was no overall development strategy, and no cohesion to government policies. By the arrival of the first United Nations visiting mission in 1950 the indigenous economy remained oriented around subsistence, on which had been grafted the European overlay of coconut, cocoa and rubber plantations. The main themes of the report of the first UN mission, the need for political advancement and secondary education, were to become recurrent issues. When Paul Hasluck, newly appointed Australian Minister for Territories, made his first visit to the territory in 1951 he recorded: 'one very vivid first impression . . . was that the habits and outlook of colonialism permeated the place. I had read about colonialism of a comic kind in other lands but had not expected to meet it in an Australian territory' (Hasluck 1976:13). For decades to come Australian (and other) observers and those public servants and politicians assigned to foster development, constantly believed that the country would be unlike colonial territories and newly independent states elsewhere; they were invariably proved wrong.

Development policies in the early post-war years focused on the coastal regions familiar to administrators, but the discovery of large concentrated populations in the fertile highland valleys quickly led to a redirection of policy. Initially the highlands was seen primarily as a source of labour and, for a quarter of a century after 1950, the Highland Labour Scheme organised the migration of young men to work on coastal plantations. On the coasts, copra had been the principal commercial crop since European contact, hence the diversification and expansion of commercial agricultural production were major post-war changes. Coffee was an almost entirely new industry, centred in the highlands, and under way by the 1950s: the 'rush for brown gold was on' (Donaldson and Good 1981:144) and it quickly spread to Melanesian smallholdings. Within a decade highlanders produced more coffee than expatriates, a situation very different from that of other tropical crops in coastal areas where plantations remained dominant.

As coffee became successful in the highlands, it spread into lowland areas, a rare example of diffusion from the interior. No other new crops have had the impact of coffee on economy and society. There were, however, other brief successes; experimental tea plots, first producing tea with 'a wet taste like the smell of a dog who has been out in the rain' (Hasluck 1976:136), became successful on highlands plantations in the 1950s, but tea could not be produced on smallholdings. Coffee in the highlands and cocoa on the north coast and in the islands gradually came to dominate the agricultural economy. Without new discoveries of significant quantities of minerals, there was every assumption in the early 1960s that the economy 'must depend chiefly on agriculture for development for some years to come' (Hasluck 1976:303). Attempts at diversification of the economy were essentially efforts to diversify agriculture (Figure 2.2).

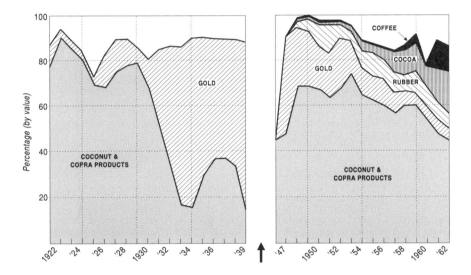

Figure 2.2 The emergence of export diversity
Note: No data are available for Second World War period
Source: World Bank (1965:15)

Achieving uniform development was one of the themes of administration policy in the 1950s. In 1951 Hasluck directed that all 'restricted areas' were to be brought under control by 1954, an impossible task, given the number of such areas, and the time that had proved necessary to achieve this else-where. Indeed it was not until 1963 that the whole of PNG was officially declared to be under administrative control (Downs 1980:126) though, in many areas, control still meant virtually nothing. It was readily apparent by the 1960s that development was extremely uneven. On the coast some parts of New Guinea were becoming relatively prosperous, notably the Gazelle

Peninsula (East New Britain), and parts of Madang, Bougainville and New Ireland. Expatriate plantations had prospered alongside Melanesian small-holders, who were growing cocoa and copra, sometimes in combination with small-scale cattle holdings. By contrast the Sepik district had largely failed with cash cropping, cargo cults were not uncommon, and labour migration to the plantations remained a major source of income. On the Papuan coast infertile soils limited the prospects for cash cropping, though a few planters had hung on, and some Papuans sold goods in the Port Moresby markets. The Papuan islands of Milne Bay were bypassed by more modern development. From there, and other parts of Papua, migration to Port Moresby had started to swell the city's Melanesian population. There were also distinctive changes within the highlands. Though this region had become the rapidly growing centre of the colony's commercial life, it was concentrated around the two largest towns, Mount Hagen and Goroka. The densely populated mountainsides of Simbu offered fewer prospects for commercial cultivation, whilst the high Enga and Southern Highlands areas remained isolated. Social service provision accentuated economic divisions, but gradually tilted towards the highlands where the dense populations enabled schools and hospitals to reach large numbers of people. Thinly populated areas between the coasts and the highlands were ignored.

LAISSEZ-FAIRE COLONIALISM

The colonial era favoured *laissez-faire* policies rather than planning. The administration contented itself with encouraging Melanesian participation in the cash economy, more by exhortation and direction than by financial incentives, and extending the infrastructure that enabled villagers to join the periphery of the global economy. Except for a brief period after the war greater concern was attached to the necessity for adequate supplies of plantation labour. The portfolio of Territories held little importance in the Australian political system; between 1951 and 1963, the Australian cabinet never held a full-scale discussion of policy in PNG. The philosophy of development was nothing more than 'directions about such practical steps as increasing local revenue or applying stricter economic standards and stopping extravagance' (Hasluck 1976:376). It was not about the evolution of social, economic and political development.

Despite benign neglect and the limitations of an uninterested colonial power, the first attempt at a development strategy for the colony had been formulated in 1948 (Territory of Papua and New Guinea (TPNG) 1948). A report, produced by Australian bureaucrats in Port Moresby, stated assumptions and made recommendations which were central to economic policies formulated in Port Moresby, if not always accepted in Canberra, for the ensuing two decades. It began from the basic principle that the territory could 'be developed primarily for the advantage of the local inhabitants . . . with the limit of non-native development determined by the welfare of natives generally' (TPNG 1948:13). Though this gained acceptance in Australian government, 'there was an apparent conflict between these general statements of principle and the specific measures laid down for their achievement' (O'Faircheallaigh 1983:2). The economic basis of the development strategy was the encouragement of rapid transition from subsistence to a more specialised commercial economy, although many tropical crops were then experiencing very low world prices.

Transition to a more commercial agricultural economy was to be attained by encouraging individual production alongside co-operatives and the establishment of nucleus estates. The overall agricultural aims, to increase the export and domestic marketing of food crops, reduce food imports, and diversify agricultural production, never fundamentally changed thereafter. Though agriculture was argued to be central to future development, it was hoped that expatriate-developed forestry and mining projects would complement agriculture and enable long-term financial self-reliance, the ultimate goal (TPNG 1948:135, 190). The report envisaged eventual industrial development, but argued that there was no prospect of this for many years and that the country's needs would principally be satisfied by Australia. By contrast it recommended that PNG export products 'supplementary to Australia's own economy' (TPNG 1948:40), a combination of policies that promised a substantial trade imbalance. None of this could be achieved without significant Australian investment, but private capital was not attracted to the colony until the 1960s. The report focused on economic, rather than social issues; it sought urgency only for a proposed resources survey and otherwise cautioned 'against haste in any sphere of development except this one' (TPNG 1948:83). Limited capital, human resources and long delays in obtaining permission from a distant and uninterested Canberra prevented progress.

In the 1950s, Paul Hasluck shifted the focus of development, arguing that economic development, little though there was, might be slowed 'until the indigenous people could share in it on a more equitable footing' (Hasluck 1976:131). Future policy gave less emphasis to expatriate development in the agricultural sector and limits were imposed on land alienation. The priority of village agriculture was promoted, despite dissent within the expatriate community, and a new development strategy emerged that emphasised cash crop production, by Melanesian smallholders rather than European planters, assisted by administrative expenditure on transport infrastructure and services. This broad approach was set out in the *First Five Year Plan* that Hasluck presented to the Australian Parliament in 1961. It set out targets for economic production and the provision of government services, and made no reference to manufacturing industry, though it sought an examination of fisheries potential. For more than a decade the same basic themes were repeated. Though now consolidated in a Five Year Plan, there was little actual planning and the 1962 visiting United Nations mission criticised Australia for failing to formulate and implement plans.

THE WORLD BANK PRESCRIPTION

Despite hesitant planning efforts the economic growth of Papua and New Guinea up to 1963 was uncoordinated. Public finance was dependent on Australian aid, though the introduction of taxation meant that a third of all public revenue came from local levies and the taxation of expatriates. Though mineral exploitation was minimal and timber resources not yet tapped, there was 'a climate of economic opportunity for expatriates and a danger that this could get out of hand' (Downs 1980:252). The International Bank for Reconstruction and Development (the World Bank) was invited by Australia to produce an economic survey of the country; delivered in June 1964, it was the first effective development plan for the colony and became the basis of subsequent policy. Different from reports that had preceded it, and in line with United Nations priorities, its major aim was 'to help the inhabitants of the Territory to become self-governing as soon as possible and to ensure that when this aim is reached the Territory will, to the greatest extent feasible, be able to stand on its own feet economically' (International Bank for Reconstruction and Development (IBRD) 1965:31). Overtly political objectives were combined with an economic programme.

Although the World Bank was partially concerned with progress towards self-government (and a greater degree of self-reliance), the team had considerable experience in other developing countries and were not bound to Australian experience, convention and practice. Nonetheless the report was still conventional. It assumed that economic development would follow expatriate initiatives and increased government services: 'It is appropriate that Australia should substantially concentrate its efforts on the advancement of the native people. This advancement will come through the native taking a much greater part in expanding production and by accelerating his training and education' (IBRD 1965:34). Just as policies were conventional, so too was the language of development. Education and training were seen as central themes, and there was no challenge to existing development practice.

The report articulated three essential principles for ensuring that appropriate policies were followed. The first was 'concentration of effort'; in order 'to obtain the maximum benefit from the development effort, expenditures and manpower should be concentrated in areas and on activities where the prospective return is highest'. These were to be in the 'large areas of good land which are relatively accessible and where development is relatively easy' (IBRD 1965:35, 36). The administration's principal role was to provide a climate favourable to economic growth, through the provision of services. The second principle, 'standards', stressed that services and facilities should relate to local conditions. Hospitals and other government buildings, and attempts to extend primary education, were more in keeping 'with those found in some countries of Europe than with those found in the less developed countries' (ibid.); more appropriate standards and salaries were required. The third principle, 'fostering responsibility', rejected previous policies and practices of both the administration and the private European sector as being largely those of 'benevolent paternalism' (ibid.:37) and stressed the need for rapid movement towards participation, principally in local government councils.

Implicitly, conservatism and continuity emerged as more important than change, for Papua and New Guinea to escape the political and economic turbulence of parts of the Asia-Pacific rim. Correspondingly the report was itself paternalistic and patronising on the future of Melanesians: 'the tendency of the indigene has been to cling to the past, to traditions, to special beliefs and to oppose the unknown' (ibid.:43), whereas expatriates were recognised to play a key role. This approach to the two dominant races in the colony was scarcely likely to produce recommendations that encouraged radical change; the report was perceived as 'incomplete as economics and unwise as politics' (Schaffer 1965:40), criticisms that the World Bank never wholly escaped in later years.

Many of the reforms and recommendations suggested by the World Bank were in place by 1968. These included the strengthening of the Department of Agriculture, Stock and Fisheries, especially agricultural extension services; the investigation of forest resource potential by external consultants; and the appointment of an Economic Adviser with a small professional staff. The Economic Adviser, A.W. McCasker, sought to ensure that economic policies embodied social principles, believing that it would not be appropriate if development policies were 'in the hands of straight hard-faced bankers and economists' (quoted in Downs 1980:288). Compared with most other countries, PNG lagged far behind in the provision of social services, the diversification of economic development and the participation of local people in the 'modern' sector, including the political system. The appointment of an Economic Adviser led to the first real development plan: *Programmes and Policies for the Economic Development of Papua and New Guinea* (Territory of Papua and New Guinea 1968). This elaborated the recommendations of the World Bank and emphasised the continued necessity for substantial aid, but it placed more stress on indigenous participation in development than the Bank report. Increased emphasis on indigenous participation and greater self-reliance was a result of the growing probability that self-government could not long be denied, and greater priority was attached to social infrastructure, especially education, recognising that the shortage of educated Melanesians had hampered economic and social development. In the 1960s the number of secondary schools increased from only two to more than sixty. In 1968 the country had just four university graduates. The obvious need for higher skills led to a decision to establish the University of Papua New Guinea (UPNG) in Port Moresby in 1966; many early graduates were destined to play prominent roles in national development.

Both social and economic policies and programmes were crucial as the monetary sector gradually became more important than the subsistence sector. Monetisation and commercial expansion in the colony had however increased the trade imbalance so that the value of imports exceeded exports by A$68 million in 1966–7. This trade gap was covered by Australian aid. The value of imports was particularly swollen by food imports which, during the 1960s, represented between 40 and 50 per cent of all imports, a measure of the manner in which the country was becoming dependent on Australia for basic goods. PNG was more obviously a part of the global and regional economy, yet development was hampered by inadequate capital investment. In a sense, 'for the first 60 years of colonial control, Papua New Guinea experienced colonialism without capitalism: for another 20 years it experienced colonialism and capitalism but without capital. The superstructure of capitalism was constructed but the engine was missing' (Denoon 1985:128). That changed with the discovery of significant mineral deposits and the hesitant move of an emergent nation towards independence.

THE ARRIVAL OF POLITICS

The first step towards political development was the establishment of a Legislative Council in 1951, which included three nominated Papua New Guineans. The expansion of the Council in 1961 brought educated Papuans, including John Guise (later to become the Governor-General), into politics, and, for the first time, some Melanesians were established and confident enough to be formally critical of Australian policy. The formation of a House of Assembly in 1964 dramatically pushed the democratic process ahead, though the electorate, less than half of whom were involved in local government councils, were largely unaware of what was at stake. Democracy and nationhood were concepts that meant nothing. Moreover the whole 'effort was typically Australian: a lack of preparation followed by frenetic activity. There were elements of farce, zeal and finally overwhelming success when a functional parliament with an indigenous majority was achieved and accepted by the people' (Downs 1980:307). There were no real political parties or national political issues and electors voted for candidates whom they knew in the hope that this would grant them access to the spoils of government. In a quarter of a century little has subsequently changed.

The election of a second House of Assembly in 1968 was marked by the formation of the Pangu (Papua and New Guinea Union) Pati, which included several young, educated Melanesians, such as Michael Somare (later the first Prime Minister), and sought immediate 'home-rule' and accelerated economic development. Older Papua New Guineans, especially in the highlands, were opposed to any early movement towards independence. Australia generally continued to regard 'self-determination' as little more than a distant possibility though its reports to the United Nations constantly noted that Papua New Guineans could have independent status if they sought it. Decolonisation in other parts of the world, and the changing status of the western half of the island of New Guinea, virtually ensured that PNG would eventually become independent. The relationship between economic change and political evolution was widely seen as important. The World Bank effectively deferred consideration of economic independence, and others found it difficult to accept any real prospect of economic viability. Overall policy was explicable 'in terms of coalition politics, torpor and negligence, or of deliberately stalling for time or long range influence – or both' (Griffin *et al.* 1979:139, 141). Much of this uncertainty was a function of the independence of Indonesia and the transfer of Irian Jaya to Indonesia, the unpredictabilities of the Vietnam War and thus the role that PNG might take in Australian defence strategy. There was no pressure on Australia to grant independence, and within Australia there was just as much discussion of PNG becoming a seventh state as of its gaining independence.

In the 1972 elections the Pangu Pati sought immediate self-government, but not independence ('until we are really ready for it'), rapid localisation, land reform, high wages and a greater commitment to rural development. However the Pangu Pati itself largely remained a group of elite, educated Melanesians and a few progressive expatriates, with minimal party organisation and no overt support at village level. The Pangu Pati was the only political party promoting national unity, yet it had little support in the highlands, and struggled to overcome provincial loyalties (Downs 1980:424), as regional sentiments moved towards secessionism. The Australian administration was in an impossible position, seeking to devolve political decision-making at the same time that it attempted to construct a new nation, whose geography was barely established. Power and authority were generally transferred from Australia before there was significant local demand.

The movement to independence was slow and difficult. Secessionism in East New Britain, Papua, and later Bougainville, conservatism in the highlands and disunity in parliament all hampered progress. Nevertheless self-government was attained at the end of 1973 and, after lengthy wranglings over the constitution of the independent state, the stage was set. The Australian government resolved an impasse over devolution by unilaterally transferring full defence and foreign affairs rights, and on 15 September 1975 Papua New Guinea became an independent state.

THE EIGHT AIMS

Despite the strengthened role of development planning and the expansion of infrastructure, two major problems beset economic development as PNG moved into the 1970s, and closer to self-government and independence: firstly, 'Papua New Guinea had none of the characteristics of a national economy when the first Somare government was formed in April 1972' (Garnaut 1981:157). Secondly, 'by 1972 it was becoming apparent that while the economy was expanding rapidly, the "share of the cake" accruing to Papua New Guineans was in fact declining' (O'Faircheallaigh 1983:10). This was obviously true of the monetary sector, where the indigenous share of cash incomes fell during the 1960s; Melanesians had gained a larger amount but a smaller share of the results of economic growth. Regional inequality remained substantial, perhaps larger than in many other developing countries, and had increased in the 1966–71 period (Treadgold 1978a). In these circumstances, with more informed Papua New Guineans entering Somare's cabinet, most did not support the existing development philosophy of McCasker, which favoured maximising growth by directing government resources to those areas that would yield the quickest returns. There was growing opposition to a policy which concentrated resources in the most productive sector of the economy but attached little concern to inequalities in local or national income and welfare distribution.

In this new context, which challenged conventional World Bank philosophies of economic growth, the Australian administration commissioned a British economist, Mike Faber, to produce new proposals. The team report became a landmark for the conceptualisation of development issues in PNG, argued for much greater local control of the economy especially through a reduction in dependence on foreign aid and foreign capital investment. No mention was made of growth, partly because the growth rate was seen as satisfactory, indigenous economic development received priority (Overseas Development Group 1973) and its egalitarian aims were entrenched in the main ideological statements of the government coalition. In the same year western models of economic and social development had been criticised by radical academics and Melanesians alike. Many argued that development should take place in terms of 'the Melanesian way'; the French agronomist, René Dumont, stressed that PNG should escape from 'the 3M civilisation – Missionaries, Militarists and Merchants'; the Trinidadian economist Lloyd Best asked Papua New Guineans to 'cease playing stereotyped roles in the exotic institutions . . . established by the Australian Coloniser' whilst Mexican theorist Ivan Illich stressed the merits of a convivial society, where more appropriate forms of education, health and housing would replace imported models. At the same time, some UNPG academics went further to consider the possibilities of 'socialist' objectives. In theory and in practice the early 1970s witnessed the most critical phase in post-war economic and political development.

The Faber Report was the result of 'a happy conjunction: an advisory team offering an alternative charter for development and a new reformist government looking for one' (Fitzpatrick 1985:22) in a global context where the whole field of development studies had newly emerged and was developing a radical thrust. *A Report on Development Strategies for Papua New Guinea* recognised that economic growth was an essential requirement but in terms of social and economic priorities, 'it took existing patterns of underdevelopment in the Third World and in Papua New Guinea and recommended that people try to achieve the opposite' (Fitzpatrick 1985:23). The most coherent focus was in some respects a negative one, the issues covered in a paper by Hart that traced the structure of 'A Model of Development to Avoid' (Hart 1974), which was the nearest thing to a theoretical underpinning in the report. Hart challenged inequality, the strength of the formal sector, centralisation, foreign control of the economy and, belatedly, the form of development that favoured men. These new ideas were beginning 'to provide an alternative charter for what it saw as the country's rightful rulers' (Fitzpatrick 1985:23). Despite parliamentary support for the report, Ian Downs, a former member of the House, recorded that 'national emotions had taken over from national economics' with many Melanesian leaders beguiled by the new economic ideologies put before them (Downs 1980:53b). At the end of the year Somare presented his 'Improvement Program' – the Eight Point Plan – and abolished McCasker's Office of Planning and Co-ordination. A new development strategy was underway.

The Eight Point Plan, or Eight Aims, were:

1 a rapid increase in the proportion of the economy under the control of Papua New Guinean individuals and groups and in the proportion of personal and property income that goes to Papua New Guineans
2 more equal distribution of economic benefits, including movements towards equalisation of income among people and towards equalisation of services among different areas of the country
3 decentralisation of economic activity, planning and government spending, with emphasis on agricultural development, village industry, better internal trade and more spending channelled to local and area bodies
4 an emphasis on small-scale artisan, service and business activity, relying where possible on typically Papua New Guinean forms of activity
5 a more self-reliant economy, less dependent for its needs on imported goods and services and better able to meet the needs of its people through local production
6 an increasing capacity for meeting government spending needs from locally raised revenue
7 a rapid increase in the equal and active participation of women in all forms of economic and social activity
8 government control and involvement in those sectors of the economy where control is necessary to achieve the desired kind of development.

The essence of the Eight Aims, and the Faber Report, were rural and regional development, local ownership and control, and equity. However the absence of any reference to economic growth 'did not accord with political demands, as almost everyone wanted more of almost everything' (Garnaut 1981:166). Their multi-dimensional nature meant that one or more of the aims was almost certain to be a part of any development strategy, hence it was impossible to have consensus on specific priorities. However localisation invariably received greatest significance, especially near the time of independence, as the Eight Aims quickly became a rhetorical device of long-term significance. The combination of decentralisation, decision-making by consensus, self-reliance and an emphasis on development rather than growth were combined into what was often regarded as the 'Melanesian Way' of development (Narokobi 1980). This was a rhetorical and populist stereotype useful for general purposes, such as political mobilisation or development of national unity, but ultimately somewhat confusing: 'half of the people who use the term believe traditional Melanesian society to be capitalist, while the other half believe it to be socialist. In fact it was neither' (Berry 1977:159). Appeals to a 'Melanesian Way' had declined by the end of the decade.

The Eight Aims took on a new role as the constitution for the independent state was drafted, and were transformed into five bland National Goals and Directive Principles, which watered down the government role though they gave early emphasis to the conservation of natural resources and the environment. The elaboration and activation of the Eight Aims became primarily a political exercise. 'Quite deliberately there was almost no consultation on these drafts with senior public servants' (Voutas 1981:36). For most members of the coalition there was only one key aim, the increased participation of Papua New Guineans in the economy, hence there was little objection to other significant themes. New concerns emerged. Julius Chan, then Minister for Internal Finance, presented alternative objectives, and expressed concern that individual initiative should be preserved and not lost through state intervention in economic development (Fitzpatrick 1985:24). Others feared that redistribution might threaten their entrepreneurial ambitions, whilst university students, a significant political and ideological force, were concerned over what they saw as 'a period of rhetoric, no action and hypocrisy'; overall, at least within the House of Assembly, 'the pseudo-socialistic overtones of the aims were acceptable at the level of public rhetoric' (Voutas 1981:46). Melanesian members of Michael Somare's Cabinet 'saw the aims as a form of nationalist self-assertion' (op. cit.:35) and, apart from Somare himself, there was little concern with securing greater equality or reducing the scale of foreign intervention. Moreover there was both bureaucratic opposition to significant change and limited administrative capacity or will to respond quickly to new initiatives. Though the Eight Point Plan and the Faber Report were elaborated into a major national economic plan, *Strategies for Nationhood*, published in 1974, and these themes were also transferred to the provinces, most obviously in the 'Green Book', *Chimbu: Issues in Development*, which advocated small business, appropriate technology and more egalitarian development (Howlett *et al.* 1976), the actual translation of policies into practice, at national and provincial level, proved extremely difficult.

'STONES NOT TREES': THE RENEGOTIATION OF THE BOUGAINVILLE COPPER AGREEMENT

Though the Eight Aims provided new themes for economic change, three specific economic issues were significant for long-term policy formation as independence came closer. The first, and the one most directly related to the Eight Aims, was the necessity to provide a stable, preferably growing, flow of public expenditure to provide a context in which specific policy actions could be evaluated. Mechanisms were needed, not only to ensure the long-term provision of overseas aid, but also to promote the accumulation of foreign exchange reserves in good years to balance the declines in recession years. The stabilisation of 'the highly volatile flow of revenue from the Bougainville mine seemed to be the most important single aspect of the stabilisation strategy' (Garnaut 1981:171). Major effort was directed into the stabilisation of commodity incomes and, by the time of independence, copra, cocoa and coffee stabilisation funds had contributed successfully to government revenue. The second area of concern was the perceived necessity to have a low rate of inflation, which necessitated policies that would become important upon the complete separation of the Australian and PNG monetary system at the start of 1976. Through the 'hard kina strategy', PNG sought to maintain the external value of the kina and avoid devaluation, despite its attractiveness in a situation of considerable trade imbalance; the hard kina policy thus tied the kina closely to the Australian dollar. The third problem was national revenue growth, which needed to increase but in a manner that did not place undue pressure on low income groups. Central to this was renegotiation of the Bougainville Copper Agreement, to generate increased domestic revenue (whilst stabilising income from mineral commodities) and ensure that subsequent agreements over resource exploitation were consistent with it. The Bougainville copper mine had quickly become crucial to a national economy that had 'inherited a level of public expenditure that was far beyond anything that could possibly be financed from domestic revenues for the foreseeable future' (Garnaut 1981:175). Its role was therefore crucial.

Until 1989 the Bougainville copper mine was the single most important component of the economy. The mine, which came into production in the same month of 1972 that the first national government was formed, generated substantial income for its owners and, by taxation, for the government. When the initial Bougainville Copper Agreement was finalised in 1969, it received widespread support in PNG, despite provision for a three year tax holiday to Bougainville Copper Limited (BCL) and the permanent exemption of 20 per cent of the income from taxation (Garnaut 1981:193). Yet even before exports had begun, BCL had experienced political problems caused by 'too much publicity and too much success' (Downs 1980:540). The Minister for Mines and Member of Parliament (MP) for South Bougainville, Paul Lapun, called for renegotiation of the agreement in a speech in 1972, and was supported by Fr John Momis, MP for Bougainville Regional, who sought increased national control of all mining ventures as an integral part of 'self-determination and real political independence'. At the time these proposals were opposed in the House on the grounds that no subsequent agreements would be considered binding and future foreign investors would be discouraged. Momis later demanded a greater PNG share of the profits of the Bougainville mine, because of the considerable profits made in its first year of operation, greater equity participation, more rapid localisation of the workforce and more processing in Bougainville. The discovery of new copper deposits at Ok Tedi (Western Province) strengthened the government's wish to renegotiate.

A new agreement was finally settled between BCL and the PNG government in October 1974, which marked some radical changes in the taxation system which were so novel that Faber, again involved in PNG development, felt that they would 'set a precedent for other mining agreements between governments and multinational corporations' (1974:446). Three of the main fiscal privileges enjoyed by BCL were abolished – automatic exemption from tax of 20 per cent of the company's income, the three-year tax holiday and capital allowances on depreciation. Measures were introduced which significantly increased government revenues from corporate income tax. New provisions covering social and environmental issues were established and the new Bougainville (North Solomons) Provincial Government was supported by the company's business advisory services. Crucial to the long-term success of the revised agreement was the establishment of the Mineral Resources Stabilisation Fund – essential as copper prices fell from their high levels in 1974 – which subsequently provided a steady and rising flow of revenue into the Consolidated Revenue Fund. Though it later proved difficult to extend this agreement to the Ok Tedi mine, the renegotiation was firm evidence that PNG would not be cowed by the power of foreign investors, could negotiate tough decisions and was able to situate these decisions in the context of an emerging consensus on national policy. For a long time afterwards the then Foreign Minister, Sir Maori Kiki, would say: 'Remember, they are stones, not trees', to emphasise the importance of receiving a reasonable return from a non-renewable resource. In view of what PNG was later to receive from forestry resources, it was unintendedly and unfortunately prophetic.

The formulation of the Eight Aims, and the renegotiation of the Bougainville Copper Agreement, suggested that the transition to independence would not be as catastrophic as some foreign observers expected, nor would it merely maintain colonial policies in a neo-colonial future. One advantage that PNG had was 'not that Papua New Guineans were rich, but that total incomes were above the bare requirements of survival by a sufficiently wide margin to allow a brief period of policy reconsideration . . . without a failure of growth directly causing great poverty' (Garnaut 1981:161). A high level of Australian aid, and the viability of villages as economic and social units, emphasised this situation. Thus PNG gained independence with an economy that had achieved a significant degree of diversity, but without either an ideological basis or a perception of difficult economic times ahead that might have led to concerted attempts to restructure the basis of development. Renegotiation of the Copper Agreement represented the high point of the nation's ability to direct the structure of economic growth. Subsequently uneven attention was given to various areas of policy-making (such as controls over foreign investment), a situation common in other developing countries. When PNG became independent, the prospects of stable economic growth were well founded, and there was a degree of consensus on the broad philosophy of development.

TOWARDS SELF-RELIANCE?

Independence marked no shifts of direction in government policy. Michael Somare, the first Prime Minister, disavowed ideology, lacked clear policies, and was not well versed in economic issues. Nor were many other parliamentarians. Political parties tended to be associated with regions and personalities rather than policies, and were prone to a process of fission and fusion that made long-term decision-making difficult. The Westminster-style democracy that Australia had bequeathed raised problems for a nation where critical decisions for most people were taken in clans and villages, and where few had travelled far from their homes or achieved an education beyond primary school. Yet dramatic changes had occurred. Almost all of PNG was now known to the outside world, though its inhabitants knew little of that world or their own nation, one of the largest mines in the southern hemisphere had started in Bougainville and the old certainties of the subsistence agricultural system and gift economy had been transformed by cash cropping and the ramifications of a monetary economy.

The central thrust of the Eight Aims sought to transform the economy from dependence on external sources of finance and technology, into one more reliant on local capital and skills, in which all Papua New Guineans would have an equitable share. Self-government and independence had resulted in a greater focus on indigenous incomes and welfare, but financial self-reliance remained a central aim, though, as ever, the means of achieving it required increased external dependence.

After the first World Bank mission of 1963, other missions visited the country. The first visit to the independent state in 1976 concluded that though the prospects for self-reliance were promising, a necessary change from dependence on Australian budgetary aid and technical assistance in both the public and private sectors would not be easily achieved. Though PNG had one of the highest propensities to import in the world, the Bank stated that there were 'ample grounds for optimism about the long-run outlook for economic development' (Baldwin 1978:64) and emphasised the necessity for fiscal viability alongside a gradual reorientation of the economy towards expectations, standards and cost levels that could be sustained with the country's own resources. The World Bank mission noted the significance of the Eight Aims as statements of national goals, but quickly dispelled the notion that economic growth was not a key objective, and argued for its centrality as the basis for social development and self-reliance, though it cautioned against the proliferation of enclave projects, which it characterised as vital but not sufficient for national development (op. cit.:69). The report was particularly cautious on social welfare expenditure, in precisely those areas that would have contributed to greater equity, rural and regional development: for the education and health sectors, 'although some minor investment in these areas can doubtless be justified, it should be held to a minimum during the next few years in deference to other government sectors with greater potential for increasing production and employment' (op. cit.:78). Though the World Bank was scarcely departing from its own tried and tested formulas, its emphasis was very different from that of the Faber Report.

The government's white paper on the *National Development Strategy*, produced in 1976, pointed to the need for greater expenditure in rural areas and increased efforts to generate rural income-earning opportunities. The strategy stated that the government would give the highest priority to developing 'farming systems which sustain subsistence production per head' (Densley 1981:290) and stressed that the strategy was not a plan for maximum growth but was to be accompanied by reductions in existing inequalities in the distribution of goods and services. In some respects this was the last formal statement of an egalitarian approach to development and, in practice, little was transformed into policies. The rolling annual National Public Expenditure Plan (NPEP), which began in 1977, increasingly diverged from a consideration of the needs of rural areas and people (Allan and Hinchliffe 1982). Successive NPEPs have moved towards objectives of economic growth, although this changing direction was never spelled out; the 1981 NPEP stated: 'The over-riding priority of the Government within the economic policy framework continues to be the provision of a stable domestic economy conducive to steady and sustainable economic growth' (National Planning Office 1981:14). In terms of the broad structure of economic management, the post-colonial state pursued policies that were similar to those pursued by the colonial administration, remaining characterised by heavy reliance on private enterprise, virtually unimpeded free trade and with the more productive sectors of the economy being privately owned and dominated by foreign capital. By the end of the 1970s the emphasis of economic policy had largely returned from development to growth, though the Eight Aims remained the rhetorical basis of policy statements.

As the pursuit of economic growth became increasingly central to development planning, the Eight Aims became more peripheral; growth with redistribution appeared no longer viable and the actual successes of the aims were more critically appraised. Policy problems were increasingly complex, many elements were not clearly understood by all levels of government (Allan and Hinchliffe 1982:23), and the machinery for policy implementation, especially in rural areas, was exceptionally weak. The most important policy successes in the first decade of independence were in increasing the proportion of the economy under national control (a process assisted by the rapid localisation, and growth, of the public service). There was expansion of Papua New Guinean ownership of business, banking and international trading and nationals owned larger proportions of urban real estate and some service activities, though there was little development of small-scale and middle-level business activities, nor was there any real sign of a Papua New

Guinean petty bourgeoisie (Fitzpatrick 1985:23). Where the significance of small-scale Papua New Guinean business activity increased, it tended to conflict with the second and sixth aims, that sought to raise revenue and redistribute the benefits of increased income (Anere 1985). However other elements of the Eight Aims were even less evident. Inequalities between Papua New Guineans and expatriates were reduced, as some individuals and groups acquired substantial assets, yet rural–urban disparities increased, both in the distribution of cash incomes and through failures in the distribution of public goods and services. Inter-provincial inequalities also grew, evident in Bougainville's early success at garnering resources after the settlement of the 1975 secession crisis. Political decentralisation has not and could not equalise regional access to services but it brought a degree of political power and authority much closer to the bulk of the population.

Despite the early promise that a stringent fiscal approach would lead to increased self-reliance, there has been no reduction in imports, overseas aid remains substantial (and is likely to continue at high levels), and technology is increasingly imported from overseas. Government spending needs are not met from locally generated revenue and the paradox of fiscal self-reliance being dependent upon foreign investment has never been resolved. Little serious attention was ever given to the most neglected seventh aim, that of enabling increasing participation by women in social and economic activity. Political parties have ignored women in their policy statements; although female wage employment has substantially increased, especially in the public service, this has not been accompanied by any significant change in the social position of women. Girls have more restricted access to all levels of the education system than boys, and social structures are patriarchal. Finally, the government secured a greater stake in key sectors of the economy, notably in the mining sector – through the renegotiation of the Bougainville Copper Agreement and the development of other mines – but that involvement did not contribute to a new structure of development. The Aims legitimised policies, provided the rhetoric for aspiring political leaders and the prologue to government plans but ultimately did not significantly influence the content of economic policy.

One of the advantages that PNG was perceived to have from late self-government and late independence was the ability to learn from the mistakes of other developing countries that had earlier achieved independence. In practice, despite the proposals in the Faber Report, there was neither any climate of radicalism in PNG nor significant informed debate on crucial policy discussions. When the House of Assembly debated the Eight Aims in March 1973, 'there was some criticism of the equalisation of incomes and government control themes as being communist' (Somare 1975:110). PNG had little choice, through the absence of skilled human resources and domestic capital, other than to become increasingly dependent on foreign capital. The principal gains from late development were necessarily limited. As in other relatively small developing countries, decisions taken outside PNG – on commodity prices, foreign investment, aid, loans, trade concessions and so on – were made without significant PNG input yet had a more crucial impact within the country than national development policies and programmes, in themselves rarely other than orthodox.

THE QUEST FOR ECONOMIC GROWTH

By the mid-1980s there was no question about the new emphasis on economic growth, especially after recession at the start of the decade, discontent over the slow progress of rural development and unwillingness to provide increased budgets for welfare provision and infrastructure development. The more cautious budgetary policies that followed reflected the government's lack of resources and declining ability to play a stabilising role in the national economy, yet ensuring stability became more important than directing, and restructuring, the economy. Deregulation of financial markets contributed to this situation, with new foreign banks entering the economy, and the Bank of Papua New Guinea playing a more restricted role (Anere 1985:35). Less significance was attached to the necessity to control the form of foreign investment and more to encouraging it; in 1983 the Finance Minister, Philip Bouraga, emphasised that 'the Government has a responsibility to create favourable conditions for investment. . . . The implementation of productive investment will remain the function of the private sector which claims, rightly I think, that commercial enterprise is best left in private hands' (quoted in Gupta and Vickerman 1983:17). Over time therefore a situation similar to that in other developing countries emerged: a growing reluctance and inability of the state to intervene directly in economic issues, as divisions within government became more pronounced, an emerging urban bias in development policy and public expenditure, less overt challenge to foreign investment and the down-playing of mechanisms for redistribution. A new element was also becoming apparent: corruption was more obvious in the 1980s. As two economists observed, 'this problem could eventually undermine many of PNG's hard-won gains, and it is not something which is amenable to normal economic policy instruments however coherently used' (Daniel and Sims 1986b:111). Problems were becoming more apparent than solutions. The Eight Aims still occasionally surfaced as rhetoric but were otherwise all but forgotten.

Government spending increased very rapidly. The exchange rate was eased downwards and indirect taxes imposed, eroding low incomes and household consumption levels, especially in urban areas (Story 1989). The parallel decline in state revenue, and the scarcity of options for capital and property formation within the country, had negative effects on economic growth, and contributed to some flight of capital, mainly to Australia. Agriculture continued to dominate the national budget, as mineral prices remained low. As the recession continued, there was a further shift away from issues of redistribution, human resource development and infrastructure provision.

Though Michael Somare's government launched a Mid-Term Development Strategy (belatedly published in 1986) that continued to stress self-reliance, equality and participation, these historic catchwords were no more than that.

The transition to Paias Wingti's government in 1985 only emphasised the primacy of economic growth. The government strategy that all-out growth through the private sector was necessary became pervasive. Wingti and the Minister of Finance, Julius Chan, emphasised tax reduction and cuts in government spending, redirection of government expenditure away from service and welfare activities, privatisation and deregulation, and a greater reliance on the private sector (Kavanamur 1993:66). PNG was again falling into line with what was happening in other parts of the world, as the era of the free market, deregulation and faith in the 'invisible hand' permeated western economies and eventually spread far beyond. In 1986 the government sought unsuccessfully to privatise Air Niugini along with other state-owed enterprises, including the Electricity Commission and part of the shipping industry (Whitworth 1989). It also undertook a series of liberalisation policies, consistent with its *laissez-faire* economic policy, to reduce public expenditure commitments and generate immediate national income. Economic policy for much of the 1980s thus reflected low levels of overall real growth and the limits to indigenous economic expansion. Real minimum wages declined by some 10 per cent during the 1980s but other wages – notably those of parliamentarians, the army, police and private sector/skilled workers and management – increased (Story 1989:56–7). Further wage reduction was resisted by better organised sections of the urban and mining workforce, contributing to substantial income inequalities, notably in urban areas, that were exacerbated by rising and increasingly overt unemployment.

After a vote of no-confidence in 1988 Rabbie Namaliu gained power and sought to jettison Wingti's development priorities and establish a more 'integrated human development'. However the new government gained power at a particularly difficult time: the recession was not over and the crisis in Bougainville was imminent. Consequently, despite obeisances towards the historic goals, and a claim that 'the Eight Aims are still a valid and a fair representation of overall Government policy', economic growth remained at the core of development practice (Kavanamur 1993:68). The 1989 budget was thrown into disarray as a result of the Bougainville mine closure, with PNG facing a major balance of payments shortfall. The mine had provided a third of the value of the country's exports, about 10 per cent of GDP and 16 per cent of national revenue; its closure placed a huge strain on the government's budget, directly and indirectly increasing the extent of unemployment and worsening the balance of payments situation. This situation was exacerbated by a continued drastic decline in agricultural commodity prices. In early 1990 the World Bank estimated that PNG urgently required external funding of $A75 million to meet its obligations. The government was forced to negotiate a 'Rescue Package' from the 'International Donor Community', under the auspices of the World Bank and the International Monetary Fund (IMF).

The mine closure thus marked the end of a period of considerable economic stability, despite the difficulties associated with long-term recession, and led to a first structural adjustment programme.

At the end of the 1980s the PNG economy was stagnant. Over the fifteen year period after independence it had shown no real growth. Indeed only the sub-Saharan African countries had performed as badly. Immediately after independence PNG had recorded reasonable growth rates; between 1976 and 1979 real gross domestic product (GDP) rose by an average of about 4.1 per cent per year, as export prices were favourable. The slump in prices in the early 1980s led to the effective stagnation of the economy, as population growth rates surged ahead of economic growth. Various estimates of economic growth suggest a negative growth rate in the early 1980s, but a slightly positive growth rate in the late 1980s, following an upsurge of activity in the minerals sector (Lodewijks *et al.* 1991:50; Stein 1991:4). Over the whole decade, what little economic growth had occurred was inadequate to provide significant improvements in general living standards. The Bougainville crisis could scarcely have come at a less opportune time.

As an initial response to the crisis the government initiated in 1989 the first phase of the structural adjustment programme, involving a K25 million reduction in government expenditure (and a further cut of K70 million for 1990), and a 10 per cent devaluation of the kina against all major currencies, a negotiated reduction in real wages, a restraint on bank credit and a search for more overseas aid. Cutting almost K100 million from the budget proved difficult, but the devaluation of the kina improved the country's international competitiveness, especially in the agricultural sector (and the value of exports increased). The Departments of Tourism and Housing were both abolished, as was the National Investment and Development Authority (NIDA), to provide a much reduced regulatory context for foreign investment. Conscious of the social costs of adjustment policies, the government initiated a series of special intervention projects officially designed to counter the effects of structural adjustment on the most vulnerable groups; these emphasised housing infrastructure and finance, urban water supply and sewerage, road maintenance, health provision, small industry and coffee development (Kavanamur 1993:70–1) but there was little evidence of these schemes a few years later and they had little direct impact on the most impoverished and marginalised groups (Connell and Lea 1993). A renewed attempt to achieve industrialisation had few positive results. Despite the difficulties of achieving economic growth, with the Bougainville crisis demanding considerable and costly attention, its primacy was again evident, with the rhetoric of integrated human development now also discarded. In terms of the magnitude of response to the perceived necessity for structural adjustment, that of PNG was 'at the upper end of adjustment programmes supported by the World Bank' (Lodewijks *et al.* 1991:45); the Bank's proposals were more ambitious and comprehensive than those attempted by other developing countries. In the absence of critical discussion in PNG they were firmly in line with the most orthodox market-oriented stabilisation and adjustment policies, emphasising deregulation, privatisation and trade liberalisation in accordance with the two principal goals of achieving early macro-economic stability and, subsequently, the development of an adequate basis for long-term economic growth.

Structural adjustment had only limited success, but it enabled the country to weather the immediate Bougainville crisis. Though real GDP growth rates rose, inflation was largely kept under control and the balance of payments moved away from chronic deficit. A significant influence on economic revival was the development of new minerals projects, which quickly began to compensate for the closure of the Bougainville mine. The adjustment process was relatively painless, but despite no serious cutbacks in welfare components of the budget (Stein 1992:29), the development of human resources, in contrast to the limited restructuring of the bureaucracy (where no net reduction of the workforce occurred), was the principal victim of structural adjustment. This was more apparent in remote rural areas, despite the assumption that the burden of adjustment fell largely on wage and salary earners in the public and private sectors (op. cit.:30), whilst the devaluation of the kina posed problems for those, mainly urban dwellers, who were particularly dependent on the import of such basic consumer goods as rice and tinned fish. Structural adjustment was also inadequate to enable a better balance in the macro-economic disequilibrium between the mining and agricultural sectors, whilst trade liberalisation was not beneficial to the forestry sector, where there was minimal regulation and extensive transfer pricing.

THE RETURN OF THE WORLD BANK

The new minerals boom of the 1990s ushered in a phase of accelerated economic growth. Rather than respond to the increasing need for more broadly based development policies, this suggested the success of growth policies and pointed to the merits of structural adjustment – despite the disequilibrium between sectors (and regions) and the marginalisation of the poor. Gold exports from the Misima and Porgera mines (and briefly from Mt Kare) led to exports reaching record levels, with a 9 per cent growth in GDP in 1991. Since wages were relatively stable, PNG became more internationally competitive. However record growth in the mining sector could not be translated into success in agriculture. The international agenda remained important as domestic policy formation was hindered by frequent no-confidence motions in Parliament which defeated attempts by any government to look beyond immediate survival, and thus the rapid delivery of the fruits of economic growth, rather than towards long-term policy formation. This made it difficult to achieve a sense of national cohesion, or to support economic diversification through infrastructure provision.

Economic growth was sustained over the period 1991–3, with the annual GDP growth rate increasing and averaging 12 per cent over the three year period, due to the continued growth of gold-mining, the emergence of oil as a major export commodity, and associated growth in the transport and construction sectors. Despite this unprecedented rate of economic growth, the national economy was in crisis, because of a series of large fiscal deficits that led to financing difficulties for governments and threatened the stability of external accounts (Economic Insights 1994). Namaliu lost power in the 1992 elections, with Paias Wingti again becoming Prime Minister and Sir Julius Chan again the Minister of Finance (until he was transferred to Foreign Affairs). The new government sought to introduce a package of economic initiatives, and immediately confronted the booming minerals sector, by demanding new resource agreements and greater equity participation, which caused consternation amongst some actual and potential overseas investors. At the same time, it pressed ahead with key elements of structural adjustment, through a radical programme of fiscal reform and new proposals for privatisation. The first tentative steps were made towards developing a stock exchange (that might discourage flight of capital). Fiscal reforms in the 1993 budget reduced personal and corporate taxes, making them some of the lowest in the Asia-Pacific rim. The Wingti government again emphasised the need for continued rapid growth and, despite sometimes confused and conflicting efforts to gain greater participation in the minerals sector, moved towards liberalisation of the climate for foreign investment. Attempts to diversify foreign investment out of mining, or to regulate its growing involvement in the forestry sector (where economic exploitation and environmental mismanagement had become the norm), were absent. After only months of the new government it seemed 'inevitable that foreign enterprise will benefit the most and that the distribution of income and assets among nationals will become even more skewed in favour of a privileged few' (Wesley-Smith 1993:418). The extent of crisis was well understood by the government.

> The crisis is not one of high inflation, or lack of foreign exchange to pay for essential imported capital goods, spare parts or consumption items. The crisis is one of low growth in all sectors of the economy not directly linked with mining and petroleum – the sectors which support the mass of the population. This manifests itself in extremely low rural incomes and high rates of urban unemployment. Real per capita income in 1992 is lower than it was in 1979.
>
> (Chan 1992b)

Despite these problems the 1993 budget was expansionary though a minibudget in early 1994 sought to restrict spending (notably by cutting back a Village Services Programme and local government funding) and to lift revenue. At the same time the decline in foreign exchange reserves became critical.

After a bungled constitutional manoeuvre to ward off votes of no-confidence, and secure greater continuity of government and personal power, the Wingti government fell in mid-1994. In a familiar shifting scenario, Sir Julius

Chan, after twelve years, again became Prime Minister, to inherit a still critical economic situation. The economy continued to be powered exclusively by the resources sector, unemployment was growing (with jobs being created for only about 10 per cent of new entrants to the labour market), tax cuts had not enabled business development (because of the shortage of skilled human resources, unreliable public utilities and poor infrastructure) and privatisation had proceeded nowhere. By the end of 1994 the country was experiencing a national economic crisis; the government was unable to control its expenditure, despite bills left unpaid and the balance of payments had worsened, despite substantial mineral earnings. PNG simply ran out of foreign exchange reserves, and there was international reluctance to provide financial support, forcing the devaluation of the kina (by 12 per cent) and a freeze on public expenditure. Three weeks after devaluation the kina was floated, after persistent speculation had resulted in a decline in foreign reserves, which had dropped to record lows under the previous government. For the architect of the hard kina policy, this was a crucial economic decision, partly designed to forestall IMF intervention and a new round of structural adjustment. Once again the new government placed considerable faith in the minerals sector, and especially the development of the Lihir gold-mine (in Chan's constituency), as the key to economic growth. It did however stress that it would relinquish all direct interests in business and reduce its holdings in mining and oil. The new government faced what had become established problems of achieving diversification and improved service delivery, with inadequate infrastructure (especially roads and urban services), an inefficient public sector, growing corruption and a serious law and order problem. Despite drastic fiscal measures, the responses – that stressed foreign investment and privatisation – paralleled those adopted in the previous decade. Changes of government had not changed economic policy and practice.

The outcome was similar. Once again the government turned, reluctantly, to the World Bank and the IMF, who devised a new structural adjustment programme, in return for a A$550 million loan. The twenty-seven-point structural adjustment programme focused on five key areas – increased spending on rural social and economic services (and shifting expenditure from recurrent to capital items), reducing constraints on international investment (but refraining from deals offering tax concessions or monopolies), adopting an effective and sustainable forestry policy, retrenchment of one-seventh of the bureaucracy and informing the community of 'the seriousness of the challenge ahead and the difficulties PNG faces', whilst developing greater government transparency and accountability. With some other options available, including floating mining and oil assets, a substantial soft loan from Taiwan (later opposed by the People's Republic of China) or relaxing constraints and accelerating logging, PNG was slow to agree to the conditions and slow to implement them. Demonstrations led by students urged the government to drop the whole programme, because of a controversial land mobilisation component (part of a separate World Bank programme).

However, a second 1995 Budget set new directions with the World Bank playing an active role in formulating the Budget itself, concerned that PNG would fail to comply with all the conditions, in the same way that it had failed in 1989. The government undertook certain reforms, implementing trade liberalisation by replacing all existing trade bans with tariffs, and dismantling the investment regime that reserved certain small business activities solely for nationals, but other World Bank concerns were not addressed, including restructuring of the agricultural sector, and a reduction in the size of the public service. The government was most reluctant to enforce a 'code of conduct' on the forestry industry, phase out the export of raw logs and undertake other related reforms. There was little real commitment to radical structural reform, especially of the agricultural and forestry sectors, on which so many rural people depended for cash incomes, relatively close to a national election. Early in 1996 the World Bank team was requested to leave by the government, there were subsequent disputes with the Bank about commitment to an appropriate forestry policy – with the Bank seeking a more independent National Forest Authority – and lack of progress on a national development plan, and thus doubt about the second phase of World Bank loan payments.

PRAGMATISM, IDEOLOGY AND ECONOMIC RATIONALISM

Over the whole post-war period economic policy in PNG has been conservative. At the time of independence there were token attempts to invoke socialist development strategies but few radical policies had been formulated and almost none implemented. Links between theory and practice were rarely made, other than by itinerant academics either working within PNG or engaged in consultancies, and, despite the rhetoric of the Eight Point Plan, pragmatism or improvisation dominated national economic decision-making. The genesis of more overtly ideological policies, however, coincided with the construction of the massive Bougainville copper mine, that transformed the economy from its historic dependence on agriculture to one where the new commanding heights were in the foreign-owned and capitalised mining sector. Continuity in economic policy and practice has triumphed over change. In terms of the broad structure of economic management, the post-colonial state has pursued policies that in fundamental respects are similar to those pursued by the colonial administration, with the more productive sectors of the economy being privately owned and dominated by foreign capital. Latter-day dissidents, who have continued to evoke the essence of the Eight Point Plan and the Melanesian Way (Narokobi 1980; Samana 1988), became conservative or powerless when absorbed into the national political system. Attempts to achieve greater self-reliance and economic nationalism have been intermittent, thwarted by the dominance of mining and the continuing dependence on aid and more recently the dictates of international agencies.

The advantages from late development were limited. Central planning has been weak, because of the lack of a philosophical base, competence and vision and persistent provincial pressure for decentralisation of economic planning and decision-making. The few plans and policies were rarely easily translated into practice. Though the central bank encouraged prudent fiscal management, in other areas the state has not taken a decisive role in shaping the rapidly changing economy, especially in the post-independence years. This situation became more problematic in the early 1980s, a period of 'swings, shocks and leaks', when the gravity of the world economic climate and the problems facing national development had become more apparent (Daniel and Sims 1986a). A small, open developing economy, reliant on primary commodity exports, has remained vulnerable to the external environment. While one 'achievement since Independence has been the flexibility of policy-making in the face of changing circumstances' (Goodman *et al.* 1985:28) that flexibility has also imposed costs, in terms of the absence of a long-term economic strategy. The costs of the transition to 'the new orthodoxy of economic growth for development' (M. Turner 1986a) have largely been those of an increasingly uneven distribution of the benefits of development and the failures of rural development. Mineral-led growth imposed significant social and economic costs and demonstrated the problems that follow even high growth rates but in a single booming sector.

Recent phases of post-war development, associated with structural adjustment, have emphasised the bankruptcy of contemporary national approaches to development. The nation has made a transition from a phase of some planning, control and government intervention to one where market forces have gradually been given full rein. The new era of economic rationalism is well entrenched. 'Even with the rapid changes of government peculiar to PNG politics, subsequent governments have sought to maintain the status quo without options for radical changes based on any ideological convictions' (Kavanamur 1993:58). Contemporary ideological thrusts, more obviously apparent in practice than the nationalism of the independence years, reflect the rationale of economic growth, privatisation and deregulation, the agenda of the World Bank and the IMF. Rural development, seemingly crucial in a country of exceptionally limited urbanisation, where industrialisation is largely absent, has faded into the rhetoric of official policy statements. This has not prevented frustrated governments from choosing to 'look north' to Asian models of industrial development, however inappropriate, and towards Asian investment, whilst simultaneously opposing unwelcome World Bank advice on the grounds that it was questioning national sovereignty. Local demands for village 'development', in the sense of increased incomes, distorted the few initiatives that favoured the rural sector. Nevertheless the meaning attached to development is very much the exclusive concern of government and international financial institutions, hence the contemporary ideology and practice of development is elitist and divorced from the concerns of most of the national population. There has been little progress in achieving sustained and equitable economic development; indeed the word 'development' is infrequently mentioned in contemporary dialogues concerning national survival.

3   Subsistence and survival

> It is a truism that Melanesian peoples in general value food in ways which transcend its intrinsic value for them as a necessity of life. Its valuation is such that it appears to be used everywhere to create, maintain and manipulate social relationships. Food has the lowest common denominator and the greatest ease of convertibility of any valuable, and as a species of wealth it is crucial to the working of most indigenous political systems. Indeed, from this source springs the organising ethic of the social system. Other values such as those vitalising prestige, individualism, egalitarianism, kinship and community, are made commensurate through and by reference to food . . . food is the measure of all things . . . it is the idiom through which other values are expressed.
>
> (Young 1971:146)

Few countries in the world are so characterised by a predominantly rural population that is oriented to subsistence agricultural production as Papua New Guinea. Though no Papua New Guineans now live beyond the influence of monetisation and the purchase of commodities, self-sufficiency still plays a substantial role for most. Root crops, and to a lesser extent bananas and sago, have always been the principal food. Sweet potato is the most important of these, though taro dominated some island regions until quite recently, and yams hold great cultural significance in lowland areas such as the Trobriand islands and the Sepik region. Coconuts are ubiquitous on the coast. Bananas grow in most parts of the country and sugar cane, indigenous to New Guinea, is also widespread. Sago production remains extremely important in the swampy western lowlands of the Fly, Purari and Sepik river systems, and as far east as Bougainville still plays some role at times of famine and feast (Connell and Hamnett 1978). Few crops produced elsewhere in the tropical Pacific are not grown in PNG, and more than 400 species are grown for food, a response to enormous variations in altitude, rainfall and soils. All traditional agricultural systems were of considerable complexity, incorporating a variety of plants, though diversity was climatically restricted at high altitudes. Everywhere some hunting and gathering, and fishing in lowland and coastal areas, were combined with sedentary agriculture. A tiny minority of societies, on the highlands fringes, were almost exclusively hunters and gatherers. Except in the most remote and inhospitable regions, subsistence agriculture is now combined with commercial cash crop cultivation.

Agricultural systems have changed, often dramatically. One of the most significant transformations was the introduction of sweet potato. In the course of about three centuries sweet potato spread from Asia replacing taro and other root crops as the leading food; this happened centuries ago in the highlands but only in the 1940s on the island of Bougainville, a thousand kilometres to the east, after taro blight destroyed the former staple. Throughout PNG, agricultural systems have continually evolved, as experimentation results in new techniques and new varieties. Indeed local agriculturalists have been described as 'pathological innovators' (Waddell 1972:192), constantly seeking out and introducing new species. Since European contact the pace of agricultural innovation has increased with new plant species and domesticated animals. In one Eastern Highlands village, where there was no direct contact with Europeans until 1928 and very little for another quarter of a century, of the eighty-seven food and narcotic crops in the village in 1984, some fifty-two had been introduced since first contact (Bourke 1990), including corn, cassava, pumpkin, beans, potatoes and peanuts. Similar changes have brought greater diversity throughout PNG.

Throughout Melanesia, trade and exchange always played a substantial role in people's lives. While monetisation did not occur until the twentieth century, shells played the part of media of exchange, and exchanges were often over great distances. The 'kula ring', described by the anthropologist Malinowski, linked a large number of Milne Bay islanders in exchanges of food and pottery. Bougainvilleans exchanged goods as far as Malaita in the Solomon Islands, and there were exchange routes from the north coast of New Guinea into the highlands. However such systems never dominated the natural economy of production and most economies were highly localised.

THE SURVIVAL OF SUBSISTENCE

Agriculture is an integral part of local culture. In many societies a significant amount of time is devoted to producing particular goods, such as long yams in parts of the Sepik region (Huber 1978:175–6; Tuzin 1972) or, more widely, pigs. In the highlands at least, pig husbandry is crucial in providing both food as 'available energy on the hoof' (Waddell 1973:30) and commodities for exchange are thus cultural capital. Many plants are grown for non-food purposes, and plants and animals have a significance far beyond their nutritional value (Lea 1969). Plants had narcotic, medicinal and ritual roles, are components of tools, houses, canoes and other artefacts and used as clothing and personal adornment; they were widely traded and exchanged and were integral components of ritual life. Eating is itself a ritual and symbolic activity; the titles alone of three different studies – *Fighting with Food* (Young 1971), *Always Hungry, Never Greedy* (Kahn 1986) and *Food, Sex and Pollution*

(Meigs 1984) – suggest the extraordinary social role of food consumption, production and exchange. Crop failures and successes are often attributed to supernatural elements; when taro blight appeared in an Orokaivan village at the end of the 1970s, villagers believed 'that a sorcerer was poisoning their crop and that general village friction and unpleasantness had led to punishment by God or ancestors' (Newton 1985:93). In the Trobriands, 'even today certain kinds of magic skills continue to be employed, for example, to direct the yams how to move the soil so their growth will not be impeded by stones, to encourage the luxuriant growth of the vines, to make it rain when a drought occurs, and even to make the soil unattractive so pigs will not dig it up' (A.B. Weiner 1988:83; cf. Kahn 1986; Tuzin 1976). Magic has also been involved in most forms of hunting, especially for the relatively large and dangerous wild pigs and cassowaries, though shotguns have rendered magic less valuable.

The essence of subsistence agricultural systems is the variety of cultivated crops that are grown, often within the same gardens. Maring cultivators, in the highlands of Madang Province, for example, used more than a hundred wild trees or forest plants (Clarke 1971). Animals complement plant species; these animals – usually pigs and chickens – are important sources of protein. In tropical diets composed predominantly of vegetables, especially starchy tubers, the amount and distribution of meat is crucial (Dornstreich 1973:260). Animals are also often important for fulfilling ceremonial requirements and maintaining social relationships. The whole operation of subsistence agricultural systems in some parts of the highlands may have been determined by the necessity to have a number of pigs available at a particular time. However, where some animals are essential at particular times, the agricultural system is significantly altered by the need to rear animals; pigs may consume as much as half of all domestic root-crop production, placing stress on agricultural systems.

Diversity minimised the risk of hazard. In the highlands especially, altitude restricts diversity and hungry periods (*taim hangri*) were not unusual; marked dependence on the single staple of sweet potato, the absence of post-harvest storage techniques and the lack of large reserves of emergency famine foods gave highlanders particular vulnerability to hazard (Bourke 1988). Where population densities were relatively high in traditional agricultural systems a number of intensive techniques were used. In western highland areas mounding is practised (which increases the availability of soil nutrients and facilitates drainage, and, at very high altitudes, minimises frost damage). Elsewhere irrigation ditches may be dug, soil retention terraces constructed, mulching and green manuring practised and nitrogen-fixing Casuarina trees planted to replace grasses as fallow vegetation. These changes have all resulted in an increased length of cultivation periods so that agricultural systems in some places closely approximate permanent cultivation. Maintenance of variety, planting in mixtures, using tools that minimise the disturbance of surface soil and the diversification of field or garden locations all helped to ensure survival. The existence of supposedly archaic techniques and strategies was often misconstrued by outside observers as backwardness, low productivity and inefficiency, whereas they constituted an effective use of what were sometimes ecologically marginal or hazard-prone environment.

Melanesians sought to reduce labour inputs into agricultural systems and have rarely been interested in long-term environmental conservation. Even in some remote areas, environments have been irreversibly damaged (e.g. C.K. Schmid 1991). In Sengseng (West New Britain) fruit trees may be cut down, rather than harvested, even before they are mature, and children destroy cultivated plants without repercussion: 'casual destruction might almost be called a Sengseng character trait' (Chowning 1980:20), whilst 'a very relaxed gardening aesthetic' (Battaglia 1990:92) is another means of describing limited labour inputs and minimal management. Melanesians have sometimes been described as pyromaniacs, and practices such as grassland burning have contributed to environmental degradation (Finch 1989:134). The practice of specific conservation measures varies; in Simbu soil-retaining barriers are constructed along contours, breaking up slopes and trapping sediment (Wood and Humphreys 1982; cf. Sillitoe 1993b:161) and several highland peoples dig grid-iron ditches to direct water flow and reduce erosion. Such practices have not always been sustained, or found appropriate, when agricultural systems have begun to change more rapidly.

Although women were the main horticulturalists in most parts of the country, men sometimes provided substantial labour inputs (e.g. Clay 1986). Subsistence activities are usually divided between the sexes, men usually doing the clearing and burning while women do the weeding and harvesting. Such divisions are often quite rigid so that on Sabarl island (Milne Bay) men working 'like women' (and vice versa) was perceived to be so unusual in its transgression of gender divisions, that it actually distinguished the Sabarl people in their own eyes (Battaglia 1991:89–90). In a few other lowland areas, such as Sio (Morobe) and Sengseng (West New Britain), agriculture was also a predominantly male enterprise (Chowning 1980; Harding 1985). The division of labour has not substantially changed through modernisation, though men have often taken the role of cash crop producers, and there has been a greater feminisation of subsistence agriculture (e.g. Polier 1996) as men have devalued its unpaid toil.

In terms of energy flows (the ratio of energy input to output of food energy) subsistence agricultural systems may have been as much as fifty times as efficient as modern mechanised agriculture (Bayliss-Smith 1977). One group of Maring cultivators have been characterised as 'the world's most efficient farmers' (Clarke 1971). Precisely this situation, where needs are satisfied with low labour inputs, prompted the depiction of 'subsistence affluence' (Fisk 1975:47) though this notion of affluence is very different from its contemporary connotations, and desires were enormously constrained by the unavailability of exchange goods.

THE TRANSFORMATION OF TRADITION

Two principal factors have influenced changes in subsistence agricultural systems, following increasingly close contact with global economy and society. Population has begun to grow steadily, especially since the 1960s; this has led to the clearance of larger areas, the intensification of existing systems and reduced fallow periods. Contact with the global economy has itself resulted in the commercialisation of agriculture. Greater areas of land were required to produce a surplus that could be sold, especially where cash crops were planted. Such perennial tree crops occupied land for decades rather than the one or two years of food crops. Together these changes increased pressure on land resources and on the subsistence system.

Other factors have also created change. Forestry practices have destroyed the natural habitat of agricultural systems and in places the imminent demise of primary tropical rainforest has been predicted (Clarke 1976:255). The decline of forests reduced the availability of hunted and gathered foods. The introduction of shotguns has rapidly depleted many wild species, such as pigs, cassowaries, wallabies and possums, that were once a major source of protein.

> There was a time when animals of the land, rivers and air were abundant for the Rao people of the Middle Ramu. The old people tell of how wild pigs and bandicoots roamed near the houses. In those days food sold at the local market was bought only by teachers, other government and mission workers. Today locals as well roam the markets looking for protein. . . . But to a great extent the local people have brought it on themselves. They killed without thought for conservation. . . . People now blame modern weapons like guns and fishing nets for the depletion of game and fish. They killed off the animals without allowing nature time to replenish the supply.
>
> (*Times of Papua New Guinea* (*TPNG*) 25 May 1989)

Other wild species once widely consumed, such as ants, frogs, grubs and various insects, are less likely to be eaten now, for cultural reasons and through losses of habitat. Nevertheless in more remote thinly populated areas, hunting remains of considerable importance (e.g. Dwyer 1985; Morren 1986). Despite parallel improvements in fishing technology, including fibre-glass boats, outboard motors, spearguns and plastic gillnets, subsistence fisheries have scarcely become more significant. Even in seemingly propitious coastal areas, many coastal peoples resolutely turn their back on the resources of the sea (e.g. Harding 1985; see also Chapter 5). Rivers too play a surprisingly slight role in contributing to subsistence production.

Agricultural technology has also evolved, though the most significant change, from stone to steel, began before contact with the outside world. In pre-contact times, clearing of timber, and other tasks, was done using stone axes, until steel axes quickly replaced them and increased efficiency.

Agriculture remains dependent on human labour without the use of livestock or machinery. Steel tools have benefited men rather than women; in Orokaiva, for instance, 'women mainly use their hands and digging sticks and place the produce in string bags in a process unaltered since European contact' (Newton 1985:96). New tools, plant and animal species, all arriving over a short time span, and new mobility, led to something of an agricultural revolution. Indeed 'the introduction of steel technology and, more importantly, the cessation of warfare ushered in a brief period of subsistence affluence' (Grossman 1984a:157), in the years immediately after contact.

In contrast to substantial shifts in crop production systems, with changes in crops, crop combinations and technology, pig husbandry has changed little. Virtually throughout the country pigs remain crucial exchange items, only partly replaced (by money, or even such commodities as cars) as a necessary component for the crucial exchanges involved in land and marriage transactions. This is particularly true in the highlands where periodic pig feasts remain central elements in the social order; as many as 2,000 pigs have been killed on major ceremonial occasions (Brown 1978:87–94; Feil 1987:40–61). Despite the economic burden of feeding pigs, their numbers have not fallen, since there has been a rise in pig prices. Though pigs now have less symbolic significance throughout the country, they play a more prominent part in the market economy.

The most significant agricultural changes have followed the establishment of a market economy, with the emergence of smallholder cash cropping and the expansion of local markets. Cash cropping has often developed extremely quickly, hampered only by poor transport facilities and poor prices, and has usually resulted in the partial withdrawal of both land and labour from food crop production. Food crops have been displaced to the periphery of agricultural systems, especially in the lowlands where cash crops are directly planted in old food gardens; as this has occurred there has been less incentive to expend labour in maintaining distant gardens (e.g. Salisbury 1964). Areas previously used for hunting and gathering have also been displaced or have disappeared (Grant 1988). Villages themselves have been moved closer to areas accessible to roads, and food production may consequently have declined. Labour has shifted into commercial crop cultivation, or into wage employment; in Enga, for example, taro production has declined because it was historically a crop grown by men who now 'prefer diversions such as politics, card-playing and modern sector activities, while women do most of the routine gardening work' (Lea, quoted by Ward 1982:331). Even in densely populated highland areas, competition between cash crop and subsistence food production concerns labour rather than land (Bourke 1988:18). These trends have weakened the vitality and viability of subsistence agricultural systems, despite their increased diversity.

Cash cropping has also led to a greater permanence of village sites, as more mobile shifting cultivators have chosen to locate close to semi-permanent tree crops. Fission within villages (as in Siwai, Bougainville) has also occurred, as lineage groups move on to their own land and away from nucleated villages. Only in the more remote and thinly populated areas, essentially those between the coasts and the densely populated highlands, does significant mobility of both village sites and people remain the norm (e.g. Morren 1986). The expansion of cash cropping has contributed to the decline of indigenous technical knowledge, and the loss of some forest species, whilst intensification of land use eventually produced a retrogression within traditional agricultural systems (Lea 1972:275) and a reversion away from polyculture and mixed agro-forestry systems. The movement towards monoculture has also increased the risk of environmental degradation and agricultural disease. Change has emphasised the increasingly strong link between evolving agricultural systems and the global and national economy. Local cultures incorporate values and practices from outside, and value more highly the artefacts of western cultures. Cash croppers seek to produce yet more, because the terms of trade are moving against them, hence the establishment of cash cropping necessarily reduces opportunities for self-reliant development, increases dependence on western nations and puts pressures on the local economy (Chapter 4). As part of this transition food production systems have exhibited a transition which, at its most extreme, is 'from subsistence affluence to subsistence malaise' (Grossman 1980:2). Labour inputs have fallen, food crops have been spatially marginalised, beer consumption and other 'distractions' such as gambling occupy lengthy periods of time and villagers become complacent about subsistence production because imported foods can be purchased in village stores. Consequently 'cash earning activities have lulled people into a false sense of security. Part of the flexibility in the traditional subsistence system has been lost, its level of production lowered and its resilience has declined' (Grossman 1980:14). It nevertheless remains central to achieving an adequate nutritional status for the bulk of the population.

NUTRITION AND HEALTH

Prior to contact, nutrition was not always adequate, and mortality rates – particularly in the highlands – were often high (Dennett and Connell 1988). The establishment of a commercial economy had a positive effect on health through improved nutritional status. Initially the key to this improved status was simply increased diversity through the addition of purchased foods to the diet. More important, however, was the fact that tinned meat and fish, rice, flour and animal fat provided nutrients that were limited in traditional diets, specifically concentrated energy and protein. A series of studies in the Simbu village of Jobakogl over a twenty-five-year period, during which time coffee cultivation had become established, revealed that nutritional status had increased, following greater protein and energy intakes with a transition from sweet potato to rice and fish, leading to better growth of children (Harvey and Heywood 1983). In a different context, at Gavien resettlement project

(East Sepik), both the dietary quality and the nutritional status of different groups of settlers improved, since the staples were low in nutrients and purchased foods had a beneficial effect; the combination of cash cropping and food production increased nutritional status (Shack *et al.* 1990a, 1990b). In other situations where diversity of income-earning opportunities has increased, there have been similar improvements in health and nutrition. (Heywood and Jenkins 1992:264). At least in the 1970s and 1980s, improved access to medical facilities and to cash incomes enabled widespread improvements in nutritional status.

Nutrition is below average in a number of districts, especially in remote parts of the Sepik region, Milne Bay and some highland districts, where cash sources are few. Growth retardation is greatest in the middle altitude zone (600–1,200 metres); the factors responsible include nutrient intake, birthweight and morbidity, all influenced by the physical environment (Heywood and Jenkins 1992; T. Smith *et al.* 1993). More specifically, inadequate nutrition is correlated with short supply of foods, limited purchasing power, poor health conditions and lack of knowledge of nutrition. In the Southern Highlands, child malnutrition is most apparent in larger households and in those with less garden area per person (B.J. Allen *et al.* 1980). Higher levels of inadequate nutrition are also apparent in areas of emigration, such as Menyamya, parts of the Ramu valley, upland Kaintiba and amongst the Maring, where social inequalities contributed to selective nutritional deficiencies (Buchbinder 1977; Levett 1992). Where there is seasonality in food purchases, or substantial diversion of incomes into other forms of consumption such as alcohol (Grossman 1991), nutritional gains from cash cropping may be slight. Malnutrition is an important health problem, in relatively remote areas and even in parts of otherwise developed provinces, such as inland Manus and the North Solomons, where a too-rapid transition to cash cropping, and hence food purchase, may be a more significant influence. This is even more apparent in urban areas where 'a serious problem of undernourishment exists'; a third of urban households get less than the required amount of energy and the poorest 10 per cent get little more than half their needs (Gibson 1995:75). By the mid-1970s malnutrition was the fifth most common diagnosis and cause of death amongst infants in hospitals (Wood-Bradley *et al.* 1980:73). Although malnutrition is not a new phenomenon, as the many historic examples of *taim hangri* demonstrate, its contemporary causes are quite different from those in earlier times. The difficulty experienced by many Papua New Guineans in achieving adequate diets, longevity and homeostasis emphasises the limited relevance of the historic notion of 'subsistence affluence'. At least in the lowlands greater ecological diversity may have provided a more satisfactory diet, especially on the coasts where fish were available. Subsequently both agricultural systems and diets have become more complex though not necessarily more rewarding.

FOOD DEPENDENCY AND FOOD SECURITY

In pre-contact times Melanesian societies were largely self-reliant (despite limited exchange) and self-sufficient in the production of basic foods. Most such societies subsequently entered a situation of 'dietary colonialism' or 'food dependency' (T.G. McGee 1975), part of a movement towards the production of goods that are not consumed (such as cocoa and copper) to the consumption of goods that are not produced locally, as village economies became part of an international economy. Although in some cases land used for cash crops was previously unused, the movement of some land (and labour) from food crops to cash crops contributed to diets increasingly being composed of purchased foods. What has been described as 'the Pacific TV Dinner', rice with tinned meat or fish (Sargent 1985:161), is firmly established as a prestigious meal. Alongside this, sugar, biscuits and bread have also become important. Hot chip shops and other fast food outlets are features of most large urban centres. On Tubetube island, Milne Bay, 'rice has become an alternative staple in times of drought; tea and sugar are commonly drunk, while tinned meat, tinned fish and biscuits must now be considered Tubetube's "fast food" ' (MacIntyre 1987:95). A substantial volume of foods are imported; although their value has steadily increased, the proportion of imports that are foodstuffs has not grown since independence, because of very high levels of imports of machinery and other manufactured goods (Table 3.1). Annual food and beverage imports have been valued at more than K200 million in the 1990s and constitute around 18 per cent of the value of all imports. The key imported foods are grains (rice and wheat), biscuits and confectionery items (including K2 million of chocolate and K4 million of ice cream in 1989), meat in various forms and tinned fish (Table 3.2). Major efforts have been made to reduce the extent of imports, especially rice, tinned meat and tinned fish, and such nutritionally inadequate foods as lamb flaps, but there has been little success.

New foods and drinks confirm a degree of status and prestige, many are prominent in exchange ceremonies, and 'imported foods are an embodiment of wealth' (Sexton 1988:131). In parts of the highlands bottles of beer have been referred to as 'small pigs' because of their useful divisibility (and identical size) in traditional exchanges, where pigs were the principal exchange good (Standish 1978a). Even before the Second World War, south Bougainvilleans would walk over 20 kilometres to obtain rice for feasts. Many imported foods are characteristically referred to as 'European foods'. Although few were ever consumed extensively by Europeans in PNG, they were first seen and eaten by migrants in plantations (and towns) and associated with concepts of progress. Processed foods are extremely convenient, especially when weather conditions are bad, where more than one household member works in the cash sector or in urban areas, where considerable time has been spent on cash crops (Sexton 1988) and where access to gardens is difficult. This is particularly true, during dry seasons or when natural hazards

Table 3.1 Imports by commodity group (1985–90) (million kina, f.o.b.)

Commodity group	1985	1986	1987	1988	1989	1990
Food and live animals	154	163	172	182	191	195
Beverages and tobacco	10	8	12	15	15	15
Crude materials (inedible)	7	7	8	9	8	9
Fuel and lubricants	153	93	112	98	64	80
Animal and vegetable oils	3	3	4	3	3	5
Chemicals	65	82	85	84	78	81
Manufactured goods	134	149	182	207	253	223
Machinery and equipment	262	308	339	425	525	423
Miscellaneous	79	91	99	111	123	110
Total	867	904	1,013	1,134	1,260	1,141

Source: Papua New Guinea Department of Agriculture and Livestock (1992), *Handbook on Agricultural Statistics 1990/91*, Port Moresby, p. 35

Table 3.2 Food imports (1989) (million kina)

Wheat	9.0
Rice	36.5
Malt	2.2
Biscuits	2.4
Lard and margarine	6.1
Sauces	2.5
Beef	16.0
Lamb and mutton	14.2
Poultry	3.9
Pork	2.5
Butter, milk and cream	9.9
Sardines	2.3
Mackerel	30.7

Note: This table includes only those products whose imported value was more than K2 million in 1989

Source: Papua New Guinea Department of Agriculture and Livestock (1992), *Handbook on Agricultural Statistics 1990/91*, Port Moresby, pp. 48–63

have damaged agricultural systems, as famine foods have all but disappeared. New foods are also often preferred for their taste, not least by children, to whom advertising campaigns are sometimes oriented, and because they add diversity to relatively narrow diets. For the Kilenge: 'as village elders long for thick, heavy taro-coconut pudding their grandchildren cry for white rice' (Grant 1988:110). New patterns of food consumption have become most firmly established in the larger urban areas, though about half of all rice consumption is in rural areas. In the 1970s some three-quarters of all food consumed in Port Moresby was imported (Flores and Harris 1982:147) although a greater degree of self-reliance has subsequently been achieved. In urban areas, imported foods are often cheaper than their indigenous counterparts.

The most dramatic form of food dependency is alcohol consumption. Since 1962, when prohibition was removed from Melanesians, alcohol has rapidly diffused from urban areas, transformed expenditure and consumption patterns and had a great effect on social relations and law and order. Different groups have particular contexts for drinking, styles of drinking behaviour and symbolism for alcohol. Between 1970 and 1978 alone, over the period of independence, imports of alcohol to PNG increased by 289 per cent (Lambert 1979:31), even though beer was being produced in Port Moresby. The rate of subsequent expansion has been little different because of the status and prestige of alcohol consumption: in colonial times, 'the practice became firmly associated in many Papua New Guineans' minds with the perceived, wealth, knowledge and power of their rulers' (Ogan 1986:21) and this attractiveness was enhanced by prohibition. Male drinkers chose the varieties of beer favoured by Europeans and spoke English or Tok Pisin during drinking rather than vernacular languages (op. cit.:25). Leaders use beer to recruit and pay followers and workers, and politicians use beer to buy votes; beer has become a liquid asset. Where socio-economic change has been particularly rapid the social impact of excess alcohol consumption is negative; around Ok Tedi, the word *spakman* (drunk) has even become synonymous with men who have moved to take up mine employment (Hyndman 1991). Perceptions of the more widespread and harmful impacts of excess alcohol consumption have increased over time, leading to laws, especially in Port Moresby (and other large towns), to regulate and restrict alcohol consumption, and whole provinces have become officially dry for long periods of time, in an effort to reduce the violence that surrounds alcohol consumption.

The establishment of food dependency has created health and nutrition problems whilst income is diverted from a development strategy that might be more productive. Food imports can be expensive. In Oro Province in the 1970s villagers sold coffee at 10 cents a pound and purchased instant coffee at $4.80 a pound (Crocombe 1971). The drain of significant amounts of income, into alcohol consumption, has led to opportunities for capital accumulation literally being 'pissed away' (T. Schwartz 1982). Income and expenditure surveys in both rural and urban areas consistently reveal that a high proportion of all household incomes goes on food and drink (e.g. Christie 1980). The cost of food dependency is even greater when purchases are made in village stores, where prices are higher.

One response to rising food prices and import volumes has been to seek some degree of import-substitution through local production (and processing). Considerable problems arise in establishing processing plants. Sometimes production is seasonal, markets are established and protected elsewhere (hence only import substitution is possible) and technology must be imported. A peanut butter factory was established in the Markham Valley which produced a fine quality product using local peanuts, but because of the cost of imported machinery, bottles and expertise, the final price was the same as that of imported peanut butter. Moreover peanut producers were able to obtain superior prices from betel nuts, thus negating the only real location factor that made the factory worthwhile. It lasted only a few years. Meat canning has proved to be possible, and tinned fish will be domestically produced, but only through substantial subsidies and higher prices (Chapter 5). Nevertheless, for many manufactured products, it is extremely difficult for such small countries as PNG to achieve self-sufficiency, let alone strive to reach export markets; cheap labour and locally available raw materials are insufficient for the economies of scale that enable competition in established markets.

Proposals have been made to reduce the cost, extent and impact of food dependency. Politicians have consistently sought food self-reliance, even in the face of straightforward comparative advantage. Nowhere has this been more apparent than for rice production. Most schemes are costly and inefficient – such as promoting traditional foods through education, 'home garden' schemes and national nutrition plans – and are often more than offset by private sector advertising campaigns and promotions. Implementing tariffs on food imports and imposing quotas or bans on certain commodities have been successful for a small number of unpopular foods, such as lettuces and tomatoes (and PNG is now self-sufficient in a range of fruits and vegetables), but have not worked for major imports, such as rice. Repeated efforts to reduce import dependence on rice, including a short-lived imposition of a rice quota in 1979, have failed. The quota produced political unrest in several areas, and a switch to other imports; consumers were reluctant to replace rice because of either preferences, prices or both (G.T. Harris 1982) and institutions, such as prisons and hospitals, which were geared to rice, were severely affected (H. Thompson 1986). Restrictions on rice imports had to be lifted in 1986 because of its dietary significance. At the same time a major feature of agricultural development has been the persistent failure of local rice production to reach markets, despite numerous efforts in many areas where rice readily grows. There have been frequent exhortations to increase local production. In 1983 for example the Minister for Administrative Services, Sir Pita Lus, berated the Department of Primary Industry, 'Anyone who thinks Papua New Guinea cannot be self-supporting in rice is a fool. Why talk about importing rice when rice can be grown within the country to save millions of kina. Papua New Guinea can be self-supporting in rice quicker than most people think if primary industry officers have a more positive attitude' (*Post Courier* (*PC*) 12 September 1983). A decade later, the agricultural policy set out in the 1993 budget aimed to replace 50 per cent of imported rice by the end of the decade (Chan 1992a), a forlorn hope where betel nuts produced better incomes in most rice-growing areas. A significant increase in domestic rice production could be achieved only by commercial production on a very large scale. Any foreign exchange savings would be negligible while a substantial subsidy would be required (Joughlin 1986; Gibson 1993). PNG's comparative advantage lies in crops that can be exported or locally marketed, unlike many Asian contexts where there are no appropriate alternatives. However the quest for greater self-reliance, undiminished by persistent failures, disappointments and lavish expenditure, has never ended.

Efforts to achieve better marketing of domestic food production have been disappointing. A Food Marketing Corporation was set up in 1976 but there were major supply problems and it collapsed in 1987 (Dorney 1990). A more complex Smallholder Market Access and Food Supply Programme, began in 1986, aimed at improving subsistence food production, nutrition and marketing in areas identified as particularly disadvantaged but also failed because of poor administration and management (Crittenden and Lea 1991). Government attempts to stimulate village food production and marketing, limited though they have been, have been dismal failures in comparison with villagers' own efforts. Without much government assistance vegetable production marketed through formal outlets increased by 40 per cent between 1987 and 1991, though it was stimulated by a New Zealand aid project based in Mount Hagen (Chapter 4). The problems of supplying fresh food to urban areas remain significant.

Attempts to reduce food dependency have been directed at symptoms of the problem, whereas the primary problem is not, in itself, the expense or impact of imported foods but that food imports occur in a context of relative poverty. Hence, in urban areas, imported processed foods do not supplement the diet, but they become the diet, especially for the poor. Equally the revolution in rising expectations has emphasised the modernity and convenience of imported, processed foods and drinks (and cigarettes and fuel). Opposition to imported foods thus threatens household economics (where imports are cheaper), dietary satisfaction and the demand for modernity. Food security is best achieved by a combination of cash cropping and subsistence farming in rural areas, by cheaper local fresh food in urban areas (which may follow infrastructure improvements, subsidy schemes for rural producers and higher incomes). In both rural and urban areas there has been little progress towards this situation. Despite rapid commercialisation, subsistence agriculture remains at the core of the economy, producing the bulk of all food consumed in the country, and remains crucial for food security.

Around the time of independence it was possible to describe Simbu, like many other areas, as a place where change could be characterised as being a partial acceptance of modern innovations into a continuing system whose essential variables had not been transformed (Brookfield 1973). Though such a situation remains true, the shift to cash cropping, wage labour (and migration) associated with population growth, has brought new variables, influencing land use and the commercialisation of rural life. Whilst environment and culture remain intrinsically and deeply interrelated, economic issues have now intervened. Subsistence agriculture continues to dominate lives and livelihoods but, despite greater diversity, without the sustainability and significance of earlier years. Hunting and gathering have also lost their social and nutritional significance, as habitats have been depleted and populations become more sedentary. Many plants and animals have retained their social and symbolic importance and the role of food in social organisation remains vital, but there is now a less holistic perspective on agricultural systems. Local self-sufficiency has declined in every sphere and the subsistence economy is no longer distinct from the global economy.

4 An agricultural economy?

When you first brought us these [coffee] trees and told us we should grow them, we scoffed at you and said 'We have plenty of trees; what use are these new ones?' But now we see we were wrong: money grows on those trees.

> (A Simbu leader, 1959, quoted in Brookfield 1968:97)

We are planting coffee ourselves. We are probably doing it wrong, but there is no point in asking the *didiman* to help us. If he started to help us we would end up relying on him, and we would have to wait too long for him to come back. He might not ever come back. We can't wait for him. He just stays in his office.

> (Huli farmer, Tari, December 1984, in conversation with B.J. Allen)

Agriculture is of enormous importance, for both food and exports. Since independence the agricultural sector has conspicuously failed to expand and – at least in terms of exports – the economy has become dominated by minerals production, and by the contemplation of even greater future possibilities in that sector. The slow and steady incomes generated from agricultural production have lost their appeal at every level, against the 'fast money' of wages and salaries, and the immediate returns from forestry. Although smallholder agricultural production has increased since independence, this has been offset by a fall in production from the plantation sector (other than oil palm). Indigenous smallholders now dominate the export of cash crops, being responsible for about two-thirds of production (outside the oil palm sector, where they produce about a third). The agricultural sector contributes around a quarter of total output in PNG, employs about two-thirds of the workforce and contributes more than 10 per cent of export earnings. Increased production and employment generation in this sector remain critical to national development; though the agricultural area in use increased by about 8 per cent between 1970 and 1985, this was a growth rate little more than half the rate at which the number of agricultural workers increased (Jarrett and Anderson 1989:31). The principal constraints to smallholder cash crop production are lack of knowledge of modern techniques and varieties, the decline of the agricultural extension system, inadequate access to capital needed to replant old trees, poor maintenance, low prices and difficulties of access to markets and land. The plantation production of copra, coffee and cocoa has declined because of limited replanting and maintenance, following uncertainties over land tenure, a shortage of managerial expertise, labour problems and falling world prices.

Table 4.1 Agricultural exports by commodity (volume) (1981–95) (thousand tonnes)

	Cocoa	Coffee	Tea	Copra	Copra oil	Palm oil	Rubber
1981	27.8	46.4	7.0	102.9	30.1	34.1	4.5
1982	28.6	41.2	6.1	74.8	42.7	88.9	2.2
1983	26.3	52.5	7.2	78.7	36.2	77.9	2.7
1984	34.1	49.4	7.3	93.5	40.7	129.9	3.4
1985	30.9	40.6	6.6	103.5	41.5	123.8	5.4
1986	31.9	53.1	5.3	93.0	41.1	129.0	5.0
1987	34.4	64.8	5.6	84.1	40.2	97.3	3.7
1988	37.1	44.8	5.8	76.8	36.3	102.6	4.5
1989	46.6	85.0	5.4	60.7	34.6	131.7	3.6
1990	33.9	63.3	5.4	55.3	34.8	142.7	2.3
1991	35.8	46.6	4.7	44.0	33.2	199.6	2.8
1992	38.6	53.0	5.6	47.5	34.8	206.1	2.7
1993	37.8	62.8	6.4	59.0	45.5	245.7	3.6
1994	26.0	64.7	3.4	50.3	32.4	230.8	3.4
1995	30.6	55.1	4.2	64.2	33.1	186.6	2.7

Source: Bank of Papua New Guinea, *Quarterly Economic Bulletins*, 1981–96

The reduced significance of agriculture in the national economy is particularly striking because of its critical role in recent economic history. In 1951 coconut products accounted for more than 60 per cent of the value of all exports, and in the 1960s PNG was overwhelmingly an agricultural economy, with cocoa, coffee and copra the key exports. Timber became a valuable commodity at the start of the 1970s and palm oil in the mid-1970s. At the same time, mineral exports first became substantial, and the agricultural economy entered into a long period of relative decline. Subsequently the export volume of the three historic cash crops never really increased significantly though oil palm exports did increase (Table 4.1). At the start of the 1970s exports from the primary sector (fisheries, forestry, but mainly agriculture) represented more than 90 per cent of the value of all exports; by the end of that decade agricultural exports represented only 50 per cent of the value of exports and minerals accounted for most of the other half, though the total value of exports had substantially increased. Minerals took over primary importance as an export earner in 1985 after a steady shift away from agriculture. At the end of that decade agricultural products still constituted 24 per cent of all exports (Table 4.2). The relative decline was much more

Table 4.2 Exports by commodity group (value) (1976–95) (million kina)

Year	Agricultural	Forest products[2] Logs	Total timber	Marine products	Minerals Gold	Copper	Silver	Total metals	Oil	Total exports[3]
1976	172.7	10.4	22.0	1.5	—	—	—	200.0	—	461.3
1977	286.3	11.0	23.2	20.5	70.4	111.9	4.6	186.9	—	555.8
1978	236.5	11.8	22.6	25.0	103.8	122.5	5.5	231.8	—	562.5
1979	274.6	20.9	36.5	21.8	163.0	184.0	12.0	358.9	—	754.4
1980	230.5	30.0	45.8	31.6	172.9	139.3	10.2	322.2	—	691.8
1981	174.8	31.5	43.9	27.4	158.9	134.6	7.0	300.6	—	565.9
1982	174.4	49.6	61.7	8.3	171.8	122.8	7.5	302.1	—	570.4
1983	231.5	43.2	54.7	9.1	200.9	161.0	11.2	373.1	—	687.4
1984	380.6	69.9	81.7	10.0	183.3	135.5	8.0	326.8	—	822.0
1985	330.2	58.4	67.3	12.1	318.8	164.2	6.9	489.9	—	926.2
1986	331.9	68.0	74.7	7.9	398.5	156.0	6.8	561.2	—	1000.8
1987	268.9	103.0	110.9	11.0	422.9	281.9	10.6	714.9	—	1123.2
1988	255.2	90.5	97.5	7.5	405.1	446.9	9.5	861.5	—	1256.1
1989	270.1	90.0	96.2	8.1	316.9	344.9	14.3	676.1	—	1111.6
1990	204.6	65.2	79.6	8.2	393.2	349.2	15.1	757.5	—	1122.4
1991	204.6	81.2	90.2	10.4	666.9	323.8	14.6	1005.3	—	1390.5
1992	223.6	140.0	148.2	9.3	745.9	313.5	16.6	1070.1	301.4	1862.6
1993	270.1	400.2	410.4	7.8	681.6	256.3	12.1	950.0	817.8	2527.3
1994	374.6	483.1	494.4	10.3	702.3	367.4	10.3	1080.0	702.7	2662.0
1995[1]	498.0	437.0	450.0	14.0	840.0	755.0	13.0	1607.0	828.0	3397.0

Notes: 1 The data for 1995 are provisional
2 Other forest products include timber, plywood and woodchips
3 Includes re-exports

Source: Bank of Papua New Guinea, *Quarterly Economic Bulletins*, 1976–96

Table 4.3 Direction of trade: imports and exports (1970–93) (thousand kina, f.o.b.; percentages in parentheses)

Imports	1970–1	1975–6	1981	1987	1990	1993
Australia	130.395(51)	161.413(47)	227.999(38)	431.7(43)	534.4(51)	
Japan	43.650(17)	49.980(14)	119.245(16)	185.6(19)	152.2(14)	
New Zealand	—	—	38.025(5)	37.6(4)	38.5(4)	
Singapore	—	—	136.116(18)	66.1(7)	97.2(9)	—
UK	9.823(4)	18.327(5)	31.658(4)	28.3(3)	26.8(3)	
USA	29.585(12)	24.388(7)	56.414(8)	80.6(8)	109.9(10)	
Other	41.226(16)	92.309(27)	78.680(11)	166.2(16)	99.8(9)	
	254.499	346.397	738.137	996.0	1,056.8	1,110.0
Exports						
Australia	43.373(43)	54.193(15)	53.205(10)	84.8(8)	313.1(26)	911.4(36)
Japan	11.813(11)	105.459(29)	211.836(39)	301.2(27)	335.4(28)	546.2(22)
New Zealand	—	—	2.804(1)	4.9(0.4)	10.9(1)	18.9(0.7)
Singapore	—	—	7.857(1)	5.9(0.5)	12.7(1)	73.7(2.9)
South Korea	—	—	—	170.4(15)	110.2(9)	255.9(10)
UK	19.567(19)	19.317(5)	27.573(5)	50.4(5)	51.7(4)	76.6(3)
USA	3.337(3)	30.663(9)	18.550(3)	22.1(2)	28.8(2)	100.8(4)
Germany	5.377(5)	90.752(25)	121.824(22)	288.4(26)	192.0(16)	163.2(6)
Other	8.465(8)	63.366(17)	101.925(19)	195.1(16)	143.8(13)	394.8(15)
	101.932	363.750	545.574	1,123.2	1,198.6	2,541.5

Source: Bank of Papua New Guinea, *Quarterly Economic Bulletins*, 1970–94

rapid in the early 1990s, as new mines compensated for lost production at Bougainville, oil exports began and the volumes of most agricultural exports declined. By 1995 agricultural products represented just 15 per cent of the value of exports. Despite the enormous social importance of agriculture, PNG is no longer a primarily agricultural economy. Manufactured exports have always been inconspicuous, a result of the dismal record of industrial development (Chapter 8) even including the processing of agricultural commodities. Exports of manufactured goods have been so trivial that they have never been recorded separately in export statistics.

Within the primary sector there have been changes in the composition of exports. Coconut products (mainly copra) were about half of all export earnings around 1960, but at the start of the 1990s copra had declined to just 2 per cent of all exports. There were no significant exports of cocoa and coffee until the late 1950s, but they contributed 30 per cent of the value of all exports in the 1960s. The decline of copra, the more recent stagnation of coffee and cocoa, and the disappointing development of tea and rubber (Table 4.1) were compensated for by increased exports of oil palm. Sugar became an export earner in 1992, whilst timber, often of slight importance, eventually became the third most important export, after oil and gold. Despite the optimism occasionally generated by the potential of new crops – notably oil palm – the national agricultural system is dominated by what can be seen as the traditional trilogy of copra, coffee and cocoa, alongside food production. The agricultural history of PNG is more or less defined by the fluctuating fate of copra, coffee and cocoa, though the future may be more influenced by the fate of oil palm.

Before independence trade was primarily oriented to Australia and, in terms of imports, that orientation has been remarkably resilient over a quarter of a century (Table 4.3). The destination of exports has become more varied, as these have become more diverse, with a shift away from the traditional western trading partners towards new minerals purchasers. Historic trade preferences with Australia and the European Union remain significant despite the slow shift 'north' towards Asia. Trade with other Pacific states, even New Zealand, has always been minuscule. Japan has been the single most important destination of exports since the start of the 1980s, despite the growth of Australia as a gold importer. Trade has shifted only a small way from the old colonial flag.

THE CLASSICAL CASH CROP TRILOGY: COPRA, COCOA AND COFFEE

Of all the contemporary cash crops, copra has been of greatest significance. The nineteenth-century history of the Pacific, and of much of coastal PNG, is bound up with copra trading and coconut production. It began in the 1880s in East New Britain, expanding to other New Guinea islands and to the north coast of New Guinea during the German era, but getting underway in

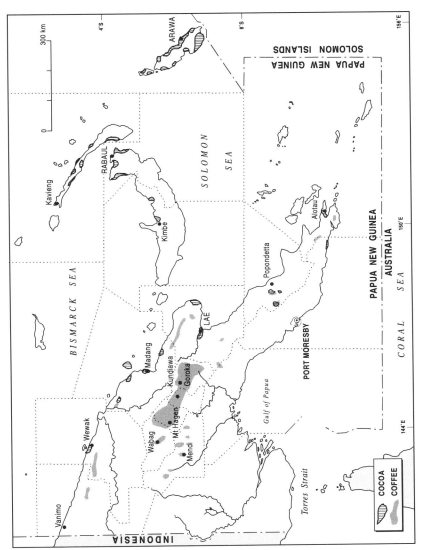

Figure 4.1 Cocoa and coffee production areas

Papua only in 1907. In East New Britain individual Tolai production of copra was so substantial by the end of the nineteenth century that European traders found it difficult to acquire enough shell valuables in exchange (T.S. Epstein 1968:35; Salisbury 1970). At the start of the century copra comprised about 90 per cent of the total value of exports, but the post-war establishment of cocoa as a lowland cash crop hastened its relative decline. Coconuts have remained important primarily because they are both a major food crop (with a diversity of additional uses, including fuel, timber, and animal feed) and a useful shade tree (for cocoa or cattle), hence copra could be produced when prices were high or there were excess coconuts. Plantations lost their pre-eminence in the 1980s, as prices fell; so poorly was the copra industry performing at the start of the 1990s that it almost became a 'dead industry' (*TPNG* 19 September 1991), with no obvious future potential, as world prices remained exceptionally low (Figure 4.2). Both smallholder and plantation copra production had stopped in several areas; even high-yielding, hybrid coconuts offer little incentive for regeneration.

Coconuts and cocoa are mainly grown in the same lowland areas, though coconuts are more widespread because of their food value and their ability to grow in poor soils. Five provinces – East and West New Britain, North Solomons, Madang and New Ireland – usually account for about 90 per cent of all copra production, both from smallholders and plantations, though the copra industry has been particularly important where there are few alternative economic opportunities, hence depressed prices have led to economic recession in a number of remote lowland and island areas (Table 4.4).

Cocoa is the second most important cash crop, established as a plantation crop in the island provinces in the inter-war years. By 1940 exports were just 213 tonnes. After the war, world demand for cocoa grew substantially, copra plantation owners diversified into cocoa and indigenous cocoa planters were encouraged. The earliest producers were again the Tolai of East New Britain, a few of whom had experimented with production in the inter-war years. Expansion was rapid; the planted area increased from about 3,700 hectares in 1951 to 50,000 hectares in 1965, and, over the same period, production increased from 485 tonnes to around 15,500 tonnes. Almost all of this, some 95 per cent, came from the plantation sector. However, from 1965 onwards, smallholder cocoa planting grew at a phenomenal rate to reach about half the total just after independence and almost 70 per cent in the mid-1980s. In the boom years of the late 1970s and early 1980s cocoa production brought an unprecedented degree of prosperity to the island provinces, especially East New Britain and the North Solomons. The end of cocoa exports from the North Solomons in 1989 (following the violent struggle for secession) was a bitter blow to the national economy and to local smallholders. After a steady fall in cocoa prices, the value of exports never returned to that of the mid-1980s. The Cocoa Industry Fund's capital, used to stabilise cocoa prices, was exhausted in May 1989, and by the early 1990s most plantations had laid off more than 30 per cent of their labour, adopted shorter working hours and

Table 4.4 Cash crop production by province (1989–91) (thousand tonnes)

	Copra	Cocoa	Coffee	Oil palm
Western	—	—	—	—
Gulf	0.3	—	—	—
Central	1.2	0.1	—	—
Milne Bay	3.7	—	0.1	13.2
Oro	0.4	0.8	0.3	44.2
Southern	—	—	1.4	—
Enga	—	—	1.1	—
Western Highlands	—	—	19.7	—
Simbu	—	—	4.8	—
Eastern Highlands	—	—	14.9	—
Morobe	2.0	0.4	3.0	—
Madang	20.3	2.2	0.5	—
East Sepik	1.5	1.9	1.0	—
West Sepik	0.7	0.3	0.2	—
Manus	0.6	0.1	—	—
New Ireland	12.4	1.3	—	—
East New Britain	46.3	21.0	—	—
West New Britain	14.1	1.2	—	115.4
North Solomons	26.8	18.4	—	—

Note: 1989 was the last year when production from the North Solomons was reasonably typical of previous years, hence 1989 has been used for the copra and cocoa data, whereas 1990–1 is used for the coffee and oil palm data

Source: Papua New Guinea Department of Agriculture and Livestock, Policy Planning and Budgeting Division (1992), *Handbook on Agricultural Statistics, 1990/91*, Port Moresby

either ended or reduced inputs such as fertilisers and fungicides (*TPNG* 29 August 1991). Rising prices in the mid-1990s offered hope of recovery. The main cocoa-growing areas in PNG are the island provinces (Table 4.4), where volcanic soils and humid, cloud-covered environments enable the production of cocoa of extremely high quality.

Of the three established cash crops, coffee is much the most recent and the only one that can be grown at high altitudes. For more than a quarter of a century it has been the nation's most valuable commercial crop. It is particularly important as a smallholder crop, since some 75 per cent of all production is by smallholders. Coffee was probably grown in PNG in the nineteenth century but it was not until the 1950s that serious attention was given to the development of an industry, beginning in the highlands in the late 1940s. After initial doubts (as in Simbu) coffee was quickly and widely accepted as a cash crop. Before 1960 most of the coffee exported from PNG was Arabica from the uplands of Morobe, and a small quantity of Robusta came from lowland areas, where it has now been largely superseded by cocoa or oil palm. Arabica coffee makes up more than 95 per cent of total coffee production, almost all from the five highland provinces, with small quantities from the upland areas of Madang and Morobe provinces.

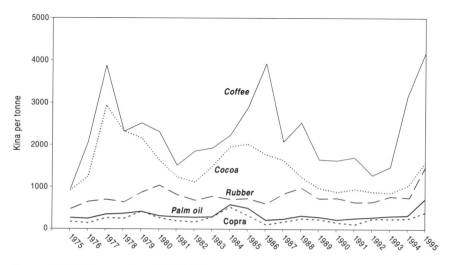

Figure 4.2 Cash crop prices (1975–95)
Source: Bank of Papua New Guinea, *Quarterly Economic Bulletins*

Since the first coffee plantations began in 1950, export volumes steadily increased until the mid-1980s, when declining prices led to a lengthy slump. Prices fell from a peak of K3,927 in 1986 (when coffee constituted 63 per cent of all agricultural exports) to K1,632 per tonne in 1990; this price, already the lowest real price for over forty years, fell by a further 25 per cent in 1992 (Figure 4.2). The collapse of the International Coffee Agreement in 1989, the suspension of the quota system and the resultant free market in coffee, contributed to the depression in prices. At the same time that prices began to decline, the industry was hit by an outbreak of coffee rust disease, accidentally introduced into the country in 1985, which led to an atmosphere of crisis, enveloping coffee growers, processors and merchants, alongside politicians (themselves often significant growers or entrepreneurs) and bureaucrats, as production threatened to collapse (MacWilliam 1990; Shaw *et al.* 1986; Stewart 1992). Declining prices and coffee rust took their toll on production and producers. In the 1990s, factories operated at less than a third of capacity; this resulted in the purchase of low quality coffee – as smallholders invested less time in management and production – hence coffee sales were discounted by 10 to 15 per cent (Grey 1993:97). Falling prices induced a downward spiral of reduced investment of time, technology and money and a further reduction in profitability. Attempts to support the coffee industry have proved difficult and expensive, yet have been politically essential. By mid-1991 the national Coffee Stabilisation Fund was exhausted, two years after that for cocoa. In the highlands, the smallholder sector was more resilient to falling prices, some indication of the limited range of alternative income generation opportunities in the region. A sharp increase in prices in

1994 – to levels similar to those of the mid-1980s – also offered prospects of revival.

Since the mid-1980s the historic trilogy of cash crops has fallen on hard times, mainly through falling world prices. Declining prices have been particularly significant in the highlands, where coffee-growing was still reaching new frontiers in the Southern Highlands and Enga in the 1980s, and in those coastal areas where there are few alternatives to copra. After the exhaustion of commodity price stabilisation funds, subsequent subsidies were unable to produce agricultural restructuring or improved efficiency, nor benefit most producers, but blew out budget deficits. 'Middlemen manipulation' reduced the benefits of the stabilisation schemes and the main beneficiaries were exporters rather than smallholders (MacWilliam 1995, 1996; D.G.V. Smith 1992; Stewart 1992:163–74). Since the mid-1980s alternatives have assumed greater significance and, relative to the traditional trilogy, several have expanded and become valuable sources of revenue. They have not achieved the economic and social significance of the earlier cash crops.

OIL PALM, LIVESTOCK AND OTHER ALTERNATIVES

With the decline of the principal export crops, oil palm has become of much greater economic significance though its production affects very few people. The industry began only in 1965, exporting after 1973, although the Germans had grown oil palm in the 1890s. It currently consists of four major estates, in West New Britain and Oro Provinces, and a number of associated smallholders. In the late 1980s new oil palm smallholder projects were also established in Milne Bay and New Ireland, and other projects are planned. Commercial development followed the recommendations of the 1964 World Bank report and, perhaps more important, the Indonesian expropriation of plantation interests in Sumatra and the resultant international interest in PNG. The schemes have the same basic organisation: a central nucleus estate, jointly owned by the government and an overseas corporation, surrounded by a large number of smallholders. Smallholders have 6.5 hectare blocks, four under oil palm and the remainder for subsistence gardens or other uses (Grieve 1986). Oil palm has been the fastest growing agricultural export crop in PNG and is 'one of Papua New Guinea's success stories' (Stein 1991:43). Exports grew by an average of more than 20 per cent per year in the eight years after independence; technological innovation and socio-economic change combined to enable output to grow more steadily than in other sectors, despite price declines. The areas of current production are all environmentally amenable to oil palms, whilst the late start of the industry has been advantageous, as the stock is of high quality, milling facilities are modern and efficient and the estates are large enough to enable economies of scale that are not possible in the copra and cocoa industries.

The traditional export crops, plus oil palm, together account for more than 90 per cent of the value of all agricultural exports (Table 4.5). Other

Table 4.5 Agricultural exports by commodity (value) (1975–95) (million kina)

	Cocoa	Coffee	Tea	Copra	Copra oil	Palm oil	Rubber	Other	Total
1975–6	28.6	42.1	4.0	12.2	7.3	6.8	2.7	0.1	103.6
1976–7	55.1	132.6	8.0	18.9	11.4	8.5	3.1	—	237.6
1978	63.0	107.2	7.8	23.0	12.4	10.5	2.6	—	236.5
1979	60.9	125.0	8.0	38.2	20.6	14.4	3.5	—	274.6
1980	46.5	118.6	8.5	24.5	16.6	12.0	3.8	—	230.5
1981	34.1	74.2	7.1	19.3	12.5	14.2	3.4	10.0	174.8
1982	31.8	77.8	6.7	12.9	12.1	21.7	1.4	9.2	174.4
1983	41.4	94.7	10.4	24.0	20.0	23.7	2.2	15.1	231.5
1984	67.0	110.7	17.1	49.1	39.4	75.7	2.4	19.2	380.6
1985	62.5	117.5	11.5	33.4	23.7	61.6	3.9	16.1	330.2
1986	56.4	208.5	7.5	10.0	10.4	28.3	3.0	7.8	331.9
1987	56.2	134.7	5.6	15.2	14.5	23.9	3.1	15.7	268.9
1988	46.0	113.5	6.3	19.4	17.4	32.9	4.4	15.3	255.2
1989	45.2	140.4	6.1	14.0	15.3	38.3	2.6	8.2	270.1
1990	29.9	103.3	6.7	8.7	11.0	32.7	1.7	10.0	204.6
1991	34.0	79.5	5.3	5.2	12.8	52.5	1.8	13.5	204.6
1992	34.1	68.1	6.6	11.8	24.2	64.2	1.9	12.7	223.6
1993	33.1	100.5	7.2	14.2	19.6	79.2	2.6	13.7	270.1
1994	29.0	204.8	4.2	14.7	20.1	77.5	2.9	21.4	374.6
1995¹	48.0	215.0	5.0	27.0	30.0	142.0	4.0	27.0	498.0

Note: 1 The 1995 data are provisional

Source: Bank of Papua New Guinea, Quarterly Economic Bulletins, 1979–96

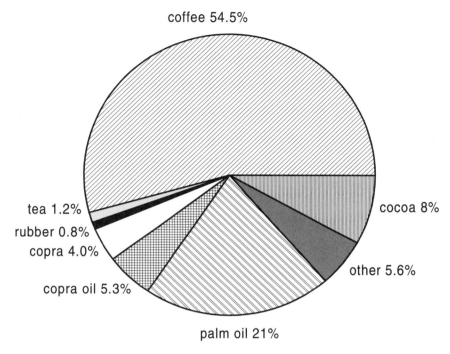

coffee 54.5%

tea 1.2%

rubber 0.8%

copra 4.0%

copra oil 5.3%

palm oil 21%

cocoa 8%

other 5.6%

Figure 4.3 Agricultural export earnings (1994)
Note: 'Other' includes sugar, chillies, cardamom, etc.
Source: Bank of Papua New Guinea, *Quarterly Economic Bulletin*, June 1995

crops are of very limited significance in terms of export value. At different times there has been considerable optimism over the future of tea and rubber, but in 1994 they represented only 1 per cent and 0.8 per cent respectively, of the total value of agricultural exports (Figure 4.3). Tea was promoted in the 1960s to encourage diversity in the highlands and contribute to import substitution, but it was never popular as a smallholder crop hence production is concentrated on seven factory estates, six in the Western Highlands and the other in the Southern Highlands (Goodman *et al.* 1985:105). The area under tea reached its peak of 3,000 hectares in 1975; exports peaked in 1978 (and again in 1984) and subsequently declined, along with employment in the industry. Ironically the principal tea-growing area, the Wahgi valley, is ecologically ideal for tea; both yields and quality are high by world standards. The tea industry has survived only because of the replacement of high cost labour by tea-picking machines (in a part of PNG where there is significant unemployment). If tea prices fall significantly the industry may disappear, the first significant cash crop to do so since the demise of cotton at the start of the twentieth century.

Rubber is a lowland industry, concentrated in Papua, and it is one of the longest established cash crops in the country; like copra it was well established before the war, and can grow on soils too poor for other crops. Planting reached a peak in the early 1960s and production in 1972. About 95 per cent of the area under rubber is in Central Province; sporadic attempts to develop a rubber industry have been made in other provinces, most recently around Kiunga (Western), despite low world prices. The small-scale, peripheral nature of the industry has meant that it has been unusually isolated from technical innovations in the rubber industry elsewhere, and labour costs are high.

The crop most recently developed on a large scale is sugar, established in the Markham Valley in the 1980s in an attempt to achieve self-sufficiency and generate local employment and income-earning opportunities. The large-scale sugar project at Ramu (Madang,) two-thirds owned by the government, produced enough sugar for local consumption and sugar imports were banned in 1983. However the Ramu sugar project was heavily criticised, in terms of its dependence on imported components: it 'appears to contradict almost all the principles set out in the national development strategy . . . it uses high technology, imported skills, overseas capital and increases the inequitable distribution of income, services, and housing' (B.J. Allen 1983:233). The cost of production was well above the world price (though this is distorted by EU and United States policies), and the price of exported sugar has been less than half the domestic price. High sugar prices have prevented the development of any secondary use of sugar, and raised costs for bakeries and soft drink manufacturers. Import substitution has been at a high cost in subsidised employment, has discouraged some industrial development and been most harmful to lower income groups. During the 1960s there were similar less heralded attempts, but on a smaller scale, to encourage tobacco production, since ecological conditions in the Eastern Highlands and the Markham Valley seemed appropriate and there was perceived to be a need for import substitution as consumption and imports increased. However the two principal companies operating in PNG – Rothmans and W.D. and H.O. Wills – were interested in manufacturing tobacco products rather than growing tobacco, and returns in the Eastern Highlands could not compete with coffee, hence the last commercial operation collapsed at the end of the 1980s, whereas local tobacco is marketed widely.

A host of other cash crops exist, including pyrethrum, cardamom and chillies. Most of these have existed for some years, without there being any significant expansion, and have tended to remain dependent on direct government purchases. Pyrethrum has the longest history, introduced in the late 1950s, and intended to be an alternative cash crop to coffee, because of marketing restrictions on the latter; costly pyrethrum 'pushes' were carried out in the Southern and Western Highlands and Enga provinces, to ensure that there was adequate volume for the economic operation of one factory at Kagamuga (Western Highlands). The industry never developed as anticipated because of climatic constraints, production quickly became rationalised and localised in the most suitable growing areas, all upland areas above 2,400 metres, especially in Enga, which produced 95 per cent of the country's pyrethrum in 1989. Though it proved its value in the highest altitude agricultural areas it was never competitive with less labour-intensive and more profitable crops.

Spices were the fastest growing agricultural sector in the 1980s. Cardamom was comparatively easy to grow and annual output increased from 10 tons in 1981 to 387 tons five years later (Callick *et al.* 1990:11.4). The price then plummeted and production fell dramatically. When the Gulf War cut off exports, production declined further, even in areas like Bundi (Madang), where it had become the major source of income (*TPNG* 16 August 1990). By the 1990s chillies had become the most successful export spice, whilst pyrethrum exports were valued at K0.7 million. There was also a small domestic market for chillies, unlike most of the other principal crops. Disappointments in diversification rarely discouraged governments, or individuals, in the search for successful alternatives to the classic trilogy, though they demonstrated why meeting niche markets is difficult.

The substantial livestock industry has never generated exports, nor was that intended. Central to the industry are pigs, but pigs have been so much a key element in social life that they long remained peripheral to the commercial economy though central to the gift exchange system. Many smallholder piggeries were established in the 1970s – perhaps as many as 500 – but almost all of them lasted a very short time, because of the low fertility and high mortality rate of pigs, high feed costs, low returns, heavy loan repayments and 'poor management' (Goodman *et al.* 1985:82). Pig owners and producers were often unable to operate on a commercial basis (even where appropriate skills existed) since they could not escape the *wantok* (kin) system, which demanded that pigs be part of the ceremonial exchange complex. A shift in the 1980s to medium-sized piggeries, on the fringes of the larger towns, finally enabled domestic pig production to achieve commercial success to the extent that, since 1985, pork imports to PNG have been banned.

The cattle industry is much more recent though it has lengthy antecedents. PNG is environmentally well suited to a tropical cattle industry since the country is free of major infections and debilitating livestock diseases. German colonists introduced cattle into the country, and the national herd grew rapidly between the wars. From the early 1960s a major effort went into import substitution and extending the expatriate-owned ranching industry and, rather later, to incorporating smallholders around these nuclei. Large pastoral land leases were granted to expatriates, especially in the Markham Valley (Morobe) and the adjoining Ramu Valley (Madang), where there was a large amount of thinly populated flat land. Despite impressive growth in the 1960s ranch herd numbers began to stabilise in the years after independence. Few ranches had any expansion potential; there was minimal interest in pasture improvement and little opportunity for acquiring additional land. National attention shifted to smallholder schemes. The smallholder cattle industry was initially concentrated in Morobe and the Eastern Highlands, two of the principal areas of expatriate ranch development, but expanded rapidly in the 1970s for a variety of reasons: prestige, the ability to control land, assumptions of profitability, ready availability of Development Bank loans and a desire for diversification. Many were unsuccessful for the same reasons that accounted for the failure of small piggeries: inadequate management skills (for both stock and pasture), lack of extension advice, disappointing incomes and high costs of debt repayment, and disputes over the larger land areas required for smallholder schemes (Connell 1979a:590–3). In some areas there was so much frustration over land tenure that grazing areas and fences were burnt down; owners neglected their animals which became feral and low profitability and alternative demands on land sealed the fate of many schemes. By the 1990s the national herd was about 40 per cent down on that in the 1970s (*TPNG* 12 December 1991). The smallholder component had fallen even more rapidly, from around 50,000 head at independence to around 17,000 head in 1991. Production fell, despite substantially increased demand. After a quarter of a century of extraordinary effort to develop the industry, 'which possibly absorbed more government extension effort than all other agricultural activities combined' (Goodman *et al.* 1985:82), the smallholder sector had almost disappeared. Outside the Markham Valley the results were particularly dismal. Ranches now provide enough high quality beef to meet the national demand for expensive cuts of meat, but imports of cheaper cuts of beef and lamb, particularly mutton flaps, have grown substantially.

There have been intermittent attempts to develop other livestock industries. In the post-war years sheep projects were begun enthusiastically in the highlands, especially in Seventh Day Adventist villages, but declined for the same reasons that led to the collapse of the cattle industry: returns were slow and slight (because of the low cultural value assigned to sheep), fences rotted and pasture degenerated, sheep wandered wild and by the end of the 1970s there were few new projects (Grossman 1984b). For a time there was some optimism about a buffalo industry, that might also produce draught animals, and a dairy cattle industry. Neither succeeded though there have been commercial dairy herds both in the highlands and lowlands. Goats have been tried, butterflies have occasionally triumphed, bees were commercially successful, mainly in the Eastern Highlands, to the extent that PNG briefly became self-sufficient in honey production, until, as in so many other niche industries, production fell away. A similar fate met the once promising silk industry (J.F. Weiner 1986). Deer and crocodiles have fared better, despite problems of market access (Ranck and Tapari 1984; Tapari 1988). A more successful poultry industry has emerged, especially around Port Moresby, making PNG self-sufficient in chicken by the early 1980s. Smallholders are oriented around a few processing companies that supply feed, chicks, processing, extension and marketing. The success of the poultry industry, even if localised near a few large towns, demonstrated that successful commercial agriculture did not have to be for export only, though the limited success of the sugar, tobacco, beef and honey industries emphasised the problems of import substitution. The real success story of recent agricultural change has been quite different: the marketing of food and vegetables by many small-holders, especially in the highlands.

BETEL NUTS, MARIJUANA AND MARKETS

Conventional analyses of commercial agriculture in PNG have largely revolved around the successes and failures of the major cash crops, all actively promoted, often at considerable expense and with an enormous input of time, by government agricultural extension workers (*didimen*). As urbanisation has continued, the purchasing power of the population increased, land tenure conflicts worsened and the prices of major cash crops have fallen, other crops – especially betel nut, sweet potatoes, peanuts and potatoes – became more important for many producers than the old export crops. Around Mount Hagen for example, where coffee prices early in 1992 were barely a quarter of the price a year earlier, villagers abandoned coffee production for vegetables (*TPNG* 20 February 1992; cf. Schwimmer 1991:154–5). However, since food crops are marketed in a vast number of ways, there are few data on the extent and value of marketed production or its regional significance.

One of the most successful cash crops in PNG is betel nut (*Areca catechu*) which, since the 1970s, has earned substantial incomes for producers, espe-cially in the Markham Valley, and the Mekeo area (west of Port Moresby). Both areas are well placed for access to most of the largest towns, and there is now a massive trade of betel nuts from the lowlands to the highland provinces where betel palms cannot grow but where betel nut consumption has become part of a new way of life, especially in the urban areas (Connell 1984a). No other legal agricultural product nets such profits to producers and traders alike. Betel nuts are exceptionally easy to grow and take up little land, labour inputs are minimal and land disputes few. The significance of the boom in betel nut consumption is perhaps reflected most dramatically in its weighting of 7.5 per cent in the consumer price index: it is a major consumer good of social and economic significance.

Betel nuts have become one of the most important components of urban food markets. There are betel nut sellers at markets throughout the country (along with sellers of lime and pepper, since these are chewed with the nuts), many specialised betel nut markets and betel nut vendors constitute the bulk of the urban informal sector. The volume of sales in the formal market, and the mess that results from chewed betel nuts being spat or dribbled onto the ground, has resulted in many urban authorities banning betel nut sales from official markets and displacing them to specialised markets elsewhere. Most betel nut vendors in Port Moresby are Mekeo for whom betel nuts are of major economic significance; even in 1968, when Port Moresby was a fraction of its present size and there was no connecting road, the 6,500 Mekeo were selling around 600 tonnes of nuts and, in 1972, were earning an estimated A$1 million (Hau'ofa 1981:17–18). The Mekeo consequently turned deaf ears to attempts by the Department of Agriculture to diversify local agricultural production, and by 1982 sales were worth at least K3.5 million (Walsh 1982). Markham Valley producers have similarly increased their earnings and are faring just as well as the Mekeo, through trade into the highlands. In perhaps no other sector of the economy have brokers, middlemen and entrepreneurs become so important.

At the start of the 1990s the most rapidly growing cash crop of all was almost certainly marijuana, known in Tok Pisin as *spak brus* (literally 'drunk tobacco'), and exported from PNG, though no export figures reveal this. In the highlands numerous mountainous areas provide the right ecological conditions and shelter the crops from police searches. High returns make marijuana an extremely attractive crop and the expansion of cultivation has followed falling coffee prices. By the mid-1980s it had 'become a feature of "social night" dances, being . . . reported to induce hilarity and mild hallucinations' (A.J. Strathern 1987a:142). Since the late 1980s there have been numerous arrests and the burning of confiscated crops, mainly in Simbu and the Eastern Highlands, where it may be almost as valuable as coffee. Illegality has not prevented a significant export trade (and its converse of imported guns) across the Torres Strait to Australia. Cannabis, known in Australia as 'PNG Gold', fetched up to A$12,000 a kilogram in Australia in 1990; in one month in 1990 Port Moresby police burnt K7 million worth of marijuana, some 700 kilograms destined for local and Australian markets. (In 1990 cocoa exports were valued at K30 million and tea exports at K6.7 million; marijuana has become of major value.) Because of its illegality, it is visibly much less important than betel nut yet the substantial incomes earned from both crops, one in the highlands and one on the coast, emphasise the manner in which cash cropping is now much more than merely the trilogy of export crops.

For a very large number of people, producers, middlemen and consumers, food crops are now the most important cash crops. By the mid-1970s only a few remote areas of PNG were not accessible to weekly markets, whilst the largest towns already had daily markets; since then markets have grown in number and frequency, especially in urban areas, but also in many rural areas and at mine sites. The larger towns have several different markets. Prices in Port Moresby markets are often substantially above those elsewhere; in 1992 prices of goods such as potatoes and sweet potatoes were three or four times the price they were in Mount Hagen and for most other goods the ratio was at least 2:1. In smaller highland towns prices were lower than in Mount Hagen (*Fresh Produce News*, 68, 7 August 1992) hence, in most cases, high prices in the capital city offset substantial transport costs. The potato industry has been another of the rare recent (and legal) successes of the agricultural sector, to the extent that PNG achieved self-sufficiency in 1987, when imports were banned, even after enormous growth in urban demand for hot chips. The potential of potatoes at high altitudes (above the coffee line) enabled rapid growth, though the remoteness of many smallholders led to marketing problems. The major market centre is Mount Hagen, but there is substantial production in most parts of the highlands, especially in Enga, where Tambul has become the 'potato capital' of the highlands. Traditional marketing preferences and a transport and commercial system that is unable to link suppliers and consumers more adequately, have led to inertia in the market system, though wholesaling of potatoes, cabbages, peanuts, mangoes and coconuts has become significant (Bourke 1986:69), with marketing chains extending from Lae to the end of the Highlands Highway.

Market sales have been dominated by a range of food crops, but markets have become more diverse, increasingly incorporating cooked food (including fish and pork) and goods otherwise available from stores (such as bread and clothes, iceblocks and chewing gum). Market vendors are now more likely to sell produce grown specifically for the market (rather than occasional surplus), be increasingly specialised and be regular participants, and engage in price determination that is responsive to cost factors, supply and demand (Bourke 1986:61; Newton 1985:168). Nevertheless the majority of participants, especially in the smaller markets, are still those who produce a 'surplus' when they are short of cash for a particular need; in Orokaiva market participation is thus most closely correlated with the frequency of village social events (Newton 1985:167). Few manufactured goods are sold in PNG markets and there is very little service activity. A *maket raun* (market round) system in the densely populated highlands, with urban services grafted on to rural produce markets, was only briefly successful (Ward *et al.* 1978) before it foundered for lack of support.

Even quite small markets have a substantial turnover. At the daily Kainantu market, in the Eastern Highlands, total sales of fresh food, betel nuts and cooked scones were estimated to amount to K228,000 in 1981–2; sales in the betel nut section accounted for just under half this total, an impressive proportion for a highlands town. Other markets have similar turnovers, suggesting that a large number of periodic market sellers earn above the minimum rural wage (Bourke 1986:63). The large number of villagers who are at least intermittently engaged in food marketing (officially 53 per cent of households at the time of the 1980 census and now rather more) indicates that market participation is an important source of income. In one Eastern Highlands village, despite being 25 kilometres from the market, every household was involved in market trading, which (after coffee) produced the most important component of household incomes, and reduced the problem of coffee being a seasonal crop (Dickerson-Putman 1988). The value of marketed food in urban areas alone was probably around K21 million by 1980 and had more than doubled by 1985. These are underestimates of trade since much is traded outside the market system and barter markets also flourish (Carrier and Carrier 1989; Gewertz 1978; D.E. Keil 1977). Local foodstuffs (and related goods) are by far the most important 'cash crop' in the country. Because of its scale, with very few large producers and a handful of substantial marketing intermediaries, this is the most crucial – yet largely unrecognised – development of the agricultural economy since oil palm. Even in the mid-1980s, when export cash crops were faring well on the world market, the value of the fresh food (and betel nut) sector was already of the same magnitude as that of the main export crops (Bourke 1986:72–3). Subsequently food sales have grown (especially in temperate areas), export crop prices have fallen and there has been a continued movement into vegetable production, hence the domestic marketing of food, betel nuts (and marijuana) has become the most important agricultural sector.

The income received from local marketing is usually seen as belonging to women, who are the principal market participants and food crop producers. Sometimes however a husband's and wife's goods are sold separately and the proceeds divided. Vegetable marketing is thus usually distinct from other forms of economic activity – such as cash cropping, trade stores and other business – where men are the prime organisers and beneficiaries: 'marketing is seen to bring only enough cash to provide for needs such as salt, kerosene and tobacco, and to make small contributions to feasts. Although they do not hesitate to appropriate them, most men see such profits as trifling and in fact single men view the activity as demeaning' (Newton 1985:1971; cf. Warry 1987:150). Marketing of food and other goods is steadily increasing, market products are becoming more diverse, the income generated is an important contribution to rural incomes in many parts of the country and may more obviously improve welfare since the initial beneficiaries are women.

THE PLANTATION SECTOR

For much of colonial history, the economy was dominated by plantations, characterised by the large size of their operations and the particular form of labour management. In the inter-war years plantations provided the bulk of export crops and gave the colonial economy its dominant characteristics. Subsequently, the plantation economy, of enormous consequence for the economic history of PNG, has become a shadow of its former self. Crucially important during the earliest phases of the transformation of the natural economy, it remained so in the early post-war years of the long boom, when the rapid economic recovery of western Europe, and later the Korean War, increased the demand for primary commodities. Plantation capital began to face a crisis towards the end of the 1960s, a crisis which coincided with the labour frontier having moved inland until, by the early 1970s, the supply of cheap labour was largely exhausted, plantation capital was expatriated and a process of transfer to national ownership began (Gregory 1979) enabling the independent state to inherit a largely moribund plantation system. It has become more rather than less moribund over time.

During the 1970s, the plantation system began to change. Following independence, the government introduced a Plantation Redistribution Scheme, and a number of plantations were purchased by nationals. Most plantations acquired under the Scheme were held by groups, in some cases by the traditional owners of the land, but in others by groups or individuals, who formed 'development corporations'. Though the target was full or part-ownership of all plantations by Papua New Guineans by 1980, that target disappeared as it became apparent that many plantations were extremely difficult to operate profitably, and the Scheme was abolished in 1980 on the grounds that it was having a disastrous effect on plantation production (M. Turner 1990:54). The average yield on copra plantations was too low for them to be economically viable hence, after nationalisation, few were restructured into productive enterprises. The coffee plantations that were returned to Papua New Guinean ownership were usually sufficiently profitable to continue in production. On balance, 'at the point when the plantation sector is in decline, nationals of the country are able to acquire plantations' (Gordon 1977:195). Plantation output declined as a result of uncertainty over investment decisions by expatriate owners and inexperienced management (especially of labour) on newly acquired plantations, the lack of land for expansion and poor commodity prices. The plantation situation deteriorated further in the 1980s as wage rates increased, but labour was not forthcoming, and cash crop prices declined; it was further exacerbated by indebtedness and inadequate management. The Highland Labour Scheme, in which labour was contracted under agreement to coastal plantations, was terminated in 1974. Subsequently provincial politicians in the highlands opposed what they regarded as the exploitative wages and conditions of plantation labourers (M. Turner 1986b:136–7) and actively discouraged labour migration. Many overseas companies sold off their plantations and plantation output declined rapidly as a number of plantations were simply abandoned by their expatriate owners (Manning 1983). In 1986 the most important trading company, Burns Philp, sold off all its cocoa and copra plantations to local interests after more than sixty years in the country: 'The sale completes Burns Philp's divestment of its Pacific plantations and continues the company's strict rationalisation of unprofitable investments' (*Sydney Morning Herald* (*SMH*) 7 January 1986). By the early 1980s many plantations had halted production either temporarily or permanently, and a large proportion of those that remained were operated (and subsidised) by missions. The decline was most significant in the former heartland, East New Britain, where many plantations closed in the 1980s, leading to increased unemployment and crime, especially against the plantations, and a downturn in general business activity (*PC* 28 August 1990), and also around Madang, where a dozen plantations were simply abandoned in the space of a decade (*PC* 27 March 1992). The unwieldy and increasingly unmanageable plantation system has gradually given way to smaller schemes characterised by indigenous ownership. Within the plantation sector, and more generally, national interests acquired assets of uncertain profitability that international companies no longer wanted and which were unlikely to become profitable again.

Plantations have continued to experience problems. A high proportion of plantation tree crops are senile and need replacement. Escalating wages, fuel and transport costs, together with crop diseases and some technical problems, pointed to the need for more sophisticated business management and crop husbandry practices. Insecure land tenure discouraged investment and the provision of national agricultural services, including extension, research and development, had deteriorated (Wylie and Sims 1981). Wages on plantations are high, and productivity low, relative to other countries with plantation economies (Manning 1991:13–14). Localisation of ownership and management has reduced authority, discipline and productivity (McKillop 1981:26–7). Plantations increasingly depend on a more casual, local labour force, that includes women and children; in highlands plantations, women are the principal workforce and some key activities, such as weeding and picking coffee, are sometimes undertaken only by women (Finch 1989:273–4). Nevertheless, despite the savings on accommodation and other amenities that have resulted from this, and an abundance of labour in some highland areas, labour costs remain more than half the operating costs of plantations (J. Johnson 1984). There has been no consensus on the future role of plantations in the agricultural economy, and an absence of policies directed at improving the system.

SMALLHOLDER CASH CROPPING

A critical phase in the transformation of the national economy was the emergence of primary commodity production on village smallholdings, because of the resultant local income generation, and the extent of economic differentiation within villages and regions that followed as the smallholder sector steadily became more important than the plantation sector. The expansion of the acreage under smallholder cash crops was most rapid in the 1960s and the early 1970s, as large parts of the highlands became incorporated into the monetised sector of the economy. The increased pace of expansion again coincided with the global post-war long boom, the expansion of Australian interest in development and infrastructure provision and the parallel growth of the plantation sector, which provided something of a model and demonstration effect for smallholders. Smallholder acreages almost quadrupled between 1962 and 1970 (MacWilliam 1986:163), the most dynamic period of agricultural expansion that PNG has ever experienced. Rapidly rising commodity prices in the second half of the 1970s brought an increase in cash incomes for many small-scale producers on a quite unprecedented scale.

Increases in production have not been sustained and various constraints limit the potential for the development of smallholder cash cropping. These include land issues (absolute shortages and tenure), labour use and availability, management and techniques, capital, prices and market access: the same issues that confront smallholders throughout the world. In a number of areas, notably in the highlands, there are absolute land shortages, and there are land-short groups throughout the country (Chapter 9). There is considerable rhetoric amongst urban populations about the difficulties of village life, land shortages and the problems of achieving an adequate livelihood in rural areas. In parts of Simbu, not long after independence, population pressure on land was such that numbers had already reached the 'maximum supportable', but the widening of livelihood opportunities beyond rural areas, there as elsewhere, ruled out any simple notions of populations passing the carrying capacity of the land (Brown *et al.* 1990:29). Northern Simbu, and some other highland and lowland areas, are moving towards a critical situation where land is likely to become degraded and eroded —because of high population pressure on scarce land resources – affecting both food crop and cash crop production (Grey 1993:93). Localised shortages are already apparent; this restricts the area available for cash cropping and has led to cash crops and cattle projects being displaced by more intensive food crop production (e.g. D.D. Mitchell 1982). The demise of schemes that have both worsened inequality and threatened adequate nutrition is welcome in terms of local control of livelihoods, but indicative of severe, localised pressures on land. As population grows, more areas will experience similar problems.

Underlying many development problems is land. The strongly maintained traditional ownership of land has effectively prevented the alienation, nationalisation or even leasing of all but the most limited areas, and then mainly for large, prestigious projects, such as towns and mines. At least 97 per cent of land in PNG remains under customary control, and that proportion has remained virtually unchanged since independence. The administrative problems and costs of leasing areas of land for projects, and dissent over tenure, have prevented many possible development projects, including roads, ranches and urban housing development. Tackling wide-ranging and complex land problems, where landowners increasingly recognise that land remains the basis of wealth and there are growing pressures on it, is perhaps the most difficult task that PNG faces in seeking to achieve development. Achieving solutions has been and will be difficult and in some places almost impossible.

Traditional land tenure normally provides all members of a clan, lineage or other social group with access to some land, that will thus provide a degree of security, work and a means of earning some income. Land is transferred within that group according to well-established principles, usually based on inheritance, and is not normally given or sold to non-members of the particular social group. Land remains owned by the group and group members have access to that land for usufruct and not in perpetuity. Over time historic land-use systems have come under pressure through the establishment of cash crops, changes in value of particular tracts (because of their new utility) and preferences by individuals for acquiring large areas of land for cash cropping, or other purposes, and seeking to pass this land on to their children, rather than adhering to other principles of group tenure. The value of land has been reconsidered; amongst the Kewa (Southern Highlands), 'Even before land had become fully exploited commercially, its potential commercial value was being felt. . . . Even when lying idle it began to be thought of as a potential commercial commodity, its usufruct no longer being granted so casually' (Josephides 1985:85). As cultivation has become more intensive and semi-permanent, and population grown, there has been a progression from fluid land rights and tenure to the formalising of rights and boundaries amongst individuals and households (Brown *et al.* 1990). In most cases this has increased conflict over land and limited some forms of rural development (e.g. Foster 1995). More generally traditional land tenure has discouraged investment in land and technology, and agricultural intensification and improvement. Land tenure constraints no longer affect the availability of loans, as PNG banks have overcome uncertainties of land tenure (Jarrett and Anderson 1989:36–8), but they have resulted in both the under-utilisation of some potentially productive areas of agricultural land and in the 'freezing' of areas of land within particular small social groups, especially where there are land shortages (Brown *et al.* 1990:46; Meggitt 1965:297). Individual ownership of land is strongly correlated with high population density and high agricultural intensity (Brown and Podolefsky 1976:221), a situation that has followed population growth and the expansion of smallholder cash cropping. In exceptional circumstances, land has become a commodity. In both the highlands, and some densely populated island areas, the market in smallholdings is already significant. Disputes over land have contributed to an increase in the extent of tribal fighting since the 1980s. All land transactions are difficult, and often a source of misunderstandings. Formal land registration lags behind demand, compensation claims have increased over many tracts of land taken out of 'traditional' use, even when this was many years previously (Chapter 9), hence security of tenure, when land use has been 'modernised', is weak and fraught with uncertainty.

Inappropriate agricultural systems, involving a reduction in plant diversity, overcropping (through reduced fallow periods) and the use of marginal areas (such as steeply sloping land), have all contributed to environmental degradation. In Siwai (North Solomons) the rapid extension of cocoa cultivation in the 1970s depleted much of the forest cover, to clear land for cocoa (and to provide fuel and housing for the growing population), thus reducing the area available for hunting and gathering and causing soil erosion and the siltation of several streams, so reducing biodiversity. Elsewhere new technological introductions (including shotguns and nylon fishing nets) have combined with similar changes to deplete land and marine environments (Grant 1987). Deforestation has proved to be an irreversible threat to the environment, in some coastal and island provinces, so that, despite intensification, food security and agricultural sustainability are problematic in a range of contexts (B.J. Allen *et al.* 1995; Bayliss-Smith 1991; Ohtsuka *et al.* 1995). Environmental degradation and mismanagement have become critical for agricultural production.

The limited ability of women to participate in the economy, a situation that is often related to their inability to own land, has, in some cases, discouraged the development of commercial agriculture, though women's groups have occasionally set up their own ventures. Amongst the Kewa (Southern Highlands), though women have undisputed rights to the crops that they produce and sell in the markets, they cannot operate large commercial vegetable projects; because they do not own the land, they cannot summon the working parties that are necessary to clear large tracts of land while extension officers (who are almost always men) do not approach women to provide any kind of assistance in their enterprises (Josephides 1985:92). Old forms of inequality have discouraged new forms of commercial development, even where men are uninvolved. However, more commonly, women have taken an increasing role in cash cropping, especially for coffee, for example in the time-consuming tasks of weeding and picking, so that in many coffee-growing areas women's labour inputs into cash cropping have been greater than those of men (Barnes 1981:275). Such changes rarely benefit women: 'crudely and quickly put, men are fast becoming capitalists and women the proletariat or sub-proletariat. Consistent with traditional patterns, men manage, women are managed. . . . Capitalism may, at one stroke, increase the productive value of women and provide men means to achieve public prestige, both individually and collectively' (P.L. Johnson 1981:333). However, increased vegetable production by women has reduced the significance of this trend and compensated for 'lost' commodity production. To a substantial extent, at least in the highlands, the development impasse has its principal antecedents in the economic and social discrimination facing women. Gender-based discrimination occurs both within the pre-contact patriarchal social order and in the context of the capitalist relations that followed the introduction of cash cropping. Consequently individual incentives are not determined by world markets but by household power structures, leading to 'gendered market failure'. Women's returns to coffee production are so low that they apply more labour to food production, hence there is an under-allocation of labour and land to coffee, and households are unable to respond to changing incentives, such as increased coffee prices, creating a 'vicious gendered circle of under-development' (Overfield 1995). More frequently the general lack of labour can limit smallholder development. In some contexts full harvests are apparently not taken because of a shortage of labour, because price incentives are perceived as inadequate to shift activity from leisure to labour or because an acceptable 'target' income has already been achieved (Stent 1984). Despite a limited propensity to save, there is otherwise little real evidence of target income production. Though the need for income to stage social events, or meet other specific goals, influences participation in the cash economy it is not the most critical determinant.

Inadequate husbandry techniques, such as pruning, weeding, harvesting, fencing, shading and draining, are ubiquitous, and an inevitable corollary of limited labour inputs. Moreover little use is made of commercial inputs, such as fertiliser, so that production levels are usually sub-optimal (Stewart 1992:55), though the use of improved techniques is correlated with cash crop prices (G.T. Harris 1979). In severe price slumps, labour is simply withdrawn; 'villagers thought that their time could more fruitfully be spent on other activities which were not necessarily commercially productive. These included socialising and organising large-scale events' (Josephides 1985:87–8), whilst coffee may be stored by households for up to a year in the hope that prices rise. Other commodity prices, the price of imported goods, and the requirements for participation in the social system all influence production; ultimately, smallholders regard themselves as price responsive (Overfield 1995), a situation that was vividly demonstrated in the late 1970s when prices rose rapidly and apparent in other ways when prices declined (Fleming 1988; Story 1990:100; Townsend 1977). Labour inputs are nevertheless rarely optimal. An increasingly inadequate agricultural extension service has provided little assistance to smallholders: the 'public extension service is almost certainly a waste of funds, particularly when it is directed at men' (Callick *et al.* 1990:11.1). It has become increasingly urbanised with about 80 per cent of the staff of the Department of Agriculture and Livestock working in Port Moresby (Economic Insights 1996:87). New seeds, new technologies, new information on market access, or even simple encouragement (as the opening quotation suggests) no longer reach the rural areas.

Transport infrastructure has been a further problem. Feeder roads dramatically improved access in the 1960s and 1970s and were the most important stimulus to participation in the commercial economy, but in the 1980s progress in road construction was not sustained and transport costs have been a high proportion of all costs (Das 1982) and a disincentive to production. Commodity prices are lower at a distance from processing centres, and the resurgence of tribal fighting in the 1980s (Chapter 10), and the growth of armed robbery, especially targeted at mobile coffee buyers, significantly reduced returns and discouraged participation in remote areas. Land that is favourably located with respect to roads, access to government services and freedom from malaria has been placed under increasing pressure, whereas more distant areas of land have sometimes been abandoned (Crittenden 1987:347–8; Grant 1988:106). Inaccessibility to transport exacerbates other constraints to production: 'lower prices than anticipated, the difficulty of transporting heavy bags over arduous foot-trails, the uncertainty of finding itinerant coffee buyers waiting at the road-head' (Healey 1986:23–4). Cash cropping has become increasingly concentrated in more accessible areas, so emphasising regional uneven development (Table 4.6).

The lack of capital for investment has discouraged agricultural development and technological innovation. Early on this was rarely a problem, since cash crop holdings were easily divisible, little technology was required, capital could be accumulated slowly and savings were often pooled by local clan groups. Capital availability has become more problematic with the

Table 4.6 Economic activity by province (1980) (% households)

	Grow coffee	Grow cocoa	Grow rubber	Sell copra	Sell food crops	Sell fish
Western	3	—	25	33	65	53
Gulf	22	2	2	32	41	35
Central[1]	22	2	3	23	49	17
Milne Bay	16	7	—	48	40	28
Northern (Oro)	69	23	7	41	56	27
Southern Highlands	41	—	—	—	50	1
Enga	31	—	—	—	44	1
Western Highlands	83	—	—	—	54	1
Simbu	80	—	—	—	66	—
Eastern Highlands	89	—	—	—	61	—
Morobe	66	5	—	19	55	8
Madang	43	26	—	33	48	20
East Sepik	65	25	3	23	52	12
West Sepik	34	14	3	15	50	11
Manus	—	19	5	52	46	31
New Ireland	—	45	1	61	40	17
East New Britain	1	61	—	63	57	12
West New Britain	2	29	—	54	58	40
North Solomons	1	77	—	45	46	11
PNG[2]	48	13	1	19	53	11

Notes: 1 Data for the National Capital District are included within Central Province
2 Some 0.1 per cent of national households grew tea, 21 per cent grew spices and 3 per cent were raising cattle

Source: Papua New Guinea (1988) *1980 National Population Census*, Port Moresby: National Statistical Office

movement to larger schemes. One source of capital available to rural producers has been Papua New Guinea Development Bank loans. However the Bank tended to provide the bulk of its loans, in volume if not in number, to urban rather than rural residents and until 1980 provided a high proportion of all loans to non-nationals in the two expanding sectors, oil palm and cattle, where large-scale development was the norm, a situation which generated resentment amongst village smallholders who were unable to gain access to loans (MacWilliam 1986:173). In 1984 the Bank was restructured and, after pressure from the World Bank and others to cease funding large-scale coffee projects and reach more equitable arrangements in other parts of the country, it became the Agricultural Bank of Papua New Guinea. During the 1980s some 60 per cent of Agricultural Bank loans were allocated to agriculture, but went to the larger commercial farmers, resulting in a 'concentration on lending to the small subset of enterprises which tend to involve farmers who are at the upper end of the income distribution for rural producers' (Jarrett and Anderson 1989:41). The number and volume of loans into coffee, cocoa and rubber have all stabilised or increased (Table 4.7); to

Table 4.7 Agricultural Bank, sectoral distribution of agriculture loans (1967–90) (percentages)

Sector	Number of loans			Amount of loans		
	1967–77	*1978–86*	*1987–90*	*1967–77*	*1978–86*	*1987–90*
Coffee	1.1	4.6	22.7	4.7	24.6	21.9
Cocoa	3.8	6.0	4.3	2.3	31.4	26.6
Oil palm	17.7	43.7	31.2	18.9	14.8	18.9
Rubber	4.8	6.0	—	1.3	43.7	—
Copra	9.4	1.7	—	3.5	0.2	—
Cattle	28.1	4.0	0.8	36.	4.2	1.9
Pigs and poultry	12.0	9.3	0.4	8.5	8.9	1.7
Other	23.1	24.7	39.6	24.7	11.5	39.0
Total	100.0	100.0	100.0	100.0	100.0	100.0

Sources: Fernando (1990a: 10); Agriculture Bank of Papua New Guinea (1990), *Annual Report*

some extent this allocation reflects the Bank's reliance on foreign lines of credit, which emphasised the key cash crops (Fernando 1990a:10). Very little agricultural credit is directed to the food crop sector, though this sector accounts for almost half the agricultural output.

The average size of loans has increased over time, from K2100 in 1967–77 to K6180 in 1987–90, although in real terms this is not particularly great; larger loans have been most significant for cocoa and coffee growers (Fernando 1990a:13). The Bank has concentrated on a smaller number of larger, low-risk loans and most funds have gone to the more wealthy provinces: lending was concentrated 'across the country's economic and social spine' from the Western Highlands to the North Solomons (MacWilliam 1988:95; Table 4.8). The province that has received the largest amount since the Bank's establishment was actually the National Capital District (with 12.5 per cent), followed by the Western Highlands, Morobe and East New Britain, with Gulf and Manus receiving the least, and West Sepik, Simbu and Western receiving very little. Though the Bank introduced a Less Developed Areas Project Scheme in 1988, this had made no real difference to the overall structure of loans by the early 1990s. Despite attempts to redirect the structure of loans between rural and urban areas, rich and poor provinces and different kinds of producers, they have effectively supported and emphasised emerging structures of inequality. Credit delivery and its effective utilisation remain major problems (Economic Insights 1994: 80), hence the Bank was again restructured in 1993, becoming the Rural Development Bank, with a new mandate to focus solely on rural areas and give priority to small and medium-sized operators.

Many rural producers have had high expectations of cash cropping, a situation born of considerable government pressure on producers in the 1960s

Table 4.8 Agricultural Bank, regional distribution of loans (1967–90) (percentages)

	No.	*Kina* (million) 1967–77	*No.*	*Kina* (million) 1987–90
Western	3.3	1.0	2.0	2.2
Gulf	1.5	1.0	1.1	0.4
Central	7.8	5.1	7.5	5.1
NCD	2.6	13.4	3.6	2.1
Milne Bay	2.5	1.4	2.6	1.7
Oro	7.3	6.3	6.7	3.5
Southern Highlands	2.1	2.6	2.0	2.4
Western Highlands	6.7	12.5	10.2	11.6
Enga	1.6	2.8	1.8	3.7
Simbu	1.7	1.6	2.0	1.3
Eastern Highlands	5.7	2.1	5.7	7.3
Morobe	12.1	13.5	7.0	9.3
Madang	2.8	2.1	2.8	4.2
East Sepik	4.8	4.6	4.4	2.8
West Sepik	1.1	0.7	0.9	0.9
Manus	2.8	2.1	2.8	4.2
New Ireland	4.2	1.6	1.6	5.5
East New Britain	8.4	7.3	6.5	12.1
West New Britain	15.4	8.6	25.8	8.9
North Solomons	5.7	5.3	5.1	4.5
	n = 31,684		n = 22,846	

Source: Agriculture Bank of Papua New Guinea (1990) *Annual Report*

and 1970s and high prices in the 1970s and early 1980s. Disappointments have sometimes been severe, especially where expectations have been artificially heightened (e.g. Crittenden *et al.* 1988:24–6; Newton 1985:239; Walter 1981a:102; see also Chapter 10). Changes in world commodity prices have affected living standards in rural areas much more substantially than any government programmes for development; this has created uncertainty, disillusionment with government and, on occasion, disengagement from participation in the cash economy and some revitalisation of 'tradition' (Josephides 1985:85–6; Mosko 1985:19; D. Townsend 1980a; see also Chapter 9). Disengagement from the commercial economy was usually short-lived and tended to stimulate the search for more effective means of incorporation, simply because the need for money has become inescapable; 'with incentives to acquire cash increasing due to pressures from stores, advertising, desire to leave the village, a liking for beer, education, government (to pay taxes) and the general intrusion of the modern sector, people become locked into some form of commodity production' (Lea *et al.* 1988:29). Sustained disengagement and withdrawal are unacceptable and impossible. Most communities have some first-hand experience of periods of booming commodity prices, when the impact on living standards has been substantial; in the highlands during 'the 1976 coffee boom' consumption of imported foods, beer, fuel and motor vehicles all rapidly increased, as did coffee planting and production rates (D. Townsend 1977), as villagers engaged in every way with the expanding commercial economy. In seeking an adequate place in the commercial world villagers are nonetheless prone to comment along the lines of 'coffee imprisons us' (Grossman 1980:4). The frustrations of marginal participants on the periphery of the cash economy have been considerable.

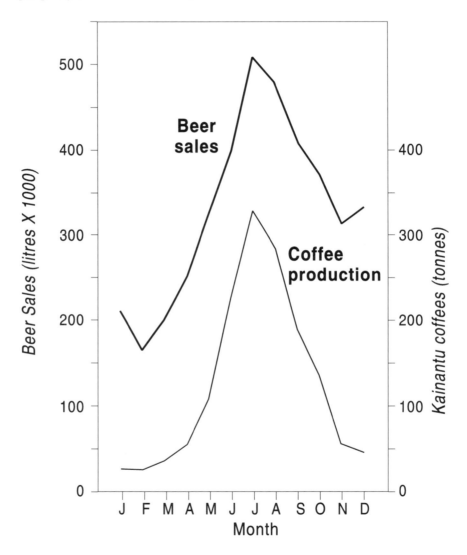

Figure 4.4 Mean monthly beer sales, Eastern Highlands (1979–84) and village coffee production, Kainantu area (1974–83)
Source: Shaw *et al.* (1986:69)

For all the difficulties attached to successful participation, cash cropping has provided an enormous stimulus to rural incomes and to commercial development in various forms, but especially of trade stores. Where cash crop production is seasonal, as it is for highlands coffee, purchases of major consumer goods – such as food, beer, clothing and petrol – are also markedly seasonal and closely follow the pattern of coffee receipts (Figure 4.4). Even in relatively small urban markets there is a strong seasonality to some forms of purchase; at the peak of coffee revenues, more betel nuts and cooked scones were sold whereas there was a downturn in sales of fresh food (Bourke 1986). Most village income is spent fairly soon after it is received, supporting anec-dotal comments from villagers that 'money does not stay in hands' and demonstrating the close correlation between cash crop incomes, especially the 'coffee flush' in the highlands and purchases of beer and rice (B.J. Allen and Bourke 1988:27).Over a long time period, in the Eastern Highlands, the second most important province in volume of coffee production and one of the most dependent on this single commodity, the effects of the decline in prices in 1990 were substantial and wide-ranging. More than eight businesses, ranging from motor dealers to construction companies, closed or moved else-where in the country, the provincial government's revenue declined, thus reducing its ability to provide services, whilst even registrations of football teams had declined as clubs could not find the fees (*TPNG* 29 November 1990). Income from cash cropping has had a very strong multiplier effect, on the commercial sector directly, and indirectly on the public sector, through provincial government taxation on such goods as beer and petrol. The extent and success of smallholder cash cropping and market participation are thus of enormous significance.

THE NEW 'MEDIUM-HOLDERS'

One response to the difficulties of smallholder agriculture, and to the demand for cash income in the rural sector, has been the consolidation of smallholder schemes and the emergence of new agricultural structures, intermediate between household activities and plantations. The consolidation of land – most apparent in the coffee-growing areas of the Eastern Highlands – began in 1978 as part of a national programme to boost agricultural output (Donaldson and Good 1988:127; Stewart 1987, 1992). The aims were to increase planting rates and production in the more developed areas, where land was already in short supply, and facilitate the introduction of better management and technology. Increased production of coffee was intended to be achieved through the development of 'blocks' (or 'mini-plantations') larger than 5 hectares, owned by individuals or groups. The Development Bank provided loans and the National Plantation Management Agency provided managerial and technical support. The stage was therefore set for the Eastern Highlands to become a model of medium-holder development.

Most mini-plantations were concentrated near Goroka around the historic centres of coffee-growing. Only 20 per cent of development applications were from individuals but prominent amongst these individuals were national politicians, the most powerful of whom could be seen as 'representatives of the rising rich rural classes, the rich peasantry and rural capitalists, active in rural capitalism in the province' (Donaldson and Good 1988:135). By the early 1980s almost 200 mini-plantations or '20 hectare blocks' had been established, covering some 10 per cent of the smallholder coffee area (Story 1990:61–3), and were benefiting from more skilled management, bank loans and the introduction of new higher yielding varieties of coffee.

As the mini-plantations emerged, so too did development corporations, and wealthy individuals diversified from smallholder cash cropping into a range of other business activities. Successful entrepreneurs often sought out political careers; indeed commercial success was 'the outstanding accomplishment' of Eastern Highlanders elected to the national Parliament in the 1960s (Finney 1973:118). A number of development corporations had very large memberships, and could mobilise substantial financial resources, to promote the large-scale ownership of land, crops, equipment and a diversity of urban commercial resources. By the end of the 1970s many councils and provincial governments had also established development corporations as business arms, and owned even more substantial economic resources, especially in the urban service sector (such as stores, hotels and car dealerships). The development corporations were both acquiring more urban commercial interests and replacing the smaller rural co-operatives which, where they survived, were also developing urban interests. The consolidation of land, and the emergence of development corporations, contributed to the process of uneven agricultural development in the highlands, and especially in the more established coffee-growing areas of the Eastern Highlands. Whilst a small number of prosperous farmers emerged as business leaders and politicians, 'in contrast with the increasing wealth of the rich rural classes, the position of the average coffee grower in the Eastern Highlands deteriorated' (Donaldson and Good 1988:154), to the extent that 'the land and surplus monies of smallholders have been "captured" by the big peasants and the *petite bourgeoisie* and . . . smallholders have been "disenfranchised" on their own blocks' (Stewart 1987:230), hinting at some regional class formation.

The mini-plantations scarcely extended beyond the Eastern Highlands. Though there were more than 250 at the start of the 1990s, they produced only about 4 per cent of the nation's coffee (D.G.V. Smith 1992). They experienced severe cash flow difficulties, when prices were low, and problems in hiring labour; landowning households refused to supply labour, objecting to low wage levels, and management companies were forced to hire labour from more distant places. Like plantation labour this tended to be unstable and unreliable. In protest over low prices and the slow progress to profitability, landowning groups sometimes moved onto the blocks to pick coffee, or stole that picked by labourers, to process with their own (H. Thompson and MacWilliam 1992:148). Smallholder households thus challenged the development of the blocks, and the accentuation of uneven development. The mini-plantations tended to experience the worst of both the worlds of plantations (labour and management) and the smallholder sector (inadequate economies of scale); though only exceptionally successful they emphasized the extent and visibility of emerging inequalities in the smallholder agricultural system.

RURAL BUSINESS

Village people have often participated in agriculture, forestry and other forms of rural development, with the hope that they would be able to earn sufficient income to establish a small business, usually a trade store. There has been substantial Melanesian participation in rural business and commercial development, ranging from sales of produce and handicrafts in local markets to the establishment of small-scale tourist projects (Chapter 8), transport ventures or commercial stores. Many small entrepreneurs have sought to combine these activities, sometimes with clubs and bars (where 'six-to-six' parties might run overnight), video or cinema ventures, bakeries and cafés. The more remote the area, the greater the tendency to refer to any small money-making project as 'business'. There are vast numbers of stores, and smaller family-owned *canteens*, though many have proved uneconomic over an extended time period, not allowing their owners to achieve the lasting success they crave. Rural businesses generally have failed to survive for long and cash crop production has remained the principal source of rural income generation.

Contemporary businesses are the descendants of earlier co-operative ventures, that had some success where cash cropping was relatively successful, as in the islands. The administration encouraged Rural Progress Societies and Co-operatives, and cash cropping in the 1950s and 1960s also had a significant communal component, with village plantations referred to as *kampanis* (Connell 1978; Foster 1992). Co-operative societies eventually declined and disappeared, under the weight of individual competition and disputes over low profitability and the distribution of dividends and revenues; failures were sometimes spectacular. By the time of independence most co-operative ventures were shells of their former success, and had largely given way to small group and individual enterprises. They were not necessarily more successful.

Participation in the commercial economy has often been a mystifying experience for villagers, especially for those who ventured beyond cash cropping into the diversity of trading experiences. Trade stores have been the most problematic. Though turnover and profitability are inevitably affected by the amount of cash flowing through the economy, this is not the only influence on success and failure. In the Maprik district (East Sepik), where cash cropping of a variety of crops has been no less erratic and sporadic than elsewhere, business enterprises, especially stores, have come and gone; none have been successful. After thirty-five years of disappointment, the explanations are typical of other areas; 'the main reasons seem to be lack of management expertise especially dissipating capital and profits in personal and group consumption, failure to make profits (due to under-pricing and failure to keep records), wantokism (satisfying the needs and interests of one's relatives and friends), personal and group jealousies, and personal addiction to store products – particularly alcohol and cigarettes' (Lea *et al.* 1988:27). Competition from other stores, especially urban stores with a greater range of goods and lower prices, high transport costs (and vehicle breakdowns) and theft have also contributed to failure and short life cycles. Shareholders in rural stores have often been disappointed by non-existent profitability, accusing owners or managers of 'eating the money', often with some justification, so hastening the process of downfall (M.F. Smith 1990, 1994:154–62). Unrealistic expectations have sometimes been influenced by cargoism, further disrupting business ventures (Connell 1978; see also Chapter 9), and by the substantial use of store goods to meet social obligations. Most store owners have never had a profit motive; though they may claim to follow commercial trading practices, some have not understood the concept (Finney 1973; McSwain 1977) and most have established stores because of the prestige associated with them and their own ease of access to modern goods.

Only in exceptional cases were individuals, or groups, able to transform the incomes gained from cash cropping into long-term entrepreneurial activity; otherwise the duration of small businesses has been much less than in more modern economies, and at every point those who have begun businesses, and especially those who have succeeded, have developed values different from those of their fellows. They were more educated, more easily able to mobilise land and capital, and often respectfully known as *bikpela man bilong bisnis*, in recognition of broad leadership skills. Those who have been successful in business inhabit a lonely world, envied and distrusted because of their success, in conflict with cherished egalitarian norms, a situation unchanged for decades (Hogbin 1958:190–1). Over time, successful businessmen have become rather more divorced from rural society, and traditional obligations, acutely depicted in *Joe Leahy's Neighbours* and *Black Harvest* (Connolly and Anderson 1989, 1992), devoting less of their time and income into social 'obligations' and more into entrepreneurial success. Conflicts, even sorcery, have sometimes ensued. Nevertheless no contemporary 'entrepreneurial class' has developed, even around the owners of the more successful businesses, as businesses have eventually failed, their assets split up between heirs or dissipated through rivalries (Finney 1987). Most trade stores, like most business enterprises, are operated by men; though women have established some collective, commercial enterprises (Sexton 1986; Warry 1987) there are few national businesswomen.

Despite the repetitiveness and familiarity of failure, potential Melanesian entrepreneurs have rarely been deterred for long, even in the more remote areas 'where development never comes'. Commodity fetishism, where imported goods play a symbolic function, has ensured that 'those with large, well-stocked trade stores feel superior to those with empty shelves. Those with empty shelves look down on those with no shelves at all' (Grant *et al.* 1986:210); hence 'the appearance of a store is itself a sign of material success' (Warry 1987:114), a visible mark of modernity. Consequently store owners seek to keep their stores open as long as possible, even though this may further worsen their precarious economic position; but, as amongst the Orokaiva, where businesses have failed with monotonous regularity, 'You gain status even by, and especially by, failing. Your business dies, its limbs and assets are spread among the multitude and increase exceedingly. It is a religious practice' (Schwimmer 1979:308–9). Stores are important to their owners primarily because of the 'symbolic value of connecting shareholders to locally-perceived processes of development rather than for any actual income derived from them' (Healey 1986:26) and to others for their utility and some degree of recognition that development has been achieved.

After trade stores, the most common rural businesses are transport ventures; indeed 'a group-owned store is seen as a service and a source of pride, but this is nothing compared with the thrill and renown achieved in owning a truck' (Newton 1985:192). Unlike the establishment of stores, the purchase of a truck demands a capital outlay that is usually well beyond the ability of an individual. Most trucks are therefore group-owned, and conflicts arising from group ownership – involving decisions on use, rates, contributions to maintenance and distribution of profits – tend to result in the demise of transport businesses and other group schemes. For a short time, transport businesses provide enormous status and convenience, but mechanical and other problems ensure that they are of short duration (Josephides 1985:85–6). The bush is littered with the hulks of not particularly old vehicles, abandoned because there is no money or accessible skills for repair, after they have not been maintained or been driven beyond endurance on inadequate roads with heavy cargoes.

In an economic rather than social sense the evidence of failed rural business development is considerable, yet the presence of stores throughout the country enables villagers to have access to basic goods. One 'result of this for women is that they get some respite from harvesting and from the time-consuming food preparation' (Newton 1985:191), and it contributes to some degree of egalitarian development within rural areas, as stores (and other ventures) are set up by more wealthy individuals and groups, lose money and eventually fail, but sooner or later the system begins again. The costs of this are considerable, whilst failures emphasise the distinctions between urban and rural life, and the dependence of rural populations on urban centres.

AGRICULTURAL DEVELOPMENT

Smallholder agricultural production has transformed the relations of production in almost every part of the country since the early 1970s. The old plantation economy has virtually disintegrated and a new more complex commercial economy arisen. The landscape too has been altered: coffee now dominates highland slopes, like the coconut canopy in the lowlands, forests are depleted, roads have linked most villages to the expanding towns, few villages are without at least one trade store and rural populations have doubled. The evolutionary changes that have followed new innovations – plant species, technology and medicine – have been allied to the transition to capitalism; simple commodity producers 'are encircled by market–price relations and capitalist relations of production, circulation and distribution' (H. Thompson 1985:8) though they are not enmeshed in them. Labour has not been separated from the land, and both the moral economy and the 'gift economy' – with their extended kinship relations, competitive and reciprocal exchange – remain in place. Indeed because of the short period of time in which contemporary commercial development has become established, it would be strange if this were not so. PNG is at the very periphery of the world capitalist system, and traditional relations of production displayed elements of 'proto-capitalism' (Chapter 9), hence labour relations were not always changed. At the national margins, as in the remote Star Mountains, 'if the market for a commodity dries up one can always eat the crop' (Morren 1986:304). Symbolically and practically this is widely true. Nonetheless land, labour – and even time – have increasingly become commodities and new inequalities have emerged. Though traditional leaders ('big men') have sometimes maintained their primacy in the contemporary economic arena, younger men (with knowledge of mechanical and accounting skills, and important political and economic contacts in urban areas) have often replaced them: 'The enchanted great men of a more heroic age have been displaced by political economic entrepreneurs' (Modjeska 1991:253). Women have tended to become more marginalised. Declining local autonomy has contributed to some degree of impoverishment, and conflict between groups, especially during the prolonged rural recession of the late 1980s. However contemporary agricultural development has largely emphasised older regional divisions. There is a distinctive geography of cash crop production (Figure 4.1, Table 4.4), that has not substantially changed since independence, especially at the smallholder level. The two island provinces of East New Britain and the North Solomons have been particularly successful, for both cocoa and copra production. The loss of production from Bougainville, following political crisis, and from East New Britain, after the Rabaul volcanic eruptions, were thus particularly serious. Coffee production is even more localised, hence the crisis that followed the discovery of coffee rust. The most concentrated major cash crop is oil palm, a new estate crop in just four provinces. More striking is the limited extent of cash crop production, even in some provinces (Morobe and the Sepik region) with large populations (Table 4.6). Although there are cash crops in every province, cash crop production and income vary substantially between provinces. The acute regional differentiation of rural economic activity in 1980 is apparent, as is the greater national significance of coffee and the role of copra in the lowlands. At a district level, where data are unobtainable, divisions are much more acute. The crucial role of food crop marketing, even before the more rapid expansion of urban markets, is marked; in no province were fewer than 40 per cent of households involved in some food marketing. Whilst there are no data on how many households play no part in any commercial agricultural activities, the low proportions in most categories in Western, Gulf (despite fish sales) and Central, Enga and Southern Highlands Provinces, suggest that these provinces are least involved in the emerging agricultural economy. Bank loans have emphasized this pattern. The evolution of commercial agriculture has consolidated regional uneven development.

In almost every way the period since the mid-1980s has been a disappointing even disastrous one for agriculture, as prices for all the key export crops slumped and a classical supply response followed as producers shifted towards local market production. Only oil palm escaped the downward spiral. The loss of export production from Bougainville meant that by the end of the 1980s agriculture had experienced a greater decline in its contribution to GDP, employment and especially exports than in most developing economies (Jarrett and Anderson 1989:111), a situation of considerable concern in a predominantly rural nation. Restructuring from export crops to local markets enabled the decline in rural household incomes to be less severe, and stabilised the volume and cost of imported foods. In adversity a more adequate domestic food marketing network was created by villagers largely without government support. However the absence of agricultural extension services, or even simple interest in and information on trends in rural areas, has hampered rural development. Ironically while local food production brought PNG closer to self-reliance, national politicians, universally and obsessively, were pursuing the notion that self-reliance in rice production was crucial to national development – an economic nonsense, that wasted enormous sums of capital without purpose (as had previously occurred with cattle and sugar schemes).

Though governments have officially pursued policies that favour the development of smallholder agriculture, practice has tended to favour larger schemes. Until well into the 1980s the National Public Expenditure Plan grouped small-scale investments under the 'Rural Welfare' category whereas large-scale developments were referred to as 'Economic Production' (Etherington and Carrad 1983:86). Agricultural policy has had an urban bias, favouring consumers rather than producers, and rural policy makers are faced 'with conflicting interests and concerns which derive from considerations well removed from agriculture *per se*' (G.T. Harris 1979:35). Agricultural policy has generally distorted the national labour market, and discouraged employment in agriculture, to the extent that it has become 'both inefficient and inequitable' (Jarrett and Anderson 1989:50) in failing to increase overall output and employment. Rural development policies have been subsumed in considerations of political stability and longevity. Despite the shift to commercial production, the dominance of smallholder activities in association with subsistence production has resulted in considerable continuity with the past, since land and labour supplies are limited. Rural socio-economic relationships are governed more by kinship ties and social obligations than they are by the dictates of commercial production, though these are necessarily linked, as small producers struggle to transcend the poverty of rural development policy.

5 Fish, forests and sustainable development

Of what use is it to talk of the environment to a man who has never in his life known what it is to have a full stomach?

(Somare 1977:ix)

PNG is labelled as one of the world's natural history museums where unique fauna and flora are less disturbed and still continue to flourish. However with the current accelerated pace of industrial mining, forestry, agricultural and socio-economic developments our natural environment and its biodiversity will be at grave risk. Our environment and life support systems would deteriorate if precautionary measures were not taken immediately.

(Navu Kwapena, *PC* 29 September 1992)

The focus of rural development practice, planning and policy has always been agriculture, and developments in the agricultural sector have been quite distinct from those in other areas. Other than rhetorical statements, and the minimal processing of some agricultural products, there has been no interest in rural industrialisation, policy on fisheries has been conspicuous by its absence – despite the large number of coastal dwellers, the significance of marine transport in many provinces and a large Exclusive Economic Zone – and forestry development has contributed much less than it might have to the economy, engendered substantial ecological degradation in several areas and been the focus of a major inquiry on corruption. Forestry became one of the most important sectors of the economy in the early 1990s, with exports valued at much more than all agricultural products together in 1994. In a situation where planning has been largely absent, integrated rural development has made no headway, except for brief periods in particular regions where there have been external pressures, and rural businesses have been only intermittently successful. The growth of the national economy and the growing significance of foreign investment in natural resource development (timber, fish and minerals) have resulted in an emphasis on growth and production rather than job creation and broadly based development, whilst sustainable development has, at best, been a slogan.

Rural development projects have tended to favour better-off rural people, or at least not the poorest people in the poorest provinces, even when rare policies have aimed at achieving greater equity. Moreover rural development has shifted away from even a tentative emphasis on the relatively poor, towards large-scale projects and income generation through the production of commodities. Though this orientation has simplified rural development policy formation it has posed problems for a country dominated by small-scale semi-subsistence agriculturalists. In other areas of rural development, such as fisheries and forestry, where considerable capital investment for necessary technological inputs is often required, foreign investment has been significant, the scale of development has been greater than in much of the agricultural sector, and the role of government is more important but much less evident. The structure of the fisheries and forestry sectors, and the implications of changes there for environmental management and integrated development, have been closely related to the presence or absence of government intervention.

FISHERIES: A FAILURE OF DEVELOPMENT

For a country with an 8,300 kilometre coastline, about 300 islands, numerous reefs and lagoons and such vast river systems as the Sepik and Fly, with more than 1,800 species of coastal fish, where fishing and fishery products have been and are of significance in the lives and diets of many people, commercial fisheries have been a dismal failure. So unsuccessful were fisheries projects, that by the mid-1980s, 'government programs to develop commercial fisheries have proved a disappointment with high costs and low returns, and no more are to be started' (Goodman *et al.* 1985:81). The fisheries sector contributes scarcely 1 per cent of GDP. Despite the long history of subsistence (artisanal) fisheries, marine fish resources have generally been under-utilised. Even coastal people have placed more emphasis on agriculture than fishing, and the proportion of the coastal population with a distinct fishing tradition or significant current involvement in fishing is small. Subsistence fishing is of importance on small islands, and in some coastal areas, including parts of Papua and the Sepik river, where agriculture is not particularly easy (Dalzell 1993; Pernetta and Hill 1983). In many respects, Melanesians turn their backs to the sea. Fish play a limited role in nutrition and social life, compared with root crops or pigs, and it is rare for Melanesians to be able to say, as in Tatana village (Central Province), that 'fishing is very much part of the personal, social and spiritual beliefs of our people' (Gaigo 1977:176; cf. Hyndman 1993; Pomponio 1992:54–72). With rare exceptions agriculture is universally more important.

There have been only crude estimates of the value of local fisheries production. In the mid-1970s it was suggested that local production was around 13,000 tonnes per year, between a quarter and a third of the quantity that was imported (Densley 1979:2). Production has subsequently grown only slightly, with increased fishing in some river and swamp systems, but probably represents less than 3 per cent of the potential sustainable yield. No more than about 12 per cent of fish catches enter the market system. Limited development of commercial fishing has resulted from the lack of a widespread tradition of subsistence fishing, alongside minimal government assistance, hence the lack of a suitable marketing and distribution system, where ice and freezers are often crucial. Problems of freezer maintenance have also meant that many group efforts have failed. On Ponam island (Manus) the introduction of a fish freezer, intended to assist in the commercialisation of the sole island resource, was a dramatic failure because of disputes over kinship obligations and marine tenure, technical problems, inadequate economic information and non-existent extension services (Carrier 1988), a situation repeated in many other parts of the country. Other factors that have discouraged the development of artisanal fisheries include mixed catches from coastal areas, seasonal variations resulting in erratic catch quantities, over-fishing of reef grass close to urban areas (especially Port Moresby) and customary restrictions on fishing rights (Densley 1979; Wright 1985). Consequently there are very few areas where marine sources contribute significantly to incomes. One exception is the isolated island of Ware, where trochus shells, beche-de-mer (sea cucumber) and, to a lesser extent, fish, made up about a third of island income, though incomes were low (Hayes 1993a). Increasing such incomes in isolated islands would be difficult without ice-making equipment and better communications.

Local production of fish has been limited, but consumption has not; fish are one of the most substantial imports and by 1989 this had grown to over 38,000 tonnes, valued at K34.5 million. More than 86 per cent was canned mackerel; PNG is the world's largest mackerel importer, and it is of widespread significance in diets. There is no food equivalent to tinned fish, with respect to protein and energy content, convenience, storability and price (Copes 1990:6) and it provides twice the protein content of locally purchased fresh fish (Varpiam *et al.* 1984:9). Substitution of domestic production, which would have to increase several-fold, is uneconomic though increased production would enable more optimal use of local resources, improve nutrition and generate employment.

The basis of commercial fishing was once the deepwater tuna fishery, which began at the start of the 1970s, with four major international companies being involved. Pole-and-line fishing was centred on the waters of New Britain and New Ireland (Figure 5.1). Catches peaked at 49,000 tonnes in 1978 but then declined until 1981, when the pole-and-line tuna industry ceased operations because of depressed world prices and the ability of the parent companies to catch sufficient fish elsewhere. Deepwater fishing began again in 1984, after the national government concluded an agreement with an Okinawan company, but lasted only two years. Since then there have been no pole-and-line operations. Taxation policy, the limited duration of operating licences (leading to problems of security of tenure and reasonable returns), inadequate infrastructure and the proscription of some good fishing grounds (to safeguard domestic efforts), have discouraged foreign investment in an

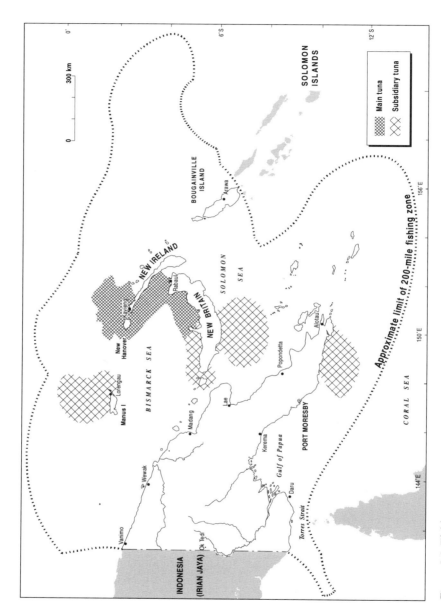

Figure 5.1 Fishing areas

uncertain international climate for fish marketing. Tuna resources, once described by the Secretary of the Department of Fisheries as 'another gold-mine waiting to be developed' (*TPNG* 7 July 1988), are still undeveloped.

Tuna are currently commercially exploited in PNG waters but by foreign-owned vessels. Rights to fish in national waters were first negotiated in 1968 between the Australian administration and Japan. The 200-mile Exclusive Economic Zone (EEZ), established in 1978, gave PNG a large fishing zone of some 2.3 million square kilometres. Since then vessels of various distant water fishing nations, including South Korea, Taiwan and the United States, have operated within PNG waters. Negotiations with the United States, which long refused to accept the 200-mile EEZ for migratory tuna, were unusually difficult. In 1982 the *Danica*, an American purse-seiner, was seized by the PNG government for fishing illegally, and disputes dragged on for five more years. Since then United States vessels have been licensed under a Multilateral Fisheries Treaty, negotiated by the Forum Fisheries Agency on behalf of Pacific states, and separate agreements exist with other nations. Since licence fees are usually based on a percentage of reported catches, there are incentives for states to monitor fish catches, and for vessels to under-report their catches. Catches have rarely been accurately measured, and Korean and Taiwanese vessels probably under-reported their catches during the 1980s (Campbell *et al.* 1994:8). From fisheries licences, the only tangible benefit from exploitation of the tuna resources, PNG earned K16 million in 1990, for a catch esti-mated to be worth about K300 million (*TPNG* 25 July 1991). Some of this revenue – which has remained much the same in subsequent years – was reduced by the costs of surveillance, enforcement, administration and man-agement. Even the limited gains from licences were not achieved without further problems. In 1989 and 1990 there was considerable concern over var-ious 'fishy deals' involving Taiwanese and Filipino purse-seiners that were illegally obtaining fishing licences, failing to pay customs duties, driftnetting illegally in local and Australian waters and engaging in transfer pricing; these activities, in which national politicians and bureaucrats were involved, resulted in losses of as much as K8 million in little more than a year, but spread over many years (M.K. Kelleher 1984). While PNG, like other Pacific island states, has an advantage in ownership of the tuna resource, it is at a considerable comparative disadvantage in harvesting, processing and mar-keting, hence its dependence on overseas capital and technology.

Proposals for a domestic tuna cannery were first mooted in 1972, but aban-doned shortly afterwards since the prospects for economic success were slight. Because of depressed world market conditions, the establishment of a PNG-based tuna industry, in competition with such low-cost existing Asian producers as Thailand, seemed particularly improbable, but in 1992 decisions were taken to establish both tuna and mackerel canneries at Alexishafen (Madang) and Lae, by United States and Malaysian companies respectively. The tuna cannery was expected to generate 1,500 jobs and result in twelve tuna vessels being relocated to PNG. The mackerel cannery, opened in 1996, employed 500 people, and lead to an increase in mackerel imports. Both companies intended to diversify into can manufacturing (linked to the meat cannery in Madang), vegetable canning and other more improbable ancillary activities.

Other than tuna, there are few marine resources which appear capable of supporting commercial fisheries. Prawn fishing however has had a longer history than that of tuna. By the 1990s around twenty national or Japanese-owned prawn fishing trawlers were locally based, all operating out of Port Moresby in the Gulf of Papua. In comparison with other nearby areas, the PNG prawn fishery is relatively unproductive, and has reached what appears to be its annual sustainable yield. It has however survived a period of 'economic and environmental disaster' when corruption was rife, almost twice as many licences were issued as the industry could sustain, and transfer pricing paralleled that in the tuna and timber industries, so that low profitability discouraged local joint venture participation. Other marine products are of slight importance, but include barramundi, mother of pearl shells, beche-de-mer, giant clams and trochus. Production of non-perishable shell enables some cash income to be obtained in remote areas where it would be difficult to gain market access for fish, hence it has significance beyond the limited national gains. It is indicative of the widespread failures of the fishing industry that the prawn industry, despite its disappointments, has proved to be the only successful component of the fisheries sector.

Fisheries exports in 1985, the most successful year in the past decade, were valued at K12.1 million – just a third of the value of fish imports. In 1993 fisheries products were valued at K5.3 million – virtually the lowest level since independence – just 0.2 per cent of all exports, and merely 2 per cent of agricultural exports (Table 4.2). Fisheries potential is as far from being realised now as it has been at any time since independence. Kearney then observed that 'PNG has a greater fisheries potential than other emerging countries in the region, and future production should be more than adequate to meet the domestic requirements. Development of this potential to provide maximum return to Papua New Guinea will not however be without problems' (1977:125). The second sentence, at least, has proved valid. Other than in the prawn industry and the bureaucracy, there is virtually no formal employment in fisheries.

FORESTRY: ECONOMY, ENVIRONMENT AND POLITICAL SYSTEM IN CONFLICT

Certain timber interests in Queensland saw the Bulolo stand as a natural source of supply for Queensland plymills, and they lobbied hard and influentially for it. The contrary view which I expressed was that any timber industry should be primarily for the benefit of PNG and not for the benefit of Queensland, and that PNG should not export logs but manufacture plywood and veneers. The fight was a hard one but I won it.

(Hasluck 1976:27–8)

Forests have been of value for millennia, providing food and materials for housebuilding, canoes, shields and other goods, vines for bridges, baskets and bags and many edible species, including medicines, and habitats for animals and birds. In many societies there were and are various practices to preserve and regenerate tree resources, through regulating access, planting and weeding around seedlings. The new era of commercial forest exploitation has competed with traditional forms of forest use. Though it has generated a significant and increasing proportion of all national export income, it has created concern because of illegal activities, the absence of sustainable resource management and environmental degradation.

About three-quarters of the 46 million hectares of land in PNG is forest covered, but the accessible forest resource is probably around 7 million hectares, almost all in lowland areas (Figure 5.2). Although the area of commercial value is smaller than in many south-east Asian states, there is a larger forest area per capita hence the potential for economic gain is greater. About 200 tree species have economic potential but the bulk of marketable timber comes from a small proportion: taun (*Pometia spp*), kamarere (*Eucalyptus deglupta*), kwila (*Intsia spp*), kauri pine and klinkii pine. Forests are unusually diverse by global standards but wood quality is often lower than in Asia. Some hardwoods are relatively unknown elsewhere hence marketing was an early problem, and returns were sometimes small. Since the number of commercially valuable logs per hectare is relatively small, and there is limited infrastructure in remote regions, the costs and environmental damage of logging have always been high. Because of excess logging in Asia, PNG – where virtually no logs were exported until the 1970s – was the last country in the Asia-Pacific region to be in a situation, as late as the early 1980s, where the rate of logging could increase without reaching the sustainable yield level, even with low rates of reforestation. It was then argued that this was 'a feature which should give it considerable bargaining power in the future' (Daniel and Sims 1986b:70); so far it has conspicuously failed to do so.

After the Second World War a 'vigorous forest policy' was introduced to enable the development of a timber industry, with public tender for the right to harvest forest areas and scope for future indigenous participation (Jonas 1985:48; Lamb 1990:48). In 1950, when this policy was being established, most sawmills were in Morobe, New Britain and Central provinces. The most important venture in the 1950s was the establishment of a large plywood mill at Bulolo – then the single largest industrial operation in the colony – half owned by the Australian administration and half by Bulolo Gold Dredging Company. Through the efforts of Hasluck and others some manufacturing was thus established in the colony. Plantations were developed by the government at Bulolo, Kerevat and Brown River, to protect the forest resource through government control in order to ward off excessive exploitation by either landowners or outsiders (Barnett 1992:90). Various factors discouraged rapid expansion of the timber industry: the diversity of the forests and difficult terrain, which demanded heavy machinery and imposed high costs. Small local companies could not compete internationally and large international companies were uninterested, especially compared with neighbouring Indonesia, where concessions were large and controls minimal (Lamb 1990:21–31). Overseas investment nevertheless expanded in the colonial era; Japan first imported timber from PNG in 1963 and a part-owned Japanese company undertook the largest log export operation in the colony near Hoskins (West New Britain). The amount of processed timber more than doubled between 1955 and 1970, accompanied by an increased scale of production and the concentration of ownership in international companies. At the time of independence almost 95 per cent of processing capacity was foreign – mainly Japanese – owned. Indeed Japan was taking an extraordinary interest in the colony as it moved towards independence

> But some of the Japanese suggestions were a bit startling. The president of Mitsui Mining and Smelting suggested that Japan should acquire a fifty-year 'development mandate' over the whole island (including the Indonesian half) under which, in return for 'developing' the island, Japan would be free to use its raw materials for half a century. Prior to this, Nayar Shiges, Chairman of Nippon Steel . . . had proposed that Japan buy PNG outright.
>
> (Halliday 1975:297)

Such dramatic overseas intervention in the global quest for raw materials may have been improbable, but this kind of approach was indicative of expanding corporate interests, contemporary attitudes to emerging nations and new perceptions of the extent of raw materials in the country.

Expansion of the industry was accompanied by various schemes aimed at developing local processing further, in order to increase the value of exports. Such 'downstream processing' activities were poorly developed though even limited successes merely emphasised post-independence failures. At the time of independence, the industry was expanding, contributing substantially to exports, attracting overseas investment, generating new employment and infrastructure expansion, and the problem of poor, diverse forests appeared to have been overcome by clear-felling for woodchip operations. Yet trade favoured metropolitan interests, processing was limited, Melanesians were employed only in unskilled, poorly paid jobs, land disputes were becoming more common as timber rights were hastily acquired (Jonas 1985) and clear-felling posed environmental problems. Subsequently such problems became considerably worse.

The establishment of pulpwood logging (woodchipping) allowed economies of scale, and offered the industry the chance to achieve some degree of profitability. When negotiations to allow the Japan and New Guinea Timber Co (Jant Pty Ltd) to develop a woodchipping industry in the Gogol valley, near Madang, were concluded in 1971, the industry appeared set for a more successful future. In the same year the Forestry (Private Dealing) Act was enacted; this allowed customary owners to sell their timber

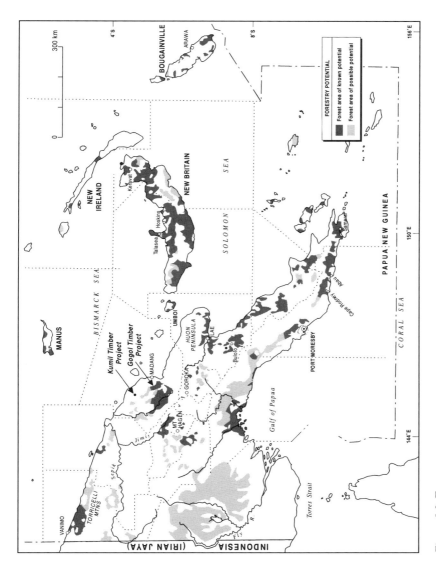

Figure 5.2 Forest resources

direct to outsiders, subject to the approval of the Forestry Minister, bypassing previous timber rights purchasing procedures which gave more centralised control (Barnett 1992:91). This was later exploited by foreign companies and individual forest ministers, who became more powerful and autocratic, and some entered into private negotiations with foreigners seeking timber export permits. The decentralised structure of the industry, in increasingly remote areas, allowed foreign intervention to be much less easily controlled and monitored than in any other area of the economy. In a very short time a promising industry became riddled with corruption, and the national government's ability to protect the environment, enforce permit conditions, control logging operations and prevent such marketing abuses as transfer pricing virtually disappeared.

Some of these problems occurred over more than two decades at the largest, most integrated and long-established project, the Gogol Timber Project (GTP). It attracted considerable criticism, but generated more export income and employment than any other single component of the forestry industry. Underlying this specific Japanese interest was the continued expansion of the Japanese forestry industry in and beyond Asia, to establish a more decentralised pulpwood industry, with PNG perceived as a low-cost location (Lamb 1990:70–4). Jant was originally interested in integrated rural development; various agricultural developments were expected to replace the cleared timber and benefit from new accessibility. Villagers who welcomed the industry saw it as enabling them to participate in a wider economic world; essentially they 'sold their forests in exchange for roads' (ibid.:96), in what became a familiar situation elsewhere. In the nearby Kumil Timber Project (north-west of Madang)

> By 'development' the people mean that all settlements in the bush should get a road, that every man should then have his own vehicle, that all goods should be easy to buy, that money should exist in abundance, that all children should go to school and that no-one should have to die because of sickness.
> (Renner 1990:17; Mullins and Flaherty 1995:95)

Demand for forestry was particularly great in rural areas where landowners perceived no viable alternative income-generating opportunities; at Arowe (West New Britain) one landowner

> said that the Arowe people are in great need of development. He said they were the forgotten people of Papua New Guinea and must sacrifice their environment, resources and social structure to see changes in the name of development. 'Our people do not have any "choice" because there is no alternative and therefore greenies have no right to interfere'. The people wanted a change in lifestyle so that they could live like those in towns and cities. He said this was the opportunity in their life for those changes to take place.
> (*TPNG* 16 September 1993)

Logging companies offered landowners the kind of infrastructure that would normally be provided by the state but as the state's performance in supplying basic infrastructure and services declined, people became increasingly vulnerable to the inducements of logging companies, whilst governments participated in the portrayal of logging companies as agents of development (J. Fingleton 1994:21). In direct comparison with the situation in Bougainville, where the copper mine was then being constructed (Chapter 6), few villagers appreciated the impact that large forestry projects would bring. Forestry proved to be analogous to small-scale mining.

The initial GTP agreement quickly created problems. There was very little environmental protection: there were inadequate or non-existent environmental guidelines and minimal environmental monitoring. Reforestation was excluded from the initial agreement, and was rare; land tenure posed problems, since land was required for around twenty years to ensure commercial viability, and the company did not commit adequate capital to reforestation, because it lacked capital or sought immediate profits (De'ath 1980:53; Lamb 1990:217). The inability to achieve an adequate rate of reforestation was critical. Subsequently Jant placed a continued demand on new forest areas to ensure the company's viability. Other problems followed: Jant had no real timetable, tropical experience or plan of operations, in part a result of an uncertain international timber situation; logging densities were too high, and neither a veneer mill nor a plywood mill were built. Clear-felling initially led to the loss of flora, but in the 1980s logging areas increased in size, minimal areas were left alongside watercourses and the environmental consequences worsened. The national economic gains were less than anticipated since Jant did not pay company tax, on the grounds that the operation was unprofitable, a conclusion that was contested.

At the village level the consequences were considerable. Better accessibility enabled services to reach remote villages but most feeder roads were of such poor quality that they rarely lasted more than a couple of years. Incomes increased, from royalties and employment, out-migration ended but rivers and water supplies were polluted and degraded. New agricultural projects had little success, and business development was ephemeral. In short there was 'little sign of an economic multiplier effect' (Lamb 1990:213) and income supposedly spent in the Gogol 'in effect has gone into the pockets of middle-class public servants, middlemen traders and outsiders in the form of salaries and commissions' (De'ath 1980:121). At Kumil, the Provincial Government tried to overrule the local landowners' development corporation, when the corporation sought to monitor contract violations more carefully (Renner 1990:50), a precursor of events elsewhere in the country. Employment opportunities were intended for local residents; 30 per cent of all timber-related jobs at GTP went to people from the area, but requirements for educational achievement reduced the ability of villagers to gain the best jobs. Villagers were particularly concerned at the small size of royalty payments (which led to road blocks, non-cooperation and other forms of opposition), the complexity of royalty distribution and its extremely uneven outcome, the periodicity of payments, their limited value and changes in procedures over time (De'ath 1980:101–5; Lamb 1990:164–7; Mullins and Flaherty 1995; Renner 1990:61). Landowners generally had expectations above reality, a result of their own misconceptions, inadequate explanations of project outcomes and fluctuations in world market prices (De'ath 1980), feared the loss of their land, but, at the same time, were anxious to see the start of forestry and obtain shares in Jant, and, despite negative experiences, anticipated that things would improve. The project brought both gains and losses but, like mining projects, the losses rather than the benefits mounted over time.

Compared with all subsequent timber projects, the amount of government and company planning that had gone into the GTP was considerable, and the local and national gains were much greater. Efforts were made to ensure local participation and Jant was reasonably enlightened; it had established about 6,000 hectares of plantations, constructed 160 kilometres of all weather roads, employed 842 people and paid out K4.1 million in royalties between 1979 and 1990 (*TPNG* 25 June 1992). Very little of this could be said of subsequent projects or the companies involved. Unlike the mining industry, guidelines and controls weakened over time, hence subsequent projects generated few of the gains and all of the losses that occurred in the Madang hinterland. Practice diverged further from what good management required, and social and environmental problems worsened.

In the post-independence years formal strategies for the commercial development of forestry were largely based on the National Forestry Policy of 1979. This sought to increase timber exports and proposed large log export quotas for companies in exchange for the construction of infrastructure and the establishment of forestry plantations. A previous requirement that logs be processed into sawn timber was waived, since processing costs in PNG were high and both Japan and South Korea had under-utilised processing capacity and preferred logs. Overseas interest in PNG's forests increased as the supply of timber in south-east Asian countries declined and those countries imposed bans on the export of logs, in order to protect their dwindling forest resources. Asian corporations 'were mainly small-scale but resourceful operators who had developed expertise in getting as many logs as possible out of a country at the greatest possible profit, disregarding government controls and revenue procedures when necessary to achieve these ends' (Barnett 1992:95). After honing such skills in Asia, especially Indonesia, such corporations were well organised for success in PNG, where regulations were few, policing minimal and sanctions weak. Little national effort and finance was allocated to resource assessment and management and more to organising the purchasing of timber rights and the allocation of timber areas for exploitation. As 'the race to export quickened' the Ministry was no longer able to negotiate and purchase timber rights at the speed that demand was increasing, and foreign companies became involved in direct negotiation; ministers eventually issued letters of intent to award permits to foreign companies, without any challenges to the viability of the project or the company, in a context where bribes were sought and given, and landowners encouraged to participate (Barnett 1992:99–100). Control over marketing abuses collapsed to the extent that companies were declaring a loss for PNG taxation purposes, defrauding the government of revenue and cheating landowners of even their limited share of profits. By 1987 the extent of corruption, fraud and scandal was so great that the Prime Minister, Paias Wingti, set up a Commission of Inquiry into all aspects of the industry. Meanwhile a new National Forestry Development Programme (1987–91) sought to double log exports by 1991. Judge Tos Barnett, the Chairman of the Commission of Inquiry, described the situation graphically:

> The control of operations was left to the newly decentralised, dismembered, disorganised and demoralised forestry service administering the toothless and out-of-date Forestry Act. Most field officers were clearly incapable of supervising the aggressive timber operations and of enforcing the operating conditions. Consequently the forestry scene in 1987–88 was fairly described by the Commission of Inquiry as one of 'rampage and pillage' by logging companies who moved from one illegal and destructive operation to another. Operations were commenced illegally: forest working plans, if submitted at all, were being widely ignored; logging tracks were being pushed through at the discretion of the bulldozer driver; hillsides and river banks were being logged; and the immature future forest resource was being bashed and trampled in the reckless haste to get the logs down to the waiting log ships. The dazed and disillusioned forest owners stood watching in disbelief as foreign operators removed their trees before moving on.
>
> (Barnett 1992:97)

In a very few areas, such as the GTP, foreign companies sought to remain for longer periods of time, were more conscious of environmental issues, the involvement of Melanesians in decision-making and the provision of infrastructure. Barnett's conclusions were however particularly true of the island provinces.

The Commission of Inquiry lasted for two years, eventually producing a twenty-volume report (Barnett 1990), which stressed that there was no obvious forestry policy, forestry planning or adequate knowledge of forestry resources, legislation was ineffective to monitor or control existing forestry practices, serious environmental damage was being caused by over-cutting and nineteen of the twenty timber companies that were investigated had been involved in fraud and transfer pricing on a very significant scale. Barnett described the mainly Malaysian and Singaporean companies as 'roaming the countryside with the self-assurance of robber barons, bribing politicians, creating social disharmony and ignoring laws' (Asia-Pacific Action Group 1990:5). Transfer pricing on log sales during 1986 and 1987 had caused a loss of about K27.5 million in foreign currency earnings and of K4.3 million in company tax on hidden profits. Moreover companies undermeasured and smuggled logs, or undervalued high value species, to defraud governments and landowners of royalties. Over the whole post-independence era, PNG had received about half the average revenue that the Philippines had received and as little as a third of that of Sabah, relative to the volumes of timber exported. A number of prominent Papua New Guineans, notably Ted Diro, the Minister of Forests from 1985, had received illegal benefits and major political parties obtained substantial election campaign funds from overseas timber companies (see p. 279). Despite the gravity of political corruption and the extent of economic disruption, implementation of the report's recommendations was lethargic, exemplifying the scathing conclusions of the Inquiry: 'forest policy amounts to no more than window-dressing for free market anarchy' and the forest industry is 'effectively unpoliceable, inherently corrupt and beyond reform' (Asia-Pacific Action Group 1990:58). Several companies that had been severely criticised for various breaches of permit conditions continued to operate, new leases were granted to them, sometimes to even larger tracts, especially in Manus and West New Britain. These two provinces and New Ireland, probably the most seriously deforested province, have lost most of their viable timber resources. De'ath's prophecy for Manus that 'outsiders will create a boom and bust timber industry which will have as its only memorial, in a generation from now, an empty logged-out area, abandoned technology and unusable infrastructure' (1983:72) is already true, not just for Manus, and well before there has been a change of generation.

A positive outcome of the Inquiry, and of World Bank involvement, was the development of new forestry legislation. A white paper entitled *The National Forestry Policy (1990)* was published and a two-year ban placed on new logging permits, though this was largely honoured in the breach (Deklin 1992; Filer 1991; Taylor 1992). The resultant National Forest Plan (PNG Department of Forests 1991) had two principal objectives: management and protection of the nation's forest resources as a renewable asset, employment creation, greater local participation in the industry, and increased onshore processing. The policy still focused almost entirely on production, rather than on forest management or the wider relationship between forest values and the environment. The Plan set up a government statutory body, the Papua New Guinea National Forest Authority, which was empowered to acquire authority over particular forest resources by means of Forest Management Agreements (FMAs), between the Forest Authority, the resource owners and the provincial government, with reference to the allocation of timber rights in particular areas. The FMAs were intended to give landowners increased ability to participate in decisions concerning their resources. The greater involvement of national government (the Forest Authority) and the landowners was intended to prevent companies manipulating resource owners directly and so preventing any outside monitoring of negotiations (Holzknecht 1994:27). Under this system widespread corruption had been entrenched and landowners gained disproportionately few benefits from their resources. The Act also sought to protect landowners from themselves, or at least from particular dominant factions.

Elsewhere global concern over the environmental consequences of the destruction of the world's rainforests had stimulated interest in promoting their use for diverse local social and economic goals, with various nations developing Tropical Forestry Action Plans (TFAPs). In PNG the process of establishing a TFAP was initiated by the World Bank (1990) whose study of the forestry industry coincided with the final phases of the Barnett Inquiry. The TFAP reflected PNG's willingness to preserve its rainforests in return for financial compensation from aid donors, crudely phrased by the Minister of Forests, Karl Stack, to the European Community:

> Okay, if you are worried about the greenhouse effect, if you want us to be responsible corporate citizens of the world, you must also understand we are a Third World nation and need the money. Give us 200 million kina a year for our budget and you can be in charge of our forests. You can set and dictate the harvest levels to us.
>
> (Quoted in Callick *et al.* 1990:13.1)

The TFAP, established in PNG as the National Forestry and Conservation Action Programme (NFCAP), embraced twenty overseas-funded projects, all designed to reduce dependence on exports, integrate forestry into other rural social and economic activities and ensure a greater degree of conservation. Projects examined the viability of non-timber forest products, such as medicinal plants and mushrooms, since the value of products extracted for subsistence purposes was regarded as greater than revenue from the sale of timber (CSIRO 1992:1). Another programme saw the introduction of mobile sawmills (*wokabaut somil*), which have provided an alternative to large-scale exploitation. The *wokabaut somil* requires no roads or heavy machinery, timber can be used for various local and export purposes, the rate of forest use is slow and there is some possibility of sustainable forestry. However sawmills are prone to mechanical failure, there are disputes over ownership, considerable wastage and it is extremely difficult for small producers to gain access to markets. By the early 1990s there were about 200 sawmills; three years later there were about 600, but only a third were operational. Capital constraints, limited human resources and commitment to sustainable development, and long established export orientation, have made such programmes difficult, especially where the National Forest Plan neither recognised, nor encouraged, small projects that used mobile sawmills (Holzknecht and Kalit 1995). There was some suspicion within PNG, especially from NGOs (non-governmental organisations), of both ministerial intentions and the motives of the World Bank (which did not oppose the export of logs) and thus the ability to achieve alternative forms of development. The powerful core of the industry remained focused on increased production.

Despite environmental concerns there was no real monitoring of projects

(Filer 1991:25). A new Task Force on Environmental Planning in Priority Forest Areas was unable to develop clear criteria for deciding what areas should be 'priority forest areas' for conservation rather than logging. Even the formalities of environmental planning were absent. Of the 316 timber projects operating between 1975 and 1990 only 22 had submitted an environmental plan, though such plans were compulsory after 1986. In several provinces, including New Ireland, there had been no environmental plans. The few plans that existed were virtually identical, with similar checklists of plants and animals and landowners with apparently identical cultural systems, even from widely separated provinces: 'a "search and replace" exercise on the word processor' that had little relationship to particular areas (Henderson 1994:50). The scale of forestry was rapidly increasing, without any consideration of sustainable development and environmental management. Despite new legislation, expediency, graft and corruption continued to characterise the industry.

Reforestation has also failed. Between 1945 and 1988 no more than about 38,000 hectares were reforested, a mere 864 hectares per year, vastly less than the area cleared (Fernando 1990b:7), and not enough to sustain a pulpwood industry. Limited reforestation was a result of government and landowners failing to make land available, uncertainty over rights to harvest future plantations (Barnett 1992:115–16) and lack of interest by forestry companies. Most of the reforested area was at early forestry sites around Bulolo and at Gogol, despite the problems there. The achievement of a more sustainable forestry industry has also been hindered by a lack of knowledge of the resource base, and hence what is an appropriate logging rate, and by the attitudes of landowners, government and industry to income generation. Because of uncertainties over forested areas, the environmental impact of logging and the period required for regeneration, the extent to which there is overcutting is difficult to assess, though both in West New Britain and Manus the rate of logging appears to be considerably beyond what is sustainable (Nadarajah 1994:53), and similar situations are probably true elsewhere (Duncan 1994; Nadarajah 1994). There has been excessive clearance for road construction, felling in steep areas close to watercourses, erosion and flooding after the use of caterpillar-tracked machines. Undersized trees have been felled, remaining trees damaged, habitats disrupted and seed sources lost. At every stage, waste of timber resources has continued, from indiscriminate cutting to rejection of wood in timber yards, prior to export. The crudest versions of economies of scale have overwhelmed environmental ethics and economics. No adequate attempt has been made to quantify the costs and benefits of logging anywhere in the country, and timber resources are disappearing before there is adequate knowledge of almost every facet of the resource base, and especially its diversity of values.

The ability to manage a sustainable system does not exist at local or national level. Landowners, especially in more remote, least developed parts of the country, where most forest resources exist, have sought 'development' more than conservation, and do not want conservation if they cannot have development. In the Lak area, on the southern tip of New Ireland and the only significant part of the province that had not been logged, where income was primarily from migrant remittances, 'it would probably be difficult to find another place in PNG where local landowners were more insistent on the need to have their trees cut down as soon as possible' (*TPNG* 3 January 1991). Consequently despite the Barnett Inquiry, the World Bank report and the establishment of a Tropical Forestry Action Plan, old habits died hard: 'The province is back to "business as usual". Logs make money, money wins votes. The logic is inescapable. So provincial politicians are falling over each other to secure timber permits for any portions of their own electorates which have not so far been penetrated by the bulldozers of the logging companies' (*TPNG* 3 January 1991). Some landowners would have to wait a long time for 'development' if projects elsewhere absorbed all the permissible harvest that sustainable yield management allows. Mechanisms to reduce the ability of contractors to 'grease' local landowners and politicians were inefficient, and local 'landowner companies' emerged that were no more than fronts for foreign corporations (Taylor 1992:141). The combination of politicians, landowners and overseas corporations has overwhelmed sustainability.

Following the development of the National Forest Plan, and widespread concern from NGOs over the extent of forest destruction, the new Minister of Forests, Tim Neville, introduced a 1993 Forestry Act (Amendment) Bill, which formulated new guidelines, that sought to ensure that projects could start only in areas identified in the Plan, and only after landowner awareness programmes had been conducted. Underlying the new Act was a renewed attempt to lower timber harvest levels to sustainable levels, reduce the export of logs (rather than processed timber) and introduce a new forest revenue system (Economic Insights 1994; Holzknecht 1994). One new measure was the introduction of a Swiss company, Société Générale Surveillance, a private sector export monitoring service, to inspect all export logs and provide market price data, in order to reduce undervaluation, sale of undersized logs and transfer pricing. The minister estimated that in 1992 K119 million was lost in revenue through undervaluing and misreporting (*PC* 28 March 1994). The guidelines also sought an improved context for production, marketing and downstream processing, but continued to ignore environmental issues. All forests up to 2,400 metres altitude were designated as production forest, despite the enormous diversity and range of uses of those forests, and high priority biodiversity areas were not separately identified. The environmental standards required of the forestry industry were not defined, nor was the means of monitoring adherence to any standards identified (Nadarajah 1994). The policy changes were bitterly opposed by the timber industry, with some landowner support. Though a private member's Bill that broadly represented these views was soundly defeated in Parliament, the Wingti government suspended the implementation of the guidelines. The institutional context deteriorated further in 1994 when the Forest Authority building in Port Moresby was destroyed in a fire, for which arson was suspected, and all forestry contracts and other data were lost. The minister faced powerful cabinet opposition, in order to implement reforms, and experienced death threats to himself and his family. One prominent opponent was the Minister of Agriculture, Roy Evara, who sought to clear around 40,000 hectares of forest in his Kikori constituency, for a subsequent oil palm project; Evara stated 'we are not going to entertain any conservation projects in Kikori because we need to utilise our natural resources to develop and improve the living standards of our people' (*Australian Financial Review* (*AFR*) 6 May 1994). Despite the presence of a minister intent on implementing reforms that would create a more sustainable industry, the political context made legal and institutional changes almost impossible to develop. Logging companies continue to hold inappropriate influence with government, corruption remains an issue and new guidelines have been difficult to implement with strong industry opposition, notably that of ensuring that landowners receive a higher proportion of the value of the timber (Economic Insights 1996:89–90). Implementation of an appropriate new forest revenue system was the major hurdle in negotiations between the government and the World Bank in 1996.

Log exports continued to increase as crucial policy elements were not transformed into practice, emphasising earlier trends. The most substantial export growth however came after 1991; exports of forest products earned K148 million in 1992, a new record level, and hit K494 million in 1994 (Table 4.2), when log prices averaged K164 per cubic metre (twice the price in 1992, and three times the price in the 1980s). Compared with an export value of at least K410 million in 1993, landowners received about K6 million in royalties (*TPNG* 3 March 1994). Timber prices were particularly high in the 1990s, because of substantial demand in Japan and a shortage of logs from Sabah and Sarawak; soon afterwards PNG and Solomon Islands became the only places in the world where logs were still being exported, hence prices increased even faster. The massive increase in the rate of exploitation of the forests in the 1990s was accompanied by the establishment and consolidation of south-east Asian logging companies, especially those from Malaysia. Much the most important of these was Rimbunan Hijau (literally 'green forest'), Malaysia's largest publicly listed timber company, which arrived in 1988. At the end of 1992 it held fourteen timber permits, covering 38 per cent of all timber operations in the country; in 1992–3 it recorded a profit of at least K300 million in PNG and had 2 million hectares of concessions. By 1994 it was considered to control about 50 per cent of the timber industry, through its own operations (and through other companies by complex, interlocking but secretive share ownership structures). The company has been strongly criticised in Malaysia and elsewhere, particularly for transfer-pricing; in PNG it established a second national newspaper in 1993 to provide it with a better public image (*TPNG* 3 March 1994). South-east Asian corporations now dominate the export industry, as Japanese corporations once did, with their modes of operation and profitability shrouded in secrecy.

The volume and value of log exports grew enormously in the 1990s, but the value of processed timber exports remained largely unchanged. In 1977 some 63 per cent of all logs were processed domestically; that figure had dropped to only 15 per cent in 1991, including the volume converted to pulp chips by Jant (Henderson 1994:10). Throughout the 1980s and 1990s the export value of processed timber was rarely more than 10 per cent of the total export value of timber, and in 1994 was a mere 2 per cent. PNG gained proportionately less income, and new employment generation, over this period, whilst Port Moresby occasionally ran short of sawn timber during the 1990s. The gains from processing that Hasluck achieved in the colonial era had disappeared. Only a fraction of the increased log prices remained in the country, substantial profits were transferred overseas, whilst the royalty rate was pegged at about K3 per cubic metre. There were numerous examples of landowners receiving less than that, and of the true volume and value being inaccurately recorded (*PC* 23 September 1993). Despite the increase in timber prices in the 1990s, the bureaucracy and the structure of legal relationships were unresponsive to this market surge, so that the price increase was a substantial windfall gain for the companies. Though the fundamental alteration in market conditions warranted a renegotiation of all logging contracts, there were no mechanisms to put this in place, though the value of forestry to the national economy increased. The share of forestry products in total export earnings rose from 4.7 per cent in 1976 to 7.0 per cent in 1991, but by 1994 it had grown to a record 18.5 per cent (Table 4.2). Timber had become big business.

A series of attempts have been made by different governments to increase the benefits to the national economy of the forestry industry, by demanding a domestic 'downstream' processing component from companies seeking to export logs, and by banning the export as logs of such high value species as ebony, teak and rosewood. They were unsuccessful because of such institutional and macro-economic constraints on industrial development as high wage rates and the high cost of infrastructure. There is acute competition from large-scale mills in south-east Asia and efficient high recovery mills in Japan. Moreover the small domestic market, species diversity and high domestic transport costs raise costs and reduce the viable recovery rate to less than half the best world standards, hence restrictions on log exports would not increase the viability of a domestic processing industry (Economic Insights 1994:104–5). Under pressure from Australia and the World Bank the government agreed to phase out log exports and encourage local processing activities, but processing – though creating new employment opportunities – may impose additional costs (Economic Insights 1996:91–2) and the industry was strongly opposed to the move. Lack of institutional capacity, and government reluctance, may prevent this transition. On various occasions companies have established proposals for new processing ventures, to turn out plywood and sawn timber, but none have come to fruition. Consequently, though about 10,000 people are employed in the forestry sector, this number actually declined during the expansionist 1990s.

Villagers have opposed some forestry developments, but usually belatedly when the full implications of clear-felling alongside inadequate infrastructure, employment and royalties, have all become apparent. Disappointments were sometimes emphasised by internal conflicts and uneven distribution of royalty payments. In one of the most remote parts of Western Province, where effective contact came only in post-independence times, forestry has only just begun and the Wawoi-Guavi people draw their only income from timber royalties

> Because there are no government officers to give advice to the villagers about ways of using the money to provide income for themselves in terms of small business projects, the money is usually spent on unnecessary items like alcohol consumption, trips down the river to Daru for shopping. There is no initiative for fishing or agriculture on the part of the local people. There is hardly any market. There are no fishing or crocodile projects despite the abundance of resources. People do not usually plan ahead for the future because there is no guidance.
>
> (*TPNG* 1 October 1992)

In many remote areas like this, forestry has provided windfall revenue, but long-term benefits were absent. In many places the 'landowner companies', set up by the timber companies to enable negotiations, became another mechanism to manipulate, misrepresent and divide resource owners and be a buffer between the timber companies and the owners. The speed of deforestation ensured that, unlike mining, the extent of the negative consequences was apparent only towards the end of the process, hence renegotiation or denial at a local level was impossible. Landowners have threatened 'another Bougainville', through the takeover of forestry projects (J. Fingleton 1994), but this has not happened. Such threats emphasise that the same kinds of problems have pervaded people–governments–corporations relationships over forestry as have occurred on a larger scale in the mining industry, but in a much greater number of sites. Landowners' attitudes have gone from demand to disillusionment.

At the current rate of exploitation, with a total commercial area of about 7 million hectares, of which about 2 million hectares (but possibly as much as 4 million hectares) had been cut by the end of 1993, PNG will have exhausted about half its forests by the end of the century. The industry was simply 'mining the resource' (Nadarajah 1994:20), particularly in the island provinces, as West New Britain retained its premier position as a timber exporter, and like two other key areas, Western Province and New Ireland, exported only logs (Table 5.1). The historic view of forests as a subsistence resource, a source of livelihood invested with symbolic meanings, had shifted to timber as an economic resource and a source of immediate revenue. The

Table 5.1 Timber exports and cuts by province

	Log exports (1991) (thousand kina)	Sawn timber exports (1991) (thousand kina)	Total permitted cut (1993) (thousand cubic metres)
West New Britain	33,203	21	2,548
East New Britain	9,563	386	889
New Ireland	6,418	—	526
Manus	1,940	—	84
Morobe	1,020	66	880
Madang	781	194	716
West Sepik	9,836	217	484
Central	8,008	61	701
Milne Bay	2,540	—	225
Oro	1,701	—	165
Western	15,371	—	380
Gulf	6,614	—	556
Southern Highlands	—	—	4
Western Highlands	—	—	4
East Sepik	—	—	230
North Solomons	—	—	60
Total[1]	96,995	1,020	8,452

Note: 1 There is no timber industry in Enga, Simbu and the Eastern Highlands
Source: PNG Department of Forests (1994) *Timber Digest, June 1992*, Nadarajah, p. 2

diverse role of forests as biological resources, sources of non-wood products, means of soil conservation and watershed protection, natural habitats for global diversity and repositories for carbon, have barely ever been considered. Asian corporations have proved more influential in generating log exports than the World Bank in enabling sustainable forestry. Concern over the operation of south-east Asian companies has mounted and has gone beyond PNG. The Australian Prime Minister, Paul Keating, at the Conference of the South Pacific Forum in 1994, criticised such companies for committing 'environmental piracy' and 'threatening the future of the South Pacific', and in turn was accused by the Malaysian Prime Minister, Mahathir Mohamad, of seeking to continue neo-colonialism in the region, by bribing countries through aid to halt the timber operations of legitimate companies from ASEAN nations (*SMH* 27 August 1994). International efforts to develop a code of practice for sustainable forestry were rebuffed by PNG at the 1995 Forum Conference, thus despite international debate and a national inquiry, the structure of the industry remained unchanged: 'the period between the Barnett Inquiry and the present day is much worse with regard to questionable forestry activity than at any time . . . an indictment of the opportunistic nature of PNG society as well as of many of the present day elected and educated elite' (Holzknecht 1994:29). Even in the provinces most seriously affected in the 1980s, notably New Ireland, the situation worsened.

A number of phenomena contributed to the rapacious destruction of forestry resources: the increase in world prices for tropical timber (as a result of the progressive elimination of log exports from south-east Asia), the consequent movement of Asian companies into PNG (and Solomon Islands), the greater interest by residents of remote rural areas in access and cash incomes (as cash crop prices fell) and new and easier opportunities for corruption. Monitoring of the industry worsened, and the rate of reforestation fell. Forestry has never been given the national priority afforded to mining. The negative experiences at Gogol, despite forward planning, a long-established industry and considerable monitoring, demonstrated the difficulties of establishing a sustainable forestry industry, yet more recent projects have been much worse. Despite the potential of the industry to provide a more diversified and long-term resource, and because of the unusually exploitative nature of the corporations currently engaged in the industry, the forestry sector is the most rapacious and uncontrolled within the country and, even in comparison with mining, the least equipped to enable more equitable local participation. Most forests will not survive the present economic and institutional regime.

ENVIRONMENTAL MANAGEMENT

The depletion of the forest industry has demonstrated that, at an institutional level, the extent of concern over environmental management has been minimal, even in a country of outstanding beauty, and physical and biological diversity. Pre-colonial management practices only incidentally conserved ecological systems, through a combination of particular techniques that maintained long-term productivity in environments prone to natural hazard, while populations remained stable. From colonial times, population growth and technological change – including shotguns, chainsaws, gillnets and chemicals – have disrupted ecological systems and led to the extinction and depletion of some fauna and flora (Chapter 3). In some places new problems have emerged, most obviously the large-scale environmental degradation caused by deforestation and mining and, in other areas, mainly on the coasts, from the localised use of bleach and detergents, the dynamiting of reefs and the disposal of liquid and solid wastes. Some urban beaches, like Ela beach (Port Moresby) are now highly polluted. There is however comprehensive environmental legislation, more developed than in other Pacific states, while the fourth national goal in the constitution proclaimed at independence was 'for Papua New Guinea's natural resources and environment to be conserved and used for the collective benefit of us all, and to be replenished for the benefit of future generations'. To this end the Office (later Department) of Environment and Conservation was established in 1974.

Constitutional commitment to environmental conservation is largely rhetorical. The government has become the sole arbiter of the conditions of resource development, 'having to balance its role as a promoter of development (and sometimes even a project equity partner) against its role as protector of the environment. Not unnaturally, the former more immediately appealing role has tended to prevail' (J. Fingleton 1992:10; see also Chapter 6). A number of NGOs have sought to strengthen and implement environmental legislation but without great effect. Despite the revision of resource laws in the late 1980s and early 1990s to include landowners in discussion of issues relating to resource development projects, commitment to growth has had negative environmental consequences whilst contemporary legislation has been ignored. Environmental plans in the forestry and agricultural sectors have been inadequate or simply absent, whilst landowners themselves have not been interested in environmental concerns.

The database for even the most general assessment of environmental change in PNG is lacking, yet the range of environmental changes is considerable. Agriculture, forestry and mining have had an impact on fresh and marine waters, forests and related ecosystems, through inundation, soil erosion, siltation and chemical pollution. Losses of cultural heritage have followed flooding by hydropower development, and resource extraction. Ecosystems have been degraded by particular forms of deforestation, agriculture and hunting and gathering, and inadequate urban waste management has resulted in health hazards, visual eyesores and the reduced recreational and fisheries value of coastal environments. It is impossible to assess the extent and significance of these changes. An attempt to evaluate environmental quality losses caused by mining and forestry alone – the most damaging land uses – indicated that even conservative estimates gave losses amounting to over 10 per cent of the value of the net production that caused them (Bartelmus *et al.* 1992:33). Losses may have been more than that, but there were inadequate data to assess changes in forest and fisheries reserves, the impact of water pollution and depletion of biodiversity.

Adopting the most straightforward approach to defining the key elements of ecologically sustainable development as, firstly, integrating economic and environmental goals in policies and activities; secondly, ensuring that environmental assets are appropriately valued; thirdly, providing for equity within and between generations; fourthly, dealing cautiously with risk and irreversibility and, fifthly, recognising the global dimension (G. Kelleher 1991:19), resource exploitation has failed to come close to even recognising the value of such objectives. Legislation that might contribute to this has been ignored at every level and the Department of Environment and Conservation poorly funded. Demand for 'development' has overwhelmed advice over caution and conservation, there is inadequate land-use mapping and analysis, to enable the identification of critical areas where conservation would be appropriate, and minimal monitoring of key changes. With inadequate policy guidelines, poor co-ordination between agencies, scarce resources and insufficient staff training and experience it has not been enough merely to have appropriate policies and laws. Agriculture and resource use has contributed to economic development – though the gains have been slight in the forestry and fishery sectors, relative to the value of the resource – but has also hastened environmental degradation in a permissive political climate, where pressure groups and private interests have been able to subvert the theory and practice of existing environmental legislation and management.

INTEGRATED RURAL DEVELOPMENT

Throughout the country even development practices in particular sectors have rarely been coordinated adequately, whilst any notion of linking developments in different sectors has been conspicuous by its absence. Formal integrated rural development projects (IRDPs) were a major element of rural development between 1976 and 1986 in five provinces – East and West Sepik, Southern Highlands, Enga and Simbu – some of the least developed provinces in the country. Though largely funded by the World Bank and the Asian Development Bank, they cost the PNG government more than K80 million. The IRDPs emerged from the Less Developed Areas strategy, formulated under the Eight Aims in 1975, and combined a mix of infrastructure (roads, bridges and buildings), income-generation (plantations, rural industries and smallholder cash-cropping schemes) and social welfare (schools, aid posts, health centres and nutrition centres). The projects sought development that would improve health, nutrition, education and the status of women, and also increase rural productivity, cash incomes, employment opportunities and the general standard of living.

The impact of the IRDPs varied significantly between provinces, according to priorities and interests. Coffee, tea and rubber estates were established, and associated processing factories constructed in the Southern Highlands and East Sepik provinces. However both the tea and coffee projects in the Southern Highlands closed; the Kaupena tea project failed because of unreliable transport and low prices (Crittenden *et al.* 1988). Most other economic projects also had disappointing results. The Gavien rubber scheme in the East Sepik, intended to benefit the landless and the isolated through resettlement, 'inadvertently locked them into a rigid production system that keeps them in poverty' (Crittenden and Lea 1990a:27); there were flaws in the implementation of the settlement scheme, compounded by worsening terms of trade for rubber, sub-standard housing, poor health facilities, erratic water supplies and little capacity for food production (Cox 1979). The exotic nature of several projects – such as tea, salt fish and buffaloes – was often outside the experience, and sometimes the interest, of local people and had little chance of being integrated into other spheres of existing or future development.

Hundreds of kilometres of roads were constructed; schools and aid posts were built, but 'it is far from clear whether the projects achieved what was promised in the appraisal reports', though the increased provision of health care facilities meant people were healthier, fewer children died, fewer mothers died in childbirth and there were more educational opportunities (Crittenden and Lea 1989:474). Formal development projects did not affect gender roles; though planned agricultural schemes might have been expected to address the question of women's subordination, the evidence from the Gavien scheme suggests that the position of women was actually worse than in spontaneously evolving village contexts, and effectively institutionalised gender bias (Ilave and Cox 1988). At considerable cost the social context failed to benefit.

Though the IRDPs contributed to rural welfare gains, they failed to provide and develop opportunities where villagers could raise their economic productivity and increase their incomes over time. Technical problems followed from the design, implementation and management of the schemes within an inefficient bureaucracy with little continuity of personnel. Consequently programme management grew more inflexible; despite costly failures the objectives were not modified and programme activities were not better managed (Crittenden and Lea 1991). The people for whom the projects were meant were rarely involved at any level and the projects were 'divorced from local ways of doing things, local customs, aspirations, hopes and capabilities, to such an extent that the projects become self-serving, mainly benefiting those who run them', with large sums of money being spent on government housing, air charters and travel by public servants, and little on village-based projects (Crittenden and Lea 1989:475). Projects benefited those already involved in related economic activities, education projects were directed to urban and clerical training that was of limited relevance in rural areas whilst agricultural extension activities declined in the IRDP areas as they did elsewhere. There was little attempt to link agriculture with the fisheries or forestry sectors. Efficiency rather than flexibility and effectiveness was emphasised, usually in accountancy terms, and equity was not about redistribution in favour of poor and remote rural people, but rather about achieving a reasonable spread of projects around a region, and achieving some balance between government departments and between welfare and income-generating projects. Policy was conservative and incremental, dependent on a 'technological fix' rather than links with existing community development. Local tribal frictions and loyalties intervened, as did disagreements between national and provincial politicians and bureaucrats, whilst 'politicians, bureaucrats and rural elites are able to manipulate planners, researchers, extension officers and projects as well as their own people' (Crittenden and Lea 1990b:154; Stewart 1992: 158). Over time the IRDPs quickly fragmented into small and unrelated projects. The disintegration of these formal schemes was symptomatic of the general process of rural development, where integration was absent, and stark and costly evidence of the failures of government intervention.

Since independence PNG has been broadly committed to free enterprise, although other ideological elements have sometimes been a part of rural development policy. Despite price support schemes there is neither a strong practical focus on rural development nor a commitment to redistribution and equity; ' "the capitalist mode of production" has been and continues to be the principal ideological wellspring of politicians, policy makers and planners'

(M. Turner 1986c:9). Rural development, policy and programmes have consisted of eclectic and ephemeral strategies and been unable to link redistribution with growth or integrate agricultural development with that in other sectors. It has also suffered from weak provincial expertise and involvement and, perhaps conversely, by 'pork barrel' politics, where particular projects were viewed by members of Parliament and their constituents as the content and context of development. Rural development is linked to political processes and political support at national and provincial level; projects are neither devised nor supported without pressure from below. Thus, for the Foi of the Southern Highlands, 'It is unlikely that the National or Provincial Governments by themselves will take the initiative in providing aid to rural areas, especially ones as sparsely populated and remote as that of the Foi. As the Foi are now aware, only their own application of political pressure will result in tangible support for such projects' (J.F. Weiner 1986:436). Without specific localised political intervention, rural development, through new income-earning opportunities or access to services, is difficult.

Service provision in rural areas has not improved significantly since independence. Agricultural extension services have become office-bound, and entrenched in bureaucracy, a critical concern by the late 1980s, where replanting programmes were required for coffee and cocoa. Forestry extension has invariably been absent, and there has been no support, beyond Development Bank loans, for rural business development. Rural health and education services have stagnated, despite the steady increase of rural populations. Investment and loans have favoured urban areas (even by rural co-operatives), bureaucrats have sought their personal development through becoming 'desk-jockeys' in the urban centres and the public service has increasingly tended to service itself rather than the public (Chapter 9). Even within the rural sector, the diminished extension advice tended to concentrate either on the largest projects or on the most inappropriate sectors of the agricultural system such as cattle smallholdings (Carrad *et al.* 1979). Government policies have only exceptionally favoured rural sectors, either in terms of policies directly oriented towards agriculture, forestry, fisheries or small business, or in terms of less direct policies concerned with public investment in technology, human resources and infrastructure, trade and exchange rate policies (Jarrett and Anderson 1989). This is partly a consequence of a situation where 'political leaders spoke of service to the rural underprivileged, [but] chose for themselves a high-cost western lifestyle and became involved in business interests which work against the welfare of rural people' (B.J. Allen 1983:234). Consequently, with a declining national and provincial political will to undertake the inevitably slow processes of rural development, and rural distrust and cynicism over broken promises and failed projects, the focus of rural development has shifted to large-scale export-oriented schemes, in agriculture, fisheries, forestry and mining, rather than small-scale programmes integrated with welfare programmes, that might have brought a more wide-ranging rural development. The returns have remained elusive.

Ultimately the disappointments of rural development are a function of landowners' participation, in their willingness to earn paltry but immediate sums from valuable resources and in misunderstanding, incomprehension or uninterest in the slow process of achieving development. Such problems are scarcely surprising, in a region where cargoism exists, modern education is limited, cash needs are many and few have sought to explain and examine the complexities of contemporary development. They are also long established. Landowners at a small-scale timber project near Vanimo (West Sepik) in the early 1970s experienced what later became familiar problems: 'Many villagers still do not understand the difference between the initial payment for timber rights and the six-monthly interest on the investment of the balance. . . . The timber mirage has had a negative effect on local initiatives and opportunities, and has damaged perhaps irreparably villagers' willingness to cooperate in their own development' (Herlihy 1976:6, 8). For two more decades such conclusions have continued to be made in areas where forestry projects have been developed, and where mining has gone ahead (Chapter 6). They have not dampened the enthusiasm of villagers in more remote areas to canvas and accept the promises from new international corporations of wide-ranging gains from integrated rural development. The credibility of government has meanwhile declined further.

Since rural development involves activities in various sectors, and resources of all kinds are limited, some co-operation and co-ordination between government and other agencies is essential to achieve success. This kind of integration and co-operation was best achieved in the highlands *maket raun* where different provincial government departments combined to bring various services to rural areas. There and elsewhere, co-ordination of service delivery and project development proved difficult as 'relations between and even within government departments may sometimes be characterised by lack of communication, negligible cooperation, rivalry, suspicion, and even hostility, all of which militate against the optimal utilisation of finance, manpower and other resources' (M. Turner 1986c:25). These problems have been accentuated by the duplication of, and conflict between, national and provincial responsibilities, which have made management failure more apparent. Government personnel, resources and development programmes have slowly withdrawn from the rural sector, leaving villagers to undertake their own development, achieving some success with vegetable marketing (Chapter 4). It was already apparent that government assistance was not crucial since the rapid and successful expansion of smallholder cash cropping in the 1970s occurred with minimal government intervention, because prices were right and markets accessible. The worst problems of rural development are exemplified in the forestry sector, where government participation has been so counter-productive that villagers have often been the compliant victims of corporate policy. A lack of evaluation and monitoring, extensive corruption and the failure to implement guidelines, have enabled a form of development to run rife, with transfer pricing, the 'mining' of timber resources, failures to achieve integrated development (whether between sectors or in terms of downstream processing) and environmental degradation as the consequences. At the very least failures in the rural sector illuminate the massive logistical problems of planning for rural development under conditions of rapid political change, severe financial and skilled human resource constraints and an entrenched, conservative and oligopolistic bureaucracy. Institutionalised planning has largely failed, at considerable expense.

6 Mining

The source of economic growth

Parts of Papua New Guinea will benefit immensely from the petroleum and mineral projects now coming on stream. Other areas will sadly miss out on such dramatic experiences and benefits. They will have to be content with their traditional low priced cash crops of coffee, cocoa, copra, palm oil and betelnut. . . . Massive monetary benefits will go to landowners of the sites where there will be oil wells extracting crude, where the oil pipeline passes through, and where mines and new townships are sited. . . . They will walk around with bulky wallets and large cheque books while their countrymen in plantations will live much the same as they do today.

(PC 24 October 1990:23)

Few countries in the world are endowed with mineral resources on anything like the same scale as Papua New Guinea. Moreover while the age of exploration and discovery is substantially over in many parts of the world, in PNG it is still continuing. Major discoveries of minerals and oil were made in the 1980s and 1990s and there is a high probability that further exploration will be rewarded. Centuries old expectations are coming to fruition. The first Europeans to sight what was probably the north coast of the island of New Guinea were Spanish sailors who named the island, somewhat prophetically, Isla del Oro (Island of Gold), but only since independence has the economy gone through its critical transition from agriculture to mining. Virtually on the eve of independence, despite the development of Bougainville and plans for a mine at Ok Tedi, there was consensus that 'enough general surveys have been carried out to bring home the disappointing realisation that the country is lacking in industrial minerals such as coal and iron, has virtually exhausted its gold deposits and has as yet been unable to locate worthwhile petroleum deposits' (Howlett 1973a:109–10). Two decades later the situation was vastly different. Copper, gold and oil are abundant; no country in the Asia-Pacific region has been so transformed by recent mineral exploitation. Mining has brought both great wealth and new conflicts over resources, localised environmental degradation and political problems of unparalleled severity. Its impact has been much more than merely economic.

Mining in PNG spans a period of more than a century. Between 1878 and

1920, it was extremely important to the Papuan economy. North Queensland miners flooded into Sudest island (Milne Bay), and there were goldrushes on other nearby islands. Though the first wave of mining has been eclipsed it never really ended. From Milne Bay alluvial mining spread as far as the Sepik, and individuals continue to pan and sluice on the old fields. This initial phase of mining boosted the Papuan economy, which had previously been dependent on the activities of missionaries, and was no more than 'a vague extension of the Queensland economy' (W.A. McGee and Henning 1990:258). For the first time there was significant economic activity in Papua rather than New Guinea which, in the half century from 1878 to 1928, produced more than half a million ounces of gold. Some 65 per cent of this was mined in the islands of Milne Bay, and the rest in Oro and Central provinces (Gregory 1982:125). The impact on the local economy was limited and short term. The profits from mining, small as they usually were, almost always left the country rather than being invested locally. The net impact of mining on government revenue in Papua was probably negative, and the same was true in New Guinea until the start of the 1930s, when mining did make a substantial contribution (O'Faircheallaigh 1982:8). For almost half a century the Australian administration subsidised the mining industry, profits were exported and the local impact was slight.

After several false starts in Milne Bay and at Laloki copper mine (near Port Moresby), capital-intensive mining finally got underway in the post-war years. From the 1920s a second wave of mining capital began to transform the Wau and Bulolo valleys, involving the development of more extensive, concentrated mineral deposits of a substantially lower grade, which meant that a larger scale of operations was required to ensure profitability. The era of the small mining team was over, at least where it involved Europeans. Mining was now mechanised and the size of the operations attracted overseas companies, such as New Guinea Goldfields Ltd, a subsidiary of what was to become Mt Isa Mines (MIM), and the newly formed Canadian company, Placer Development Ltd, who floated the public Bulolo Gold Dredging Company. The degree of foreign investment in the industry increased considerably, alongside an increased commitment of human resources, encouraged by the colonial administration, since copra prices had slumped in the wake of the Depression. Australia was experiencing a trade deficit that could be met only by gold exports while international gold prices were rising. In this unusually favourable international economic climate mining boomed, more than 1,200 indigenous labourers were employed at a time and by 1933 gold had displaced copra as New Guinea's main export, accounting for 77 per cent of the total value of exports. In 1940 gold accounted for 82 per cent of all exports, the highest proportion in history. Even so, mining's contribution to the economy was still limited, though the search for gold had opened up several parts of the country and took the first European explorers, the Leahy brothers and Jim Taylor, into the highlands in the 1930s. This second phase of mining only really ended in 1965 when the gold dredging at Bulolo, that had begun in 1932, finally came to a close. European miners' fortunes were made and lost and 'local communities evaded them, worked for them, traded with them, fought them and slept with them' (Nelson 1976:266). Nearby Melanesian communities could scarcely avoid the transformations wrought by the gold-rushes. Relationships with the miners were often ambivalent, sometimes difficult and violent and rarely entirely harmonious; early experiences provided prototypes for the rest of the century.

Mining remained in a state of uncertainty for two decades after the Second World War; gold prices were low and the best alluvial deposits appeared to have been largely worked out. In the 1960s it appeared that the industry was experiencing a terminal decline. Production of minerals had decreased to just A\$0.7 million in 1971, with the mining industry contributing less than 1 per cent of the GDP (Downs 1980:301). Agricultural development, especially coffee in the highlands, offered much better prospects for Melanesians and Europeans, though geological exploration had increased, primarily because of administration subsidies. There were moments of optimism. A minor goldrush in 1948 took government officials and others to the remote Porgera area, six days' walk from Wabag (Enga), but the results were disappointing. Downs concluded: 'the country is inaccessible, high, cold, sparsely populated and extremely rough. Many other metals make this area a mineral "fruit salad", but none are in large deposits' (1980:174). Until geological survey techniques, extraction technology and world prices improved, commercially viable deposits were unknown and, in several areas, Melanesians were encouraged to take over what seemed to be increasingly unproductive alluvial gold-mining.

The most outstanding minerals prospect resulted from the discovery in 1964 of substantial low-grade copper deposits in the mountains of Bougainville. Coming at a time when the industry was at its lowest ebb it was perceived to be 'the greatest single event in the economic history of Papua and New Guinea' (Downs 1980:340). Technological progress, enabling the mining of low grade (less than 1 per cent mineralised) ore, effectively created new reserves whilst nationalisation of major producers in Chile and Zambia had caused concern over global copper availability. Mine planning began in 1966 and Bougainville Copper Limited (BCL) was established by Conzinc Riotinto of Australia (CRA) in 1967. After eight years of exploration, evaluation and construction, involving a new port, two new towns (Arawa and Panguna) and a new highway into the mountains – 'the most formidable industrial management task ever undertaken by Australians' (Downs 1980:341) – mining began in April 1972 with BCL quickly recording enormous profits, a situation that largely continued until its abrupt closure in 1989. By global standards Panguna was one of the last great copper mines to be constructed. Expectations rose as PNG's third phase of mining got underway.

Copper and gold deposits at Ok Tedi were identified in 1968 but it was not until 1981 that the construction of the first mine in the highlands finally got underway. The mineral deposit was initially identified by the US-based

Kennecott Copper Corporation, but in 1975 Kennecott withdrew after lengthy negotiations with PNG's first national government, concerned that the project was marginal in economic terms and that nationalisation might be considered (Jackson 1982a). The Prime Minister, Sir Julius Chan, enthusiastically announced that 'Ok Tedi represents the pot of gold at the end of the rainbow'; it was a prescient phrase, for gold prices were about to boom and there was no shortage of rainbows in the rainforests of the Star Mountains, close to the Indonesian border. In 1984 Ok Tedi began producing gold and silver; without its 'gold cap' it might not have become a mine. As quickly as 1987 what had started out to be a copper mine became for a time the largest gold-mine outside South Africa, until the gold cap was removed and that title was later taken by Porgera. The fourth mining era thus began in the highlands in the 1980s. Crucial to the new 'goldrush' was the dramatic rise in world gold prices in 1980–1, which levelled off but soared again in 1986 and 1987, precipitating a new wave of mining and exploration.

The construction and operation of the Ok Tedi mine was more difficult than any other in the country. The mine is on Mount Fubilan, more than 2,000 metres above sea-level, in extremely rugged terrain and dense forest, where rainfall is heavy, cloud cover the norm and moderately severe seismic activity not unusual. Copper must be piped as a concentrate more than 150 kilometres to Kiunga and then taken by barge to the mouth of the Fly river. Despite local support and national enthusiasm for diversification away from Bougainville, numerous problems have threatened to end mining there. Foremost amongst these have been environmental problems surrounding the non-construction of a tailings dam and waste disposal in the Fly River (see pp. 161–4)) but other problems involved local pressures for infrastructure changes, concern over the number of outsiders, land disputes and court action for increased compensation.

A brief restoration of mining at Wau and Bulolo in the 1980s was part of a new goldrush, that initially resulted from a rise in gold prices and subsequently from technological innovations in prospecting and mining in difficult sites. The new goldrush produced positive results as four more gold-mines: Porgera (Enga), the smaller Mt Kare (Enga) and Misima (Milne Bay) mines and the tiny Mt Victor (Eastern Highlands) mine went into production. Of these new mines, Porgera has been much the most important though, like the others, it is in a very remote part of the country, previously without road access. A number of difficulties slowed the establishment of the mine, including disagreement over the necessity for a tailings dam to be constructed and concern over the appropriate distribution of compensation payments and business opportunities. During the early life of the mine there were strikes (one of which left seven people injured from a shotgun battle), problems over local pollution and a week-long closure after an explosion killed eleven people. When gold production began in 1990, it immediately became the largest gold-mine in PNG, producing 1.2 million ounces of gold in 1991, and production subsequently increased with improved recovery rates. Mining

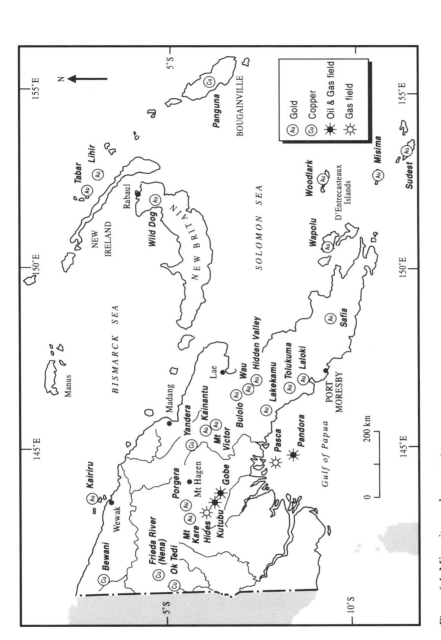

Figure 6.1 Mine sites and prospects

has been unusually profitable at Porgera with costs of production falling to as low as K86 an ounce, less than a third of the industry average in Australia (*SMH* 6 May 1992), compared with K190 an ounce at Misima. The Porgera Joint Venture (PJV) has been an extremely important source of profitability for the national government and the three principal shareholders – Placer, Renison GC and Highlands Gold (MIM) – enabling them to write off losses elsewhere. The smaller Misima mine produced its first gold at the end of 1989, reached peak production in 1994 and was expected to have a ten year life, with a quarter the production of Porgera.

The most dramatic circumstances of mine development were at Mt Kare, where a goldrush eventually gave way to a more formal gold-mine, that began in 1991 but closed at the start of 1992, after landowner disputes and an armed attack on the mine. Prior to that, in 1988, hundreds of Papua New Guineans poured onto a bare and remote mountainside, some 3,000 metres above sea-level, on the borders of Enga and Southern Highlands provinces, and carried off vast quantities of alluvial gold. The series of events at Mt Kare dramatically emphasised the substantial incomes to be earned from mining. The gold deposit was unusual because of both its richness and its easy accessibility to the simplest extraction techniques – little more than buckets and spades – and hence enabled direct and immediate Melanesian participation. When local villagers arrived in Mount Hagen 'carrying buckets full of nuggets causing banks to temporarily run out of cash, motor vehicle salerooms to empty and salesmen to froth at the mouth' (Jackson 1991b:29) it marked the start of a 'modern Stone Age goldrush' (Murphy 1988). It was the only distinctly Papua New Guinean goldrush, vastly different from the Australian ventures a century earlier. Potential miners flooded into the area. Stores were rapidly established on the site, selling goods at several times their price elsewhere in the country; frozen chickens reached over K50 and prostitutes, flown in by helicopter, cost upwards of K40. Disputes were not uncommon, though conflicts over landownership were rare; most arguments revolved around card games – where the stakes were measured in thousands of kina – or were over women. Home-made shotguns appeared on the site; at least one person was killed and many were injured in brawls. At the start of the rush some individuals were earning as much as K2,000 per day. For some miners, however, such as the Huli, gold was associated with impurity (analogous to menstrual blood, and a cause of illness) and the income could not be spent on *bisnis*, but rather on consumption, particularly on beer, gifts for relatives and friends and airline tickets. Such gifts affirmed social relationships, and were thus not 'wasted', yet the belief that they were unproductive, even amongst the Huli themselves, is 'a metacommentary on a particular experience of colonialism' (Clark 1993:749) and a familiar situation throughout the country. Bride prices rapidly inflated, and there was a subsequent spate of divorces as new wives discovered their husbands' income had run out (Vail 1993). Much money was spent on store goods at greatly inflated prices, on travel as far afield as Japan, or on investments in property – even at Cairns in Queensland – and cars quickly became an ideal status symbol for newly rich miners. Early in the rush an 8 year old was reported to have arrived in Mount Hagen with a bottle containing 21 kg of gold – worth almost K200,000 – exchanged it for cash and gone straight off to the local Toyota dealer accompanied by his driver (Callick 1988). A 9 year old was reportedly earning K2,000 an hour (P. Ryan 1991:3) and men were apparently listening to short wave radios giving London metal prices. Whilst such reports may sometimes have been exaggerated they were indicative of the drama, novelty, excitement and wealth that accompanied the goldrush. By late 1988 about 6,000 people were jammed into a tiny area of a hundred or so hectares without water, sanitation or any facilities. Government facilities at the mine site were restricted to one overworked medical aid post. The principal beneficiaries were the middlemen, some of whom were politicians, paying on site little more than half the world market price, and store and helicopter owners also made substantial incomes. The PNG government, as an entity, gained no direct benefits. A significant quantity of gold was smuggled out of the country to avoid taxes. In the eighteen months to late 1989 about K50 million of gold was taken from Mt Kare, but by the middle of the year the goldrush was virtually over as the surface workings were largely exhausted. The most spectacular of PNG's new mining developments drew to a close and CRA and the local landowners reached an agreement for the subsequent more formal development of the site.

Reaching agreement between CRA and the Mt Kare landowners proved difficult; there was opposition from certain landowner groups and from the Enga Provincial Government. Despite no habitation being within 10 kilometres of the site before the goldrush the number of landowners was considerable, as distant groups sought to share the new resource. The eventual agreement resulted in a complex and delicate organisational structure with CRA's wholly owned subsidiary, Pacific Minerals, taking up 51 per cent shareholding in the joint venture, and the landowners taking up 49 per cent. Within days of the agreement being reached in December 1989, the Enga Provincial Government Premier had objected to the terms of the agreement, invoking Bougainville parallels and suggesting that the landowners should have received more than a 49 per cent share. A Special Mining Lease was eventually signed in 1990 and the new Mount Kare Alluvial Mining joint venture began; the expected mine life was not much more than five years. Only sixty-five people were employed, mainly from the local area, no road was constructed and all the machinery, fuel, labour and gold was flown in and out. Mining began in 1991 but was plagued by disputes and violence; the mine closed in January 1992 after a night-time attack by fifteen armed men, who held the staff at gunpoint and caused more than K3 million worth of damage. The attack was praised by one Member of Parliament, who sought changes in the mine-ownership structure to give landowners 100 per cent ownership, and criticised by others who were concerned about criminal issues, greedy landowners and 'hired gunmen' (*TPNG* 30 January 1992). CRA closed down the mine, fearing that the problems would recur, and subsequently sought to sell three-quarters of its 51 per cent stake in Mt Kare to the three joint venture partners in the nearby Porgera mine, but withdrew entirely from Mt Kare in 1993 after legal challenges from landowner groups supported by the small Australian companies, Ramsgate and Menzies Gold. The mine has remained closed, with legal problems unresolved.

Despite the difficulties attached to mining in PNG, evident at all present mine sites, other small mines have been established during the 1990s in a new phase of mining. The first was at Tolukuma, 100 kilometres north of Port Moresby, where there is a high grade gold deposit and a working life of perhaps six years. Within months of its first producing gold in 1996, local landowners had disrupted workings, in a dispute over compensation. Wapolu on Fergusson Island (Milne Bay), a small epithermal gold-mine, also began, and Ewatinona, an extension of the Misima mine, got underway. By far the most valuable mine is Lihir, the anticipated jewel in the crown of the new era. Deposits are estimated at more than 25 million ounces, in the world's largest undeveloped gold reserve with a life of thirty-seven years. Exploration on Lihir did not begin until 1982, and gold was discovered a year later, but development of the proposal was slower than expected because of falling gold prices, the Bougainville crisis (so close to Lihir), uncertainties over the size of the deposit, the difficulty of raising international loan funds, with both political and law and order problems being raised by investment bankers, changes in policies over equity by the PNG government (see pp. 145–7) and landowner demands for 20 per cent of the equity. The agreement was eventually signed in 1995 and construction began. Development is difficult since the Lihir site is a collapsed volcano, where temperatures are extremely high and a quarter of coastal gold deposits are engulfed in boiling water; waste disposal into the ocean will pose problems.

More mines are certain to follow. Later in the decade copper mines, such as Frieda River (West Sepik), and small gold-mines could begin operations. Economically feasible deposits exist at Woodlark (Milne Bay), Kainantu (Eastern Highlands), Hidden Valley (Morobe), and Wild Dog (East New Britain), while Laloki (Central Province) and Lakekamu (Central Province) may be reopened, because of the development of new techniques for mineral recovery. Numerous other prospects also exist. In 1990 gold was discovered in underwater volcanoes in the waters of Milne Bay province at depths of 2,500 metres below sea-level; though these are currently too deep to mine economically their discovery suggested the wider presence of gold in the area. Most of the new mines of the 1980s and 1990s are quite different from the old alluvial workings or the mining of lodes. They are closely associated with hot springs and ancient volcanic activity – the rim of fire – at the mobile junction of the Australian and Pacific geological plates, and took mining into new areas (Figure 6.1). Discovery of these epithermal mines demanded new geological techniques and processing requires new chemical skills. There are few parts of the country where mineralisation is absent and good prospects have not been claimed. The era of exploration, discovery and the establishment of new mines is far from over.

At various other sites there has also been relatively successful small-scale mining activity of different kinds. The Mt Victor mine, south of Kainantu (Eastern Highlands), operated by Niugini Mining Ltd, lived out the whole of its life in just two and a half years. The company extracted about 21,000 ounces of gold, made a profit of K490,000 and spent some K2,200,000 in the local area (*TPNG* 12 April 1990). It had a workforce of 125, all but 5 of whom were Papua New Guineans, issued 200,000 shares – most of which were taken up by the business arm – Kainantu Komuniti Bisnis (KKB) – of the Kainantu Local Government Council and landowners from seven villages on the outskirts of the mine. In late 1988, half-way through its operation, the Managing Director of KKB concluded that the mine was successful because it had involved local landowners: 'I think the whole mining act needs to be reviewed so that the landowners get a bigger share than they do' (*TPNG* 3 November 1988). It was a prophetic comment. Since then landowners elsewhere have been involved in mining in a variety of ways.

In a number of areas alluvial gold-mining has gone on for years. The most prominent such area is Wau-Bulolo where mining continues to involve around 1,500 families, who produce about 70 per cent of PNG's alluvial gold, worth around K20 million per year. Smaller alluvial operations occur in many parts of PNG. Typical of these operations is that in the lower Jimi valley (Western Highlands), where mining has been going on since the 1970s; by the mid-1980s twenty-four men were involved in gold working teams, selling gold to itinerant purchasers from Mt Hagen. Though gold production was the most important local source of cash income, more so than coffee, sales were irregular and after four years few teams (of up to three men) had made much more than K1,000 (Healey 1986:27). Such workings are a far cry from the large mines, though many operate in their shadows, but large numbers of people are involved on a short-term basis, they contribute to export diversity, mining is undertaken alongside other work and it rarely results in conflicts over land tenure and environmental damage.

The combination of new exploration, gold price increases and the necessity for the PNG government to extend mining development beyond Bougainville guaranteed the wave of drilling, construction, negotiation and share issuing that marked the 1980s. At the start of the 1990s more than 40 per cent of PNG's land area, and some of its sea area, was covered with prospecting licences, one indication of how many areas may yield new resources. Without domestic capital and technical skills, virtually all elements of mining have been a function of international capital and expertise. Transnational corporations (TNCs) multiplied in the highlands and islands. New deposits of gold, oil, natural gas, copper, nickel and platinum are continuing to be discovered in what may be commercial quantities. Exploration and mining have been slowed by inhospitable terrain, the absence of infrastructure, limited knowledge of geological formations that are different from other world

Table 6.1 Mines, mine ownership and mining phases (1996)

	Location	Time period	Mineral	Ownership
I	Laloki	1878	gold, copper	
	Misima	1888–1942	gold	
	Sudest	1887–99	gold	
	Woodlark	1895–1942	gold	
	Lakekamu	1909–39	gold	
II	Wau	1928–90	gold	New Guinea Goldfields
	Bulolo	1928–90	gold	(Renison Gold Fields Consolidated)
III	Panguna	1972–89	copper, gold, silver	Bougainville Copper Limited (CRA/RTZ) (54%) PNG Government (19%) Shareholdings (27%)
IV	Ok Tedi	1984–	gold, copper, silver	Ok Tedi Mining Limited (OTML) Broken Hill Proprietary Limited (BHP) (50%) PNG Government (30%) German KE Consortium (20%)
	Mt Victor	1987–90	gold	Niugini Mining Limited (RTZ)
	Mt Kare	1988–92	gold	KPDC Landowners (51%), Ramsgate/Carpenter Resources
	Misima	1989–	gold	Placer (80%), PNG Government (20%)
	Porgera	1990–	gold	Highlands Gold (MIM) (25%) Placer Pacific (25%) Renison Gold Fields Consolidated (25%) PNG Government (20%), Landowners (2.5%), Enga Provincial Government (2.5%)

Table 6.1 continued

	Location	Time period	Mineral	Ownership
V	Tolukuma	1995–	gold	Dome Resources
	Wapolu	1996–	gold	Union Mining (51%), Macmin (49%)
	Lihir	1997–	gold	RTZ (23%), Niugini Mining (17%), PNG Government (17%), Lihir Gold (public company) (43%)
	Woodlark	1997–	gold	Highlands Gold (60%), Nord (40%)
	Frieda River (Nena)		copper, gold	Highlands Gold (75%)
				OMRD Frieda (Japan) (25%)
				Affinerie A.G. (Germany)
	Hidden Valley		gold	Hidden Valley Gold (CRA) (51%), Carpenter Pacific Resources (49%)
	Laloki		copper, gold	Newmex
	Ramu		nickel	Highlands Gold (62%), Nord (38%)
	Lakekamu		gold	City Resources
	Kainantu		gold	Niugini Mining
	Tabar (Simberi)		gold	Kennecott (62%), Nord (30%), Niugini Mining (8%)
	Wild Dog		gold	Niugini Mining
	Wafi		gold, copper	CRA

regions and fluctuating gold prices. So large have the new ventures been, and so substantial the costs of construction (alongside extensive additional infrastructure provision) in difficult environments, that new projects have invariably necessitated funding from various sources in new joint ventures. The mining boom thus also led to changes for the international corporations themselves, creating through mergers a new generation of extremely powerful mining giants, of which CRA, BHP (Broken Hill Proprietary Ltd) and Placer have been the main players. Three of the largest gold-mining companies in the world are thus prominently represented in PNG, a measure of the extraordinary significance of gold and its role in global trade. PNG has the potential to move from seventh place to become the third largest gold producer in the world, behind South Africa and the Commonwealth of Independent States, by the end of the century.

OIL AND GAS

New mines promised 'pots of gold' by the end of the 1980s, but what had never been expected was the wealth of resources that oil exploration would bring, although the presence of oil was first recorded in 1911, near the Vailala river (Gulf). By 1940 an estimated £1,850,000 had been spent on oil exploration which had led to the discovery of substantial amounts of oil and gas, but never quite enough for commercial development. Exploration continued in the post-war years, until 1960 when the main exploration company, Australian Petroleum Company Ltd, which had spent £30 million since the war in exploration costs, finally abandoned the search. A year later the *South Pacific Post* concluded that oil exploration in PNG had ended forever. Three decades later it was a different story.

More wells were dug in the 1970s, almost all unsuccessfully, so that as recently as 1988 the consensus was that 'the oilfields still have to remain in the marginal category' (*TPNG* 21 January 1988). Three main companies, the US-based Gulf (now Chevron Niugini), Oil Search and BP (British Petroleum), continued the search, though without the series of global oil shocks and the Gulf War, both of which greatly increased world prices, these exploration bids would have been abandoned. As in other facets of the mining industry the agenda was dictated overseas. Ultimately oil was first discovered in large quantities at Juha (Western Province) in 1983 and in nearby areas in subsequent years, heralding the first main discovery at Iagifu (Southern Highlands) in 1986, followed by strikes in adjacent structures, Hedinia and Agogo (Figure 6.2). During the 1980s there was a high success rate by world standards, and in the second half of the decade these were turned into commercial operations, in the Southern Highlands and the adjacent Gulf Province uplands. Gas was found at Pasca and Pandora in the Gulf of Papua in the early 1990s. Oil reserves were estimated at 1,000 million barrels in 1991 (Jackson 1991a); whilst further exploration may increase this figure, substantially greater volumes are not yet proven.

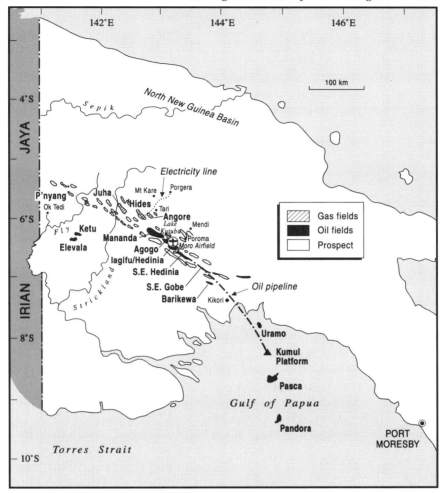

Figure 6.2 Oil and gas lease areas

Construction began in 1990 on the first two wells, a 270 km pipeline to Kikori in the Gulf of Papua and an offshore tanker terminal. By 1992 there were three related oil and gas fields: the Iagifu-Hedinia oil field at Kutubu, the Gobe oil field and the Hides gas field. The most substantial oil discovery and development was the Iagifu-Hedinia field (Southern Highlands), the major component of the Kutubu oil field, along with Usano and Agogo. The joint-venture partners in the project include Chevron and BP (each with 19 per cent) and the state-owned Petroleum Resources Kutubu with 22.5 per cent. The first commercial oil was produced in mid-1992, the start of yet another significant phase of national development, though PNG produces just 0.2 per cent of the world's oil. Indeed the total resource base at Kutubu represents just three or four days of global oil consumption (Kennedy 1996). Oil production was expected to peak in the late 1990s. By 1992 two small refineries had been constructed at the project site, mainly producing aviation fuel and diesel oil for local use. The Hides gas field (95 per cent owned by BP and 5 per cent by Oil Search) came into production in 1991 and may last for twenty-five years. There has been some uncertainty over the uses of the gas whose volume far exceeds national requirements, and more is likely to be discovered. The first successful wells at the third field, Gobe, were drilled by Barracuda Pty Ltd (a subsidiary of MIM) in 1991. The potential of the Gobe field is similar to that of Iagifu-Hedinia – a volume comparable with the best offshore discoveries made by Australia in recent years – and could be developed at about a quarter the cost of Kutubu. Chevron is expected to bring it into production in 1997, to maintain national oil production as Kutubu begins to decline.

The oil and gas industry has some potential for processing within PNG itself, a possibility that does not exist for the mining industry, and construction of a refinery began at Motukea island in Port Moresby harbour in 1995 (despite global refinery overcapacity). There has been extended consideration of construction of a gas pipeline to major markets in Queensland. Limited industrial and technological capacity has discouraged direct productive linkages with other sectors of the economy, despite the obvious immediate utility of oil and gas. The service sector, and especially the transport and construction sectors, have been the principal beneficiaries of oil and gas discoveries.

The centre of oil and gas exploration and development is around Lake Kutubu, one of the more isolated parts of the Southern Highlands province. Services have been developed where neither the colonial government nor the national government had hitherto achieved much more than a token presence. Just as mining had already done, oil and natural gas exploration and production have changed the face of remote, rural PNG. There have been costs. Disputes over land tenure and compensation have been considerable; at Kutubu the local people objected strongly to a share of royalty payments that gave them 30 per cent of all royalties, with the Southern Highlands Provincial Government retaining 70 per cent (*TPNG* 28 May 1992). Compensation payments were invariably late, and distinguishing landowners was difficult: 'agreements were signed and money paid to persons who had little or no accountability to the local groups they supposedly represented' (Knauft 1993:188), causing frustration for legitimate claimants. Large sums of money were spent without obvious benefit. Disputes were consequently frequent and 'if it were not for the capacity for Chevron to throw money and manpower at problems . . . things might have been different' (*Pacific Report*, 7, 25 July 1994) in terms of disruption of the project. The local economic benefits from the project have been limited, despite the trivial cash incomes in the area prior to oil and gas development. Nevertheless 'many locals feel the company is more accountable and amenable to their needs than the pre- or post-independence governments of the area' (Kennedy 1994:56), who ignored them.

Consequently Chevron 'increasingly performs the role of surrogate government and the landowners increasingly expect the company to fulfil this role' (*Pacific Report*, 7, 25 July 1994; cf. Tree 1996). The roles and responsibilities of companies and governments have never been adequately clarified, and have led to mining companies playing a broader role in development than they would have wished and than has occurred in other parts of the world.

Indicative of the manner in which the future potential of oil and gas production is far from being realised, is continued uncertainty. After the success of the second well at Gobe, it was recorded that 'the strike represented a good call, according to industry analysts. It was largely a shot in the dark due to the lack of availability of seismic data. The rugged terrain and difficult geology make the area unsuitable for seismic surveys' (*SMH* 15 November 1991). Exploration is continuing and present oil and gas production may be only a fragment of future production. Of all sectors of the economy this is the most rapidly evolving hence predictions of future changes and their impacts are almost impossible.

THE BOUGAINVILLE CRISIS

No mining development in PNG, and few in the world, has been as important as the Panguna copper mine in influencing the structure of economic growth and development in a single country. Though there were special issues in Bougainville that have few parallels in other parts of PNG, there were also many similarities with the situation at other mine sites in the country. The closure of the Panguna mine raised major implications for the future of the crucial mining sector, and other large projects, within the country. After construction began in 1967 the mine grew rapidly to become the largest in the southern hemisphere, directly employing almost 4,000 workers (and indirectly contributing to the employment of more than double that number). When PNG became independent in 1975 the Panguna mine was the only one in operation, and there were no immediate prospects of others coming into operation. Panguna was then responsible for more than half the value of all exports from the country, it was the only significant economic venture outside the agricultural sector, much the largest single economic enterprise in the country and the modern flagship for the era of independence. By the end of 1988, the last full year of operation of the mine, Ok Tedi had begun operations but Panguna still produced the bulk of mineral exports. Moreover it had produced over 40 per cent of the value of all exports and provided about 16 per cent of the GDP during its lifetime. After seventeen years of production – about half the anticipated economic life – its contribution to national and regional development was unparalleled. The economic impact of closure was enormous, and all subsequent debates over mining have been overshadowed by the potential precedent of the daunting Bougainville crisis, where the social, economic and environmental implications of mining had catalysed a major political and economic problem for the island and the nation.

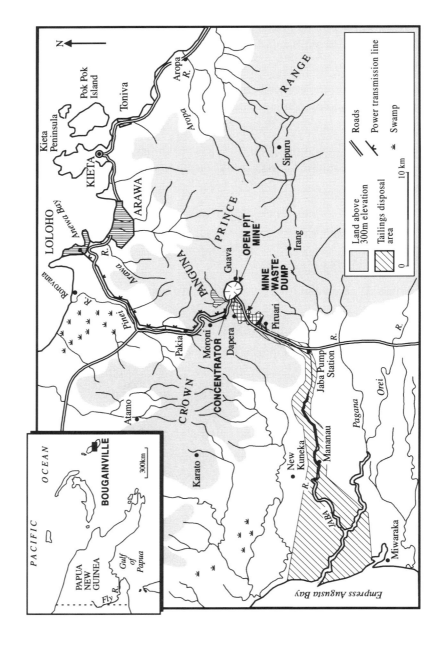

Figure 6.3 Bougainville copper mine

Though the immediate cause of the crisis was disagreement over compensation payments for environmental damage near the mine site, the genesis of this disagreement stemmed from the social and political context when the mine began. In a context of isolation, separation, distinct ethnicity and local frustration with limited development, mineral exploration in the central mountain chain of Bougainville was met with hostility (Connell 1991:56–7). Mine construction operations got underway in 1967, initiating substantial changes in most aspects of society and economy. The population grew rapidly, new urban centres and transport infrastructure evolved. The most dramatically affected villages – Moroni and Dapera – were relocated away from the mine site. Bougainvilleans took up prestigious wage employment and expanded cocoa growing. Such changes reduced the self-reliance and cultural distinctiveness of village societies and, through education, brought the area into a wider social and economic arena. Crime and violence increased, in part following the growth of dominantly male mining towns. Traditional values came under increased pressure, linked to the rapidity and comprehensiveness of change. Many of the effects of mining and modernisation were psychological, associated with the vastness of the BCL enterprise and the manner in which it was often referred to by villagers as an octopus sending its tentacles into every part of people's lives. Leo Hannett, a former Provincial Premier, well expressed some of this feeling:

> Our once peaceful, non-violent living is now forever shattered: we are constantly harried by day and haunted by night with continual acts of violence in our midst. Where we once walked with our heads high, now we move around with our heads hanging low . . . never quite knowing what to expect from these outsiders, heartless outsiders with their heartless machines slowly eating out like a cancerous growth the soul of our community; degenerating, humiliating, and dehumanising us with their 'development' at our expense. We are now made strangers in our own land.
>
> (Hannett 1975:288–9)

Over time many Bougainvilleans worked there, passed through and became familiar with the operations of the mine, though few came to accept it or approve of it as anything more than a temporary part of their lives.

The quest for compensation and resettlement

Land was the most critical element in negotiations for mine construction and the subsequent operations of the mine. Three Bougainvilleans expressed this well at the outset:

> Land is our life. Land is our physical life – food and sustenance. Land is our social life; it is marriage; it is status; it is security; it is politics; in fact, it is our only world. When you [the Administration] take our land, you cut away the very heart of our existence. We have little or no experience of

social survival detached from the land. For us to be completely landless is a nightmare which no dollar in the pocket or dollar in the bank will allay; we are a threatened people.

(Dove *et al.* 1974:182)

Though compensation was paid for land leased and damaged, subsequent debate grew over the extent of the damage and the level of compensation payments. Most payments were quite small and compensation money was distributed in a very uneven manner (Connell 1991:63–5), though during the early stages of mine construction and operation, these were, by contemporary Bougainvillean standards, substantial sums of money. Over time frustration with the amount of compensation increased, as other problems emerged: the inadequacy of the resettlement villages, the pollution of rivers and land over wider areas, the growing recognition that land considered to be leased no longer existed and the enormity of the hole. Compensation payments had little relationship to profitability, would end when the mine did, had not been converted to long-term development and were often inaccessible to a new generation of landowners. This combination of factors contributed to new, more vociferous demands for increased compensation payments.

What appeared to be the fate of villagers in and around the resettled villages gradually became another issue. Housing conditions were perceived to be inappropriate and inadequate, and villagers elsewhere were uncertain about the future direction that mining might take and hence where and how they might be expected to live (Connell 1991:65–7). Villagers increasingly emphasised that the standard of housing and other facilities provided by BCL in the resettled villages was inadequate, in comparison to that provided for migrant mineworkers. As owners of the resource they sought the best housing, and more opportunities for business development, not in competition with the mine 'company stores'. Planning for resettlement was inadequate, attention to the concerns of resettled villages declined over time and provision of services was lacking. Dapera was relocated on a waste dump. Relocation held out the promise of a new life which might have put them on the same footing as the urban residents of Panguna and Arawa, but this never materialised.

The environmental impact

During the life of the mine it was constantly reiterated by villagers that land was crucial to livelihood since Bougainvilleans were primarily dependent on agriculture and would again be more dependent on agriculture when the mine closed; loss or damage of land was seen as threatening the basis of future survival. The main concern was the absolute decline of productive land areas, as mining operations expanded. Tailings disposal contributed to the loss of land in the Jaba river valley and with it drinking water, timber and hunting and fishing areas. Deposition of tailings blocked tributary streams, causing flooding and the loss of fish, and made access to some regions difficult and dangerous; the area occupied by tailings became much greater than people believed it would be. Experiments in revegetation were failures in terms of the growth of species of some nutritional or commercial value, and neither the tailings area nor the mine site could be restored to its original state. Crop damage, the death of flying foxes and an epidemic amongst coastal fish were all seen as a measure of the extent of chemical pollution caused by BCL (Connell 1991:67–8). Health problems too were attributed to the mine. Changes in fauna and flora emphasised the perception that the impact of BCL was much more pervasive and harmful than could ever have been contemplated.

The increase in what appeared to be environmental problems, dramatically apparent in dead fish and flying foxes, added to long-held concerns over the extent to which the tailings would spread further across and beyond the Jaba floodplain and how far coastal drift would carry tailings. Global debate over 'acid rain' accentuated these fears. Villagers predicted that at the end of the mine life, Bougainville would be a lifeless island, seared in the centre by an enormous hole, the barren Jaba flood plain and a new delta, surrounded by areas of land and sea depleted of wildlife and fish and useless to the human population. Beyond this, the mine had contributed to a degree of dependence and passivity; many people felt that 'the mine is so big and we are so small' hence self-determination was impossible.

The outcome

Discontent over the impact of the mine was concentrated primarily in a few villages close to the mine, where the impact was considerable. Initially the villagers, in three different linguistic and cultural regions, were poorly organised until the Panguna Landowners Association (PLA) was formed in 1979. Its early demands for greater financial benefits met an unfavourable response from BCL and in 1980 there was some dissent and disturbance in which the Panguna supermarket was looted and damaged. As the issues concerning villagers grew in number and sensitivity, sporadic violence increased in opposition to BCL. In 1987 a more militant new-PLA was established in opposition to the old-PLA and youthful leaders embarked on greater opposition to BCL in almost every sphere of its operations. Such younger men included Francis Ona, a graduate surveyor employed by BCL. They were better organised, understood the operations of the company more clearly than their predecessors, shared all the concerns of the villagers and articulated them more vigorously.

The transition to the new-PLA, and the intensification of discontent, was exacerbated by the 'Melanesian Initiative' of Father John Momis, a Catholic priest, cabinet minister, regional MP for Bougainville and leader of the Melanesian Alliance political party. Momis called upon BCL to increase its financial support for the North Solomons Provincial Government, and denounced the social and environmental impact of mine operations (Quodling 1991:51). The lack of positive response to the 1987 Initiative, from BCL or from the national government, stimulated further frustration and discontent. The new-PLA placed greater pressure on the company, over a range of issues, including demands for better services (education, housing, health care, etc.), increased localisation of employment, more employment and business contracts to be awarded to landowners, greater control of erosion and pollution and a new land survey. BCL took note of these wide-ranging demands but requested more time to consider them; the demands escalated to include 20 per cent PNG government share ownership in the mine and K10 billion compensation. A wide-ranging independent inquiry failed to resolve the dispute, whilst the new-PLA argued that BCL continued to 'hide behind the Bougainville copper agreement and deny us the conditions it promised our parents even before the agreement was reached with the government' and that the PNG government was so dependent on income from the mine that it ignored the demands of landowners for a fair share of wealth from their land. Eventually this view developed into a demand for secession.

Violence escalated with a series of destructive events late in 1988, including the arson of mine buildings and the destruction of power pylons which intermittently closed the mine in the succeeding months. Ona incorporated the demand for secession into his previous demands. Violence mounted, tension increased, a number of incidents led to the first of many deaths, and the arrival of police and military forces from PNG exacerbated an already difficult situation. In May 1989 BCL closed the mine following renewed attacks on mine installations and mineworkers. What had begun as opposition to the perceived injustices of large-scale mining was transformed into a political and military struggle (Chapter 10), in which mining no longer played a significant part, despite its role as the catalyst of crisis. A localised dispute over services and compensation payments for environmental damage had become a national and regional political nightmare.

The Bougainville crisis has had substantial implications, many negative, since there was recognition by landowners, companies and governments that a similar situation could recur elsewhere. The loss of national income, and the subsequent problems for service provision, were considerable. Otherwise the immediate impact of mine violence was largely predictable; mining executives issued warnings about the future of investment in PNG if unrest continued and the PNG government was unable to resolve the issues and restore investor confidence. The world's largest insurance group, Lloyds, downgraded PNG's credit standing. By contrast landowners at Porgera, and at other sites, gained a better share of royalty payments, greater compensation payments, promises of significantly improved infrastructure and more participation in decision-making. Mines could no longer be started without the completion of an appropriate environmental impact statement. Despite a new legislative context and greater participation of all involved parties in preliminary discussions, there remained constitutional uncertainty over the ownership of mineral rights and various disagreements subsequently occurred; mining companies, governments and landowners had quite different aims and objectives.

THE ECONOMIC CONTEXT: NATIONAL INCOME AND FOREIGN INVESTMENT

By far the most important contribution of mining to the development of PNG has been its ability to generate national income. The expansion of mining diversified the economy from its reliance on agriculture exports, a change of great significance during the 1980s with the decline of agricultural commodity prices. In the year that the Panguna mine commenced production (1972–3) the mining sector contributed 55 per cent of the value of all exports, compared with 1 per cent just two years earlier. That proportion increased to reach over 70 per cent at the start of the 1990s; the value of mineral exports has subsequently remained at 73 per cent of the total, as gold and copper prices fell, and timber production increased (Table 4.2). During the 1980s the export economy of PNG thus became increasingly dominated by minerals, and even more so by gold, especially after the shift from Panguna to Porgera. The more rapid growth of GDP in the 1990s was driven by the mining sector, as Porgera entered full production, there were spin-offs for the construction and transport industries from the development of the Kutubu oil project, and oil exports began.

The principal objective of post-independence mining policy was to maximise revenue flows from minerals in the long term, so that mining income could be used for investment to meet other broadly based development goals, which included the creation of rural income-earning opportunities and a reduced dependence on Australian aid. The construction of an appropriate fiscal regime occurred largely through the renegotiation of the BCL agreement (Chapter 2) and the negotiations over the establishment of Ok Tedi (Daniel 1985:6). No mining agreements in PNG have been achieved without enormous, and seemingly endless, negotiation, controversy and protracted discussion. Through the renegotiation of the Bougainville agreement in 1974 the PNG government devised what was widely perceived to be an appropriate tax regime, but it was not followed by further successful negotiations there or elsewhere. A year after the Bougainville Agreement was renegotiated, Kennecott abandoned the Ok Tedi project; much later there were lengthy discussions over the Porgera, Mt Kare and Lihir agreements, a partial result of the inclusion of more interested parties (landowners and provincial governments) than in earlier years, and the necessity to include a greater range of issues, primarily environmental, than had been at stake in earlier agreements.

At the core of minerals policy has been the concept of resource rent; the aim of policy was to channel resource rent to the government and minimise its diversion to other claimants. In the early post-independence years the PNG government never sought equity ownership in mining operations, though it took up minority ownership in all the main mines (Table 6.1), believing that equity was neither necessary for the desired degree of national control nor the correct route to revenue maximisation. Governments also sought to persuade the TNCs to undertake as much infrastructure investment as possible, to minimise the risk of any withdrawal if prices fell, whilst the government would provide only those services which would otherwise have been provided in the absence of mining. Despite these precautions even the minority equity shareholding in Ok Tedi presented difficulties in the 1980s because of the low profitability of the mine and the extent of debt servicing which became a burden on the government. Through its emphasis on resource rent, lack of interest in significant equity participation and disinclination to provide infrastructure, the government had 'demonstrated great reluctance to risk its own budgetary resources or borrowing capacity to promote mining projects' (Daniel and Sims 1986b:48), which gave it a better fiscal regime than in nearby Asian developing countries.

The legal framework for access to minerals was centred on the principle that all minerals were the property of the state, and therefore that the national government was responsible for all policy matters concerning their development and could acquire land for mining purposes. Like the financial regime, the legal framework proved satisfactory in the early years, enabling TNCs to have security of tenure and the national government to develop resources efficiently (Daniel 1985:24), but later came under considerable pressure, because of its denial of mineral ownership to the landowners and the consequent centralisation of the principal financial benefits of mining. The early success of the fiscal and legislative regimes was also associated with substantial profits for BCL, rising world mineral prices and the considerable national income generated by the mining sector.

In many respects the mid-1980s marked the zenith of mining and other economic activity in PNG, with two large mines in production, the discovery of a major gold deposit at Lihir, the continued success of cash cropping and fiscal, legal and political regimes that offered stability. This period was also marked by the floating of shares in Placer Pacific in July 1986, which prompted an extraordinary rush for participation. Shares specifically set aside for PNG investors were eagerly taken up, but just as quickly sold off to foreign buyers by government ministers, politicians and public servants, in search of quick profits. Shortly afterwards the discovery of alluvial gold at Mt Kare led to an extraordinary indigenous goldrush. However there were environmental problems at Ok Tedi and dissent was becoming consolidated into more widespread opposition to BCL in Bougainville. The future of mining came under threat, as provincial governments and local landowners began to assert greater authority and pressure, with reference to the financial and legislative regimes. Relations between different levels of government have become more complex, and a new tier has been introduced, with the growing influence and participation of local landowners, coupled with their increased ability to forcefully determine the outcome of mining situations.

Administrative and managerial problems have sometimes compounded this situation. Over time therefore the national influence on mining became more important than international influences and, whilst that national interest was better able to accommodate the interests of landowners, the uncertainty attached to landowner decision-making severely reduced the attractiveness to TNCs of the existing financial and legal regime.

The emergence of the landowners and a greater concern for environmental issues posed some threats to TNCs, whose projects and practices were increasingly opposed more directly. New demands were motivated by an increased understanding of the financial and legal regimes associated with mining and, above all, by the desire that the economic gains be localised, through the recognition of local ownership of mineral resources. The Bougainville precedent was inevitably raised elsewhere. After a mining agreement was reached at Mt Kare in 1989 the Enga Premier stressed:

> CRA will rip the gold out of this corner of the province and go, leaving behind them the sort of political and social disaster they have created on Bougainville. The Enga Provincial Government will never accept this deal. We want these people out of the province. . . . They use their big money to fly selected landowners to . . . secret meetings, while the real traditional leaders are left behind and kept in the dark . . . CRA are not doing anybody a favour by offering landowners 49 per cent of their own gold. It is an insult to our national independence. . . . We need the expertise and financial resources of these big multinationals to develop our hard rock deposits not shift a bit of mud.
>
> (*PC* 14 December 1989)

Though the agreement was signed these concerns remained, and similar demands recurred elsewhere.

The provinces where mining has taken place have gained substantial direct financial benefits, primarily through royalty payments, but also through new infrastructure and business development, enabling those provinces to commit more funds to other areas of development. Provincial governments were primarily concerned with deriving revenue from mining operations, rather than regulating them, and have given only limited attention to the needs or wishes of local populations. The interests of the provincial governments and landowners rarely coincided, and at almost every mine site there have been conflicts between landowners and the provincial government. For example, at the end of 1987, the Min people of the Ok Tedi area threatened to close the mine (with road blocks), arguing that the border provinces of West Sepik and Western, and especially the Telefomin and Oksapmin areas, were relatively undeveloped, the Ok Tedi mine was contributing little to local development, there were few training opportunities, environmental conditions had not improved and the provincial governments were not using their resources to assist them (*TPNG* 12 December 1987; cf. Jorgensen 1996). In several cases threats to disrupt or close mine operations have been used as bargaining tools against provincial governments. Everywhere there have been disagreements over the local, regional and national distribution of revenue. This emphasised the local and regional inequalities that followed mining development and the friction over vast new incomes and access to jobs and contracting services, and substantially increased the tasks involved in developing legal and financial regimes for new mine operations. Indeed 'the government dealt more satisfactorily with the MNCs than with the local population when it failed to anticipate local discontent toward the central government's large share of the mineral revenues' (Auty 1991:97). Difficulties primarily lay in the shift of real power over mining from the national government to provincial governments and landowners.

Throughout the 1980s the national government largely sought to maintain the existing mining regime, whilst making necessary concessions to increasing the formal participation of provincial governments and landowners, and encouraging the continued involvement of TNCs in mineral development. As the agricultural economy collapsed this became more crucial. Following the Bougainville crisis, PNG devised a new institutional structure, to take greater account of landowners, and to formally recognise their role and that of provincial governments. New mining development agreements were introduced in 1989 that made specific provisions for equity shareholding by both provincial governments and landowners and sought to ensure a distribution of royalties, infrastructure provision and development opportunities that was more responsive to local needs. Mining landowners can now receive 20 per cent of royalty payments, half of which is paid into an investment fund for future generations of landowners. In addition the government introduced a special support grant, first used in Enga province, for infrastructure projects, a fifth of which would be in mining lease areas. Securing even initial consensus has often been difficult; even defining landowners poses problems (see p. 155) and power is relatively dispersed and fragmented in many Melanesian societies. This is partly a function of scale and uncertainty about which areas, and people, should benefit from particular projects.

The international financial community has also been a player of significance. Development of the Ok Tedi mine became problematic in 1984 when major banks became disillusioned with both PNG and the project, which low world prices then suggested was risky. Subsequently the closure of the Panguna and Mt Kare mines, the necessity for improved environmental standards (at existing and future mines) and concern over future demands from landowners, have made mining a source of economic and political uncertainty. Moreover successive governments have repeatedly intervened to review various facets of the mining industry: 'the debilitating effect of frequent ad hoc government intervention in a range of areas from financing through to cut-off grades, reached a peak in the first year of the Ok Tedi project. Unfortunately it is continuing in some measure' (Callick *et al.* 1990:12.3). The government became increasingly anxious to control the minerals sector though it generally dealt pragmatically with periodic crises.

The mining industry has experienced five crises: the first in 1974, when the boom that coincided with the opening of the Bougainville mine went bust, the second in the early 1980s following a fall in copper prices and a rise in interest rates, the third in 1989, when landowners and secessionist violence closed the Bougainville mine (Auty 1991), the fourth from 1992 to 1994, when Paias Wingti's government sought a massive increase in equity in mining ventures and the fifth in 1995 when environmental problems at Ok Tedi resulted in international legal action, followed by new fears over heavy metal discharges at Porgera (Figure 6.4). The first two shocks were a result of external price fluctuations, the second followed local landowner dissent (associated with political divisions), the fourth – and to a lesser extent the fifth – were partly self-inflicted, as the government challenged the power of the mining companies or failed to enforce environmental safeguards. In response to the first two crises PNG displayed fiscal caution, though it failed to cut public expenditure, and revenue fluctuations were mitigated through the Mineral Resources Stabilisation Fund, which enabled PNG to manage the problem of revenue instability more successfully than most broadly comparable mineral exporting countries (Daniel 1985; Fairbairn 1994). However the 1979–83 shock was accompanied by a sharp deceleration in economic growth, creating enormous pressure for the establishment of the Ok Tedi mine. The third shock – the closure of Bougainville – abruptly terminated the improving fiscal situation and the trade balance; early in 1990 the kina was devalued by 10 per cent, government spending cut by 8 per cent and restrictions were placed on wage increases and credit. Eventually the crisis was again averted, primarily because Misima and especially Porgera came on line. The fourth and fifth crises raised new questions over local intervention and the feasibility of TNC participation in the mining industry. Overall, although PNG had responded fairly well to the necessity for macro-economic management of the earlier mineral shocks, the national economy had become increasingly influenced by fluctuations in the mining sector, that were less easy to respond to with conventional economic instruments.

The macro-economic context for mining became more difficult, when confrontation with the companies, through demands for greater equity, proved counter-productive in a difficult national financial situation. The decision of Wingti's government in 1992 to seek significant equity participation overturned historic mining policies. Following larger than expected gold production at Porgera in 1992, the government reopened negotiations over its equity share in the joint venture, which eventually resulted in its equity participation increasing from 10 per cent to 25 per cent (Table 7.1), and also took up 22.5 per cent equity in the Kutubu oil project. This had an adverse impact on investor confidence, and led to a large reduction in the value of PNG stocks. Progress in developing the Lihir mine was slowed, and there was uncertainty over the South East Gobe oil field. The government at one stage sought an equity share in Lihir as high as 50 per cent but later agreed to 30 per cent. Though it is normal for states to simultaneously entice and restrict

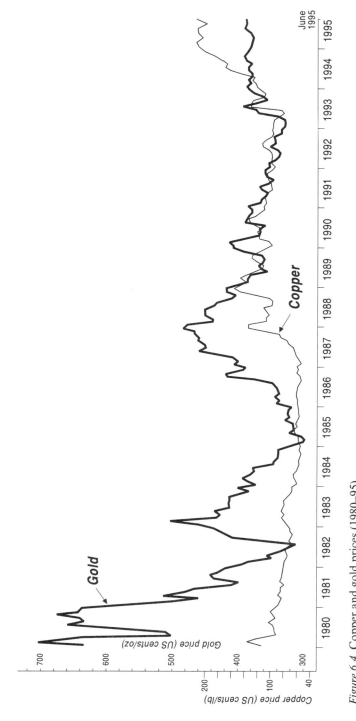

Figure 6.4 Copper and gold prices (1980–95)
Source: Bank of Papua New Guinea, *Quarterly Economic Bulletins*

global capital, with inducements including infrastructure support and tax holidays and restrictions including commitments to local employment and training programmes, PNG's fluctuating policies, and especially the demand for much greater equity participation, were widely seen as unreasonable, especially by mining companies (Economic Insights 1994:102). Whilst the government stressed its enthusiasm for mining, the companies involved were simultaneously being described as exploiters, environmental despoilers and people of bad faith. The IMF reviewed the fiscal regime for mining oil and gas in 1993 and was critical of the quest for greater equity, recommending that the state rely more heavily on royalties and more effectively enforce its tax regulations. It pointed out that the Ok Tedi mine, opened thirteen years previously, had yet to return the government's 20 per cent equity (*TPNG* 15 April 1993). However the government maintained its pro-equity stance, and increased its share in Ok Tedi from 20 to 30 per cent, after Amoco withdrew. A number of companies ended or reduced their interests in PNG, and expenditure on geological exploration fell to its lowest level in two decades because of high costs and political uncertainties. After the Wingti government fell in 1994, the new government quickly overturned past policies, announcing that it would 'fast-track' the Lihir project (to grant a special mining lease early in 1985) and substantially reduce its equity share to 10 per cent, with local landowners also holding 10 per cent, and take out less equity in future mines. Almost immediately the small Tolukuma mine received a mining lease and the Prime Minister, Sir Julius Chan, sought new CRA interest in reopening the Panguna mine. Placer Pacific welcomed what it described as a shift 'from political machinations to economic pragmatism', engendered both by a national financial crisis and international pressures.

In contrast to the relatively successful management of the mining sector, at least until the fourth shock, and overall fiscal management, the weakest area of national economic management has been in the diversification of the economy. Three principal factors constrained developments in other sectors (primarily agriculture and manufacturing industry), each of which in some ways extended the colonial legacy: relatively high wage rates, a high exchange rate and restrictions on overseas investment. High wages discouraged manufacturing industry, agriculture declined (mainly through depressed world prices) and tourism never developed. Financial and human resources have become more concentrated in one sector and, in a different way, in one or more mining regions; Sir Julius Chan has pointed out: 'To build the road from Kiunga to the Ok Tedi mine cost us one hundred million Australian dollars. It was necessary but that kind of outlay hurts . . . if a similar amount of money had been diverted towards effective agriculture and educational development, then perhaps a large part of our current social problems which have developed over recent years may well never have existed' (1992b:5). The inability to reverse the economic trajectory and diversify the economy out of mining, and the much greater importance of mining since independence, moved that sector from a role of economic bonus to one of economic backbone (Auty 1991, 1993; Fairbairn 1994), taking the country closer towards a 'Dutch Disease' scenario.

The essence of the 'Dutch Disease' is that rapid and wasteful spending of windfall revenues from a mineral price boom is difficult to avoid, and that the over-rapid absorption of these revenues produces various problems including wage inflation and exchange rate appreciation. This leads to the decline of non-mining export goods, such as those produced in agriculture and industry, since their costs rise relative to the cost of local production. It also reduces the ability of domestic manufacturing industries to withstand competition from imports. This decline in turn makes any adjustments to the losses of revenue and foreign exchange that occur during a mineral price downswing difficult to achieve. Skill shortages, which are hard to overcome, lead to higher wages and substantial problems for the agriculture and manufacturing sectors in retaining or attracting labour. As a high-wage enclave sector, employing many expatriates, the mining sector creates high expectations in other sectors, and in nearby areas, that contribute to social tension and conflict. Whereas in the 1970s and early 1980s mining made a substantial contribution to economic diversification, by the end of the 1980s diversification out of mining had become essential.

Though PNG governments have consistently stressed that agriculture should be the basis of national development, the reality has never matched the rhetoric. Channelling mineral incomes into other sectors of economic growth has proved difficult. The high priority given to minerals projects distracted policy formation from the necessary task of developing the fisheries, forestry and agricultural sectors, and there are few linkages between these sectors and the minerals sector. Mining has raised the cost structure of the PNG economy, as the construction boom and an increase in mineral revenues led to excess demand for goods and services that could not readily be imported; these included some local transport services, urban land, electricity, some foods and even betel nuts (Daniel 1985:51). Such impacts were small in the first decade after independence, but increased in the second decade with the expansion of the minerals sector.

LOCAL DEVELOPMENT, CAPITAL LOGIC AND THE PROJECT CYCLE

If mining has been beneficial in national terms, because of the enormous increase in revenue and despite 'Dutch Disease', the effects are more ambivalent locally and regionally. Mining has had a substantial spatial impact, since recent mines – and projected mines – are mainly located in previously remote parts of the country, which had little cash income and few services. Mines have generated local employment, directly or indirectly, hence incomes increased. Infrastructure improvements, primarily designed to benefit the mines, such as highways and airstrips, have also benefited local people; schools and dispensaries have been specifically constructed for them.

In particular places there have been rapid changes in society, economy and in the environment; most have been similar around different mine sites, but on a smaller scale to those that previously occurred in Bougainville.

Elements of the modern economy are now located in some of the more impoverished parts of the country. The Prime Minister, Paias Wingti, stated: 'Most of our mines, actual and prospective, are in remote areas. Mining is a means to what we regard as real or true development' (quoted in Connell 1988b:22). Before mining the Ok Tedi area was 'something of a black hole' to which the first government patrol had only set forth in 1963. Government officers regarded a posting there as a punishment, its administration were 'beggars', with development largely left to missionaries, and its people were 'expected to migrate to find a better way of life, or face gradual extinction' (Jackson 1982a:3). Porgera, Misima and Lihir are all in isolated, thinly populated areas and Mt Kare is the epitome of remoteness and inaccessibility. Even Tolukuma, a 100 kilometres from Port Moresby, was totally isolated. A new national geography has thus emerged, in which mining has reduced the extent of uneven development at a national scale.

Urbanisation near and far

The mines themselves, and the environmental transformations that they engender, have been the most obvious impact of mining. New mining towns have also transformed the landscape. Arawa, the prototype mining town, had grown from nothing to around 17,000 people at the time the mine closed. It was little different from similar towns elsewhere in the world: a somewhat sterile collection of houses of various kinds, with numbered sections rather than named and distinctive suburbs, and an extremely heterogeneous population. Despite steady growth in size and a greater diversity of functions Arawa never quite lost its aura of being a company town that was benefiting a distant rather than a local population. Other smaller and more recent mining towns are more obviously company towns. Tabubil (Western Province) is similar but in a very different mountainous environment (Figure 6.5), grown beyond its 'artificial' start, with substantial migration from Oksapmin and elsewhere, to the fringes of the town. Nonetheless, 'the cultural climate of Tabubil is decidedly colonial; the social hierarchy of the company and town is racialized, ethnically stratified, male dominated, and the superiority of expatriates is broadcast in crude and subtle ways. Though most workers in town are Papua New Guineans, the upper ranks are predominantly white, and nationals are regarded by the Europeans as a foreign race, alternately "diverse", quaint and menacing' (Polier 1996:3). Spontaneous migration was even more visible at Porgera, where in the five years before mining began there was a 50 per cent increase in the local population, mainly of Enga and Tari migrants, to the extent that landowners eventually sought company help in removing outsiders (Banks 1993:323) and some squatters were forcibly removed, in the development of a 'cordon sanitaire' around the mine site.

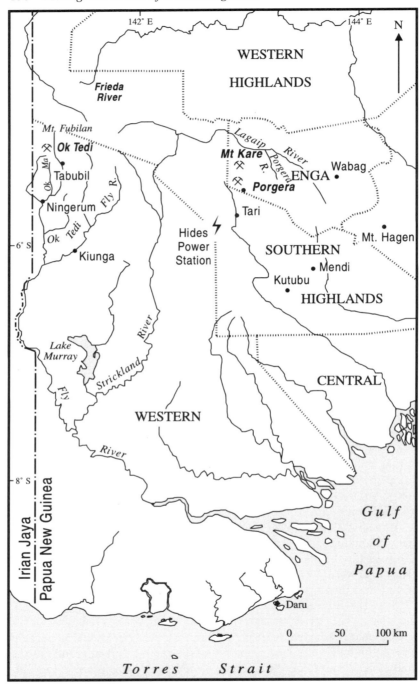

Figure 6.5 Mt Kare, Ok Tedi and Porgera mines

Urbanisation has often occurred at a distance from the mine site. Because of the high cost of constructing facilities at Tabubil, itself 20 kilometres from Ok Tedi, some mine support functions were located in Kiunga and Port Moresby, which also meant that some private urban costs were transferred to the public budget, and there was a speculative boom in house prices there (Pintz 1984: 161). Away from the mining towns themselves, the most rapid mine-related growth has been at Mount Hagen, which has benefited from mining activities at Porgera, Mt Kare and Kutubu. Lae, at the end of the Highlands Highway, has also been boosted by the import and export demands of the mining boom, but it is probably Port Moresby, as the base of many head offices, supply companies, ancillary services and transport ventures, that has been the single greatest recipient of the urban impact of mining growth.

The establishment of 'commuter mining', through 'fly in–fly out' (FIFO) schemes based on Cairns in Queensland, reduced the local impact of mining. Since all the mining companies are transnational corporations, numerous specialised high-level operations attached to mining are undertaken overseas. FIFO schemes expand this offshore activity. For mining companies commuter mining is more economic since it reduces the initial costs of town and infrastructure construction and substitutes recurrent costs, whilst industrial and personnel relations also benefit (Gerritsen and MacIntyre 1991:42) as expatriate mining personnel may prefer family residence overseas rather than in PNG. In 1993 at least 550 residents of Cairns were employed in PNG under FIFO schemes. Both at Misima and Porgera there have been local demands for a mining town, rather than FIFO, because of the contribution to local economic growth. At Porgera landowners demanded that if the FIFO scheme continued, they should be compensated for the losses to the Porgera community (*TPNG* 11 June 1992). There are economic losses; 'in Misima the impact of the mining project appears insignificant as is evident in the lack of economic activity in Bwagoia whereas Tabubil is a thriving community. Spending by the expatriate employees of Misima, Porgera and Kutubu takes place at their home bases during their breaks off-site' (*TPNG* 28 January 1995). Expatriates rarely venture beyond these mine camp boundaries, whereas Tabubil has a range of social activities, with local multiplier effects. Mining has boosted economic growth in northern Australia, at the expense of PNG, as there is less impact on the construction and service sector, with expatriate expenditure being largely transferred offshore. Through 'commuter mining' the mining sector is more obviously an enclave industry, without local linkages.

Business development

Other impacts of mining on the regional and national economy have been typical of mining regions elsewhere. Mining and exploration have generated demand for machinery, transport equipment, chemicals and paints. Thus one company alone employed more than twenty people and supplied 11,000 tonnes of explosives to the mining industry in 1991, somewhat less than half the demands of the industry. Transport of these and other goods provides a further boost to the economy, and the road transport industry has become largely locally owned. Transport activities, from small local ventures supplying consumer goods to the mines and mining towns, from barges on the Fly River to trucks on the Highlands Highway, but above all air services, have all grown rapidly. Air services have been particularly important for Porgera and Kutubu. Symbolic of these developments was the introduction of giant Russian-made helicopters into the highlands, by the appropriately named Hevi Lift PNG Pty Ltd; it was the first time such helicopters had been used outside the former Soviet Union.

Mines have created other demands for services in the local region, notably for fresh foods, hence most have established markets of one kind or another, enabling local produce to be sold. In the mid-1970s the Panguna mine was being supplied from as far away as Buin, some 80 kilometres to the south, and villagers were developing market gardens (some using hired labour) specifically to supply the mine. At Ok Tedi in 1983 the project was purchasing vegetables worth $500,000 from local suppliers, many of whom had no previous outlets for agricultural production. The people of Oksapmin had increased their production tenfold; produce was flown into Tabubil by light aircraft belonging to Cloudlands Aviation Developments, 40 per cent owned by local, village-based business groups (Jackson 1983:29). Agricultural production and transport development were linked.

At Bougainville the mine had a considerable impact on industrial development. Soon after mineral exports started in 1972 more than 40 factories were employing over 1,200 people, in such areas as machinery repairs, cement goods production, clothing, fibre glass and plastic products (Treadgold 1978b:26–8). Industrial expansion subsequently grew more slowly, but diversified into a range of other areas, mainly related to services such as cleaning, printing and food processing. No other mine has had anything like this impact on the nearby region; only the larger mines have contributed to some kind of industrial development, but usually at a distance from the site.

Mining has generated few linkages within PNG, even within the construction industry, which might have been expected to be the principal beneficiary. At Ok Tedi a lack of information on the requirements of the mine made it difficult for local firms to participate; there was a lack of skilled labour in the country, the majority of firms that were involved were subsidiaries of foreign companies, and many goods provided by local suppliers were imported, hence relatively low levels of domestic value were added (Pintz 1984:154–7). During the establishment phase of the Misima mine, a Port Moresby MP called on the government to ensure that contracts associated with the project were awarded to companies in PNG, to avoid what was described as 'the Ok Tedi fiasco' where many contracts and services that could have been performed by local companies were offered to offshore companies (*TPNG* 28 January

1988). Official preference is given to local companies but there is little evidence that such preferences have been effective.

At a much smaller scale a number of projects have been successful, where villagers have combined as partners in businesses, such as service stations and engineering companies, that have paid considerable dividends. Most of these have involved landowners from areas close to the mine sites, who have more substantial incomes to invest (Jackson 1993:140). The extent of linkages and their significance is poorly understood. At Misima business development did not live up to villagers' expectations, partly because of the lack of entrepreneurial skills amongst the villagers and partly because of inter- and intra-clan hostility. Those that were successful, however, eroded 'the communitarian nature of Misiman society' (Gerritsen and MacIntyre 1991:50), but were unlikely to survive the end of mining. Despite significant business development around Porgera – mostly involving stores – local capital accumulation has been limited, a situation true of most mining areas. All store goods are imported from Mt Hagen or beyond; half the value of sales is immediately lost to Porgera, and much of the remainder leaves soon afterwards. The multiplier effect of business development around Porgera is thus trivial, despite local businesses employing almost as many people as does the mine (Banks 1996), and playing some part in developing the few linkages between mining and the wider economy.

Employment

Beyond its obvious visible effects the most immediate impact of mining has been on employment. As a classic capital-intensive industry, mining makes a limited direct contribution to employment; overall the mining sector employs less than 1 per cent of the national workforce. The number of workers directly employed by the mining companies is very small. Panguna, with almost 4,000 at the time of closure, was exceptionally large; Ok Tedi employed 1,875 in 1993 and Porgera just over 1,770. By contrast Misima then employed 675 and Mt Kare employed fewer than 100 workers when it closed. Yet even these numbers compare favourably with relatively large Australian mines such as Kidston and Big Bell (that jointly employed about 400 people in 1993). By contrast informal mining operations in PNG may well have a workforce of about the same size as in the formal mining sector. Mine workforces have tended to decline, rather than increase, over time, so emphasising the attractions of well-paid, skilled mine employment. By 1984, after the construction phase was over, Ok Tedi was referred to by the local Wopkaimin people as 'the place without work' (Hyndman 1991:86; Polier 1996:5) where the unskilled, uneducated local people had been placed at a considerable disadvantage.

Competition for scarce mining jobs has been considerable. Most unskilled jobs at the mine sites have been reserved, where possible, for local residents; this minimised the numbers of outsiders, a source of early resentment in Bougainville, and usually enabled local workers to upgrade their skills.

Typical of this kind of situation is that at Porgera where the mine provided direct employment for 1,770 people, of whom 78 per cent were from PNG (and 70 per cent of those were from Enga Province, just over half being from the Porgera district). At Ok Tedi 88 per cent were citizens and at Misima the comparable proportion was 80 per cent. At Ok Tedi, in 1991, some 40 per cent of the national workforce of 1,630 were from Western Province, though employment policy favoured workers, or Preferred Area Employees, from the Kiunga and Telefomin areas. During the goldrush at Mt Kare effective informal regulation resulted in local workers having priority. The majority of workers were therefore from nearby areas of the Southern Highlands and Enga, but workers came from most other provinces: 'As interlopers, foreigners, they seem to have been accepted by the locals with considerable tolerance. They were to some extent discouraged from digging in the richest ground, but had a free go in reworking old holes; in some cases they appear to have been charged an informal "rent" or "royalty" by a local man' (P. Ryan 1991:52). In a very different context, the employment structure at Mt Kare, without any formal regulation, replicated that at the sites of transnational mining projects. A crucial question, that continues to pose considerable difficulties in some mining areas, such as Porgera, is who are the 'local' people, specifically the landowners, in terms of allocating employment and business opportunities and paying compensation. Concern with the migration of 'outsiders', and antagonism to them, was greatest where they were from other parts of PNG, since their skills were less likely to be recognised as superior by local residents, for whom employment in the mining sector was invariably a major goal. In the highlands especially there was widespread concern over migrants from other parts of PNG, especially from the richer coastal areas, seizing the best jobs and profiting at local expense. As employment remained static such conflicts intensified.

A significant proportion of mining-related employment is in the construction phase, and is largely unskilled and temporary, hence mining has made a limited contribution to skill formation. However it has substantially contributed to skill formation amongst the long-term mine labour force; when the Bougainville mine closed many workers quickly found jobs elsewhere. The PNG government has taken little interest in the employment and training situation at the mines, and training programmes within the mining sector have followed company initiatives. However the financial imperatives of project schedules minimise opportunities for local people who have no time to acquire the necessary skills and qualifications (Gerritsen and MacIntyre 1991). Where distant migrants received such opportunities, relative deprivation was an inevitable outcome, since mine jobs, skilled or unskilled, have offered considerable prestige, relatively high wages and skill acquisition. Mine hard hats have become a distinct status symbol in the outside world. As something of a labour aristocracy, mine workers have infrequently taken strike action and have tended to hold on to this employment rather than engage in forms of 'circular migration' that are more common elsewhere.

The employment of a predominantly local labour force has created some problems because of the distortion of the local employment structure (and the decline of other sectors); mining has drawn workers out of agriculture (and other activities), contributing to the local component of 'Dutch Disease', as mineworkers and landowners increasingly disdained some kinds of agricultural activity. The release of large numbers of workers into the local economy, when the construction phase ended or mines closed (especially if closure was not anticipated), and the difficulty for potential workers from the local region in securing mining jobs, intensified local tensions.

Compensation and development

Compensation payments have been paid for the lease of land and for various forms of damage and disruption that have followed mining. Establishing the social and geographical basis for the allocation of compensation payments was often difficult. Invariably there were initial problems in defining landowners and local people (Jackson 1982a:161–70), especially at Mt Kare where there was no local population (P. Ryan 1991:96–7). Normal procedures for establishing land ownership are difficult enough in PNG, as ownership is defined by the membership of clan and lineage groups (and there are different ways in which such membership might be gained and claimed), and boundaries that had never been surveyed or demarcated were often contested.

The number of land claimants at mine sites was often considerable. At Kutubu as many as 1,100 people from 49 clans were identified in the oil development area, alongside a further 2,000 people from 60 clans along the pipeline route (*PC* 17 March 1992). At the Ok Tedi mine site over 700 people in 7 villages were identified as landowners (Pintz 1984:163) but during the 1980s many people from areas as distant as Oksapmin migrated into the villages closest to the mine site and pressed for inclusion in the list of those to receive payments; local village leaders were sometimes powerless to prevent this (Jackson 1993:67). It was even more complicated at Mt Kare where some 6,000 landowners (about 2,000 more than at Bougainville) were eventually organised into 63 separate business groups: 'an object lesson in the complexities which social organisation in PNG imposes on otherwise straightforward business undertakings' (P. Ryan 1991:133). Divergent claims over land tenure contributed to the closure of the mine. Invariably land disputes increased over time.

Actual compensation payments (for lease of land, damage and so on) were generally quite small, inadequate to enable their recipients to engage in any form of development with long-term sustainability and usually quickly spent by villagers with many unsatisfied needs. At Mt Kare, 'entitlements descended as low as a couple of kina' (P. Ryan 1991:111). Even at Ok Tedi where relatively few villagers were directly affected by mining, cash payments were often around K250 per head in the 1980s: that is around 1 kina per person per day for those most involved. Payments rarely went to individuals, most going to family or sub-clan groups; subsequent processes of distribution have caused local conflicts, and contributed to individualism and social disintegration. At most sites compensation was boosted by migration into anticipated development areas, as at Lihir where there has been a form of 'real estate speculation' through movement into the caldera, and more generally by rapid planting programmes in future mining areas. Nevertheless in real terms payments have usually declined over time, whilst the number of claimants and the range of demands, has increased. There is very little indication that compensation has enabled most landowners to establish ventures that would enable them to achieve and maintain new economic status during and particularly after the mine life.

Damage usually did, and was always perceived to, increase over time. At Kutubu, even before oil had been exported, villagers stated:

> Our rivers run muddy and we don't catch fish. We have fished here all our lives, and we could get two baskets of fish in an hour's time. Now our men fish during the day and our women fish at night, and we don't catch enough to feed our children. The animals [that we hunted] have become frightened and run away. We are river people here. When Chevron is finished here, they will go back to their white man's houses where they will have whatever they want, but without fish in the river we will have nothing.
>
> (Quoted in McCoy 1992; cf. Connell 1992)

Provision of facilities for mineworkers or displaced villagers, has also posed problems. At Ok Tedi the provision of what were perceived to be low quality, single quarters for migrant mineworkers contributed to strikes in 1988. The strikers burnt down the premises of the Golf Club and the Hash House Harriers, which catered for the sporting and social needs of expatriates, as 'symbols of the unfair and unequal treatment given to Papua New Guinean workers' (*TPNG* 29 September 1988). Following the subsequent construction of improved housing for the militant mineworkers, the Ok Tedi landowners launched similar demands for free housing, complete with appropriate amenities. Mining has invariably contributed to and intensified new and increased demands, alongside relative deprivation.

The 'local' people, and the 'local' region, have meant different things in different contexts and in different places. In terms of land leasing, and compensation payments, companies have sought narrow, localised definitions to minimise costs; in terms of employment a wider concept of 'local' workforce is more valuable. Landowners, however defined, and governments had different perspectives. All projects have had particular benefits for the provinces where they operate, mainly in terms of shareholdings and equity participation. At Porgera the joint venture partners introduced a new scheme, by which the company spends part of the money it owes in taxes on approved items of public works, usually nominated by the Provincial Government and local communities. The company set up a provincial works unit, and mainly hired Enga contractors for work on various projects, from roads to schools; thus its impact is apparent throughout most of the province, rather than on that directly influenced by mine operations or indirectly by multiplier effects. Mines have also tended to result in mining companies giving special concessions – such as the provision of schools, aid posts or other infrastructure – beyond the specific mine impact areas. Finally there are the landowners in those areas used, and leased, by mining projects, who have received compensation, royalty payments and preferential assistance in terms of employment and business development, but have experienced the bulk of the environmental disturbances. For the highlands mines, these disturbances may be very distant from the mine site itself.

Infrastructure and the project cycle

Governments and mining companies have naturally attached great importance to the economic gains from mining. While the government has sought to maximise taxes and royalties, the desire to swiftly develop new mines also stemmed from the 'capital logic' of mining. That is, mining projects are moulded by financial flows; 'the source of the money, the timing for repayment of loans, the need to make a profit, all force a particular negotiating outcome and timetable and as a consequence provide a characteristically "legalistic" regime that encourages deferred dissatisfactions among local people' (Gerritsen and MacIntyre 1991:37). Landowners are invariably placed under pressure from governments and companies, whose timetables are based on financial flows and who seek to maximise the economic gains. Moreover landowners usually had relatively little understanding of the costs and benefits of mining and inadequate information to make or participate in complex decisions; at Ok Tedi, the local MP complained: 'we have not been given enough time and consultations before the decision was made compared with other mining areas within the country' (*PC* 5 October 1989). After an early phase of general satisfaction, when land is relatively little disturbed, pollution minimal, compensation apparently generous (and old and new needs satisfied) and employment aspirations met, dissatisfaction has become more evident. Eventually conflicts emerge over environmental stresses and the distribution of income (from royalties, compensation and profits) which contribute to frustration, apathy, hostility and occasionally violent opposition to mining activities, initially through the construction of blockades. At all contemporary mines, anxieties over access to the spoils of development led to actions that conflicted with unwieldy legislative procedures. The legislative and political systems were unable to keep up with rapidly changing situations in wholly new contexts. Western-style legal arrangements, with strict boundaries and formal contracts, have posed problems, as at Misima: 'For Misimans unfamiliar with the rigidities of commercial contracts, the appeal to the letter of the law is not only baffling, it is anti-social. More specifically it fails to take into account the prevailing notions of reciprocity and the customary indebtedness of guest to host' (Gerritsen and MacIntyre 1991:44). Moreover even after two decades of 'modern' mining in PNG, landowners in new mine locations had little or no experience of commercial operations, negotiating with large corporations or, in the most general terms, of what could be expected from mining. Thus at Mt Kare

> the most common problem encountered in the early days of negotiation was instilling an understanding of basic business philosophy in people who had no concept, and had never dreamed of becoming involved in a business . . . the Paielans had practically no idea what CRA was getting at when it first attempted negotiations.
>
> (*Pacific Resources* January 1992:17)

At Misima, before construction, 'as this project was being set up by an independent Papua New Guinea government [villagers] believed their interests would be protected and their voices heard in places that had been dominated by whites. Few knew about Ok Tedi; even Bougainville was little more than a name' (MacIntyre 1988:28), hence the experiences gained in other parts of PNG were not easily transferred to new mining regions. While technological skills could be learned and transferred, the involvement of local people invariably started anew.

The isolation of mining regions from each other had a number of effects. At every site, other than Panguna, the local people were enthusiastic initial supporters of mining development, believing that mining would generate considerable improvement in living standards, though such beliefs declined over time, after wide-ranging demands were made on mining companies and governments. Other misunderstandings emerged, for example over the manner in which environmental damage might be assessed and thus compensated for (Connell 1992). Technical operations were invariably the source of further misunderstandings. At Mt Kare, diamond drills were perceived by some to be a form of vacuum-cleaner, removing gold from deep in the ground; others felt that CRA was using a helicopter to spray the area with a secret chemical so that gold would sink into the ground beyond the reach of the local miners' hand equipment (P. Ryan 1991: 112). At Bougainville there were occasional fears that the sea would rise up through the mine pit and the island would drown.

Underlying the dissatisfactions of landowners at mining sites were situations where neither governments nor mining companies readily sought to respond to villagers' requests for infrastructure, since both were anxious to maximise profitability and minimise 'overheads', whilst the division of responsibility for infrastructure provision was not always clearly specified. At most sites the companies fulfilled their responsibilities more successfully than governments. Consequently landowners redefined their relationship with the mines in terms of exacting new demands upon them (Gerritsen and MacIntyre 1991:45–6; McCoy 1992). The lack of direct government involvement in planning in mining regions posed problems for people and companies alike, and ensured that in some contexts they appeared as direct antagonists rather than collaborators in the development of resources for mutual gains.

The prospect of establishing a mine at a particular site put new perspectives on old problems; long neglected and unmet local demands for infrastructure again became relevant as part of a new agenda. Mines promised access to new resources, and the resolution of problems not yet solved through normal recourse to political channels. What resulted was 'garbage-can anarchy', where new situations had old problems grafted onto them, and matters irrelevant to the mine became part of the politics of managing the impacts of the mine. The inability or unwillingness of the mining companies to respond to wide-ranging requests was 'usually expressed in terms of disbelief that such an obviously rich entity as the mining company cannot countenance new, apparently trifling claims' (Gerritsen and MacIntyre 1991:41). Moreover the situation tended to worsen over time, as minerals were steadily exported and anticipated infrastructure and employment did not always materialise. Pressures for local development and infrastructure invariably exceeded those proposed by companies, intended by governments or actually constructed. To meet wide-ranging demands would be costly for either companies or governments; companies have different interests whilst governments have similar concerns but in a much wider geographical area and with limited finance and technical support. At each mine site, the companies have become, at least in part, a quasi-government, as governments have failed to exert their influence or deliver services. For years this was apparent around Panguna; the Lower Ok Tedi/Fly River Development Trust is a surrogate government agency alongside the Fly river, and the Porgera Joint Venture has been involved in high school development, capital works and infrastructure provision as far away as Lake Murray (Figure 6.5). At Ok Tedi company officials even produce 'patrol reports' like those once produced by patrol officers (*kiaps*), and perceive themselves to be the 'safety-valve' of the company.

At the most remote sites, where operations were not expected to last long, companies preferred to move equipment, personnel and even output by helicopter to reduce costs, minimise population movements around the site and, exceptionally, reduce environmental damage. At Kutubu, Chevron did not intend road access (at a cost of K40 million, that was inessential to mining operations) but local pressure ensured that it be built. The road improved local access, but also led to more general access, hence contributing to new problems of alcohol consumption, theft, poaching and squatting, and thus to new demands from landowners that Chevron provide security services (McCoy 1992). Mines have also set up more wide-ranging development projects. Following the Bougainville model, Ok Tedi Mining Limited established the Ok Tedi/Fly River Development Trust in 1989 'to contribute to village development funds and establish community and business development projects. Only traditional village communities on either side of the Ok Tedi and Fly Rivers who demonstrate they need assistance will receive funds' (*Niugini Nius* (*NN*) 9 October 1989). Between 1990 and the end of 1995 the Lower Ok

Tedi/Fly River Development Trust spent K17 million in the area, to support projects ranging from village halls and women's clubs, to solar-powered water pumps and the construction of a rubber-producing plant at Kiunga, in a successful attempt to revive rubber production – the only viable cash crop in the region. Elsewhere new schools, aid posts and roads have all introduced new forms of development. Though such activities, highly developed at the most established mine sites, have been directly beneficial they have increased the confusion over the division of responsibilities between mining companies and governments. Some of those who have gained most and lost least (including shareholders) have been distant from the mine sites such as those in remote parts of provinces who have gained new services. Otherwise, closer to the sites, where there have been environmental costs, unless companies display 'a genuine commitment to mitigate the causes of its impacts, rather than the symptoms, such [village-level] projects must be viewed as tokenistic and diversionary' (Rosenbaum and Krockenberger 1993:19). Perceptions of costs and benefits vary widely, and are both subjective and highly political.

Other social impacts of mining have often been predictable and generally harmful, despite the new educational, recreational and health opportunities. 'Fighting, vandalism and disturbance of the peace are now commonplace on Misima when men are flush with their new pay cheques and liquor is available at licensed outlets. A black market in beer has emerged in a few villages and young men are particularly prone to offensive or socially disruptive behaviour when drunk' (Gerritsen and MacIntyre 1991:47–8). Even in the construction phase Lihir was hit by a rapid increase in alcohol-related crimes (*PC* 19 June 1996). At the mines drinking has become an industrial problem and accounts for some degree of absenteeism. At Ok Tedi men no longer had men's houses and 'aggressive drunken behaviour, black-marketing, fighting and adultery associated with heavy beer-drinking now threaten family life' (Hyndman 1991:84). Similar situations followed the unequal distribution of cash and other benefits from the mine. At Porgera individuals with good access to compensation payments gained prestige and, amongst relocated households, polygamy increased substantially (Banks 1996). Domestic violence also increased. At Ok Tedi, and to a lesser extent at Bougainville, discontent was channelled into broadly based movements of social protest. At Ok Tedi this took the form of an indigenous Christian revival movement, affirming a more traditional order in opposition to the consequences of rapid economic change.

Nowhere was there an equable transition to mining, two mines closed unexpectedly and at most sites some problems had emerged, as at Kutubu, where 'Chevron is enmeshed in countless jungle disputes – some of its own making, others caused by corruption, inertia, cultural misunderstanding and ancient tribal enmities' (McCoy 1992). The changes to which mining contributed occurred much more rapidly than other forms of change and development in PNG. At every site, as at Misima, 'national government was inadequate in protecting Misimans from the adverse effects of mining policy' as the 'capital logic' of the project cycle meant that it sought to maximise national income especially in the early years, and 'inefficiency, incapacity and intergovernmental rivalry characterised governmental dealings with the Misiman people' (Gerritsen and MacIntyre 1991:51–2). Gains and losses from mining were usually highly localised. At Ok Tedi the lease payments, share of royalties and compensation payments given to people in two villages provided them with an income three times the national average (Pintz 1984:164). Similar situations occurred elsewhere, though such villagers often lost much of their land and experienced other environmental disadvantages. By contrast, not far away, 'life goes on with very few of the promised advantages for people who have no land for the mine to lease, no trees for the company to fell or no skills with which to gain employment' (MacIntyre 1988:29). Inequalities thus increased substantially and quickly, as the bureaucratic elite, of politicians and public servants, has been the principal beneficiary of mining. When Placer Pacific shares were floated in 1986, 'so many eminent Papua New Guineans were involved in buying pre-issue shares which they then sold within the first few days of normal trading at profits in excess of 100 per cent that great difficulty was experienced in finding people who had not so participated to staff the subsequent Committee of Inquiry' (Jackson 1989: 91). The limited attention to environmental standards indicated the unwillingness of this elite to compromise between profitability and conservation.

THE ENVIRONMENTAL CONTEXT

The Bougainville copper mine demonstrated the significance of mining for national and local income generation, and the problems attached to uneven development, but it even more obviously displayed the environmental problems that mining created, and the manner in which environmental damage could have political implications. Environmental degradation is no new phenomenon in PNG, and has long been associated with the forest industry (Chapter 5), but nowhere has it been more dramatic than at the largest mine sites in the country. Environmental damage has also been substantial over a wide area at Wau and Bulolo, after more than half a century of mining, and the Bulolo river, flowing through a boulder-strewn wasteland, has long been 'dead' because of the discharge of largely untreated cyanide into the river until the closure of the mine in 1990 (Hughes and Sullivan 1989:51; Kreye and Castell 1991:53). Disposal of waste tailings, alone or contaminated with heavy metals and other waste materials, has damaged river systems, unsightly waste dumps have occupied valuable land areas, dangerous chemicals and heavy metals have occasionally been released into the environment, and environmental legislation has been difficult to transfer from paper to practice.

Debate over the environmental implications of mining largely focused on Ok Tedi since the construction and operation problems have affected a wider area than elsewhere. The whole history of mining at Ok Tedi has been sur-rounded by controversy over the environmental impact, stemming from the non-construction of a tailings dam and the deposition of sediment below the Fly river confluence – where the river is less than 20 metres above sea-level. A partially completed dam was destroyed in a landslide in 1984 and the national government then agreed to an interim tailings disposal system. Ok Tedi Mining Ltd (OTML) argued that the high cost of a tailings dam, in an area geologically unsuitable for dam construction, meant that construction had to be deferred, though the company was simultaneously stressing its ability to produce low cost copper (Pernetta 1988:6). With the Bougainville copper mine closed, the government, faced with what appeared to be the ecological necessity to construct a tailings dam, was confronted with what was per-ceived as an 'environment or economy' decision; it chose not to burden the mine with a K380 million bill for a permanent tailings dam, but rather to ensure that mining went ahead, with discharge of waste into the Fly river 'sacrifice zone' at very high levels, in exchange for compensation. Landowners briefly closed the mine in January 1990, in opposition to this 'ecocide deci-sion' (Hyndman 1991:82), but mining continued. In this *ad hoc* manner operations at Ok Tedi were specifically exempted from the conditions of the first two pieces of environmental legislation that had been passed by Parliament in 1978.

From the mid-1980s pollution of the Ok Tedi and Fly rivers increased, threatening river fisheries staples, gardens and sago palms along the river-banks (Hyndman 1991:79). At much higher reaches of the river, such as at Tabubil (Figure 6.5), the contamination levels from various pollutants, including arsenic, were said to give 'shocking figures and represent industrial effluents on a scale not permitted in any river in the western world' (Kreye and Castell 1991:43). Fish biomass in the Fly river immediately downstream of the Ok Tedi confluence has been reduced and species composition altered as a result of the mine; fish numbers have also fallen through commercial fishing, with potentially serious ecological consequences (R. Smith 1991; H. Thompson 1990). Sediment has entered the floodplain, bank erosion and channel changes have occurred, and heavy metals may have reached the Gulf of Papua in high concentrations. Such conclusions probably represent a worst-case scenario; a subsequent report by the German Starnberg Institute suggested that higher losses of biomass were possible but long term company environmental assessments reached more positive conclusions (Kreye and Castell 1991:45–7; Eagle *et al.* 1992; Economic Insights 1996:218–22). Conditions in the Fly river are also influenced by mining at Porgera. Due to the rugged topography and unstable terrain at the site a permanent tailings dam was not constructed there either, but waste is deposited into the Lagaip river, which flows into the Fly below Lake Murray. (The only mine where a tailings dam was constructed was Mt Victor, a very small mine in the Eastern Highlands, where the daily production of tailings was less than 1 per cent of that at Ok Tedi.) The Porgera mine environmental scientists concluded that environmental damage below Lagaip would be slight, though some tailings would reach the Gulf and mercury levels in Lake Murray would increase (Ross 1991). By 1994 there was some suggestion that mercury and arsenic, entering the river system in high quantities in the absence of compliance critera, were contributing to ill-health and deaths downstream (L. Thompson 1996) but the origin of the mercury was in dispute (Economic Insights 1996:226–7). At every site, there has been extensive debate over the validity and significance of all environmental data.

At various times there have been national and international protests over the environmental impacts of mining at Ok Tedi; in 1989 and 1990 there were protests by landowners, and the mine was closed for three days. Indonesia has formally requested the PNG government to ensure that greater safety and environmental precautions were taken on the use of the Fly river (*PC* 29 November 1989). In 1990 an Australian Parliamentary Committee expressed its concern that it was inappropriate for the monitoring of environmental issues at Ok Tedi to be carried out by the Department of Mines and Energy, which was scarcely a disinterested body, but that it should be undertaken by the Department of Energy and Conservation. Two years later, the Australian Prime Minister, Paul Keating, passed a protest letter from the Australian Conservation Foundation to the PNG Prime Minister, Rabbie Namaliu, which claimed that 'BHP would not be prepared to operate in Australia with the same lax standards it employs in Papua New Guinea. The Ok Tedi mine sets a dangerous precedent with the rationalism to pursuit of profit [*sic*] overriding minimum standards of environmental protection' and should therefore be closed. Criticism of the environmental issues took a new form in 1994 when a group of landowners alongside the Fly river launched a class action against BHP and OTML in the Victorian Supreme Court, alleging damage and injury from Ok Tedi's operations. The writ alleged that pollutants had caused the river and its flood plains to become 'impure, unclean and noxious', that the river was less navigable, and flooding and erosion more serious. The compensation sought was A\$4 billion, making it the largest single claim in Australian legal history. The company responded with a K100 million compensation package, negotiated with the national and provincial governments, that involved a lump sum payment of K10 million and at least K4 million in every year of mining, to be distributed in a wide area down to the Fly estuary. The government produced controversial bills making it illegal for landowners to pursue subsequent claims against OTML, and outlawing legislation in foreign courts. The tailings dam remained 'under consideration'.

Environmental issues are closely related to economic considerations. At Ok Tedi, especially in the wake of the closure of the Bougainville mine, 'maintaining production and securing monetary earnings and receipts took precedence over measures indispensable for the protection of the environment' (Kreye and Castell 1991:34). More generally it was concluded, at a time of low minerals prices, that 'it is probably not appropriate for Papua New

Guinea and other developing countries to adopt the environmental standards found in Japan, the United States and other developed countries until they are also enjoying the same high standards as these countries enjoy in other areas, such as public health, education and housing' (Tilton *et al.* 1986:47). This perspective has prevailed. Mining companies have consistently pointed out that they have operated within government guidelines; 'the Porgera gold mine operated throughout the year in compliance with all regulatory requirements set by the PNG government' (Placer Pacific 1992:24), yet such regulations have nowhere been demanding or consistently monitored by an independent body. The Department of Minerals and Energy itself concluded that the state had been unable to set up an adequate management system to assess all aspects of development at Ok Tedi, that the adoption of a 'fast-track' approach to development resulted in both significant financial losses and inadequate environmental safeguards and that environmental considerations were either ignored or played a secondary role to income generation (B. Townsend 1988). Nonetheless, when conflicts have arisen, the Department has usually taken the position of the state as shareholder rather than as the advocate for environmental protection.

Contemporary large-scale mining in PNG has had a relatively short history. Its environmental impact will be long term and the effects of some changes, such as the build-up of heavy metal and sediment concentrations at particular sites (marine or riverine), remain in the future. Whilst the environmental damage from mining is highly localised, in most cases it is quite severe. At Ok Tedi however environmental damage is not localised, but spread over a wide area, at least as far as the mouth of the Fly, to influence areas where the benefits of the mine (employment, royalties and business development) are minimal or non-existent. The lower the profitability of mining, the less likelihood there is of environmental safeguards being put in place. Over time the highest grade deposits will have disappeared; other things being equal this will increase the costs of mining. Only lenient environmental restrictions (and political stability) will interest international mining companies in marginal investments. The closure of one mine reduces the probability of environmental constraints at another; after the 1989 decision not to demand a tailings dam at Ok Tedi the minister, Jim Yer Waim, stated: 'The Government is sandwiched simply because of the economic crisis – there was no alternative. Bougainville diminished our ability to protect the environment. In a country like PNG with a big demand for social services and infrastructure, we just can't forgo the harvesting of a resource like Ok Tedi'. Local environmental and social costs have been seen by governments as necessary and therefore acceptable sacrifices in the interests of national development; in the wake of the Bougainville crisis environmental standards became no more stringent. The tasks of protecting the environment and ensuring sustainable development in PNG are considerable, and will increase if minerals prices fall or if growth is over-dependent on that single sector.

EL DORADO OR TIME BOMB?

Despite being a classic enclave economy, employing few people and with few linkages to other sectors, mining is the most important sector in the economy. On its success or failure hinges the future of national development. By the 1990s PNG was the eighth largest gold producer in the world, and a major mining economy in the global scene. Future mineral discoveries may still be considerable. Disputes over the mining of these and existing resources are likely to continue. The mining sector, because of its dependence on TNCs, is unusually dependent on political stability at local and national level, and on world prices. The industry has changed extremely quickly; in just four years between 1988 to 1992 a major goldrush occurred, two mines closed at Panguna and Mt Kare, two opened at Porgera and Misima, gas was produced and piped to Porgera and oil, virtually ignored at the start of the period, was being exported. Several remote areas were opened up, and landowners played a new role in development. In such a changing context the planning and management of the minerals sector, and its influence on other sectors, have been extremely difficult and sometimes beyond the capacity of the national government.

The overseas ownership of the industry has meant that a substantial proportion of the revenue from exports flows out of PNG in the form of profits, purchases of imports (whether mining equipment, food or other goods) or even transport hire. A substantial proportion of expatriate wages and salaries are remitted outside the country; for the Bougainville copper mine, at the start of the 1980s, this proportion was estimated at 45 per cent (O'Faircheallaigh 1984). FIFO commuter mining symbolises the external linkages, but without which only a small alluvial gold-mining industry would exist. The extent of foreign investment in such a profitable sector has increasingly become a source of contention. TNCs have been concerned with generating and exporting profits, with minimal investment in infrastructure or environmental management beyond limited legal obligations. National governments regard mining as the key source of economic growth, whilst provincial governments and landowners have seen particular mines as means of generating local income, employment and infrastructure and redressing uneven development. Different expectations have contributed to discord; this was almost inevitable where people perceived that 'their natural resources were to become national resources' (Hyndman 1991:79). The conflict between the government's several roles, as tax collector, equity shareholder and regulator of the public interest (on environmental, employment and equity matters), ultimately therefore as both trustee and developer, has made financial and legal regulation of the minerals sector difficult. As mining grew in importance the government's enthusiasm for its regulatory role declined. So crucial had the stability of the mining industry become by 1992, and so volatile the situation at some mines, that the government established a special elite Rapid Deployment Unit police force to respond quickly to difficult circumstances at mine sites.

The closures of the Panguna and Mt Kare mines after landowner action, and dissent elsewhere, led to fears of a social 'time-bomb' at mine sites, associated with the capital logic model and increased environmental degradation, and the notion that PNG was a high-risk environment for capital investment. Julius Chan stressed to Lihir islanders in 1986 that they might experience 'a worse time-bomb than Bougainville' (Filer 1990:78). At Bougainville a significant degree of dissatisfaction took more than a decade to surface, and bring the mine to a halt eighteen years after its completion. By contrast the Mt Kare mine closed only four years after the start. At other present and future sites frustrations and tensions will occur, though not necessarily with the devastating impact of those at Bougainville and Mt Kare, as the national government seeks to exert greater control over dissidents at mine sites.

The impact of mining has been vast and rapid, and more disruptive than changes in other sectors of the economy. Indeed one somewhat extreme parallel has been drawn between mining and war. Only mining and war in PNG have stimulated migrations of such magnitude, suddenness and masculinity, and to such isolated places. Both employed the most advanced techniques and technology, miners and soldiers went through complex adaptation to the social and physical environment, war and mining were violent, and the nature and degree of the violence were only partly determined by foreigners (Nelson 1992). In the transformation of particular localities to meet national and international demands, new opportunities, challenges and dilemmas emerged from the consequences of these changes, for peoples whose land had been transformed. While the injection of substantial capital and infrastructural resources into previously neglected areas provided enhanced access to the benefits of national social and economic development, there have been no circumstances where landowners' development goals have been successfully linked to those of the mining corporations. This disjuncture, and the final destiny of the enormous wealth that mining has brought, poses problems for the future of mining, and hence for the future of PNG.

7 Mobile Melanesians?

Population growth and migration

Villagers . . . see children as the most reliable form of income insurance. In contrast to industrial societies where people decrease their reproductive rates in obvious association with their economic goals, the Kilenge see consumption and reproduction as directly connected; having more children protects your ability to consume after you cease to produce children yourself. Since children can help in the gardens and in other activities after they reach the age of 7 or 8, their parents perceive them as a productive asset, rather than the consumptive drain we fear in our societies. . . . Village residents cannot consume such a wide range of imported goods [as urban migrants] and thus see little benefit in family planning.

(Grant 1987:256)

Until very recently there were few demographic data on Papua New Guinea. The first comprehensive national census was not undertaken until 1980 and the only subsequent national census in 1990 was incomplete and inaccurate. Early population data were gathered by census patrols, but there is virtually no information on population change until the 1960s. Fragmentary historical records show that in some places there were population declines in the years after contact, but probably not on the scale that occurred elsewhere in the Pacific. Only in the tiny western islands of Manus was there a virtual extinction of populations (Cilento 1928), but a slow and steady population decline occurred in parts of New Ireland, where malaria and gonorrhoea were the principal causes of the decline (Scragg 1954), and subsequently in some parts of the highlands (Bowers 1971). More recently there were declines in societies contacted only in the 1970s and 1980s (Jenkins 1987). The 'fatal impact' that followed contact has therefore been quite widespread.

The total population is likely to have been more or less stable until well after the Second World War. The war may have resulted in significant population declines in a few coastal and island areas, where there was considerable fighting and blockade conditions. Between 1950 and 1966 administrative control within PNG was rapidly extended. During this period there was some evidence of mortality decline and the start of a phase of population growth that continued in subsequent years, and was increasingly better recorded through censuses and sample surveys. In the 1960s and 1970s the rate of annual population growth increased though it probably never reached much more than 2 per cent. At the end of the decade the population passed the 3 million level. Subsequently the growth rate increased beyond 2 per cent and the 1990 census revealed that the population was well over 3.5 million, with an annual growth rate of around 2.3 per cent. The total probably reached 4 million some time in 1995. PNG has only recently entered into a period of more rapid population growth, and begun the first phases of the demographic and epidemiological transitions. In a country without emigration, the impact of recent and more rapid population growth is becoming apparent.

Almost all the population are Melanesian with a very small number (a couple of thousand) of indigenous Polynesians from the atolls north of Bougainville. A non-indigenous population, only 17,000 in 1990, was mainly of European ethnic origin with the remainder being Chinese, Indian or Filipino. There are enormous cultural variations within PNG and quite substantial physical variations between populations in different parts of the country, and especially between the highlands provinces and the North Solomons. Local and regional ethnic and cultural variations are usually much more important than overall similarities.

POPULATION GROWTH

Though it was generally assumed that the whole population of PNG was enumerated in 1980 and hence that this was the first accurate national census, a small number of remote groups, such as the Hagahai, were excluded. The 1990 census was never undertaken in the North Solomons province, and there were additional problems, as in New Ireland, where cargo cultists refused to be counted. The difficulties of census-taking were further emphasised when enumerators recorded a group of people who had not been contacted by the government for twenty years. The patrol was carried out in the tributaries of the appropriately named Nomad River in Western Province, and counted some 75 people, on one occasion travelling for two days to a hamlet of 19 people (*TPNG* 21 February 1991). No census has yet been wholly complete and, because of problems attached to the analysis of unreliable and incomplete data (McMurray 1985), the value of the population data is sometimes limited.

The total population of PNG grew from just under 2.2 million in 1966 to about 3.76 million in 1990 (Table 7.1). Growth rates varied widely between provinces during 1966–90, principally through migration but also because of variations in the rate of natural increase. Low rates of fertility characterise most of the provinces with low growth rates, especially in the highlands, where education levels are lowest, health services weak and female autonomy limited. Excluding the National Capital District (NCD), the fastest growing provinces have been the coastal provinces of West New Britain and, until the end of the 1980s, the North Solomons, both of which experienced significant

Table 7.1 Population growth rates by province (1966–90)

Province	Population				Annual growth rate (per cent)				Area (sq km)	Population density 1990
	1966	1971	1980	1990	1966–71	1971–80	1980–90			
Western	61,860	70,900	78,575	110,420	2.7	1.1	3.4	99.300	1
Gulf	55,310	58,560	64,120	68,120	1.1	1.0	0.6	34.500	2
Central	146,330	193,840	116,960	141,240	5.3	2.9	1.9	29.500	5
NCD			123,620	195,570			4.6	0.240	815
Milne Bay	100,160	109,460	127,975	158,700	1.8	1.7	2.2	14.000	11
Northern (Oro)	58,575	66,510	77,440	96,240	2.5	1.7	2.2	22.800	4
Southern Highlands	184.100	192,850	236,050	317,180	0.9	2.2	3.0	23.800	13
Enga	291,440	134,590	164,530	235,560		2.2	3.6	12.800	19
Western Highlands		211,460	265,660	333,830	3.4	2.5	2.3	8.500	39
Simbu	167,245	160,245	178,290	186,110	−0.8	1.2	0.4	6.100	30
Eastern Highlands	204,030	239,640	276,730	300,515	3.4	1.6	0.8	11.200	27
Morobe	209,070	249,030	310,620	377,560	3.5	2.4	2.0	34.500	10
Madang	152,050	170,950	211,070	256,370	2.3	2.3	2.0	29.000	9
East Sepik	157,930	181,890	221,890	255,010	2.8	2.2	1.4	42.800	6
West Sepik	99,610	93,980	114,190	140,050	1.2	2.1	2.1	36.300	4
Manus	20,680	24,870	26,040	32,840	3.7	0.5	2.4	2.100	16
New Ireland	50,300	59,540	66,030	87,000	3.4	1.1	2.8	9.600	9
East New Britain	109,930	113,750	133,200	185,020	0.7	1.7	3.3	15.500	12
West New Britain	44,190	61,515	88,940	130,625	6.6	4.0	3.9	21.000	6
North Solomons	72,480	96,360	128,790	155,000	5.7	3.2	1.9	9.300	15
Papua New Guinea	2,184,980	2,489,950	3,010,730	3,762,980	2.6	2.1	2.3	462.850	8

Note: The 1990 census excluded North Solomons Province hence its population and growth rates are estimates
Source: National Statistical Office (1991:9); Hayes (1993b:21)

in-migration and had high rates of natural increase. Between 1980 and 1990 there was also substantial growth in both Enga and Western Provinces, where new mines were established. The more densely populated highland provinces (and districts), especially Simbu, have generally had lower growth rates and out-migration played some part in this. Apart from Central Province, the mainland coastal provinces have also experienced relatively slow growth. Urbanisation has accompanied population growth, reflecting changes in the structure of administration and economic development, though it has been less rapid than in most countries in the Asia-Pacific rim. By 1990 the urban population was over half a million; though PNG remained a predominantly rural nation, there was no longer concern that the rate of urbanisation was inadequate.

Population density varies considerably between regions. More than a third of the population is concentrated in the five highland provinces (Enga, Southern, Western Highlands, Simbu and Eastern) with densities in some localised areas of much more than a hundred people per square kilometre. By contrast the population density of Western Province is barely one person per square kilometre and the overall PNG population density is just eight persons per square kilometre (Table 7.1); few countries in the world, and even fewer less-developed countries, have a lower population density. However high densities in several areas have sometimes contributed to warfare, inadequate nutrition and rural–urban migration, and the carrying capacity of many areas is severely limited by mountains and swamps, and by land tenure constraints. Despite its overall population size and density PNG experiences some of the problems associated with high population densities apparent in the more densely populated Pacific rim nations.

The slowly increasing population growth rate has resulted in a youthful population, with 43 per cent of the population being aged under 15 in 1990, and only 2 per cent over 65, an age structure similar to that of other nearby Melanesian states. In 1966 the overall fertility rate was estimated at 40 and the mortality rate at 18; since then the former has fallen to an estimated 35, although there has been little sign of any decline between 1980 and 1990, while the mortality rate has fallen to around 12. The total fertility rate (TFR), the number of children per woman, has barely changed between 1966 and 1980, declining from about 5.5 in 1966 to about 5.4 in 1990. The highest TFRs, of over 6, occurred in the New Britain provinces (National Statistical Office 1991:11). Rural fertility is higher than urban fertility, probably because of the greater uncertainty of survival in rural areas, though urban populations are less influenced by either traditional practices of child spacing or longer periods of breastfeeding. This is indicative of an early phase of the demographic transition, from high mortality and fertility rates to lower rates, accompanied by a higher rate of population growth.

After the war life expectancy rose from about 32 years for males and 31 years for females in 1944 to an average of 52 for males and 51 for females in 1990. Life expectancies are relatively short, compared with most of the

Asia-Pacific region, and they have scarcely changed since 1970 (when the respective figures were 49 and 51). The average life expectancy of 49.5 (in 1980) varied considerably between provinces; in the West Sepik and the Southern Highlands the respective figures were only 42 and 44, whereas in the North Solomons, Central and New Ireland it was 60, 59 and 58 respectively (Table 9.1). In some isolated areas life expectancies may have still been in the mid-30s until quite recently. Over the period 1966–80 the infant mortality rate (IMR) declined from 150 to 72, a level that was still extremely high in comparison with other countries in the Asia-Pacific rim, but by 1994 it had risen to 83, an extraordinary reversal (*PC* 27 February 1996). Again there were major variations between provinces; in 1980 the Southern Highlands had a rate of 116 and West Sepik had 104, while the North Solomons had a rate of 33 and the NCD had 35 (Bakker 1986; see also Chapter 9). There was a continuing transition from high to low mortality into the 1980s, most apparent in the coastal and urban areas, and attributable to increased standards of living and the extension of preventative and curative medical services. Between 1971 and 1980 rates of infant and child mortality declined in every province. In the more remote and recently contacted areas, distant from primary health care, infant mortality remains extremely high. In the 1980s a rate of 568 was recorded amongst the Hagahai (Madang) (Jenkins 1987); more than half of all children died before the age of one. Amongst the Hagahai, and the similarly remote Bogaia (Southern Highlands), where mortality rates appear to be equally high (Sillitoe 1994: 41–5), population numbers are falling. More generally there was a decline in mortality rates from the 1960s, but in the 1990s at least infant mortality again increased.

The improvement in the IMR since the 1960s led to larger family sizes. For example, in Ongaia village (West New Britain) women who had married in the post-war period had, on average, two more children than women who married before the war, as the duration of their fertile period was longer. Moreover more of the post-war babies survived to maturity, because of improvements in local medical facilities, hygiene and nutrition. The average woman could expect to bear eight children and raise seven to maturity (Grant 1987:247–8), suggesting that TFRs could even be increasing in some places, laying the basis for further more rapid population growth in the future.

There are considerable variations in the rates of population change within PNG and substantial differences in fertility and mortality between regions. In 1990 the fertility rate varied from 28 in the five highlands provinces to 38 in the islands provinces (Manus, New Ireland and New Britain), whilst the mortality rate varied from 13 in both the highlands provinces and the northern provinces (from Morobe to Sepik) to 10.5 in the islands (National Statistical Office 1991:12). Birth rates have risen in many areas as traditional customs and taboos, which tended to space and limit births, have declined and disappeared. Prediction of future rates of change has proved difficult in the past and it is far from clear how the structure of population change in PNG will change in the future, other than that it is likely to grow relatively quickly.

Trends at the start of the 1990s suggested that the population would reach around 4.5 million by the end of the twentieth century, and double in a further thirty years, before stabilising.

FERTILITY CHANGE IN A POLICY VACUUM

Despite problems associated with rapid population growth, national support for family planning is at best ambiguous, as in many other South Pacific countries. To some extent, population policies are regarded as an imposition from outside the country. At the end of the colonial era the National Health Plan had made family planning a 'national health objective', but the limited programme was plagued by an inability to reach most of the relevant population, lack of co-operation with church groups and a suspicion that 'other motives' lay behind the dissemination of contraceptives (Sharpless 1992). A population section within the Office of Environment and Conservation was established in 1978 but terminated in 1981 through lack of support. The government then decided to abolish the token family planning programme at the national level and transfer this function to provincial governments; decentralisation was akin to disappearance.

Indicative of national interest in developing a population policy was the Prime Minister, Michael Somare's, message to the 1984 International Conference on Population:

> Papua New Guinea shares many population features of other developing nations despite our potential material resources. Our prime concern is ensuring better health for our people especially mothers and children in interior rural areas. The primary health care approach we have adopted calls for opportunity for all couples to consciously choose the number and spacing of their progeny. Any let up now when the past trends of population growth are slowly changing in the right direction could be calamitous.
>
> (Somare, in UNFPA 1984:112)

There has been no evidence of any change 'in the right direction'. Prominent national politicians and religious leaders were much more likely to advocate population growth. When a tentative movement towards family planning was hinted at, the former Governor-General, Sir John Guise, wrote

> The policy impinges on the basic individual rights of freedom of choice by every married couple. We should not be in a hurry to imitate rich developed nations who may no doubt find themselves outnumbered in their own country in the not too distant future. One can only trust that this national policy of regulated family planning will not be a barrier to the further increase of the nation's ethnic and Melanesian population. We need to grow from 3.3 million to over 20 million or more in order to occupy our vast area of uninhabited land. We are neighbours with a nation which has a population of over 160 million people and still rising yet we have the

audacity to adopt a policy of deliberate enforced and regulated family planning on our side of the border. We need to remember the calls made by a well known leader to his underpopulated nation, a call which equally applies in this troubled day and age to Papua New Guinea. 'You populate or you PERISH'.

(*TPNG* 26 March 1987)

It is this advocacy that is generally accepted, and there is still enormous consensus behind these sentiments, rather than demands for limitation.

Mildly expressed external concerns on the lack of a population policy were not therefore shared within PNG until the late 1980s, when the economic situation was worsening, urban growth and urban crime increasing and settlement schemes had largely failed to eventuate. Rural–urban migration, increasing pressure on both rural land and urban services, rising youth unemployment and high levels of maternal mortality (as high as six per thousand births in some areas at the end of the 1990s) produced a more favourable climate for establishing a population policy (McMurray 1992:13). At the same time there was increasing external pressure on PNG to develop a population policy and even a suggestion that some forms of aid would be jeopardised by the failure to do so (Hayes 1993b:11–13). In June 1991 PNG launched a National Population Policy, which stressed that

high population growth is a deterrent to the attainment of an improved standard of living and quality of life of the people. . . . A high rate of population growth reduces health status through resource depletion and deterioration of the environment, increases pressure on land, water, food, housing, education services, jobs and so on.

(PNG 1991: 12–13)

The government gained assistance from the Asian Development Bank, the World Bank and AIDAB (Australian International Development Assistance Bureau) to design a population and planning project that would enable the government to implement the policy and attain its objectives. These included increasing contraceptive prevalence to 63 per cent by 2000, from its estimated level of 6 per cent at the start of the 1990s: a 'wildly unrealistic goal' (Hayes 1993b:44). An equally ambitious target involved reducing the TFR from more than 5.0 per woman to 3.2 by the end of the century. A number of goals are valuable, including improvements in the status of women, universal completion of primary education (also by the end of the century), and reduction of infant and child mortality. However the factors that are most conducive to successful population policies – integration of population and development policies, improved rural development and communications to spread new values, the reduced economic significance of children, formal sector employment opportunities for women, the rising educational status of women, female autonomy and increasing age of marriage (Ahlburg 1992; Hayes 1993b) – are largely absent. The new policy remained 'top-down, centralised, elitist, technocratic and bureaucratic in spirit . . . long on abstract principles, but short on programme details' (Hayes 1993b:15, 32), hence successful implementation is difficult.

As in other neighbouring Melanesian states there is relatively little acceptance and utilisation of modern family planning techniques, though the use of traditional forms of population control, including infanticide, abortion, use of medicinal plants as contraception and, above all, sanctions on postpartum intercourse and too close child spacing, were widespread (e.g. Bulmer 1971; Connell 1978; McDowell 1988; O'Collins 1980). Whilst traditional controls on population growth have weakened, new family planning techniques have scarcely begun to intervene. Modern contraceptives were introduced in a pilot study in 1962, after requests from women in Port Moresby, but by the start of the 1990s, less than 5 per cent of women aged between 15 and 49 were using contraceptive techniques, and use of male methods was less than 1 per cent (McMurray 1992). Most users are in urban areas. The low rate has several causes. The status of both men and women is partly influenced by the number of children they produce. Although there is a preference for sons, daughters have considerable economic value, especially in rural areas, and children remain of social and economic support for parents in their old age. Men typically want more children than women, who prefer fewer children because of the work, mortality and morbidity associated with raising many children (Callan and Wilks 1984), whilst men oppose contraception where they perceive it to be a licence for promiscuity (McDowell 1988). In several rural areas villagers with few or no children may find themselves in need at some point (Grant 1987:256). Control of both migration and population growth also has a conscious material rationality, with ideology equating an economic return (remittances) with an economic investment (child-rearing for migration): 'Ponam is not a society passively allowing or suffering the migration of its members. . . . [Ponams claim that] children are our garden and we survive by eating the fruit' (Carrier 1984:49). Over time, lengthy birth intervals have significantly declined (Connell 1978), primarily as social pressures have weakened; 'many of the controls on sexual activity have gone, and thus many of the ideological justifications for such controls are no longer relevant or part of the instruction received by young males' (Read 1986:224; cf. Hayes 1993a; A.J. Strathern 1989:146). As social taboos weaken, nuclear families have increasingly become the norm and, where access to health care systems improves (cf. Chapter 9), there is still potential for fertility to increase.

In many areas, especially in the island provinces, high population growth, and therefore increased population pressure on resources, have long been recorded. In the case of the Tolai, landlessness grew substantially in the quarter of a century after 1960 (A.L. Epstein 1988:35). By contrast, in Simbu, where growth rates were lower, 'it is only because the Chimbu have already sought their own solution to the problem by migrating to other areas that the pressure on existing areas is tolerable' (Howlett *et al.* 1976:40). Elsewhere in the highlands, 'migration out of Enga would appear to be the only limiting factor to further population growth' (Lea and Gray 1982:52; cf. Standish 1981:294). Both indigenous and non-indigenous attitudes to population growth are thus viewed in terms of migration, rather than direct controls on population growth.

INTERNATIONAL MIGRATION

There has been significant overseas migration to PNG, mainly of Europeans and, more recently, of Asians to take up contract employment. In the German colonial era Malays, Chinese and Javanese were briefly introduced from the Dutch East Indies and Singapore. A thin trickle of Chinese migrants continued after the war but the present Chinese population is mainly descended from long-established migrants. The role of the Chinese in commerce has been paramount and even small towns such as Wau had a little Chinatown. By the time of independence most Chinese had become Australian citizens and concern over their economic future prompted considerable emigration to Australia.

In most conventional senses, PNG was not a settler colony, but there was, for most of the twentieth century, a flow of intendedly permanent settlers, mainly from Australia. This was especially so in the immediate post-war years when special provision was made for the settlement of ex-servicemen: the last colony in the world where settlement was still encouraged. However in the years around independence and afterwards, many long-term settlers left. Localisation further reduced the amount of expatriate labour employed within PNG from 30,000 at the time of the 1971 census to around 9,000 at the start of 1982 (Kekedo 1983:12) resulting from increased numbers of graduates from secondary and tertiary education institutions and the closure of some commercial ventures. Since then decline has proceeded more slowly.

As the European population declined, the number of Asians increased, resulting in various objections to Asian, and especially Filipino, migrant workers, mainly that members of their families take up other jobs and that they engage in other commercial activities beyond those related to their employment. Even in government circles this migration was referred to as the 'Asian invasion' and the 'tip of the iceberg' (Lifu and Nakikus 1982). There have been recent Melanesian migrants to PNG, including perhaps as many as 10,000 from neighbouring Irian Jaya, most of whom were refugees from Indonesian military activity, but with traditional ties across an extremely artificial border. At the other end of the country, there was some migration of Solomon Islanders across another artificial border both to seek employment in the Panguna copper mine and to maintain traditional ties with kin in south Bougainville. Nevertheless, the number of migrants has remained few, mostly concentrated in a small number of urban areas, and PNG remains undeniably, and increasingly, a Melanesian state.

Just as immigration is minimal, so Melanesian emigration – other than some illegal migrants across the Torres Strait – is conspicuous by its absence, even though at the end of the nineteenth century there was some labour migration from the New Guinea islands to the plantations of Samoa and Fiji, and even as far as Tanganyika. PNG is largely uninfluenced by international migration.

INTERNAL MIGRATION

The basic pattern of migration has not fundamentally changed since the 1960s when a national pattern was first apparent: a centrifugal movement from the densely populated centre towards the coastal towns of the mainland, especially Port Moresby and Lae, and to a lesser extent towards areas of resource development. A steady movement away from areas of restricted economic opportunities, especially in the west of the country, whether coastal or highland, has concentrated migration destinations in a number of more favoured provinces. Much migration remains temporary or circular, a situation particularly true of plantation labour migration, though that era has largely gone. Economic factors, specifically the perceived gap between urban and rural incomes, are the most important determinant of population migration. In a growing number of areas, principally in the highlands and the thinly populated Gulf and Central Provinces, population pressure on resources is such that since the 1970s there has been a 'demographic push' on migration (Connell 1985a:81–2). Problems of access to land limit the possibility of resettlement hence migration flows are increasingly towards the towns. Migration is steadily becoming a long-term phenomenon, emphasising the more permanent urbanisation of the population (Connell 1985a; Connell and Lea 1993), and the problems of rural development.

By the start of the twentieth century there were demands on labour primarily for plantation labour, but also for domestic service and administration employment, for example in the police force and as mine labour. With the exception of the police force, where some jobs were held for relatively long periods, almost all employment in the inter-war years was on plantations and for periods of less than three years. Because plantations required cheap labour power to generate profits indentured labour was recruited in conditions once described by Sir Hubert Murray as being 'really rather like slavery' (Fitzpatrick 1978). By the 1950s it was becoming difficult to obtain highlands labour, because of the problems of adjustment to the coastal environment itself, the arduous, boring work, the lack of income and prestige gained by later migrants and the introduction and establishment of cash cropping (May and Skeldon 1977:6). At the end of the 1960s the main sources of contract plantation labour were the Southern Highlands, remote districts of other highlands provinces and West Sepik. Apart from a few remote areas, of recent contact, the labour frontier had been pushed back almost as far as it could go. Labour had to be contracted from the most inaccessible parts of the country, such as Wovan (Madang) where migration to plantations did not begin until 1975 (Flanagan 1981). Elsewhere Papua New Guineans preferred to carry out cash cropping on their own land, where this was feasible, and engage in business activities, or to participate in independent migration, unconstrained by indenture.

As migration to plantations declined, other kinds of migration increased in significance. The growth of towns in the 1970s, and the new mining industry, created new demand. In both contexts wages were invariably higher and, especially in towns, social conditions were often regarded as superior to those in villages and plantations. Job opportunities were no longer confined to unskilled and semi-skilled activities, hence considerable differentials emerged in wages and conditions. By the mid-1960s there were more permanent migration movements, especially from some of the poorer districts of the Papuan coast to Port Moresby. Despite more permanent migration, migrants remained closely associated with their home societies. Migrant workers, restricted by linguistic ability, skills and wage levels, were only exceptionally able to gain more than tenuous participation in the urban market economy hence their earnings were remitted to, or invested in, their home areas. Even when urban migration became more usual, those who migrated to towns continued to engage in a rural-oriented strategy of urban migration because they wished to participate in rural development by expanding their own cash-crop smallholdings (Salisbury and Salisbury 1972) or establishing trade stores and building modern houses (Polier 1996). By the 1970s urban migration had superseded migration to plantations, and new welfare provisions, including housing, enabled migrants to remain in town and also invest there.

There has been a growing centralisation of population, as people in remote island, upland and interior areas have migrated for better access to administration services and land for cash cropping. In the early colonial era these moves were encouraged, or ordered, by the administration or missions; increasingly they have been voluntary. In the highlands movement down from mountainsides was stimulated by access to markets and employment and, because at high altitudes, particularly above the coffee line, income earning opportunities were few (A.J. Strathern 1982:146). A parallel trend is the movement away from small islands, and especially the reefs and atolls of Milne Bay and the North Solomons. The spatial structure of migration has never really changed since independence, but there has been an increase in migration from the highlands provinces; by 1980, out-migrants from the five highlands provinces represented 34 per cent of all out-migrants. Almost a tenth of the population were living in a province away from their birthplace, as migration increased in volume, distance and permanence. Seven provinces had an overall gain of migrants: National Capital District, Western Highlands, Morobe, New Ireland, East New Britain, West New Britain and North Solomons (Walsh 1985). Migration destinations have become increasingly concentrated in a number of more favoured provinces. These trends continued through the 1980s and early 1990s, only diversified by the movement to new mine sites. With the exception of the growth of urban centres, migration has had little impact on national population distribution.

THE RATIONALE OF MIGRATION

The centrality of economics in explaining migration has long been apparent (May and Skeldon 1977:19). Migration is often perceived as a means of obtaining income (and sometimes skills) that will be useful in rural areas. In many areas migration has been seen not so much as a movement away, but more as a means of diversifying village incomes (and to some extent increasing insurance and diversifying risks) or sometimes simply as a means of obtaining a particular 'target' income for a specific end, which was usually the historic situation on plantations. In reality many migrants remain for a long time in urban areas without accumulating savings, or return with very little, so that the rationale does not always explain the reality (Connell 1985a, 1988a). At a regional level there are obvious economic variations in migration streams. The rate of migration in the late 1960s from the highlands, and especially from Simbu, was about three or four times faster than that from the mainland coastal areas (Garnaut 1977:83) and particularly the islands region, where rural incomes were high.

Population pressure on resources is generally higher in the highlands, especially in Simbu, where economic opportunities are more limited, hence the greatest areas of 'demographic push' are there. However, there are other places where local income-earning opportunities are extremely limited, either because of very poor land resources (much of Gulf and Central Provinces), extreme remoteness or localised land pressure. Migration has been more pronounced and most long established, generating more apparently permanent urban residents, from the sago-dependent areas of Sepik, Gulf and Western provinces, where subsistence is difficult and alternative sources of income almost non-existent (May and Skeldon 1977:15). These relationships are not straightforward but depend on land quality, alternative sources of income and the type and extent of cash cropping.

Social factors influence migration movements. Migrants may move away from home areas to obtain enough money for brideprice payments or for the staging of other ceremonies. Social tensions and dislike of the constraints of traditional society stimulate migration, which may also be a 'rite of passage' between adolescence and manhood, comparable to earlier initiation ceremonies and thus a means of obtaining status and prestige (e.g. Lewis 1980:213–14; Schiltz and Josephides 1981:138). In some areas of the highlands movement away was traditionally regarded as an 'escape from women', involving both long hunting trips and the seclusion of initiates, and labour migration has become a modern expression of this (e.g. Clark 1993; Gillison 1980:146; P.L. Johnson 1990). Some social factors have tended to become more important over time, as family ties have strengthened in urban areas hence children may be adopted there, and marriages between members of different language groups also stimulate migration (Connell 1988a; Hayes 1993a:167; Morauta 1981:214). The presence of relatives in urban areas provides not only an incentive to rural–urban migration but a means of initially obtaining accommodation and access to employment opportunities. Without kin support, migration would be difficult if not impossible.

Education and migration are closely related, because of migration to superior education facilities elsewhere and because of the migration of those with better education. Moreover, especially in remote areas, 'for most high school students, secondary education implies a complete break with village life and returning to the district implies failure. And indeed most of those who did return to their district did so only because they could not find work elsewhere' (Jackson *et al.* 1980:205): an ideology of return may take time to acquire. Migrants are increasingly more likely to be better educated than the average in their own societies, whilst access to skilled employment is increasingly likely to be determined by educational achievements. Access to education was much earlier in coastal regions, continues to be better there and has contributed to the relative success of those from coastal and island areas in higher status urban employment.

As the national economy has become more complex and diversified so migration has increased in complexity, with an increasing degree of segmentation in the workforce – one educated and urban, migrating between villages and towns, and the other rural, making occasional visits to town (Ward 1980:130). Education has altered the employment aspirations and chances of people. Where local income-earning opportunities are few, as in Manus, the demand for education as a means to migration has been very great (Carrier 1981). Demand for education is partly a function of income opportunities. The acquisition of education and hence formal-sector employment, and/or cash crops have enabled some groups to withdraw from the unskilled labour market. Initially these groups were almost entirely coastal, such as the Yega of Oro (Dakeyne 1967), and the Siwai of Bougainville (Connell 1985b), but the subsequent expansion of coffee production into the highlands enabled many highlanders to withdraw from the migrant labour system.

In a growing number of areas it is apparent not only that economic factors are increasingly influential, but also that the 'push' factors are often overwhelming. Thus amongst the remote Ilakia Awa (Eastern Highlands), 'the underlying force which compels members of this village to seek employment outside the village is financial necessity' (Boyd 1981:75) and, further west in the highlands, the 'lack of work opportunities in Enga will continue to "force" many people to leave the province and seek work in other provinces' (Lea and Gray 1982:54). In such areas remittances are crucial; in the case of migration from Kukipi (Gulf), urban Kukipis are 'sending home part of the means of subsistence. . . . This is quite a different pressure on urban incomes from one where gifts to people at home are luxuries and the timing of them more or less immaterial to the recipients' (Morauta and Hasu 1979:31). While definitions of 'necessity' vary, and migration is related to relative and not absolute deprivation, pressures towards rural–urban migration have tended to increase in many parts of the country.

SETTLEMENT SCHEMES

No countries in the South Pacific region have had greater experience with settlement schemes, though this experience pales in comparison with that of Asia. A variety of land settlement schemes have been established for different reasons, including increased agricultural production (on unused land) and the relief of population pressure (for example on Bougainville atolls). At the end of the 1950s the colonial administration began to take an interest in the concept of settlement schemes as a means of promoting the individualisation of land tenure and more large-scale economic development (Hulme 1982). At the same time large blocks were allocated to European ex-servicemen in some coastal areas (Howlett 1965; Ploeg 1971). Rather later, in the early 1960s, new large-scale schemes were established for the production of cocoa (primarily in East New Britain and Oro Provinces) and rubber (in Gulf and Central). A small number of schemes in East Sepik and Central provinces were initiated for people regarded as land-short. Almost all these were small-scale schemes in terms of area, settlers and cost, with little infrastructure and minimal planning. Settlers usually earned low incomes, often on land of poor productivity with limited assistance in terms of capital, infrastructure and extension advice, in situations where unfamiliar crops, such as rubber, demanded high inputs of labour. Many soon abandoned their blocks.

The largest group of settlement schemes were those associated with the cultivation of oil palm, introduced to PNG in the 1960s. These schemes were larger, more carefully planned and controlled and marked 'a quantum leap' in the administration's approach to land settlement. The first nucleus estate and associated smallholder oil palm schemes began in 1967 near Hoskins (West New Britain) as a joint venture between the government and a British company. The administration considered that the scheme was a success and consequently established a second oil palm settlement scheme at Bialla (West New Britain), and a third at Higaturu (Oro) (Hulme 1982). These three large-scale schemes were the only significant settlement schemes to be consolidated and established in the 1970s. By the 1980s the phase of settlement schemes was over.

The low cost schemes have had a limited impact on population distribution. The Wosera scheme (East Sepik) resulted in the resettlement of only forty-four families in five years and others were even less successful and just as costly (Hulme 1982). In the period between 1966 and 1971, in terms of population redistribution, the schemes 'catered for about three months' increase in population at current rates of growth' (Ward 1971:97). The high cost oil palm schemes have been most successful in achieving apparently permanent resettlement; at Hoskins priority was initially given to settlers from more densely populated areas of East New Britain, Simbu and East Sepik. The more successful settlers have been from the most distant provinces, especially the Sepik provinces and Simbu, which are relatively impoverished, where the prospects for return migration were poor and hence the incentive to succeed was greater. In terms of agricultural production both the low and medium-cost schemes had limited results. Schemes like those at Wosera and Gavien made some contribution to improving food production, although at Gavien health and nutrition problems persisted (Cox 1979:32), but did not significantly contribute to increased cash crop production. The oil palm schemes (where resettlement costs were K5,000 or more per settler family) were rather more successful. However even there migration was not without social problems, and there was invariably conflict between settlers and existing residents.

The crucial issue affecting all settlement schemes in PNG has been land and the lack of available land, rather than concern over the impact and value of settlement schemes, has prevented the development of any schemes since the 1970s. It has been virtually impossible for the government to buy or lease land for resettlement schemes and at Popondetta, for example, villagers long held a claim against the government for K1 million compensation for land on which the oil palm scheme was located (Hulme 1982). Elsewhere land is simply not made available by the traditional owners (in part because of concern over the resettlement of migrants from other cultural areas), even for movement within provinces. Not only are there tenure problems, but any land that is suitable for settlement schemes, in terrain and accessibility, and not otherwise used, is very rare. Further schemes are extremely unlikely as there is little prospect of them becoming more socially acceptable, despite some economic success. Jackson has concluded that 'in many ways, the highlands of Papua New Guinea are that country's Java' but population redistribution 'seems to be so weighed down with political animosity that it must be, for the movement, ruled out as a practical policy' (1982b:52). Settlement schemes are no longer political options for social and economic development.

THE IMPACT OF POPULATION MIGRATION IN RURAL AREAS

The impact of migration is dependent on its structure and is difficult to disentangle from other concurrent trends, especially population increase and socio-economic change. There is still a sex bias in migration in favour of males. Work conditions and wages in urban areas tend to favour single males rather than females or families. Migrants are usually young adults, many in their late teens and twenties, and the overwhelming majority between 15 and 34. For some people migration is intentionally over by the age of 35, before it is too late to return and make some mark on village society (Heaney 1989). Migrants have higher educational qualifications than those who have remained in the provinces where they were born. Migration to some extent has spread the distribution of educational abilities, with more highly educated people moving to the highlands and less educated people moving in the opposite direction, although any equalising impact of this is restricted by the concentration of more educated migrants in urban areas (Skeldon

1979:96–9). The increased difficulty of obtaining urban employment has biased the labour market towards those with education and skills. Consequently migration from villages increasingly represents a loss of skills and expertise, a 'brain drain' of the most highly educated and dynamic members (Morauta and Ryan 1982; Weinand and Ward 1979). As migrants have increasingly held on to scarce urban jobs, this loss has become more apparent.

The ubiquity of the education bias, despite the relatively short history of formal education in parts of the country, suggests that it is likely to continue while the 'diploma disease' simultaneously worsens (White 1990). However in some contexts the rewards to education have been disappointing; attitudes to it are ambivalent, in view of both the limited rewards that may accrue, especially to those other than the educated, and the manner in which it distances children from parents and from society. In West New Britain 'a classic love–hate relationship wrenches the fabric of village social order; . . . although the school may facilitate the gradual process of modernisation, it does so at considerable cost in individual frustration and social discontent' (Zelenietz and Grant 1986:47–8; cf. Carrier 1984: 50). Nevertheless the upward social and economic mobility gained by many migrants is rarely discouraged. Success in an alien world is highly prized by migrants and kin alike. Amongst the relatively recently contacted Baruya (Eastern Highlands), there is 'a new kind of "big man", those with new skills in prestigious employment outside, who are gradually becoming folk heroes . . . Prestige now goes to the young men who like the *aoulatta* [great warriors] before them have conquered in the outside world' (Godelier 1986:205–18). Though many older values and practices remain vibrant, villagers are usually proud of those who have gained tangible rewards from migration.

Obtaining cash incomes is the most generally offered explanation of migration (Clunies-Ross 1984; G.T. Harris 1985), but limited savings are usually made by migrants. A common metaphor is that wages are 'eaten' in town, being spent on a variety of small trade store goods or other forms of expenditure, such as gambling and alcohol consumption. In parts of the highlands migrants often returned empty-handed having lost their earnings in card games or given them away (Zimmer 1990a). Only in exceptional cases, as on Ponam island, have remittances significantly improved economic and social life (Carrier and Carrier 1989:168). Few remittances have been invested in economic growth, since in many areas a history of failed projects has discouraged new investment, marketing facilities are poor and the more educated and highly skilled have moved away (A. Turner 1984:143). Though there is a transition in remittance use from consumption towards economic development (Boyd 1990; Hayes 1993a), few investment opportunities and the limited skills of many return migrants have reduced the significance of this transition.

The absence of predominantly male migrants has had an impact on the division of labour throughout PNG and has therefore influenced the status and prestige of women. Women have accumulated additional agricultural tasks; increased pressure on women's time is particularly apparent in areas where there has been group migration on long contracts to distant plantations (Boyd 1981, 1984; Young 1983) resulting in both women and big-men opposing extensive out-migration (Hayano 1979; M. Strathern 1972). In Imbonggu (Southern Highlands) there was minimal opportunity cost to the migration of young men since they did little other than gather firewood and some communal work (Wormsley 1978:313) so that, in these circumstances, the absence of men reduced the labour required from women. In other parts of the country, where male labour inputs were greater, their migration imposed an extra burden on women and children who remained at home (e.g. Maclean 1981). Where the extra work undertaken by women included the harvesting of cash crops this has however given women some control of financial resources, and ultimately increased their prestige as independent entrepreneurs (e.g. Schiltz and Josephides 1981:140). In at least one case, in the Eastern Highlands, the increased responsibilities and thus perhaps the status of women, have resulted in a significant decline in what was previously an unusually high suicide rate (P.L. Johnson 1981). However the complexities of migration and of PNG are such that the variations in the extent to which women gain enhanced status and prestige, if they have extra control of land and other resources, or lose power and authority and gain in workload (Connell 1984b) are very considerable.

Migration has not only contributed to the increasing availability of cash in rural areas but also led to the introduction of a variety of 'modern' values, in the use of that money, in economic and political organisation and also in social organisation. It has contributed to greater individualism in terms of the declining significance of wider social groups (clans, etc.), extended families and even nuclear households. A greater emphasis on material possessions has transformed social relationships; in a village only recently having experienced labour migration, returnees felt exploited by those who remained in the village and older people felt neglected and abused by their children (Boyd 1990). Societies and cultures have become more homogeneous and more internationalised (Chapter 9), though there are also cases where the absence of migrants, who are predominantly young men, has enabled traditional societies to escape their influence on modernisation and retain traditional values (Josephides and Schiltz 1982:79; M.F. Smith 1982:286–7) but this may be only a temporary respite. However crude contrasts between 'tradition' and 'modernity', and between disengagement and incorporation, point to the manner in which migration simultaneously acts as a force of conservation and dissolution: 'it preserves, while at the same time amputating, the principles which used to underpin the thought and workings of a society in order to withstand the march of history' (Godelier 1986:206; cf. Polier 1996). Mobility itself has not necessarily disrupted the historic social order. Remittances maintain social ties and act as insurance premiums for migrants, fuelling an ideology of return; their use strengthens traditional values and, since migration emerges out of inequality, this tends to reinforce, as much as conflict with, the social hierarchy (Zimmer 1990a). Remittances both conserve societies through emphasising historic structures of land tenure and dissolve social economies by stimulating economic change and the transformation in tastes.

Return migration is normal. At the village level few migrants are seen as permanently outside rural society and in urban areas most migrants intend to return, to participate in rural economic, social and political activities, where, for most, the only real status, security and wealth are to be obtained (cf. Howlett *et al.* 1976:56–59). Though intentions do not always become practice, there are relatively few permanent urban residents (Chapter 8). In many places the situation is much like that of the remote Miyanmin who 'expect [every] member of the community to return. And this is because they believe that their society offers such immense satisfaction and comfort that it could not be otherwise' (Morren 1986:305). Attitudes in opposition to urban life are perhaps more strongly held in PNG than anywhere else in the Pacific rim. In areas that are closer to town or with relatively poor resource bases, such as substantial parts of Western, Gulf and Central Provinces, and for some highly educated individuals, migration is more likely to be permanent, but most have vested interests in retaining their village connections, even when their urban jobs are secure. Although migration may remain transient, and its significance for changing the national population geography is still slight, its impact has been considerable in social, economic and political terms.

TOWARDS THE CITY?

The population geography of PNG remains highly uneven, primarily in terms of population densities, but also in mortality and fertility. As the country enters into the demographic transition, population growth rates, that at a national level have hovered above 2 per cent per year since independence, are probably increasing slightly. Even this rate of population growth was in excess of the rate of economic growth for much of the 1970s and 1980s. Fertility may continue to increase, especially in the highlands, and mortality decline. In response to growing population numbers, substantial concern over rural–urban migration and localised pressure on land resources, PNG adopted an official population policy in 1991. To translate this into an effective programme has proved difficult, because of objections to population policies, management inefficiencies and the continuation of preferences for large family sizes. As population increases, commodity prices stay low and the plantation economy remains stagnant, migration to cities – and to mines – becomes a more attractive proposition.

Migration is of particular significance in the more remote districts where there are few local income-earning options. Even so opportunities for unskilled migrants with very limited education have declined whilst the returns are often meagre. Nevertheless migration and education provide a dual strategy for increasing incomes, especially in relatively remote islands (Carrier 1984; Hayes 1993a), where education has been keenly sought out. An economic rationale transcends yet incorporates many social reasons. Major influences on migration have been radical changes in expectations over what constitutes a satisfactory standard of living, a desirable occupation and a suitable mix of accessible services and amenities. Aspirations are now almost always likely to involve some imported food and other goods (clothes, vehicles, oil, etc.) and access to schools, hospitals and, sometimes, modern entertainment, all of which demand some cash income. For many Melanesians, 'the ideal life-style to be sought after is that of their leaders – urban, materialist, consumer-oriented' (Bedford 1980:63). Agricultural work throughout the country has lost prestige and the relatively limited and declining participation of young men in the agricultural economy is ubiquitous. Migration has thus become accepted, a chain reaction as much as a chain migration, and a response to changes in the national and local socio-economic system. It has taken a spatial form, dependent on the penetration of capitalist forms of production, and a social form, since the existence of previous migrants in the destination is critical to the probability and viability of migration.

Despite the ideology of return, migration has tended to become more permanent. Even with poor social and economic conditions in the cities, rising unemployment, crime and sometimes violent unrest, migration is perceived to be a means of escaping limited domestic economic opportunities and of diversifying or transferring human resources into more productive areas. Although virtually the only jobs for uneducated, unskilled migrants are poorly paid, demand for work is substantial (Boyd 1990; Zimmer 1990a). The educational filter, that limited access to skilled and better-paid jobs, has also served to differentiate migration streams and stratify the social and economic structure of the cities. Tolai migrants, especially those from Matupit Island (East New Britain), who are relatively highly educated, and who come from the first part of the country to be engaged in the modern capitalist economy, have been able to gain access to many prestigious and salaried positions, to the extent that work has become a career and, within Port Moresby at least, 'in their life-style they were plainly stamped as members of the new urban elite' (A.L. Epstein 1988:33). Others have been much less successful and new inequalities have emerged. Migration has worsened rural–urban inequalities, themselves often emphasised by 'urban bias' in government policy. Increased material rewards, which may be transient, cannot be balanced against the disruption of traditional production and exchange relations (even with their often implicit inequalities) and the emergence of new forms of differentiation, characteristic of the various transitions to capitalist production. In the highland fringes of Wovan, inflated brideprices have made young women more inaccessible to men; in the absence of cash crops, Wovan men must remain away for increasingly longer times to earn adequate brideprice payments though, whilst men are away, women are encouraged to marry outside Wovan society. The migration pattern there has become 'a vicious circle which becomes increasingly difficult to break' (Flanagan 1983:46). The Wovan may earn little but their distant earnings are better than anything possible at home. For most Papua New Guineans however the situation is somewhat more positive; migration has increased options, expanded social worlds, enabled the purchase of a range of new goods and exceptionally led to successful careers. Slowly, and not very surely, population growth and migration have contributed to a more urban future for PNG.

8 Urbanisation, urban life and the urban economy

Do we really want to become a country of big cities? In all the 700 languages of our country we have never needed words for air pollution, for slum or for unemployment. Do we wish to build the kind of country that needs these words?

(Somare 1973:2)

The most distinctive characteristic of urbanisation in PNG is its recency. There is no evidence of urban development in pre-colonial times, despite extensive trading networks, including the famous kula ring of the Trobriand islands and the 'Stone Age trade' of the New Guinea highlands (Hughes 1977). There were no significant functional specialisations beyond village level, nor were there traditional state structures, but a proliferation of tenuously linked small-scale societies. Until the 1930s the few towns were tiny coastal trading and administrative centres; this emphasised their colonial origins, and the dominance of external ties, as they were poorly integrated into nearby regions. Port Moresby, located because of its ease of access to Australia, but otherwise with access only to a tiny part of Papua, epitomised this situation.

In the colonial era the most rudimentary, unskilled employment was generally available to Melanesians, who were actively discouraged from becoming urban residents. Bachelor wages, the provision of single men's quarters, compulsory repatriation after a maximum period of employment, restriction of occupational mobility and the denial of political rights, including the rights to organise and strike, made it necessary for the worker and his family to maintain a long-term dependence on the rural village economy. These sets of regulations controlling the employment and mobility of wage labour, against the background of a colonial society based on a colour bar, profoundly affected the conditions under which the indigenous urban workforce was employed and accommodated. The urban male to female sex ratios, even towards the end of colonial rule, reflected this. In Port Moresby in 1966 the ratio was 185 males per 100 females, an imbalance that changed only after independence and which was replicated in the smaller towns. Low bachelor wages were paid to all but a few public servants until 1972, as the few unions, formed under tight government control, were ineffective. This encouraged a high turnover of the unskilled urban labour force (Connell and Curtain 1982). Until after independence the towns were places of uncertainty and insecurity for most Melanesians.

The beach communities of the nineteenth century and the administrative centres of the first half of the twentieth century were expatriate creations and expatriate centres. They were white men's (and sometimes white women's) towns. Papua was very much a northwards extension of Australia. At its extreme, Samarai in Milne Bay was a by-product of the decline of the Queensland mining town, Cooktown, houses being literally transplanted from one town to the other (Nelson 1976). The towns were small-scale and peripheral colonial endeavours at the ends of empire: seedy and dusty outliers of a largely uninterested colonial power that was itself a series of colonies when urbanisation began. Nevertheless towns were 'administered by expatriate models. Public health, public order and the maintenance of so-called "standards" required, it was thought, an element of insulation from the indigenous population' (Ward 1973:366–7). Different measures were devised by the colonial authorities to ensure the continuity of 'urban apartheid' (Griffin *et al.* 1979:55), a division that was much more rigid than the more casual race relations of rural areas, and emphasised the European city in opposition to the Melanesian village, where migrants were officially recorded as 'absentees': 'the towns were toeholds of an alien society at the same time as they were bases for alien control' (Brookfield with Hart 1971:390). Distinctiveness was regulated; assimilation, sexual relations and marriage between different groups discouraged, and multiculturalism wholly implausible. Colonial towns, whilst simultaneously offering some forms of economic and social development, established and regularised an ordered and largely intransigent inequality.

THE RECENCY OF URBANISATION

Urbanisation has been such a recent development that studies of urbanisation conducted a few years before independence stressed the necessity for towns to grow as centres of economic development and social change. Before the war only two or three places could be regarded as urban, and these were little more than administrative centres; Port Moresby, in the inter-war period, was still 'a small sleepy colonial backwater functioning mainly as an administrative centre' (Oram 1976:51). Rabaul was a more substantial town until the 1930s. In the post-war years, new government activity, employment and spending contributed to economic growth and thus urban development, whilst restrictions on the movement of Melanesians into town gradually disappeared. Even with a generous definition of urban centre there was still an urban population of barely a hundred thousand in 1966 (Brookfield with Hart 1971). At the time of the 1971 census only three towns (Port Moresby, Lae and Rabaul) had populations of over twenty thousand. Two decades

Table 8.1 Urban centres (1971–90)

	1971	*1980*	*1990*
Port Moresby (NCD)	76,507	123,624	194,295
Lae	38,707	61,617	80,655
Madang	16,865	21,335	27,057
Wewak	15,015	19,890	23,224
Mt Hagen	10,621	13,441	18,977
Goroka	12,065	18,511	18,368
Rabaul	26,619	14,954	18,186
Daru	5,744	7,127	8,490
Kimbe	1,172	4,662	8,363
Vanimo	1,877	3,071	7,908
Popondetta	4,494	6,429	7,627
Bulolo	4,001	6,730	7,421
Kavieng	3,301	4,633	6,486
Alotau	2,499	4,311	6,435
Mendi	2,493	4,130	6,192
Lorengau	4,323	4,547	5,804
All urban	276,000	370,000	537,000

Notes: Connell and Lea 1993:39 1980, 1990; Papua New Guinea towns with fewer than 5,000 in 1990 have been excluded from this table, as have towns in the North Solomons Province. The largest of the small towns are Tabubil (4,670), Kiunga (4,000), Kundiawa (3,987), Kerema (3,952) and Wau (4,268). Some urban populations are known to have been under-counted in the 1990 census; Lae almost certainly had a population of over 95,000, probably about 105,000, and the population of Tabubil was closer to 10,000. The three Bougainville towns – Panguna, Arawa and Kieta – had a population of over 20,000 (16,350 in Arawa) at the time of the 1980 census, continued to grow until 1988 but were almost deserted in 1990. The boundary of Rabaul was redrawn between 1971 and 1980.
Source: Censuses of Papua New Guinea

later the urban population had increased to more than half a million, some 15 per cent of the national total (Table 8.1). Even excluding the Bougainville towns PNG has seventy recognised towns, only twenty-nine of which had populations of more than two thousand; moreover twenty-nine had populations of less than a thousand, but they were 'uniformly stagnating or declining' (King 1992b:23). Of all the countries in the Asia-Pacific rim, PNG has the smallest proportion living in urban areas but has belatedly experienced more rapid urban growth in the largest towns and thus considerable pressure on urban services, growing problems of urban unemployment and social dislocation.

The rate of urban population growth is difficult to evaluate accurately because of changing urban boundaries. The two largest cities, Port Moresby and Lae, are growing faster than the smaller towns which, with a few unusual but obvious exceptions, such as Kiunga, Vanimo and Kimbe, have grown more slowly than the rate of natural increase. Of the larger towns, Mount Hagen, influenced by the mining boom, grew particularly quickly between

1980 and 1990. The annual urban growth rate between 1971 and 1980 was around 7 per cent, some three times greater than the national population growth rate (Walsh 1983b:30). Since 1980 the rate of urban growth has slowed, but growth was more concentrated in the three largest cities. Port Moresby has become much the largest city, with a population of around 250,000 in 1996 and Lae, the second largest city, had more than 125,000 people. The relatively slow rate of urban growth has been advantageous for a country with an even slower rate of urban job creation and inadequate urban planning.

A number of factors have discouraged migration to the cities. Urban areas have a socio-economic system that is quite different from rural areas, there is an extraordinary diversity of social groups and widespread concern over urban social problems and violence. In most rural areas it is possible to maintain a reasonable standard of living through a combination of subsistence food production and cash cropping; real rural incomes are substantially higher than in most parts of the South Pacific (and some parts of Asia). Where urban employment opportunities have expanded this has been within the government and service sectors. Since most of these jobs are skill-intensive, demanding relatively high education levels, the probability of many potential migrants obtaining such jobs is limited (especially since rural opportunities are often least in areas where education standards are also relatively low), whilst the 'informal sector' is weakly developed. Cost-of-living differences (such as housing, education, food and services) vary significantly between urban and rural areas, favour the rural areas (although standards of living may be lower there) and are well known in most rural areas (e.g. Connell 1980). The largest city, Port Moresby, is an urban enclave in an often dry and dusty region with limited agricultural potential and with poor access to much of the rest of the country: an oppressive physical environment, to which access is costly.

Until well after independence urban growth was almost entirely a result of increased migration. The vast majority of males in the urban labour force were fully employed. Migrants from the poorest areas, such as parts of Simbu province, were prepared to endure much lower wage levels (and employment rates) than migrants from other areas, an indication, even in the 1970s, of the problems of rural development and income generation in Simbu. Unemployment rates were not however increasing significantly and few urban migrants were then 'trapped' or 'dispossessed' (Garnaut *et al.* 1977:56), in the sense that they could not return to their home areas. Over time a larger component of growth has followed the transfer of fertility to the cities. Natural increase is now more important than migration as a source of urban population growth, though migration remains of great significance in the largest cities. As children have been born in the cities, urbanisation has also become a more permanent phenomenon. One of the more striking trends in urban growth has been the normalisation of urban sex ratios. In Port Moresby, for example, the masculinity ratio fell from 185 in 1966 to 137 in 1980 and 125 in

1990; similar falls occurred elsewhere. Trends towards more long-term residence, especially in Port Moresby, have contributed to growing differences between towns and rural areas.

Urban conditions have improved with higher wages, social activities have diversified and governments have encouraged home ownership for some elite workers, yet these attractions are not available to all. In a number of rural areas, cash-earning opportunities have declined, especially as cash cropping has 'frozen' some areas of land, particularly in densely populated areas, to the extent that migrants have increasingly come from remote impoverished areas, often the boundaries between provinces, and swollen the numbers of the urban poor. In some very remote areas migration has even threatened to result in depopulation (Sillitoe 1994; Tilbury and Tilbury 1993). Within urban areas there are two disadvantaged groups: some of those born there and those migrants (without skills or education) from rural areas with limited development opportunities. In the years since independence the combination of improvements in urban wages and welfare and disappointment with rural cash crop incomes has encouraged rural–urban migration and urban permanence, but alongside urban poverty.

As urban permanence increased, a distinction between those permanent urban residents who are usually relatively poor (including some urban villagers and migrants from poor rural areas) and the bureaucrats and others who are relatively well off has become more apparent. Only this latter group are relatively mobile whereas the least mobile migrants have been the least successful. The unemployed or poorly paid in town return rarely and find it difficult, if not impossible, to re-establish a rural existence. By the mid-1970s a quarter of the children born in the large towns of Port Moresby, Lae and Rabaul had never visited their so-called 'home villages' (Garnaut *et al.* 1977:9) and this proportion has scarcely changed since then (King 1992a). Migrants' values and tastes have changed (for example in attitudes to diet, housing and work) and many have 'come to see the urban way of life as their own way of life not as an alien interlude' (Morauta and Ryan 1982:49). Those who are least able and likely to return to their home areas are migrants from the poorest areas, where rural opportunities are few; they are also the poorest migrants who can least easily meet social and economic obligations to rural kin. Those who are apparently permanent migrants to town, and solely dependent on wage employment, form the urban proletariat, many from low income and poorly serviced rural provinces, such as Gulf and East Sepik, who had neither enough land or income to maintain close ties with their rural home area (Curtain 1980:54–5). Many of those who are most likely to be permanent or apparently permanent urban residents are now 'trapped' and 'dispossessed'.

The availability of urban employment opportunities for second-generation urban residents, with only tenuous ties with the rural areas, has increasingly posed problems. Children born in towns often have few real opportunities elsewhere, hence 'a generation of town-born unemployed has now emerged, especially in Port Moresby and Lae, without the land rights, agricultural skills and aspirations, cultural appreciation and language abilities necessary for rural life. Even before independence some urban-born Buang children had never learned their "home" language' (Zimmerman 1973:115) though children may be sent home specifically to develop these and other cultural skills (Gewertz and Errington 1991:116). Moreover urban-born, urban residents experience difficulties in obtaining employment, a situation that provides 'a glimpse of the future in Papua New Guinea's towns' (Morauta and Ryan 1982:54). That future is one of growing urban unemployment, especially for the urban-born population who might have been expected to have superior opportunities.

PNG exhibits limited urban primacy, and Port Moresby does not obviously dwarf and dominate other towns and cities. There have been no great discrepancies between the growth rates of Port Moresby and other large towns in the post-war years, mainly because of the success of Lae, as a competitor to the capital. Geography has ensured that Lae is 'the undisputed national centre of coastal shipping, of road transport and of telecommunications as well as being Papua New Guinea's only real manufacturing centre and only true regional centre' (Jackson 1976:9). Collectively the larger towns have become more powerful, tending to dominate as the end-point for most migration streams, other than those of 'directed' public servants. There is little evidence of step migration, as migrants have generally bypassed the small towns en route to larger urban centres with apparently greater economic opportunities and more opportunities for absorption within the *wantok* system.

Port Moresby is the centre of political, intellectual, cultural and, to a lesser extent, economic influence. The more important of the two national universities is there, much of the tertiary sector of the national economy is in the capital and public sector bureaucracies dominate its employment structure. The 'formal' and 'informal' sectors of the capital offer greater employment opportunities, including crime and a more lively social life (videos, restaurants, brothels and organised sport) than is available in provincial towns and rural areas. The predominance of Port Moresby is emphasised by its bureaucratic and trading role. Decentralisation, in any form, has been difficult, and plans to relocate the capital have come to nothing. It remains poorly integrated with other towns and villages, so that there is no real urban hierarchy. The establishment of the provincial government system emphasised bureaucratic and commercial development in the provincial capitals, at the expense of smaller district centres. Thus, within provinces, there was also some degree of primacy as in Milne Bay, for example, where Alotau grew at the expense of Samarai (Hayes 1993a). It has been suggested that 'in a country of fledgling unity such as Papua New Guinea it may be that primacy and the concentration of services and administration in one centre is the pragmatic road to development, if by that we mean holding the country together as an economic and social and political unity' (Skeldon 1980:276). In such a fragmented country this is difficult, and the weak urban hierarchy plays little part in national integration.

EMPLOYMENT, INCOMES AND THE URBAN ECONOMY

Large cities, and especially capital cities, have obvious advantages for industrial and commercial development, yet PNG has experienced urbanisation without industrialisation. The employment structure in the towns and cities is tripartite: an administrative and service sector (which is characteristic of all towns, was the principal reason for the establishment of most towns and is the principal function of the smaller towns), a small manufacturing sector and the 'informal' sector. Alongside the transition from colonial towns to Melanesian cities has gone the diversification of the urban economy. What most characterises this is the dominance of formal employment in the service sector – the bureaucracy and commerce – a reflection of the relative recency of urbanisation and the failure to develop a significant industrial sector. The urban economic structure can best be understood with reference to the overall national structure of employment.

Formal employment in plantations was one of the earliest colonial innovations in coastal New Guinea and parts of Papua, but very slow to become, in any sense, attractive. Many Melanesians had to be initially persuaded of the worth of new commodities, and also taxed, to take part in the system. In extreme cases, as in parts of German New Guinea, 'smoking schools' were set up to entrench the use of, and thus need for, new goods. Until after the Second World War there were few urban employment opportunities. The first legal minimum wage was set in 1945, when the formal indenture system was replaced by an agreement system. By the early 1950s, the transition to a cash wage system was under way (McGavin 1991:32). During the 1960s the demand for urban labour slowly increased and urban wages followed suit, though it was not until 1972 that it was generally accepted that the urban minimum wage should be based on the needs of a family unit, rather than of a single man. In the last years of the colonial era, urban wage determination had thus shifted to a 'needs' basis alongside 'wage indexation' – where shifts in wages were related to movements in the Consumer Price Index. A year before independence what has been described as 'the fatal Australian system of wages indexation' (ibid.) was in place, leading to a very substantial increase in wages and salaries in the same year, but without any evident productivity gains. Though the government sought to reduce minimum wages, an inflexible wages policy, that inhibited economic growth, was effectively institutionalised. High urban wages slowed the growth of wage and salary employment. Between 1973 and 1976, when the new scheme was established, there was a decrease of 9 per cent in private sector employment, other than in mining (Table 8.2), and both government and employer groups urged a reduction in the minimum wage. Attempts to modify and stabilise the 1974 minimum wage determinations were made, but without altering the basic

Table 8.2 Formal wage employment (1968–91)

Year	Public sector			Private sector				TOTAL
	Public service	ELCOM and PTC	Total	Agriculture	Mining	Manufacturing	Total	
1968	28.093	918	29.011		1651			161.540
1969	32.763	1411	34.174		2229			174.648
1970	33.804	1556	35.360		2693			182.642
1971	36.335	1588	37.923		3465			183.633
1972	37.452	1716	39.168		5163			178.594
1973	40.516	1612	42.128		4468			176.734
1974	43.389	1599	44.988		5182			176.008
1975	46.465	1760	48.225		5153			175.429
1976	49.759	1833	51.592	38.466	4523		123.233	174.825
1977	49.700	1913	51.613	46.150	4654		133.547	185.160
1978	49.742	2288	52.030	43.730	4860	15.415	134.913	186.943
1979	50.936	2189	53.125	45.032	4893	16.253	141.004	194.129
1980	52.862	2744	55.606	48.059	5034	17.729	157.394	213.000
1981	54.728	2659	57.387	50.900	6101	19.205	149.429	206.816
1982	52.858	4724	57.582	47.500	8742	17.071	138.923	196.505
1983	49.493	4746	54.239	51.691	9496	16.712	142.255	196.494
1984	51.460	5001	56.461	53.880	6387	16.533	144.410	200.871
1985	51.682	4672	56.354	56.162	5867	17.231	148.418	204.772
1986	49.926	5072	54.998	59.096	7040	17.151	153.113	208.111
1987	50.099	5363	55.462	59.306	8019	17.231	157.446	212.908
1988	49.076	5288	54.364	64.196	9247	18.467	163.743	218.107
1989	49.274	5199	54.473	66.850	8084	19.643	174.117	228.590
1990	50.309	5143	55.452	61.170	5331	18.905	163.505	218.957
1991	50.823	4879	55.702	62.310	5283	18.985	157.515	213.217

Notes: ELCOM is the PNG Electricity Commission; PTC is the Posts and Telegraph Commission
Source: McGavin (1993:74–5)

structure, until a new wages determination in 1992, which sought industrial relations reform as a means of achieving improvements in productivity and thus employment growth. The 1992 wage determination set a national adult minimum wage for new entrants to the labour market, abolished previous distinctions between large and small urban centres and rural areas and sought a productivity-based system, with wages being determined through workplace-based collective bargaining. A key element of this was the introduction of a national adult minimum wage for new entrants at the same level as the previous adult rural minimum wage: a shift from viewing wages policy less as an incomes policy to more of an employment policy (McGavin 1993) allowing the greater regulation of employment by market conditions.

Over the long period when plantations provided almost the sole source of employment, the proportion of the potential workforce who were formally employed remained very small. Before the war the total income-earning workforce never passed 50,000. Afterwards, when agreement labour replaced contract labour, the number increased, though it was not until the mid-1960s that the workforce passed 100,000. By 1968 the indigenous workforce had reached more than 130,000 out of a total of more than 160,000 (Table 8.2). It then expanded relatively quickly, outside the agricultural sector, as the public service grew but peaked at the start of the 1970s. The late 1970s marked a revival, as construction activity associated with infrastructure development increased and elements of a more obviously urban commercial sector took shape. Employment stagnated again in the first half of the 1980s, and subsequently grew only sporadically, so that the 1991 employment level was only the same as that of 1980. Since shortly after independence the size of the public service workforce has remained more or less constant, despite intermittent government rhetoric concerning reductions. Employment growth in the post-independence years has been entirely associated with the private sector. In the early 1990s, after long years of little growth, formal sector employment involved less than 250,000 people. In 1994 there was an increase in the employment level of just 0.8 per cent, still the highest of the decade, and no hint of significant long-term improvement. Population growth is considerably more rapid; at a national level it has been approximately eight times that of employment growth since 1980, whilst for Port Moresby the discrepancy was more than tenfold. PNG remains characterised by a workforce that is primarily rural and outside the market structure. Only about 10 per cent of the economically active population (and a much smaller proportion of women) are in the formal sector, and that proportion has declined since before independence, whilst there are higher levels of increasingly overt unemployment.

Women's participation in the formal sector is small; women constituted no more than about 14 per cent of wage employment at the time of the 1980 census (McGavin 1991:60), though this proportion has since increased. Women were excluded from plantation employment and in the early years of urban growth unskilled jobs went to men. Women were less likely to be educated, especially beyond primary school, and were usually discouraged from seeking jobs outside rural areas, if they sought to do so (e.g. Connell 1985b:131). Since independence female employment has diversified considerably. Most employed women are in the public sector (especially in health and education) where they constitute approximately 12 per cent of the workforce. Though there are women in middle management and executive positions, 'glass ceilings' prevent movement out of relatively unskilled, poorly paid jobs. Although equal wages are paid to women and men, the concentration of women in the least skilled categories of the workforce (such as the coffee-processing and clothing industries) has resulted in the average female wage being at least 10 per cent lower than the average male wage (Barnes 1982:260), and women workers having rather less status and prestige. There is an inflexibility and rigidity in most workplaces, that anti-discriminatory legislation has not overcome and which has limited the contribution of women to national development.

The formal workforce is relatively youthful. There was always a tradition of early 'retirement' from the plantation workforce, and this has been retained in several economic sectors, where many workers return to the rural sector at an early age. In 1980 only about 6 per cent of the employed workforce were aged over 45 though, because the workforce has grown only very slowly, the young are also under-represented (McGavin 1991:61). The structure of the labour force is unusual because of the very low level of literacy and education. It was not until 1978 that the first localisation policies were introduced; localisation has subsequently increased the availability of employment but, without adequate training (in technical and management skills), has often proceeded faster than the ability of the workforce to absorb the rate of departure of expatriates. Most of the workforce are citizens because of the high costs of employing expatriates and the deterrent effect of crime on overseas workers and their families. In all sectors of the economy, and in both the private and public sectors, there are skill shortages that have reduced the competitiveness of the national economy.

The concept of unemployment has little meaning in most parts of the country, and there have been no consistent attempts to identify the extent of unemployment or under-employment. There are no realistic data on unemployment, though what little there is demonstrates a rapid increase during the 1980s. Census data for ten provinces point to an increase in those enumerated as 'unemployed' between 1980 and 1990 from 3 per cent to 10 per cent. More specific data for Morobe Province and Port Moresby (NCD) indicate that, over the same period, unemployment in those areas increased from 13 per cent to 41 per cent, and from 9 per cent to 34 per cent respectively (McGavin 1993:59). A third of the population in the capital were officially searching for formal sector employment, though some of these were probably employed in the informal sector (UNDP/ILO-ARTEP 1993:231). Those who are most likely to be unemployed are those in the 15–19 age group, many with little or no education (Lodewijks 1988:385). A substantial number of urban households are without urban wage or salary workers: in Port Moresby and Madang in 1983, a quarter of all households in many settlements were without any employed member. Many of these households were dependent on gifts and transfers from others (McGavin 1991:52–7) or from more intermittent earnings in the informal sector. The extent of urban joblessness has subsequently increased, especially amongst unskilled youths, many of whom have grown up in the urban areas. Visible evidence of unemployment exists in the number of jobless youths in the cities, and in the prevalence on gates, especially of factories, of signs stating *Sori Nogat Wok* (Sorry, No Work). Such signs show that demand for work exceeds supply but also that urban wages are not too low (McGavin 1991:156). Since informal sector wages and earnings are much lower than in the formal sector (ibid.:165–7) the demand for formal employment is considerably in excess of job supply. The declining rate of job creation in urban areas has emphasised the differences between those with jobs and those without jobs. Urban unemployment varies significantly within the towns, for example, between relatively unemployed highlanders and employed coastals in Port Moresby. Such variations in urban unemployment may well emphasise existing regional income inequalities.

Access to formal sector employment, even in the public sector, is substantially influenced by *wantok* ties, that is the relationship between an employed individual from a particular village or language group, and others from the same area. The unemployed, whilst poor, have some support through the *wantok* system, most evident in the larger towns. Otherwise associations created and sustained by ordinary people to protect and promote specific interests, including trade unions, are largely absent. The emergence of a class terminology is similarly absent. Only the pidgin term *pasindia* (passenger), with its connotation of the 'urban yet rootless unemployed', fills this kind of gap, but does not demarcate a class. The close rural ties that are maintained by many long-term urban residents are not merely of sentimental value but stem from the intention of migrants to return, as a response to the bleak prospects of access to housing, insecurity of urban land tenure, low or no pension payments or health benefits after retirement from wage employment. They also relate to notions of obligation and identity. One result of the maintained strength of ethnicity is that the urban poor are not yet in a situation where they can co-operate to defend their social and economic interests.

The economy as a whole, but especially the urban economy, is dominated by the national government, because of the enormous significance of the public sector, which is to some extent matched at the provincial level. At independence scarcely any manufacturing or service sector enterprise was partly or wholly owned by PNG nationals and the heights of the private sector remain largely managed, if not owned, by expatriates, in some contrast to the public service, which is almost entirely localised. There has been little attempt to achieve privatisation; protection is seen more as a stimulus, rather than a constraint, to growth, and as a route to self-sufficiency and diversification. Though governments have stated their official support for privatisation, the state has interests in mining, agriculture, fisheries, forestry, transportation and finance, alongside the utilities. After 1995 there were renewed attempts at privatisation, with sales of government shares in RoadCo transport, Ramu sugar and other ventures. In the following year the government sold off oil palm holdings, undertook the partial privatisation of the Mineral Resources Development Corporation (though retaining a 51 per cent share in the holding company, Orogen) and announced plans for the privatisation of Air Niugini. More than a quarter of all formal sector wage employment is in the public sector, though this proportion has declined since independence. There was some growth of the public sector in the early 1980s, mainly with the expansion of provincial governments, but this was counteracted by national cutbacks at the end of 1982, one of the rare occasions when the public service has been pruned. (Under the Structural Adjustment Program it was intended to reduce the public service from 62,460 in 1996 to 45,000 by the year 2000 but cuts announced in 1995 never occurred.) Job security, high wages, considerable freedom, pleasant working conditions and access to 'fringe benefits' (such as telephones and vehicles) have ensured that this is the most sought after area of employment, second only to being a Member of Parliament. Whilst public service employment is concentrated in Port Moresby, it dominates many smaller towns, where commerce usually provides the only alternative source of wages and salaries.

At the time of independence, the second largest area of employment was in plantations. Employment in the rural sector has increased since independence (Table 8.2), because of the large number of informal and often poorly paid income-earning opportunities, hence agriculture has retained its primary significance for employment. Nevertheless two-thirds of formal wage and salary employment is in the urban areas. After government and agriculture the most important source of employment is in 'finance, trade and services'. Unlike all other sectors except mining, this sector has grown through the 1980s and 1990s, with the continued expansion of transport and retail services, and the consolidation of the building and construction industry (in urban and mining areas). At the start of the 1990s, with 45,000 people employed in retail and wholesale services, transport and finance, and a further 24,000 in building and construction, the service sector accounted for 32 per cent of all wage and salary employment, rather more than agriculture.

A large part of the commercial sector is still dominated by giant commercial companies, including the 'big four' of Burns Philp, Carpenters, Steamships and Morris Hedstrom (some of which also have financial interests in plantations, transport activities and overseas banks). Much of the remainder of the commercial economy is also dominated by expatriates, operating with Melanesian partners, though Papua New Guineans have increasingly become sole owners. Corporate investment by overseas companies in services, both retailing and finance, has been at the very core of the national economy, a situation even more apparent in the mining industry (Chapter 6). The current extent of foreign involvement in the service sector is difficult to assess. Banking and other finance sector activities are still generally dominated 'by Australian affiliated companies', with Australian banks such as Westpac and ANZ particularly significant. Banking is typical of the service sector as a whole where employment is primarily urban but extends to, and is significant in, even the smallest towns. Despite the economic significance of mining, its direct contribution to employment has been slight, especially after the closure of the Panguna mine, though wages and salaries are very high in this sector. The absolute number employed in mining was scarcely greater in the 1990s than it was two decades earlier. Services – both public and private – dominate employment and the whole urban economy; production remains rural – and primarily agricultural – emphasising the distinctions between rural and urban areas, and the absence of a manufacturing sector and a tourist industry.

There are considerable regional variations in participation in formal sector employment. At the time of the 1980 census the formal sector workforce represented 9.6 per cent of the total population, but in Port Moresby (NCD) the proportion was 44 per cent with the next highest proportions being recorded in the North Solomons (19 per cent) and East New Britain (18 per cent); the only non-coastal province that had a proportion above the national average was the Western Highlands (10.5 per cent). The highlands provinces generally had far fewer people in the formal sector, with the three lowest proportions being recorded in Simbu and Enga (both 3 per cent) and the Southern Highlands (4 per cent). Both Sepik provinces also had relatively low proportions (McGavin 1991:234). The provinces with the lowest numbers of their workforce in the formal sector – Gulf and Manus – are characterised by out-migration. In both these provinces fewer than 3,000 workers were employed in the formal sector, compared with over 34,000 in Port Moresby and 25,000 in Morobe (mainly in Lae). Towns are the centres of formal sector employment. Since 1980 the extent of formal sector employment has grown most rapidly in the highlands (primarily associated with the growth of mining) whereas the rate of growth in Port Moresby has been below the national average, especially in the early 1990s. Formal sector employment has not therefore become more concentrated in the capital, though more of the better paid, high status jobs are there.

In an economy of such complexity, where most of the population continue subsistence and monetary activities, and many transactions are informal and unrecorded, the task of measuring incomes is difficult. No detailed assessment of incomes and income distribution has been undertaken since 1980, and that was dependent on much earlier data, though the basic structure of national incomes has not substantially changed. In 1971 income distribution was very skewed but not greatly unequal. Over 90 per cent of all income recipients (including subsistence farmers) were in the lowest income bracket and received 57 per cent of all incomes (Table 8.3). The upper 10 per cent of income earners received 43 per cent of total incomes. The average incomes of agricultural employees were less than a third of the wages of other employees,

Table 8.3 Income distribution (1971)

Income bracket (K/week)	Number of income recipients in bracket (%)	Total income in bracket (%)	Cumulative number of income recipients (%)	Cumulative total income (%)
0.00–6.50	90.6	56.8	90.6	56.8
6.51–8.50	3.3	3.4	93.9	60.2
8.51–10.50	1.0	1.2	94.9	61.4
10.51–17.50	1.8	3.3	96.7	64.7
17.51–39.50	1.4	4.4	98.1	69.1
39.51–80.00	0.5	4.6	98.6	73.7
80.01–150.00	0.5	13.2	99.5	86.9
150.01 and over	0.5	13.1	100.0	100.0
Total	100.0	100.0		

Source: D. Jackson (1981:146)

Table 8.4 Provincial per capita incomes (1966–83)

	1966–7	1971–2	1983
Western	126	157	673
Gulf	119	154	198
Central	374[1]	492[1]	528
NCD	—	—	2115
Milne Bay	123	151	280
Oro	135	158	413
Southern Highlands	96	135	256
Western Highlands	119[2]	182[2]	337
Enga	—	—	267
Simbu	99	142	264
Eastern Highlands	144	184	290
Morobe	206	257	473
Madang	149	184	387
East Sepik	132	163	320
West Sepik	101	15	255
Manus	222	269	416
New Ireland	213	222	534
East New Britain	289	360	770
West New Britain	136	301	483
North Solomons	175	621	1973
Papua New Guinea	160	232	520

Notes: 1 Includes National Capital District
        2 Includes Enga
Source: Treadgold (1987:6)

hence there were significant rural–urban variations in wage and salary incomes, evident in particularly high wages in the public sector (D. Jackson 1981). The differential between mineworkers in Bougainville and other employees was widening; this has continued with the opening of new mines emphasising this particular inequality. The decline of cash crop prices in the 1980s, and the collapse of the plantation sector has subsequently reduced rural wages relative to those in urban areas.

Regional variations in income levels are little more than indicative, being based on estimates of market and non-market (subsistence) production and some data on wages. The proportion of income in 1971 derived from subsistence agriculture varied from 53 per cent in the Southern Highlands and 51 per cent in Simbu, to 8.5 per cent and 7 per cent in the North Solomons and Central provinces respectively; these differences coincided with the poorest and richest provinces (Table 8.4). The richest province was the North Solomons, followed by Central Province (including Port Moresby) and the New Britain provinces, characterised by extensive cash cropping. Increased mining activity further emphasised provincial variations twelve years later, though island provinces again fared well. The greatest change over the period was the rise of Western Province, following the development of the Ok Tedi project. Subsequently the development of the Porgera and Misima mines has had a similar impact in Enga and Milne Bay, which may have slightly reduced interprovincial income equality, whose 'overall severity reached a remarkably high peak in 1980' (Treadgold 1987:12). Nevertheless the greatest income inequalities are within provinces and between rural and urban areas.

Just as there are no adequate measures of incomes there has been no analysis of what constitutes poverty. The growing extent of unemployment, the growth of the informal sector, including begging and crime (see pp. 280–88), and a range of anecdotal evidence, suggest that poverty is now of some significance in urban areas, and especially the capital. It may be less evident in rural areas, where the 'subsistence safety net' remains in place, but where there are land shortages, malnutrition, and inadequate access to services and income-earning opportunities, poverty is absent only because it has gone unobserved and unrecorded. In many rural areas, a number of people are relatively disadvantaged, especially the old (e.g. M.F. Smith 1994:36–7, 134–7). In urban areas the popular romantic view of an 'urban safety net' of the extended family, or *wantok* system, ensuring through redistribution that kin are never hungry or destitute, is no longer valid (Monsell-Davis 1993). However a poverty line might be defined, a number of households now fall below it, especially in urban settlements, where some households regularly experience hunger and poverty (Chao 1985; King 1992a:15). Whilst many urban households have some access to subsistence incomes, and benefit from kin support, long-term disadvantaged households, who have lost their ability to reciprocate favours, may be disowned and ignored by close relatives. 'A familiar sight in Papua New Guinea's towns are ageing, sometimes decrepit panhandlers and bottle collectors. Less visible are elderly hospital patients with apparently no close relatives to attend to their needs, and older people who have been dumped in town to be looked after – or not – by migrant kinsmen' (Zimmer 1990b:205). A number of situations are indicative of poverty, and outcomes of it. Suicide levels, domestic violence and crime have become more common in urban areas. The *rabisman* (a worthless person, or beggar) is more apparent as unemployment has increased. The cities, but especially Port Moresby, have become new centres of high incomes, conspicuous consumption and destitution, and sites of considerable inequality and poverty.

INDUSTRIALISATION

Recent years have seen a declining rate of urban job creation. Shortages of development capital and skilled personnel have slowed the growth of new industrial employment opportunities. Beyond basic import-substitution industries (especially for foodstuffs) there has been little expansion; export markets are protected and distant, and wage levels are too high to attract multinational manufacturing industries. Other constraints to industrialisation include a small and fragmented domestic market, with relatively low incomes, and high domestic freight costs. There are few possibilities for economies of scale, hence import-substitution has occurred only behind tariff barriers, and is consequently expensive.

The industrial sector (excluding mining) contributes about 13 per cent of GDP and about 8 per cent of formal employment. About 60 per cent of the value added in manufacturing is in food processing for the domestic market. Most other factories are concerned with either metal or wood products, and few employ more than twenty people. Engineering factories have recently become important, primarily to serve the needs of the growing transport and mining industries. The main industrial products, beyond engineering, are primarily such traditional goods as coffee, wood products, bottles, cigarettes, beer and a variety of food, thus less than 5 per cent (by value) of manufactured goods are exported. Industry is highly concentrated in Port Moresby and Lae. Manufacturing has been much the most disappointing sector of the national economy, since neither the number of establishments, the amount of employment or the contribution to GDP has grown significantly since independence.

An acute shortage of skilled human resources remains a constraint to industrialisation. Many of the skills required in the industrial sector, and in other parts of the urban economy – such as accounting, management and engineering – must be expensively imported. Wages are very high in relation to productivity, compared with nearby countries. Productivity, low as it was, declined during the 1980s. In the same period the Newly Industrialising Countries (NICs) of South Korea, Hong Kong and Singapore were paying non-agricultural wages about 60 per cent of those in PNG (McGavin and Millett 1992:14–15, 31). Moreover over 90 per cent of the workforce in manufacturing are men, a very different situation from that in Asia (Temu 1993). Wages have remained high because of the long experience of wage indexation, the demonstration effect of high public service and mining wages, localisation procedures in which high expatriate salaries have tended to provide a norm for subsequent wage and salary packages, the high 'reserve price' of most rural labour (because of the relative ease of maintaining a mixed subsistence-cash livelihood in most rural areas), resentment of the poor returns to wage labour (Stevenson 1987), the cost of extended family obligations in urban areas and the security risks and costs of housing in urban areas.

The 'hard kina' policy, adopted after independence to keep down inflation and the cost of living, also discouraged industrialisation through the appreciation of the local currency. Security and insurance are expensive; a brewery in PNG requires twenty times as much expenditure on security as does one in Singapore and insurance premiums are also up to twenty times greater (World Bank 1992:74). Despite weak unions there are few multi-shift industrial operations (outside the mining sector) hence capital is often idle for two-thirds of the time. Institutional constraints have further restricted industrialisation. Land tenure and land administration procedures have made it both difficult and expensive for individuals or companies to secure land for business ventures. At the same time, there have been few institutional supports, particularly financial incentives, for industrial development and public utility costs are high. The manufacturing sector has had low priority in national development, compared with agriculture in colonial times, and later mining.

At various times incentives have been proposed and introduced by governments though most were effectively defunct by the 1990s. During much of the period since independence the National Investment Development Authority, established in 1974, sought to promote and regulate foreign investment though, in practice, it achieved very little, functioning more like a policing agency than a stimulus to new investment (Dahanayake and Mannur 1989), and was abolished in 1991. The emphasis on import-substitution, behind tariff barriers or with quotas and import bans, has led to economic distortions and considerable costs, especially with the establishment of several agricultural processing industries, including animal feed and sugar production. Employment creation has been small, little if any foreign exchange has been saved, since inputs have had to be purchased abroad, and the value added has been at higher than international cost. In the case of the two meat canneries established in Madang and Port Moresby in the 1980s

> There is no saving of foreign exchange. They have imported their capital equipment and are importing substantial proportions of their intermediate inputs (in this case, meat and cans). Imports of canned meat competing with their products have been banned. The rural families which depended on cheap meat for their protein input have been hurt. The higher prices charged consumers behind protective barriers make for inflationary pressures contributing in turn towards higher wages and therefore higher costs. The only beneficiaries are the companies.
>
> (Callick *et al.* 1990:16.3)

Similar import-substitution and protectionism have long existed for breweries and have more recently been extended to fish canneries, where the results are likely to be similar. Comparable disadvantages exist for a new cement factory in Lae. There are foreign exchange losses (as production is about twice that of domestic requirements and must therefore be exported at international prices), a 50 per cent rise in the price of domestic cement (especially in Port Moresby and the island provinces, where transport costs make imported cement substantially cheaper) and substantial subsidies that make the limited employment gains trivial (Jarrett 1991). Ties between politicians and business people are unlikely to reduce the significance of similar forms of protected industrialisation, despite global trends in opposition to protection, import bans and tariffs.

The phase of import substitution has largely passed (especially without state protection). Exports have been minimal, and largely confined to specialised goods such as coffee and other processed natural resources, rather than more complex manufactured products. Market access is scarcely a problem since PNG has various preferential agreements with Australia, Europe and North America. Because of the limitations of export agriculture, mainly those of world prices, and the potential and real problems of mining, including limited mine life periods, environmental degradation and the generation of relatively few jobs, industrial development, at least in theory, offers both possibilities for diversification and suggests a route to development that has been highly successful in some Asian countries. Yet during the 1980s private sector investment in manufacturing decreased and its share in total investment declined from 7.6 to 3.4 per cent. 'Papua New Guinea is at a serious or even severe competitive disadvantage in the international economy against key nations that export similar products or that provide alternatives for internationally mobile capital. This is not a new conclusion.' (McGavin 1991:129), but it points to the very considerable difficulties that PNG faces in seeking to achieve industrial development.

THE INFORMAL SECTOR

The combination of migration, growing urban permanence, few new urban employment opportunities and the lack of industrialisation might have been expected to have resulted in the emergence of an 'informal sector' (where wages and conditions of work are unregulated). However there is an 'almost total absence of handicraft workers and the small-scale traders, shopkeepers and service-repair establishments that provide such a large volume of employment, especially urban employment, in many other countries' (World Bank 1978:55). The most visible elements of the informal sector are crime and its converse, security provision, betel nut selling and bottle collecting (all of which are particularly evident in Port Moresby), alongside house-building, transport, newspaper selling, window-cleaning, prostitution and gardening. The informal sector overall provides incomes and employment for a very large number of people, usually at wages and incomes below those in the formal sector.

The absence of informal sector activities is partly due to restrictive legislation. There is a 'common and pervasive bias against small-scale industrial ventures that are carried out within the purview of the so-called "informal sector"' (Fairbairn 1992:24). Whilst, in most countries, a range of informal economic activities exist that are not subject to the rules and regulations that govern businesses in the formal sector, in PNG they receive no official recognition or promotional assistance, are over-regulated or simply disrupted. This is especially true of food selling, where tough colonial legislation remains in place, and betel nut selling. At the start of the 1990s there were considerable efforts to close down and remove illegal 'tuckershops' in Port Moresby, which had no licences and were operating on state land. Mobile vans must move every eight hours and not operate within 100 metres of each other. From time to time there have been health bans on the selling of cooked food in streets and markets, and betel nut vendors are routinely harassed, have their goods stolen or confiscated or are banned entirely. In 1993 the National Capital Development Commission brought in a law to license street bottle collectors and restrict their trading to 8 a.m. to 5 p.m. on weekdays and 9 a.m. to 5 p.m. on weekends (*TPNG* 30 December 1993), a law virtually impossible to administer effectively with or without harassment. Other reasons for the limited significance of the informal sector are low consumer demand for some services, the relative affluence of the rural subsistence-cash sector (which takes some of the burden off the urban unemployed) and, perhaps, an absence of skills in some areas (such as shoe repair or sandal manufacture) where demand is only emerging.

Where there is no restrictive legislation informal sector activities have grown rapidly. This is particularly true of vehicle transport, since there is no state or municipal public transport sector in the cities. Throughout urban and rural areas most passenger transport is in passenger motor vehicles (PMVs), which are regulated according to routes and fare structures, but not according to ownership. In the larger towns, notably Port Moresby, there are hundreds of such mini-buses, many of which are owned by wealthy individuals and business groups from the highlands, and linked to other entrepreneurial ventures. Driving is regarded as a highly prestigious job and wages may, in some cases, be above those in skilled formal sector activities (M. Strathern 1975:113; cf. McGavin 1991:157–67). One of the most rapidly growing areas is the provision of security guards. In these areas, and in bottle collecting and betel nut selling (Chapter 4), there is considerable hierarchical organisation, with intense competition for sites and markets, a highly capitalist structure that has restricted earnings and depressed most informal sector incomes.

Vendors in urban markets are part of the urban informal sector since, other than in their payments for renting market stalls, their presence is unregulated and sometimes intermittent. A number of market vendors are urban

residents, either 'middle-women' or those who have produced food themselves. Relative to other parts of the world, 'the paradox of the informal
sector in Papua New Guinea's towns is that so much of it is based on an
abundance of natural resources, such as unused peri-urban land and fisheries,
whereas in other countries the scarcity of such resources forces many urban
dwellers into service and trading activities more typically associated with the
informal sector' (Conroy 1982:16). In the mid-1970s the average urban household purchased 12 per cent of all its goods from markets and street vendors
(Walsh 1983a), hence much trade was informal. In the early 1980s there were
around 1,000 market vendors in Port Moresby on peak Saturdays (Walsh
1982) and other towns also had large numbers. A decade later the number of
formal markets, and informal market places (often on the edge of towns to
avoid regulations about betel-nut spitting), had increased, the number of
vendors was much greater (as was the diversity of markets) and the volume
and range of goods considerable. Firewood, in several places, was a valuable
and specialised commodity; gambling in market-places was a common 'service' sector activity, though manufactured products are still rare. Markets
play a very much greater role in the urban economy than they did at the time
of independence. At a slightly larger scale, there are large numbers of small
stores throughout the towns, many unregistered (operating out of houses
and backyards). Though small and often short lived, they generate considerable employment, mainly of youths and often of women. A few have grown,
partly by engaging in black market operations, by incorporating pool (bil-
liards) tables (Ranck 1982) or through particular entrepreneurial skills in
good locations.

Crime, and the resultant acquisition of goods and wealth, is also an informal sector activity in both towns and many rural areas. The widespread
significance of gangs (Chapter 10) points to their considerable organisation:
'Commercialism, *bisnis*, appears to be driving and transforming virtually all
structures of Rascal organisation' (Nibbrig 1992:119), in which breaking and
entering are central. Crime has, inevitably, contributed to the rise of informal
security services, with walls and chain fences, burglar alarms, large dogs and
guards having become new elements in the urban landscape. Begging has
gradually become more significant, though less visible, importuning and
organised than in many Asian cities. Busking, despite its prominent role in the
film *Cowboy and Maria in Town* (McLaren and Owen 1991), is of trivial significance compared with that in rich-world cities. The skills are absent and the
market is small. Prostitution has grown in significance, especially in Port
Moresby, based around hotels and discos. Prostitutes are from squatter settlements and urban villages, from 'broken homes' or very large families, single
mothers or with unemployed husbands. Potential earnings were substantially
above those in the lower income levels of the formal sector, with prices ranging from K20 to K200 (*TPNG* 21 September, 5, 19 October 1989). At the start
of the 1990s prostitution in Port Moresby was reported to involve over 200
women, including some Asian migrants (*TPNG* 8 November 1990) and has

grown steadily, if largely invisibly, there and elsewhere (Hammar 1992) since independence.

The informal sector is growing, particularly among urban groups charac-terised by high levels of poverty (Williamson 1977; Norwood 1981). In most urban settlements, informal sector activities are a greater source of income than formal sector employment (Vavine 1984). The number and diversity of street vendors has demonstrated the rapid growth of the sector from the 1980s, in direct contrast to formal sector employment. The informal sector has become more visible, more significant for income generation, more organised and regulated, but poorly understood or supported.

TOURISM

In contrast to the informal sector, tourism has been encouraged but has declined rather than grown. No country in the Pacific region has so much tourist potential and gained so little from it. Despite the scenery and wildlife of the highlands, beaches and diving opportunities on the coasts, and dis-tinctive and varied cultures, the potential is unlikely to be realised in what national tourist promotions have designated 'the land of the unexpected' and 'like no place you've ever been'. Tourism has never been a priority for any government, despite intermittent market pushes in response to problems in other sectors; concern over cultural impacts meant that it was a 'last resort' (Lea 1980). Various national tourism organisations have foundered. Yet another, the Tourism Promotion Authority, was launched in 1993, with a K2 million budget, an intention to revive the industry and stimulate rural employment (which mining and the timber industry had failed to do) and focus on the highlands, Rabaul and Madang alongside small-scale resorts in the islands. Aspirations remain well ahead of achievements. High costs and law and order problems have discouraged tourists. (In 1992 both Australia and the USA officially cautioned their citizens against travelling to PNG because of these problems, warnings which resulted in the Minister of Foreign Affairs, Sir Michael Somare, issuing a caution to intending PNG vis-itors to the west coast of the USA.) Virtually no reports on the future of the national economy discuss the potential of tourism any more.

Tourist numbers have never been high. The number of pleasure tourists since the 1980s has ranged from 6,800 to 18,000. Numbers have declined from a peak of 22,000 in 1974. Few other countries have recorded compar-able declines in an age of tourism and even such small Pacific island states as Vanuatu and the Cook Islands consistently recorded higher figures in the 1980s. The majority of all visitors to PNG (around 40,000 per year in the 1990s) are on business, and many tourists are relatives and friends of expa-triates living in the country. Half of all visitors in 1992 were from Australia, though 39 per cent of all pleasure tourists were from North America and 27 per cent from Australia. Most of these are affluent; the average expenditure of all visitors in 1991 was more than K1,200, the highest ever recorded in a

South Pacific state (Samaranayake 1992:16). The reluctance of governments in the 1980s to grant landing rights to airlines – especially from Asia – with the potential to bring tourists into the country, and a small number of international flights, have pushed up the cost of tourism. Domestic air transport, essential for tourism, is one of the most expensive in the world in terms of distance and discourages wide-ranging travel. Both cost and security problems have contributed to tourism being principally confined to expensive package tours, in a small number of locations. Ecotourism and low-cost 'backpacker' tourism have largely been priced out of the market. One guide for bushwalkers stresses that in much of the highlands 'hold-ups of course aren't guaranteed, but in many of these places they're frequent. . . . The one unfortunate generalisation you can make about formal accommodation in PNG is that it is too expensive' (Pérusse 1993:54–5). Such perceptions are widely shared and a real deterrent to growth.

Tourism is concentrated in certain areas, briefly in Port Moresby (the destination of almost all international flights), the Sepik district and the highlands. Tourists stay in expensive hotels and there is little alternative accommodation. Local development initiatives, such as the guest-houses at Tufi (Oro), have largely failed because of declining tourist numbers, lack of knowledge of their existence, absence of government support, inaccessibility, cost and local conflict, whilst proprietors have had trouble maintaining properties, organising food supplies and preventing malaria (Ranck 1987; J. Schmid 1990). The rare survivors are often European operated (e.g. Errington and Gewertz 1989; cf. Errington and Gewertz 1995) and those with specialist functions – including hunting and fishing – that also have a local market, such as the Bensbach Wildlife Lodge in Western Province (Tapari 1988:28–36). Melanesian guest-houses have fallen prey to small markets, lack of capital and management expertise and to the same range of problems that have plagued most small business ventures, such as trade stores.

Despite the small number of tourists there have been economic gains from tourism. International tourist expenditure was estimated at K16.2 million in 1987, about half of which was absorbed by accommodation costs. Since most major hotels are foreign-owned, there is considerable leakage of this revenue. The direct expenditure of all visitors generated over K50 million during 1987, about equivalent to the value of cocoa exports, and indicative of the considerable significance of visitor expenditure (Milne 1991). In 1992 total foreign exchange earnings were around K49 million, more than 1 per cent of GDP and equivalent to about 3 per cent of the value of exports, hence visitors were the fifth most valuable source of foreign exchange earnings. More than 5,000 jobs were directly sustained by the tourist sector in 1992, despite the small number of visitors. There are significant linkages with other sectors of the economy, including the artefacts industry, which is increasingly an urban phenomenon. The bulk of revenue from the industry remains with the major urban stores, and middlemen have similarly been well positioned to take advantage of some popular performing groups, such as the Asaro Valley 'mudmen'. The economic significance of tourism is generally small, and substantial only in the most popular areas, such as the Sepik river (Coiffier 1991), where access to alternative income-generating opportunities is difficult.

The social impact of tourism has been slight. There is little evidence of tourist-generated prostitution, drug abuse or the emergence of a servile and resentful population. In the few areas where tourist numbers are significant – the main towns and the Sepik river – tourism has stimulated handicraft production, and the retention of some cultural forms, albeit in artificial form (Gewertz and Errington 1991). It has also challenged villagers' images and representations of themselves, demanding that tourists be accommodated by villagers dressing up and acting as savages, staging tribal fights and so on (Kulick and Willson 1992); in some respects 'the Chambri were of value to tourists only because they were different and unequal. They would remain of interest only as long as they remained primitive, only as long as they remained a vanishing curiosity in the modern world' (Gewertz and Errington 1991:56). Papua New Guineans have however asserted control of their own cultures in fostering this difference, both in performance and in artefact production, as others search for authenticity and difference. Much is made of this in the tourist promotional literature, as in a *Trans Niugini Tours* 1992 advertisement for the expensive Karawari Lodge (East Sepik): 'Down in the mysterious Sepik region, this time warped mixture of the primitive and modern is the perfect base for jungle, river and village exploration. Locals pole dug-out canoes, the drums throb, the wild birds call and the traditional village lifestyles continue relatively unchanged'. Though some tourists are not well disposed to indigenous customs, including those depicted in the film *Cannibal Tours* (O'Rourke 1987), one anthropologist has written of organised tours in the Southern Highlands that 'excursions to witness Huli life are a model of sensitivity and a successful attempt to allow the outsiders to savour the unknown with minimal effect on the integrity of the observed' (Feil 1990:30). On balance tourism has contributed to those socio-economic changes sought by Melanesians, by providing finance, but slowed the pace of some elements of change.

AGAINST URBANISATION

A pervasive anti-urbanism has invariably been at the heart of national development policy and, to a much lesser extent of practice, though it scarcely accounts for the slow rate of urban population growth. It is a direct legacy of colonial opposition to urbanisation, when there were administrative restrictions on migration, and particularly on the establishment of settlements in urban areas, in order to achieve administrative efficiency and an effective deployment of labour, primarily designed to increase the production of cash crops on plantations. Policies and practices opposing migration to the towns remain, more out of implausible attempts to preserve an aura of 'urban respectability', by reducing crime and the visible evidence of urban unemployment, than out of any desire for rural development. Squatter settlements are widely perceived to be haunts of criminals and the feckless unemployed, though there is limited evidence of this. A significant proportion of employment is in the informal sector, but this is rarely regarded as appropriate or genuine employment (Connell and Lea 1993:81–2). As controls weakened, and urbanisation and urban settlements increased, fears grew over the increase in urban crime, unemployment and insanitary accommodation. This prompted attempts to prevent migration, primarily by repatriation of migrants from towns alongside some emphasis on rural development.

Throughout Melanesia there was extensive control over migration to towns in the pre-war and post-war years (Connell and Curtain 1982). It was illegal for Melanesians to live in town without a job or a permit and vagrancy laws were enforced at least as recently as 1973. As migration to the towns increased there were new demands for its greater control and suggestions that a formal pass system be introduced. In the 1970s some district councils sought to introduce pass laws, and the carrying of identity cards, alongside repatriation of the urban unemployed. Little came of these and other similar proposals that demonstrated widespread opposition to inter-provincial migration (Connell 1975a:107–8). Even in the migrants' home areas this opposition was occasionally accepted in classic colonial terms that justified the necessity for Port Moresby particularly to be 'a clean and respectable place' to live in.

Opposition to urbanisation continued in the post-colonial era, from both urban authorities and influential leaders. Policies towards urban migration had turned full circle by the end of the 1970s, but instead of being directed by a colonial administration, they were now the preferred solutions of some provincial governments. There was, however, as there has always been, a paradox: 'Everyone blames the squatters for the sudden increase in crime. Some have petitioned the government to get rid of these settlements, yet politicians visit these same places at election time with money, beer and rice bags to win their vote' (*TPNG* 25 October 1984). At different times in the 1980s and 1990s most urban authorities sought to eject at least some squatters or unemployed migrants. In 1991 the Morobe Premier tried to eject illegal settlers from Lae: 'My plan to eject settlers is a genuine one for the sake of my people who want a trouble free environment for their children. . . . As for Papua New Guinea which has a large area of land, I do not see why people should move from province to province. I am sure there are better things to do in their own villages or towns' (*TPNG* 6 June 1991). This was not the settlers' perception. In Rabaul illegal settlers were ordered to be evicted for the same kinds of reasons. The East New Britain Premier stressed that the exercise was being undertaken for the good of both the province and the settlers: 'We want to help the settlers so that they can have dignity and that they can grow their own cash crops in their respective villages. Villages are still the best and least expensive places to live. Furthermore we want settlers to understand that they were not born to be slaves in towns. However they are making themselves slaves' (*TPNG* 29 August 1991). Settlers were forcibly evicted, and settlements destroyed at the start of 1994, as the Provincial Government sought to make employers responsible for housing provision (*PC* 11 February 1994). Similar statements, attempts at eviction and opposition to rapid urbanisation have been numerous, though only rarely have attitudes been transformed into action. By contrast to the widespread opposition to urbanisation – at least in the form of settlements – there has been minimal support for the rights of those in settlements, other than from the settlers themselves (Connell and Lea 1993:87). Forays into the considerable complexity of urban welfare provision have been rare and the pervasive opposition to urbanisation has delayed and discouraged the development of co-ordinated plans for urban management.

Whilst the effects of increasing urbanisation are often seen as social problems, their causes are both economic, a result of emerging inequalities between urban and rural life, and a result of natural increase in urban areas. To discourage migration infrastructure costs of urban development have been passed on to urban consumers in higher electricity and water charges. During the 1980s the National Housing Commission was instructed to do without government subsidies, economic rents were phased in and private land developers had to supply their own roads, all policies that tended to place urban services further beyond the reach of the majority of the urban population; however 'the government's control of urban migration through budget cuts on urban services to date does not seem to have any effect on the continuing migration into the urban areas' (Aruga 1992:13) but it has increased urban poverty. The lack of institutional response to urbanisation has therefore been similar to, though more limited than, that in other less developed countries. There have been few real attempts to manage urbanisation since independence, when there was more interest in both regional development and the development of small towns, in line with ideas about regional integration and equity. It was envisaged that

> If smaller towns can be encouraged to grow to a size which makes increased production of goods and services viable, they will become relatively more attractive to urban migrants than Port Moresby and Lae and will foster a more even distribution of urban-based services throughout the country.
>
> (Papua New Guinea 1978:107)

Since then, interest in spatial equity has given way to demand for economic growth, and explicit spatial policies have disappeared. Regional planning no longer exits. Urbanisation has been limited, primarily because of inertia, social diversity and the existence of reasonable income-earning opportunities in many rural areas. However expenditure in urban areas is quite disproportionate to urban population sizes. Policy formation directed to mitigate urban bias and urban growth has not occurred even where most politicians have extremely strong rural economic ties, where an alienated urban elite is only emerging, and where migrants are at least as conservative and poorly organised as elsewhere in less developed countries (and hence place limited pressure on urban service provision).

URBAN SOCIETY

As early as 1875 Port Moresby was grandiosely described as 'a regular metropolis and a complete babel' (quoted in Inglis 1974:46). Over the subsequent century, the capital city, and to a much lesser extent other towns, have become both more metropolitan and more cosmopolitan. Most urban residents are migrants who live with fellow migrants, identify with their social concerns, speak their 'home' language by choice and experience city life via a world of kinship contacts. Employment is primarily a male phenomenon – enabling men to cut across social ties in the workplace – and migration of women is mainly passive, thus social life in the city has remained a gendered world.

In most towns, there are clear expressions of ecological segregation, contemporary parallels to earlier racial segregation. Squatter settlements are primarily based on ethnic groupings: 'most of the smaller . . . settlements (there are over forty in Port Moresby alone) consist of people from one particular area or even one particular village. The large ones are usually internally divided on quite clear lines into separate village groups' (Jackson 1976:63). Such 'urban villages', the places of 'urban tribalism' (Imbun 1995), albeit with significant economic ties in the urban area, reinforce rural–urban ties rather than assist in the establishment of social ties to the wider community. Over time the urban squatter settlements have even become more like rural villages – rather than suburbs – as kinship ties in towns become more elaborate, residential patterns replicate village life, trees and gardens reach fruition, rituals are enacted in an urban setting, incomes are turned to social objectives, urban leaders emerge and 'village' courts provide social control. Most migrants combine nostalgia, ideology and alienation in the retention (and modification) of custom and the re-assertion of identity. The physical enactment of rituals – often with music and dance – may generate a crowd, or at least a widespread recognition that a particular cultural group retains its traditions in some form, thus also emphasising the identities and distinctiveness of others.

In many employment situations migrants from the same area work together, and access to employment is often gained through kinship or *wantok* associations. Even elements of the 'modern' sector, such as the hundreds of buses that ply the roads of Port Moresby, are owned and operated by extended kin groups. Although kinship ties may develop into formal and informal associations which cut across traditional affiliations, this does not affect residential location and associations may well co-exist with, or be superimposed upon, traditional ethnic ties. The establishment of trade unions might have been expected to foster intergroup relations since unions cut across ethnic boundaries and directly encourage solidarity across them.

However unions are few, rarely militant, primarily associated with the upper echelons of employment (such as bureaucrats and mineworkers) and rarely involve workers at the point of production. The early unions in Papua New Guinea, such as the Lae Workers' Association and the Madang Workers' Association, were largely ineffective not only because of high rates of circular migration, rigid control by the Department of Labour and discouragement by employers, who occasionally fostered ethnic divisions (Plowman 1979), but also because of individuals' limited perceptions of the value of such organisations. This has changed only slowly. Political parties, that might involve individuals with similar aspirations, do not exist at grass-roots level. Since church groups and sports clubs are often regionally or ethnically based, the contexts for social, economic or political relationships across ethnic divisions are few.

In the two largest cities of Papua New Guinea there have been suggestions that a sense of disadvantage may cut across ethnic and regional origins; thus 'signs of a fusion of class and ethnic consciousness are to be found amongst the Gulf and Goilala people in Port Moresby and the Chimbu in Lae' (Townsend 1980a:24) but there are few indications that this is expressed in any concrete form. Class consciousness remains much weaker than ethnic and regional affiliations. The urban gang is 'one of the few structures in which tribal lines are blurred in favour of larger social groupings' (B. Harris 1988; Goddard 1992; Nibbrig 1992). Urban residents can live the bulk of their lives as members of their own cultural group and most choose to do so. Even for those in formal sector employment, the ideology of return reinforces group affiliation in town. Virtually none have rejected, discounted or ignored their cultural identity (D. Ryan 1989) or are able, or allowed, to choose to do so.

In Port Moresby, at least, growing security concerns have provided a contrary differentiation of the city. Europeans, other expatriates and elite Melanesians have increasingly withdrawn to the confines of Tuaguba Hill and barricaded themselves behind high walls and fences, with guards, guard dogs and elaborate security systems. Many have moved into the increasingly common tower blocks with their shared security: a 'siege-like architecture' that is a 'visual provocation . . . to those whose existence has been deemed to lie outside' (Dinnen 1993:79). Altitudinal differentiation, in diverse ways, has become apparent. The neo-colonial city has reverted to something akin to the more segregated colonial city. In quite different ways both security and tradition enable the replication of the old order.

Life in Melanesian cities may be more exciting than a rural existence but it is also hard and difficult. Many urban residents, above all those in the squatter settlements, come from economically marginal areas where income-earning opportunities are few, and where social services like education are inadequate and are, therefore, poorly equipped to gain employment and cope with urban life. City incomes are often barely adequate to support the migrants let alone provide for remittances. Urban life may also be dangerous. Crime is more common in urban areas and there is a widespread perception, evident in *Cowboy and Maria in Town* (McLaren and Owen 1991), that urban life is violent and rural life relatively harmonious. Though the idealisation of rural life may be implausible, commitment to urban life is far less than absolute with such an ideology powerfully in place. Recent urban history, geography and the gulf between 'traditional' and 'modern', however such elusive concepts are defined, have made any notion of community of interest beyond ethnic groups largely invalid. In many respects city life is part of a distant rural social world, and is insecure and temporary.

THE UNPLANNED CITY

Town planning has broadly followed historic British principles. Little land was alienated for urban areas, and much of that was occupied in a piecemeal manner as towns expanded. Most urban boundaries include some traditional village settlements and additional customary land, hence plans and planning practices must respond to a considerable diversity of cultural circumstances, and the great difficulty and cost of obtaining enough appropriate land for contemporary development. Demands for compensation payments – often retrospective – have further discouraged urban development. Urban land is in short supply and land tenure has become the single most important problem discouraging the growth of private investment in urban areas (Kaitilla 1993). Most urban centres have no development plans nor even guidelines on which to base the zoning of land and the allocation of services, and responsibility for urban services and infrastructure is spread over a number of national, local and provincial agencies, and is particularly complicated in Port Moresby, where there is no provincial government for the NCD. Finance for urban development has primarily been allocated from the national government to provincial governments. This has resulted in substantial mismanagement and maladministration, with revenues collected in urban areas being significantly less than expected (Connell and Lea 1993:73–6). Despite the visibility, and gravity, of problems of urban service provision, of which water supply is most obvious, solutions have usually been put in place only in response to crisis situations. Urban management became expensive crisis management, rather than the 'good housekeeping' of planned and monitored urban service provision and development.

In many urban areas there is an acute shortage of land. In Port Moresby traditional ownership of land within the city boundary has prevented its use and made service provision in adjoining areas more expensive. Land acquisition problems have recurred in every facet of urban management; the National Housing Commission has often been unable to find land for housing, the Waterboard land for pumping stations, treatment plants and sewage disposal areas and in many towns there are problems in locating garbage dumps. Land problems in Port Moresby are more severe than elsewhere, because of the city's long history, its establishment adjoining, and later surrounding, traditional villages, and its size and recent growth. The customary landowners in Port Moresby, the Motu-Koitabu people, fear they are gradually losing possession of their land, have no way of protecting it against further alienation and have no control over the migrants who have settled there. They have lost their fishing grounds and most agricultural land and, to some extent unwillingly, have become permanent urban residents with nowhere else to go when they are old, poor, sick or unemployed, as do other Melanesians. The absence of formal mechanisms to deal with these perceived problems, and especially the absence of a democratic political system within the capital, have prevented responses other than incomprehension, despair and occasional violence. At the same time the combination of disputed landownership, increased claims for compensation from landowners (who often perceive this to be the most valuable source of income) and mismanagement have slowed the process of urban development, and rendered it much more complex and expensive than it is in most other countries. Schemes have been developed to increase the speed of access to land but they have been largely unsuccessful. There is very little institutional mediation between landowners and potential developers. The inability to identify, mobilise and transfer – and therefore use – land with productive potential has constrained urban development, made infrastructure construction more complicated and costly and thus hindered economic development: 'the emergence of a modern economy, with rising demands on land administration threatens to overwhelm the present system' (Papua New Guinea Department of Lands and Physical Planning 1988:7). Land tenure problems are not conducive to adequate urban development and management, or the expansion of the urban economy.

Throughout PNG there are problems of access to housing and variations in character within towns are in part determined by, and reflected in, the availability and provision of housing. There are enormous variations in residential standards within, for example, Port Moresby, from the extremely expensive homes and multi-storey luxury flats of Tuaguba Hill, through low-cost National Housing Commission (NHC) buildings to the flimsy plywood and other constructions of shantytowns. Everywhere 'marginal' housing reflects status: illegal or barely tolerated, and hence somewhat insecure, and occupying marginal land, too steep, remote, swampy or flood-prone to be used for other purposes. Yet even between settlements there are enormous differences; the provision of finance for housing is a political issue, funds are scarce and some settlements are populated by groups who are believed to be 'trouble-makers' and criminals, hence their claims on finance for residential improvement, through service schemes and social amenity provision, are less likely to be met. Scarcity of finance and therefore of housing (and related services) reflects, and has often entrenched, urban inequalities.

National housing policies have nowhere been able to cater adequately to the needs of the urban poor and have, in practice, tended to discriminate in favour of middle- and upper-income groups. This was abundantly true at the end of the 1970s (Connell and Curtain 1982), and, despite policies aimed at remedying this situation, is even more apparent now. In the meantime squatter settlements have substantially grown. The performance of government housing policies has fallen well short of expectations and needs. Management and administration of funds have not always been adequate, and rents have rarely been adequately collected. High housing costs have led to public service salaries being extremely high, thus raising the costs of government; similarly high private sector wages, to meet housing costs, have discouraged the establishment of some economic activities, especially manufacturing. Very little housing is privately owned; for example, only about 16 per cent of households in Lae own their own homes, and two-thirds of these were in squatter settlements. Most either rent homes or live in employer-provided housing, because of the high costs of home ownership and commitments to return migration to rural areas (Kaitilla and Sarpong-Oti 1994). Almost all housing consists of detached homes, a model transported from Australia, a situation that has led to very low density urbanisation, and substantially increased the cost of providing infrastructure.

Demand for housing has invariably been substantially greater than supply. Access to the small amount of national housing stock is necessarily limited by costs and other factors; it is unequal and 'an elite is therefore established. It may be an elite of those who can speak English, or it may be an elite which happens to have *wantoks* in the Housing Commission. Whichever it is it makes meaningless the idea of queuing for access to housing' (Bryant 1977:50). The limited availability of rental housing, and very high rents, ensure that there is limited renting of accommodation; 'even a highly paid expatriate employee, earning twice the salary of a Papua New Guinean counterpart, would not be able to afford to pay the market rent for a medium-cost three bedroom house' (Dahanayake 1991:2). In the mid-1980s the government sought to move away from the massive extent of government intervention in the housing market; it sought to rationalise housing policy and facilitate the emergence of a free market in housing, but after political and trade union pressure, policies were weakened and only the sale of government houses was actually implemented (op. cit.:14–16). Inadequate land availability, and provision of housing loan finance, led to the failure of the policy to achieve its original objectives. Subsequently housing policy has again tended to favour large-scale intervention in the market through subsidies rather than attempts to remove the causes of market failure and enable it to function efficiently. Moreover 'the dominance of large foreign building firms, the use of imported building materials and high building standards have discouraged the development of a low-capital building industry' (Asian Development Bank 1992:53). Irrespective of tenure constraints there is difficulty in identifying and obtaining suitable plots of land.

The informal housing sector has become the most substantial part of the larger cities. There are 'squatter settlements' or 'shantytowns' in every town, and neither tentative efforts to upgrade them nor more determined efforts to remove them have been particularly successful. By 1979 settlements in Port Moresby housed about 30,000 people, around 25 per cent of the indigenous population (Matwijiw 1982:293), and similar proportions occurred elsewhere. Since then numbers and proportions have grown substantially and there are dozens of settlements in large towns. In the late 1980s even the small Milne Bay provincial capital of Alotau had twenty distinct settlements. Squatter settlements have been characterised as demographically unbalanced, and inhabited by transients but, in practice, this is a caricature since 'family life is better developed in the informal settlements than anywhere else in the towns' and sex ratios are often more balanced in the settlements than elsewhere in the urban areas (Jackson 1977:29–31). At Bumbu (Lae) more than 90 per cent of the settlers had been living there for more than ten years (Kaitilla 1994), and over half of Toaripi (Gulf) migrants in Nine-Mile, Port Moresby, had never lived in 'their village', had none of the 'survival skills' for village life (or land or close kin there) hence were likely to remain urban settlers (Chao 1985). Older settlements have been expanded, and upgraded, as their occupants develop more political sophistication and acquire higher incomes. Employment levels are little different from those in the city as a whole, though the informal sector plays a more important role. Many settlements have a relatively well-established population in terms of duration of residence, situation within the workforce (and even incomes) and the extent to which residents had constructed relatively permanent homes. They are not simply transient components of the urban scene. However the marginality of the settlements, their recency and illegality and their migrant population have induced considerable hostility to their presence and a widespread unwillingness to provide the circumstances in which they might be upgraded and accepted.

There was some success with 'site and service' housing developments in the 1970s, alongside the upgrading of infrastructure, but early difficulties in obtaining land. The cost of providing even basic services, and growing political opposition to servicing and hence the formal recognition of urban settlements, restricted the success of many schemes. Despite their growing significance, there has been no identification of appropriate policies for settlements or their residents. Provision of other urban services is similar to that of housing. Despite the significance of adequate water and sanitation facilities, these and other basic needs have had no priority, other than when services break down. There is limited investment in service provision: water supplies, sewerage facilities and environmental management (street and stream cleaning and garbage disposal) and also in the provision of open space, transport services, roads and electricity. Moreover there is a very strong correlation between access to formal housing and access to other urban services, with substantial differences between formal housing areas, where water is supplied to every block of land, and settlements, where the capacity to pay for water is less, the supply least adequate and toilets often absent (Bukenya 1993; Connell and Lea 1993:135–42). At best policy could be described as benign neglect; at worst it is inadequate and biased.

Settlements with reasonable service provision, in Port Moresby at least, are much more likely to be those of migrants from the Papuan coast, though even groups like the Goilala, who have a bad reputation, have been able to trade votes for services (Norwood 1981:85–6). In general however amenities in the Goilala and highlands settlements are poorer, and overall they are worse in the settlements than in the formal housing areas.

There is no national water system and there are water supply problems and high costs in small towns. In Port Moresby shortages and disruptions are not unusual in the dry season; this has contributed to health problems and imposed considerable costs on hotels and industries, as the colonial public works system has creaked and rusted into obsolescence. Throughout the urban areas there are inequalities, both in access to housing (owned or rented) and land for construction (legal or illegal) and in the availability of services. All expenditure on urban housing and service provision (especially when there is no expenditure on rural housing) constitutes a subsidy to the urban sector, though the absence of urban planning and housing policies reduces the impact of urban bias. The government has been too poor, too committed elsewhere and too poorly organised, to embark on adequate infrastructure and housing schemes, but this lack of planning has been costly for national and urban social and economic development.

THE URBAN CONDITION

The process of urbanisation has been very much a function of external linkages, in most extreme and dramatic form at the mining towns. The cities and towns have gone through a period of colonial bureaucratic domination towards one of commercial domination, but the city defined by industrialisation is absent. Bureaucracy and commerce dominate the towns, in a way that is rare outside the Pacific region. The informal sector, despite constraints, has become almost as important as the formal sector for income and employment generation, especially for the poor, but the hustle and bustle of Asian and African cities are largely absent. Some characteristics of urbanisation are typical of developing countries: the tendency towards a primate city, the lack of a functional urban hierarchy, the visual if not functional 'dual city', characterised by the growth of the informal housing sector, and management problems in all areas from housing to transport. Not one town has a public transport system. Modern offices, new tourist establishments and the expensive dwellings of the elite co-exist with low-income settlements and place huge demands on the poorly developed service infrastructure. Complex and highly differentiated urban mosaics are rarely under the jurisdiction of a single municipal authority or controlled by planning legislation, despite intermittent attempts at regulation.

The pattern and extent of urban migration in the post-colonial era have been regarded almost ubiquitously as causes of problems, rather than solutions, and hence not as indicators of (or forces behind) economic growth and structural transformation of the economy. Migration, even though limited and discouraged, has still been such that urban labour markets cannot provide a sufficient number of productive jobs, whilst urban services are inadequate and deteriorating. Urban populations have remained characterised by mobility and transience, rather than permanence, though many settlement populations are stable. The emergence of a proletariat has been mainly restricted to those born in the towns or with very poor rural income-earning opportunities. Classes have been detected in urban areas along the lines of: 'the egalitarian Melanesia of old is fast disappearing as class formation cuts across descent group, linguistic and tribal boundaries' (Moore 1992:30; cf. Amarshi *et al.* 1979; H. Thompson and McWilliam 1992). Melanesians too have observed similar trends; Paias Wingti, for example, has said: 'Now we are getting to a system where a rich man may not feel comfortable talking to a poor man. Papua New Guineans who are well off . . . don't want to know about their clansmen. . . . They have already turned into the black bourgeoisie' (quoted in Hegarty 1989:11). Most politicians regard themselves as something of a class. As one Port Moresby member told the 1992 Parliament: 'I represent the elite people in this country. I don't represent the *kanakas* [backward rural folk]'. The army and police also regard themselves as elite groups, but there are tensions within these groups. There are also acute perceptions of difference; 'similar ideas are expressed by rural villagers and the urban poor' (Standish 1993:217; cf. Kulick 1993). However though the better off may be becoming an elite, and provide less support to their rural kin and *wantok* groups, there is little evidence that they function as a class to defend their interests. Equally, few other groups do. The cities remain primarily characterised by fragmentation along ethnic and cultural lines, rather than by such modern divisions as class and wealth.

The urban legacy of colonialism has proved to be an inadequate basis for achieving the objectives of economic development and national (or regional) integration in Melanesia since it provided for the development of an entrenched, structured inequality. Independence resulted in a radical change in the racial composition of those with political power, but little impact on the mechanisms that maintained a small group's dominance. However, in the absence of significant industrialisation, the slow rate of urbanisation has been of positive benefit to social and economic development, but the pace of urbanisation is quickening, with a concomitant increase in the pressure on, and demand for, urban services. Fragmentation and tension between landowners and migrants in the face of land shortages, growing urban unemployment, bureaucratic ineptitude and political corruption – hastening privatisation – have all contributed to disarray and division. Most aspects of infrastructure provision can be addressed only with the support of the urban population as a whole, and there are no institutional processes through which this might occur. Diversity and spontaneity have been more apparent. Not only have the introductory questions that Michael Somare raised before independence become even more relevant, but also all the words that he feared have become needed, and 'poverty' might now be added. The word *pasindia* has also filled a gap, whilst criminal *raskals* are primarily an urban phenomenon. New words and new problems have emerged; effective new policies to generate urban economic growth or reduce social problems have not.

9   Uneven development

Government officials in Papua New Guinea say they have discovered
another 'lost tribe', just months after stumbling upon the Liawep people of
the Sepik. The latest group, dubbed the Toulambi tribe, apparently was discovered in a remote area of thick jungle in the Papua New Guinea
Highlands. . . . Two near-naked members of the tribe were 'scared to death'
when taken by a hunting party to the nearest government station to taste
store food and view white men and aeroplanes for the first time. . . . But
some people remain sceptical. They believe the group may belong to known
isolated border tribes but have been left off the latest census.

(*SMH* 22 October 1993)

No country in the world experiences greater challenges to achieving development and equity across the nation than PNG. Late colonial rule, belated
contact with a large proportion of the population, many languages and cultures have all emphasised diversity, enhanced and encouraged by difficulties
in communication across mountain barriers, seas and swamps. Acute spatial
differentiation has marked three phases of change: pre-colonial, colonial and
post-colonial times. In the pre-colonial era there were differences in living
conditions. Those who occupied more favourable areas, mainly coastal environments offering a combination of terrestrial and marine resources, were
better off than those elsewhere. Even within many local areas, such as the Tari
basin, there were variations in access to resources (B.J. Allen and Crittenden
1987). Pre-colonial geography was marked by great differences in population
density, and by the advanced and intensive agricultural practices of the highland valleys. Colonialism and capitalism resulted in the exploitation of
coastal land areas for plantations, and also mines, initially using labour from
nearby areas, resulting in significant contact with the outside world. The traditional order changed with the introduction of new religions, foods,
technology and ways of life. After the war the highlands was drawn into the
colonial endeavour, as a source of labour and a location of plantations, but
more belatedly absorbed into the infrastructural and social development that
already existed in many coastal areas. The post-colonial era brought little
change to this overall structure, despite the establishment of significant gold

and copper mines in remote places. Many areas of the country, some with quite large populations, have few physical resources and are handicapped by their isolation. Between the coasts and the highlands, thinly populated areas of mountains and swamp were and are largely ignored, as development efforts focused on relatively large, accessible and nucleated populations, that were usually on areas of productive agricultural land. A few tiny population groups, as the above quotation suggests, may still be virtually without contact with the rest of the nation. Over time the concentration of resources in more accessible areas has emphasised uneven development, at local, regional and national levels.

DECENTRALISATION AND INEQUALITY

At independence the new nation 'inherited an economy severely distorted spatially and sectorally' (B.J. Allen 1992:58). The main sources of income were cash crops from the coasts, especially the islands and a few upland valleys, whilst mining was a rare inland economic activity. New inequalities were created during the 1960s when the policy of maximisation of economic growth in favoured areas was being pursued. By the early 1970s it was apparent that marked economic variations between provinces (Wilson 1975) necessitated some form of political or administrative decentralisation. Around independence the government sought to reverse the social and economic trends of the previous decade, that had favoured centralisation, by stressing policies of redistribution, self-reliance, rural development and decentralisation (Chapter 2) but, despite the rhetoric, and the establishment of provincial governments, spatial considerations and regional issues were absent from development planning. Moreover the notion of decentralisation was 'ill-suited to the political culture, the country's economic and financial balance and the available human resources' (Standish 1983:236; see also Chapter 10), and provincial governments had no influence on national equity issues.

During the 1970s, with government emphasis on decentralisation, there was some movement towards greater equality in the provision of services, but no progress towards equalisation of highly unequal incomes. Indeed the four principal forms of government expenditure – the capital works programme, the rural improvement programme, Development Bank lending and allocations from the National Public Expenditure Plan (NPEP) – gave no significant preference to the poorer provinces (Berry 1978; Berry and Jackson 1981). For the subsequent period, 1980–4, NPEP expenditure went to reasonably well-off provinces, notably Central and West New Britain, whereas the four worst-off provinces had poorer allocations (Axline 1986). Attempts to divert funds to the least developed provinces through a national Fiscal Commission failed (de Albuquerque and D'Sa 1986). Specific programmes were abandoned, to some extent replaced by integrated rural development projects in the poorer provinces, though these were no more successful

(Chapter 5). Poorer regions were poorly served by national political and economic decisions, and did not 'catch up'; their interests had few effective advocates. Regional, provincial and district inequalities – of incomes and human development – are likely to have increased further, since the early 1980s, though the evidence is difficult to assess. In the late 1960s and early 1970s, data on agriculture, health and education services and accessibility showed that development was most apparent in and around the urban centres of each province and that the least developed areas were more isolated areas of late contact, such as many highland fringe districts (Wilson 1975). Uneven development was more apparent within provinces than between them. There have been no subsequent comparable studies. By the end of the 1970s inequality within and between rural areas was both entrenched and apparently increasing, the 'more developed' areas fared better than the 'less developed' areas (Colebatch 1977:18), whilst the process of development also favoured richer people who had achieved some degree of economic success, thus 'concentrating wealth and experience in the hands of a developing class of largely rural entrepreneurs' (Barnett 1979:778). At all levels, national policies accentuated rather than removed inequalities.

Subsequent assessments of inequality have mainly been at provincial level because of the lack of data for districts, hence it is no longer possible to assess the extent of rural–urban inequality. Factor analysis of twenty-eight socio-economic indicators (grouped as demographic, agricultural, economic, educational and health) from around 1980 concluded, predictably, that the five most developed provinces were the island provinces, whilst the least developed provinces were the highlands provinces (other than Western Highlands) and West Sepik. This situation had scarcely changed between 1971 and 1982; the highlands remained the most disadvantaged region, Manus had improved somewhat whilst Central had slipped back (D'Sa 1987). An attempt to construct a Human Development Index using just three indicators (income, life expectancy and primary school enrolments) for 1972 and 1980 reached very similar conclusions, with the islands provinces again most successful and the Southern Highlands faring least well in both years (Fernando 1992). In terms of income alone there were clear indications of growing inequalities between provinces over a similar time period, to the extent that they provided 'a disturbing picture of regional imbalance' (Treadgold 1987:vi) since income inequality was entrenched and more severe. Both incomes and more broadly based human development have probably become increasingly concentrated in the same provinces, but since 1980 there have been no data to demonstrate this proposition.

At the district level the situation is more complex, not least because the eighty-seven districts themselves vary considerably in size and population. Five factors accounted for much of the uneven development in 1978–80 – education, urbanisation, access to basic services, status of the rural commercial sector and 'dependency' (linked to migration) – and further emphasised, in a different way and at a different scale, the substantial differences between highlands and islands provinces. The 'more developed' districts tended to be coastal, with some exceptions, while the 'less developed' districts tended to be inland, and/or districts with poor access to a town of larger than about 3,000 people. Districts with towns, even small towns, tended to be more developed. A broad belt of less developed districts stretched from the border with Irian Jaya, through the highlands to Milne Bay (Figure 9.1). By contrast, in the islands, only Kandrian and Pomio were 'less developed' districts. This spatial structure of development was as predictable as that for the provinces, with development being a function of colonial contact, differences in the distribution of resources, transport infrastructure, plantation activity and the impact of urban centres (de Albuquerque and D'Sa 1986). Substantial variations occurred within almost all provinces, hence entire provinces were never entirely 'least developed'. Few recognisable changes had occurred since independence, but subsequent mining in Ok Tedi, Porgera and Misima has contributed to more broadly based development.

Since independence, a number of developments have favoured urban areas, but the extent to which rural–urban inequalities have increased or decreased is difficult to assess. The location of towns (and especially isolated Port Moresby) has continued to reflect the colonial economy and is unrelated to the needs of national development. Urban services have increased relative to rural services and have served the urban rather than the hinterland population (Jackson 1979), since governments prefer investment in urban areas, where developments are likely to be more profitable and taxation more easily achieved, whilst the growth of urban populations strengthened the case for urban policies. By far the most important trade union is the Public Employees Association, followed by other public service unions, and there are no rural unions. The larger unions are the most successful in terms of achieving better conditions for their members. Urban Members of Parliament have become more influential than rural MPs, in part because of their relative sophistication and ability. At the end of the 1980s the two largest aid projects in the country – the Rouna hydro-electric scheme and the reconstruction of Port Moresby General Hospital – were both solely for the benefit of the capital city. Wage employment has mainly increased in urban areas. Financial institutions have tended to provide credit to the urban sector rather than the rural sector. In Morobe Province, for example, the city of Lae was particularly favoured for the allocation of Development Bank loans (and also capital works expenditure) in the late 1970s (Connell 1979a:598). During the 1980s loans generally favoured urban areas to the extent that a restructuring of the Bank was necessary (Chapter 5). Public expenditure, especially in the transport sector (see pp. 226–30), has also been heavily concentrated in urban areas; Port Moresby has been the major beneficiary. A number of services, such as electricity and piped water, are almost entirely confined to urban areas and some areas are particularly favoured. Reticulated water supplies are non-existent in rural areas and absent too in some small towns. Roughly half of all electricity generated in the late 1980s was for use at the Ok Tedi and

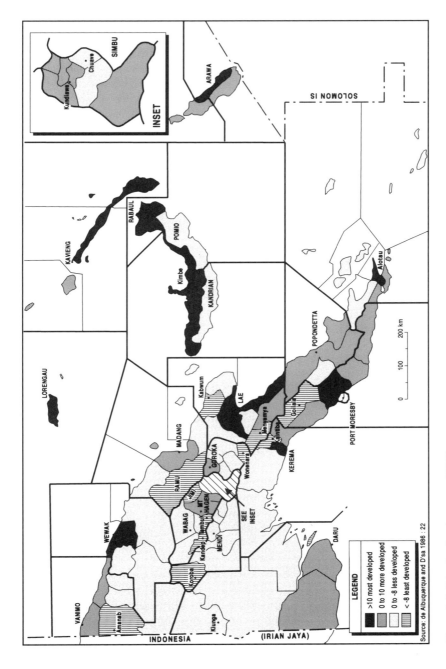

Figure 9.1 District development (1980)

Source: de Albuquerque and D'sa 1986 : 22

Panguna mines. The remainder is supplied by the state electricity company, ELCOM, based on two grids, one covering Port Moresby and the other supplying Lae and the highlands. ELCOM also supplies provincial towns but its mandate for financial soundness of investments (World Bank 1992:83) prevents the extension of electricity supply into rural areas. By mid-1992 just twenty-six villages in three provinces – Central, Madang and East New Britain – had gained electricity, despite a specific ELCOM budget of more than K1.5 million for rural electrification (*TPNG* 7 May 1992). The provision of health, education and other services has become more centralised, and also of poorer quality in more remote, 'difficult' areas (see pp. 231–46). According to the few measures that exist, the 'more developed' areas are moving further and further apart from the 'less developed' areas, as the colonial bias in the distribution of government services and public investment (Connell and Curtain 1982) increased in post-colonial times. Weak planning capacity and pork-barrelling (Chapter 10) have emphasised trends towards the centralisation of the 'modern' market economy.

Within a few years of independence, despite the prevailing rhetoric, it was well established that 'urban areas have received a disproportionate share of the national wealth and any guidelines that are drawn up for future urbanisation must deal with a need to reduce expenditure per head on urban dwellers' (Papua New Guinea National Planning Office 1977:12). As the rhetoric has weakened so urban bias has increased. It was less well established that 'not *all* urban dwellers benefited from the expenditure' (ibid.). Overall public sector expenditure is heavily concentrated in urban areas yet two groups particularly have received a disproportionate share of government expenditure: expatriates, in both the public and private sectors, and national public servants who, following expatriate 'models', have been able to secure government housing at heavily subsidised rentals. Unequal access to housing is matched, and emphasised, by uneven access to all other services. Nevertheless, if rural incomes and lifestyles are widely perceived as inadequate, worsening, and producing considerable frustration (e.g. Kulick 1993), they have not led to substantial rural–urban migration. The costs and uncertainties of living are much less in rural areas. Urban poverty exists alongside rural affluence. The urban legacy of colonialism has proved an inadequate basis for a more spatially equitable development, but has rather provided the context for internal colonialism.

TRANSPORT AND COMMUNICATIONS

The extraordinary fragmentation of PNG has given communications a key role in national development and national unity. Transport costs and accessibility are critical for economic and social development. More so than in almost any other country in the world, air transport has played, and continues to play, a prominent role in development. In large parts of the country the aeroplane was the first form of modern transport; in some areas vehicles are still unknown. Between the wars PNG was a world leader in civil aviation. Aeroplanes were important for early exploration of parts of the highlands, for developing the gold-fields at Wau and Bulolo and more recently both for basic communications to remote communities, mainly on the fringes of the highlands, and in opening up new mining ventures at Porgera and Kutubu. There are more than four hundred airstrips in the country, most simple grass airstrips, and twenty principal airports. Air services have proved crucial for health in rural areas; most of the ninety-two patients airlifted within Milne Bay province alone, over a two year period, would have died if flights had not been available (Barss and Blackford 1983). Helicopters, and single-engined aeroplanes, reach the remotest airstrips, where passengers and cargoes are weighed to determine the viability of particular flights and crashes, in difficult terrain and weather conditions, are not infrequent. There are still many 'frontiers' within the country.

Since the late 1960s, and especially with the completion of the Highlands (Okuk) Highway from Lae to Goroka and eventually beyond, the primacy of air transport has been eroded (Figure 9.2). In more remote provinces, such as Enga, this transition did not occur until the 1970s. By 1950 there were about 4,300 kilometres of vehicular roads (many suitable only for four-wheel drive vehicles), but by 1990 this had increased to about 20,000 kilometres, although definitions and measurements of roads are highly flexible. A number of major roads, such as between Madang and Kundiawa, have been proposed for years but construction costs alone are prohibitive. The major 'gap' in the road network is between Port Moresby and the Highlands Highway system, but there are grave doubts about even the economic benefits that might be derived from high-cost construction. Expenditure has tended to be focused in urban areas and many major projects are deferred indefinitely. By contrast to lavish expenditure on grand urban schemes, returns to which do not justify the investment, the decline in self-help labour in many rural areas and limited provincial finance have resulted in problems in maintaining the present feeder road system. In some areas, the network has effectively contracted as in the Asaro valley (*PC* 7 June 1996), symptomatic of and contributing to the decline in other rural services. Road transport has become increasingly centralised. Passenger and freight movements are growing most rapidly along the Highlands Highway and in and around Port Moresby. Urban transport, other than for pedestrians, is entirely by road. PNG has both bypassed the railway age and ignored low-cost bicycle transport (so contributing to the high cost of fuel imports, traffic congestion and some degree of air and noise pollution in Port Moresby).

There is no great tradition of maritime trade and transport, other than in parts of Papua (cf. Harding 1967), so that coastal shipping services are both new and undeveloped for a country where land transport is difficult. Shipping services ply between Port Moresby and other main ports, such as Lae, Rabaul, Wewak and Kavieng, but feeder services to smaller ports are irregular. More than half of all coastal freight (around 70 per cent by 1992) is

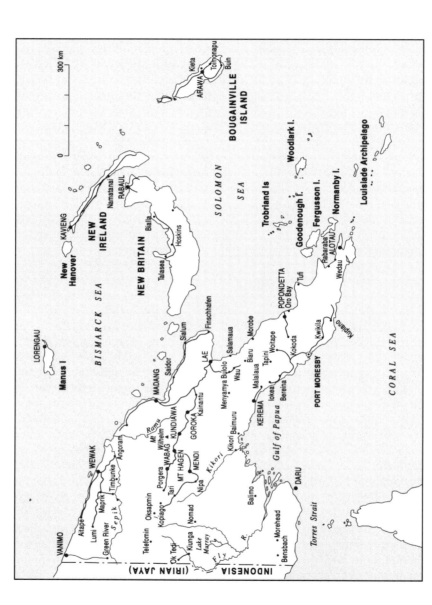

Figure 9.2 Main roads

loaded and discharged at Port Moresby and Lae, a concentration that has increased since containerisation in the 1980s, leading to greater costs in other ports, and hence their marginalisation from the system. By the start of the 1980s some eleven of the sixteen ports operated by the Papua New Guinea Harbour Board were operating at a loss, and only political and social factors kept them in operation. At a local scale, improvements in marine technology and access have been few. At Wanigela (Oro), for example, a government launch from Tufi, 40 kilometres away, collected cash crops just two or three times a year 'if we were lucky and by then much of the bagged produce would be weevily' (Sheen 1984:44). Despite village demands for improved transport, social and economic problems have hampered small transport ventures throughout the country.

All freight and passenger transport (with the exception of Air Niugini) is privately owned. Sometimes ownership is highly localised and privatised. When a bridge on one Simbu main road was washed away by floods, 'a temporary wooden bridge [was] erected by Kagul youth. A sum of K2 is collected from anybody who crossed that one-trunk bridge. Others take the cheapest route by crossing the fast-flowing river on *gumi* (tyre-tubes). A handful of village boys, who own tyre tubes, provide this form of ferry service and charge passengers K1' (*PC* 12 February 1994). In places villagers demand payment for access to particular roads. The extent of private ownership and very different and separate modes of transport, have contributed to the absence of planning and the lack of integration of the overall transport system. Private ownership is regulated but scarcely controlled, and national investment in all facets of the transport system is small for a country so fragmented. Transport costs are high and increased by the limited connectivity of the transport system, and the need to use several modes of transport.

Large numbers of villages remain distant from modern transport facilities. Gapun village, just 10 kilometres from the north coast of PNG, is typical of many isolated villages: 'surrounded on all sides by rainforest and sago swamps, connected to other villages (the nearest of which is about a two hour journey away) and to the outside world by narrow, choked waterways and slim bush paths subject to flooding' (Kulick 1992:7; cf. Pomponio 1992). Since roads and feeder roads, and the movement of vehicles and people provide a structure over which information and commodities travel, frustration over inaccessibility is widespread (Kulick 1993). Not surprisingly 'road' has long been, for many, both metaphor and reality of development. Finding the 'road to development' is a common theme and a universal goal that might involve various strategies, from the *rot bilong bisnis* (business road) to the *rot bilong raskal* (criminal road); even 'walkathons' have been seen as catalysts for development (Goddard 1995). Especially where roads remain absent, 'the road-to-be is a symbol of salvation, of endless economic gain, a path toward material wealth and increasingly accessible consumerism' (Hayano 1990:2; Hirsch 1994). The failure of economic development in more remote areas, as much as anything else, can be attributed to government failure to introduce effective transport systems; 'many villagers have returned, in frustration, to purely subsistence farming, following the loss of successive crops while awaiting transport' (Callick *et al.* 1990:15.1) or moved closer to road access points. The impact of roads has been ambiguous. Improved transport provision has resulted in increased prices for cash crops, better market access and reduced prices for imported commodities. Other perceptions of road construction, notably in the highlands, have been particularly gloomy; though new transport 'may promote regional and national awareness [it] brings its own problems. Accidents and associated inter-tribal and inter-racial violence, theft of cargo and the spread of prostitution and syphilis follow with increasing traffic' (Southern 1973:75). Despite such disappointments demands for improved access are ubiquitous. Though the feeder road network may have stagnated since independence, personal mobility has increased enormously, in distance and volume. Large towns have a commuter workforce, rural access to stores, markets and services (including entertainment) is of growing significance and many villagers have become familiar with some facets of urban life. Before the war only a few men had left their culture areas for extended periods of time; in post-independence years mobility has become more central to everyday life.

Transport is marked by incomplete integration, great distances and difficulties, whereas telecommunications are instant and effective, and have enabled PNG to go from pre-literacy to post-literacy, in some contexts without an intermediate phase, because of difficulties in the diffusion of education services. Throughout PNG the radio has become an essential household item, incorporating personal information and messages in particular programmes, and vastly more important than newspapers which remain largely urban and elite phenomena. Despite their early introduction, 'their effective reach has been largely limited to the urban literates and readership has not extended far outside the main towns' (Centurion and Philpott 1994:90); in rural areas they are at least as important for rolling local tobacco into cigarettes. The telecommunications system is highly sophisticated, with PNG a world leader in the field of solar-powered telecommunications and repeater stations (Ranck 1984), though – somewhat ironically – these have been prone to attack by dissident landowners seeking compensation. By the mid-1980s there was international competition to establish television. Large transnationals sought out new markets and domestic television broadcasting eventually began in 1987, through EM-TV, owned and operated by Australia's Channel Nine (part of Kerry Packer's Publishing and Broadcasting Ltd media empire), though cable viewers can also tune in to Australian channels. The arrival of television enhanced the already substantial market for videos. Their growing prevalence – and the primarily imported TV content – predictably gave rise to 'community concern that there are too many videos available which are incompatible with and possibly inimical to PNG society' (Centurion and Philpott 1994:93), whilst television advertising was unduly emphasising consumption, materialism and imported goods and concepts. Television has not been consciously either developed, or manipulated, to serve national goals, and is very much an imported institution (cf. Sullivan 1993). In every area of communications – telephones, television, newspapers, etc. – there is extensive urban bias and rural access has been limited; though policy is aimed at redressing this bias that task is as difficult to achieve as in other areas of service provision. With limited literacy and without electricity the rural areas are likely to remain poorly served; the new cultural orientation beyond PNG, shaped through television, has tended to marginalise rural areas.

HEALTH

PNG experiences a range of health problems, traditionally characterised by infectious tropical diseases, some of which remain common (whilst there has been a resurgence in yaws and malaria), but increasingly also marked by an 'epidemiological transition' from infectious to 'modern' non-communicable diseases (NCDs), such as diabetes and cardiovascular disease. The incidence of disease is unevenly distributed, especially between the coasts (and the urban centres there) and the highlands, just as are the preventive and curative systems, which have both indigenous and introduced components. Health status has not improved substantially in the post-independence years, and the health system has disintegrated in many remote areas.

There are considerable endemic health problems, typical of tropical countries, historically characterised by the extent of such diseases as leprosy, yaws, malaria and hookworm, in coastal areas. A range of infectious diseases continues to be the major cause of sickness and death. The most important causes of mortality are the common infectious diseases, including pneumonia, malaria, gastroenteritis, tuberculosis and measles. Accidents and trauma are of increasing importance, with the former having become as important as malaria, through continued traditional reasons (falling coconuts or pigs' tusks), the growth of the forestry industry (where basic precautions are often not taken), a resurgence of tribal fighting (and the steady shift from bows and arrows to guns) and an increase in vehicle accidents, since the accident rate is thirteen times that of the United Kingdom (Dyke 1993). Morbidity rates from acute respiratory infections, diarrhoea and malaria have all increased in recent years. Recent population growth and new mobility in most communities have significantly increased the rate of transmission of diseases and the extent of morbidity (Aitken 1991:24–6) though, until recently, this increase was paralleled by improvements in the health service.

Changes in health status have had geographical components. In 1978, when pneumonia was the leading cause of death in hospitals, followed by gastroenteritis and related diseases, both modernisation and regional differentiation were apparent in the manner in which accidents and violence were more important in Port Moresby, whilst pneumonia was primarily a highlands disease (Riley and Davies 1982:160). Population mobility in the late twentieth century resulted in the more rapid transmission of some coastal diseases, including malaria and sexually transmitted diseases (STDs), from the coast to the highlands. Tuberculosis reached the highlands only in the 1960s. Mobility has also increased the severity of epidemics of influenza and measles in the post-war years. This diffusion of disease has tended to emphasise the growing extent of tropical, and other, diseases in the highlands producing a rather more homogeneous pattern of diseases within the country.

Whilst there has been some movement towards homogeneity of diseases, there are still enormous variations, especially between the urban areas, where 'modern' diseases are becoming important, and remote rural areas, where the pattern of illness has changed little from pre-contact times. One such remote group, the Hagahai, constitute a declining population with a heavy disease burden, including respiratory tract infections, tinea, malaria, tropical ulcers, otitis media, conjunctivitis, colds and diarrhoea; a number of diseases, including filariasis, malaria, Ross River virus, hookworm and several cold viruses are endemic (Jenkins 1987, 1988; Jenkins *et al.* 1989). Not only were health conditions in many pre-contact populations poor, but also they initially deteriorated with contact with the outside world. In other remote areas, health status remains much worse than in other parts of the country, partly as a result of poor nutritional status, inadequate access to health services and the recency of 'new' diseases.

There was historic success with the eradication of some tropical diseases, but a number have staged revivals. Yaws (a skin disease) was once prevalent throughout the country and was highly contagious. A yaws eradication campaign continued until 1959 when it was effectively eradicated. However in 1984 it again had to be restored as a reportable disease, after there were outbreaks in a number of rural areas, including Sepik (Garner *et al.* 1986). Leprosy has proved even more difficult to eradicate, though a prevalence rate of 7.6 per thousand in 1973 was reduced to 1.8 in 1988, and new therapies have resulted in some optimism that it would have disappeared by the end of the twentieth century. The experience of yaws suggests that the eradication of most endemic tropical diseases is extremely difficult, however, especially in coastal and island regions.

Malaria further exemplifies this situation, since it remains particularly significant in coastal areas, though in the 1950s it spread into most parts of the highlands following the return migration of infected plantation labourers. Until then areas above 1,300 metres were free of malaria, though below that altitude the virulence of malaria is such that it has been the most important historical determinant of population distribution in the country (Riley 1983). After independence the malaria control programme was reduced and malaria again became an important cause of disease and death, to the extent that it returned to a level similar to that of the 1950s, and became a more serious problem than ever before. At the start of 1994 a malaria outbreak in the Trobriand Islands (Milne Bay) resulted in more than a hundred deaths, a result of low immunisation rates, lack of drugs and few patrols because of fuel and staff shortages, in a situation where 80 per cent of the population tested positive to malaria (*PC* 28 March, 8 April 1994). Following the arrival of a chloroquine-resistant parasite from Asia the eradication of malaria has become more difficult than at any time since independence.

Acute respiratory infections are the commonest diseases, and include respiratory viruses, such as measles and influenza, and major diseases such as pneumonia. Epidemics of tuberculosis and pneumonia are not unknown, as on Karkar Island (Madang), where the island was declared an 'epidemic area' in 1993 after an outbreak of tuberculosis, affecting more than a hundred people, combined with a high incidence of STD cases and two deaths from AIDS (*TPNG* 29 July 1993). By contrast, the extent of mortality from pneumonia has declined, because of the widespread use of antibiotics, especially penicillin. Influenza can still have a substantial effect on small communities. A 1969 epidemic in the highlands cost around 2,000 lives (Hayano 1990:111–12) and at the start of 1994, an influenza epidemic killed more than 170 people on the north coast. Whilst isolation and remoteness have helped to prevent the spread of infectious diseases, they have also prevented the delivery of medical services, either preventive or curative, in the most distant places (see pp. 235–40). Both tuberculosis and pneumonia have tended to affect the poor; an early study demonstrated that the prevalence of tuberculosis was two to three times higher amongst people living in squatter settlements in Port Moresby than those who lived in old-established settlements (Mylius and Wigley 1971), as a result of poor nutrition, hygiene and sanitation. That situation is still true.

The arrival of new diseases into the country has substantially changed the national health position, as the transmission of malaria to the highlands had earlier transformed the regional health situation. Tuberculosis reached PNG only in the late nineteenth century, the precursor of other new diseases, and part of a continuing process. Sexually transmitted diseases, the 'pox britannica', were not generally significant until the 1960s when there was a syphilis outbreak in coastal and highlands urban areas, partly reflecting the spread of prostitution to highlands towns, whilst urbanisation, changing forms of housing, clothing and nutrition have all increased susceptibility to infection. Most recent changes in health status have also resulted from lifestyle changes; asthma is now evident, alongside stress, obesity, cardiovascular diseases, alcoholism, dental caries and various forms of cancer. Malnutrition is not a new problem though its contemporary, more urban, distribution is different from its historical extent (Chapter 3). There has therefore been the onset of an epidemiological transition, from a health structure characterised by infectious diseases to one where 'modern' diseases play a more important role; this transition has posed problems for the national health service because the cost and difficulty of treating the latter prevents easy or rapid solutions.

One of the more severe problems that PNG faces is that of the increasing incidence of STDs and above all AIDS, though the present situation is better than in many developing countries. The incidence of STDs has grown rapidly since independence and they are particularly prevalent in the larger urban areas where their significance has become comparable to that of pneumonia or gastroenteritis. A quarter of all STD cases were in Port Moresby, but there were disproportionately high rates in the Western and Eastern Highlands. The spread of STDs is occurring in towns, secondary and tertiary educational institutions, along transportation routes and in those parts of PNG where premarital sex has been traditionally acceptable (Lombange 1984; Gillett 1990). AIDS appeared for the first time in 1987, the number of known HIV-positive cases has doubled in each succeeding year and there is considerable potential for further rapid spread, as prostitution increases and most sex is without condoms. At the start of 1994 there were fifty confirmed cases of AIDS and more than a hundred HIV-positive cases, though the real number was probably ten times as great (*TPNG* 10 February 1994). The extent of sexual networking (relations with multiple sexual partners) has shown no sign of decreasing and is likely to worsen the present deteriorating situation, where there is national denial of its presence and significance.

Most non-communicable diseases were rare until the post-war years. Diabetes now has a reasonably high prevalence in coastal urban areas. Cardiovascular disease was unknown in the post-war years, and the first case of ischaemic heart disease was not reported until 1964. It remains primarily an urban phenomenon. There has been a considerable increase in the incidence of peptic ulcers, vehicle (and other 'modern') accidents and appendicitis; each of these problems increased at least fourfold in the quarter of a century after 1961, reflecting 'the impact of transition from village to urban lifestyle on the morbidity patterns' (Sinnett *et al.* 1992:382). Cancer is being diagnosed increasingly frequently, and the increase in cigarette (rather than home-grown tobacco) smoking is likely to lead to an increase in lung cancer rates. Cigarette consumption has increased substantially, following commercialisation and active advertising campaigns (Vallance *et al.* 1987). The proportion of the adult population that smokes is one of the highest in the world and the female rate (with about 80 per cent of women smoking) is the highest in the world. Alcohol consumption is relatively recent (Chapter 3), and the 'drinking explosion' is more recent still, hence the consequences of long-term heavy drinking, such as alcoholism and cirrhosis of the liver, are not yet considerable. Nevertheless by the 1970s heavy expenditure on alcohol was cutting into the food budgets of some urban households, with negative nutritional consequences (Morauta and Olela 1980), and domestic violence has also ensued, contributing to problems of family breakdown. The extent and severity of non-communicable diseases are related to socio-economic change, including changes in activity and consumption patterns. Consequently they are most prevalent amongst urban public servants, especially in Port Moresby, and there are considerable differences between the coast and the highlands and, to a lesser extent, between urban and rural populations.

Throughout the country there are both introduced and indigenous medical systems though in some places there were, and are, few traditional specialists or practitioners. Indigenous medical systems are, or have been, of considerable sophistication in terms of both the specific skills that are involved, including bone-setting and trepanning, and the aetiologies and cures. Disease aetiology and process are still conceived in traditional cognitive models yet participation in the modern health system is commonplace. What has emerged in many places is a dual hierarchy of alternatives, perceived as complementary (other than by a number of practitioners in each system), which has enabled much greater diversity and flexibility in response to illness (L. Schwartz 1969; Hamnett and Connell 1981). Traditional systems have tended to give way to modern systems, since drugs such as penicillin provide new and effective therapies and explanatory systems. Accessibility and convenience are also important variables in choice of therapy. Women are less likely to use modern health services, especially obstetrics, since it is perceived to deny their competency, invade their privacy, violate their modesty and denigrate their own knowledge, authority and skills (McPherson 1994). Traditional systems have not been linked into the modern system, since healers have preferred their financial autonomy, missions have opposed the ideologies attached to traditional systems and there have been few studies of the effectiveness of traditional therapies (Jenkins 1992; Wesche 1987). Medical pluralism is only one part of wider pluralism involving a variety of social, economic and political phenomena.

Medical services were effectively introduced only in the twentieth century. Before the Second World War the number of doctors had reached twenty-two, but there were few indications of any positive impact in terms of greater life expectancy and lower mortality and morbidity rates. A programme of hospital construction was initiated in 1947 though the first major hospital was completed only in 1957 in Port Moresby. The first hospital in the highlands was opened in 1966 at Goroka. During the 1950s and 1960s life expectancies began to increase and some major diseases, such as tuberculosis and yaws, were reduced or eradicated. The 'golden age' of medicine had reached PNG; massive and optimistic campaigns were launched against malaria, yellow fever, sleeping sickness and other diseases; there were widespread assumptions that 'total victory' was possible (Denoon 1989) and some victories were achieved.

At independence health was regarded as an important issue, and the 1974 National Health Plan focused on expanding the provision of health services to rural areas and thus achieving more or less universal access, a policy similar to that proposed for the educational system (see pp. 241–6). There was some movement towards such egalitarian goals. Increased expenditure was allocated to health services. Between 1975 and 1984 government spending on health care increased from 5 per cent to 9 per cent of budget expenditure, and continued to increase between 1985 and 1990 but at a rate slightly slower than that of population growth, hence per capita expenditure has fallen (Naylor *et al.* 1993:170). The growing expenditure on health care in the 1970s paralleled a shift from campaigns against diseases to a focus on primary health care

(PHC), with greater consideration of the social and environmental context of health. During the 1960s and 1970s there was rapid localisation, the emergence of Melanesian doctors, and the closer integration of mission and government facilities. Decentralisation, with rural services being shifted to the control of provincial governments, was less successful. Despite the movement towards PHC the largest component of health capital expenditure has increasingly gone towards hospital construction. Salaries consist of more than 70 per cent of recurrent expenditure and over 95 per cent of health expenditure is on recurrent costs (Thomason and Newbrander 1991). Supporting PHC activities has become increasingly difficult. Each province has a hospital, and increased expenditure on aid posts (dispensaries) and their staff meant that the percentage of people living more than two hours' walk from an aid post halved from 14 per cent of the population in 1973 to 7 per cent in 1984 (Goodman *et al.* 1985). There were regional variations; some 18 per cent of New Ireland's population were beyond the two hour limit, compared with just 1 per cent in densely populated Simbu and none in the NCD (Table 9.1). Real access to health services cannot easily be measured (in the same way that access to education can be measured) since demand is variable, and health status is intangible.

The medical system is hierarchical. Most towns have a hospital of some kind. In the first decade after independence there was an expansion of health centres, sub-centres and aid posts, with an increase in hospital beds. Since 1984 the rate of expansion of facilities has slowed considerably. Between 1973 and 1990 the number of hospital beds per capita remained relatively steady (increasing from 217 per bed in 1973 to 243 in 1990) whilst the number of people per aid post fell from 1,678 to 1,633. However the number of staff has fallen since independence, substantially worsening the staff per capita ratio. This has been particularly significant for doctors, whose numbers fell from 266 to 260 between 1973 and 1990, hence the population per doctor rose from 9,760 to 14,390. This has become a serious problem since there were only around 15 medical graduates per year between 1988 and 1992, overseas recruitment is difficult and expensive, doctors are increasingly entering the private sector and most are in large urban centres. There are considerable regional differences in health provision. Very high per capita expenditure occurs in the NCD (the location of the national referral hospital) and also in the island provinces. By contrast some provinces with larger populations, such as Western Highlands, Madang and East Sepik, have low per capita levels of expenditure (Table 9.1). These differences do not necessarily lead to poorer health outcomes in particular provinces, nor do they reveal the considerable variations at district level, though they do suggest that in the highlands, and in some fragmented provinces such as Milne Bay, the basic availability of health care is probably poorer than in many parts of the coast and islands. There are also variations in quality.

At the base of the hierarchy there are more than 2,200 aid posts (dispensaries) throughout the country offering basic services – anti-malaria tablets,

Table 9.1 Health and disease indicators by province

	Infant mortality (1980)	Life expectancy (1980)	Malaria incidence (%)[1]	TB per 100 population	Births in hospital or health centre (1980) (%)	BCG vaccination coverage (1982) (%)	Population more than two hours from PHC (1979) (%)	School Dental Health Service coverage (1981)[2]	Population per medical officer (1990)	Health expenditure per capita (1988) (thousand kina)	Primary school enrolment (1985) (%)
Southern Highlands	116	44	16	0.1	18	47	6	1	39.714	12.4	51
West Sepik	104	42	52	2.0	11	45	15	5	34.650	14.8	59
East Sepik	94	49	39	3.0	25	41	6	24	46.967	12.6	72
Enga	91	47	8	0.2	23	42	4	24	47.400	9.9	52
Simbu	87	50	19	0.6	27	53	1	9	11.278	8.7	60
Western	83	48	31	7.0	30	48	7	17	19.112	17.2	76
Western Highlands	81	52	31	0.2	20	53	2	62	15.400	7.7	71
Gulf	71	47	59	4.6	24	53	19	15	20.000	21.1	67
Oro	67	49	49	2.8	23	63	9	23	17.160	11.6	67
New Ireland	62	58	36	1.7	55	—	4	100	22.958	16.1	86
Madang	62	51	53	2.5	23	45	7	39	20.317	12.2	58
West New Britain	60	51	39	2.5	35	67	19	74	8.610	15.9	75
East New Britain	57	52	32	3.0	95	46	12	8	16.550	15.6	79
Manus	55	52	39	0.7	42	84	2	23	12.623	25.3	84
Eastern Highlands	55	53	25	0.6	—	43	2	9	13.586	11.5	63
Morobe	52	51	27	2.6	38	40	20	25	27.767	14.9	61
Milne Bay	50	57	42	3.2	15	65	19	54	22.071	13.2	63
North Solomons	33	60	22	2.5	41	56	8	12	144.600	20.7	73
Central	—	59	32	2.5		39	15	31	—	8.9	79
NCD	35	57	36	2.5	67	77	0	49	—	—	75
Average for Papua New Guinea	72	50	32	2.2	34	49	—	29	28.744	14.2	68

Notes: 1 Percentage of positive blood slides, all ages (1981)
2 Percentage coverage of children in school

Sources: Richardson (1987:30); Thomason et al. (1991:94, 143); P.K. Townsend (1985:11, 21, 25, 48, 69); M. Turner (1990:73)

aspirins, treatment for cuts and sores and, occasionally, family planning sup-plies. In most of rural PNG the aid posts are the nearest sources of introduced medicine and basic health care. The effectiveness of aid posts in providing health care is highly variable, dependent on the extent to which orderlies have been trained, the availability of medicines, the compliance of patients to treatment regimes and accessibility. Less than 20 per cent of chil-dren below the age of four attend Mother and Child Health (MCH) clinics and a third of all children are beyond an hour's walk of a MCH clinic. Coverage of children probably reached a peak around 1980 and has subse-quently gone through a slow decline, because of the difficulty of attracting and retaining staff in remote areas, the lack of staff enthusiasm for 'difficult' rural patrols, tribal fighting, decreased public support for clinics and the withdrawal of travel budgets (P.K. Townsend 1985:19–21). Within provinces the extent of inequality in access to health services is greater than that between provinces. There are no financial or other incentives to attract good health workers to remote areas, where languages and cultures are different, and the task of providing services to remote areas is considerable. Aid posts are most inadequate in the more remote places. Funding may not be forth-coming, aid posts are closed for unknown reasons, orderlies not replaced, supervised or trained and services are not maintained (Jenkins 1988; Lombange *et al.* 1987). Since aid post orderlies were once sent to remote posts as punishment for inadequate performances elsewhere (Macpherson 1981), some lack of commitment is not surprising, a situation also true of teachers in remote schools (see pp. 244–5). Orderlies vary in competence, whilst many feel neglected in terms of supplies, supervision and general sup-port, not forthcoming from senior medical officers or from the communities. Lack of downward communication characterises the health system, both from the centre to provinces, and from provincial capitals to health centres and aid posts, despite attempts at decentralisation; centralisation is as true of technology and supplies as it is of participation, discussion and decision-making (Welsch 1986). Reduction in the availability of finance for rural centres, and the decline in travel budgets, have severely weakened even the limited ability of aid posts to provide adequate health care. Other factors which have resulted in determining the services provided to a particular com-munity include distance from the provincial centre, and elements of the social environment such as public demand and political expediency, professional pressures, private and community customs and beliefs and the extent of socio-economic development. The outcome of all these factors has been the operation of an 'inverse care law' where availability is the converse of need (Radford 1980), at different scales throughout the country, and increasingly apparent as the health budget declines and its urban concentration increases.

Urban bias in health care provision has worsened since independence when 'each rural health worker was required to serve, on average, five times as many people as each urban health worker' (Riley and Davies 1982:179). Though urban hospitals are obviously relatively accessible the only available evidence indicates that they disproportionately serve urban populations within a very limited radius (Driscoll and Winyard 1979; Marshall *et al.* 1988). Moreover patients from distant locations are likely to be least able to afford medical (and travel costs), to be more unfamiliar with hospital procedures, to discharge themselves before treatment regimes are complete and thus least likely to benefit from the health system (Tefuarani and Smiley 1989). Improved accessibility would significantly improve health status, yet the converse has occurred.

The concentration of the health budget in urban areas has not resulted in adequate urban health care. Every provincial hospital experiences weaknesses in management and administration; there is instability in management teams, few appropriate management skills, minimal health information activity and poor financial control, few links to health centres, poor hygiene, inadequate stocks of essential drugs and poor maintenance of technology (Thomason and Edwards 1991). At smaller rural hospitals equivalent problems stem from inadequate supervision. Administration of the whole health system has proved difficult, with supplies often being unavailable, compounded by a decline in the number of graduates from health training programmes and the movement of scarce, skilled professionals into the private sector (or even overseas). At the end of 1993 the Kerema hospital, serving Gulf province, had been closed for more than a year because of its deteriorating state, and Popondetta hospital (for Oro province) had not been rebuilt after being burnt down in 1991; seriously ill patients must increasingly travel to Port Moresby.

Access to health services, and adequate nutrition, have implications even beyond physical well-being. Amongst the Abelam (East Sepik), for example, ownership of wealth was correlated with body size. The poor are poorly fed and therefore most likely to get the disfiguring skin disease, tinea. Largest clans have the lowest rates of tinea, as do families with large numbers of pigs. Males with tinea find it harder to get wives, due to discrimination against such men for employment. Workers have wealth and can get wives more easily; their wives are unlikely to have tinea so that it is not reproduced in their children. There are therefore links between infectious disease, social differentiation and even 'class' formation (Gorlin 1977). A particular inequality is the relative ill-health and low life expectancy of women. PNG is one of very few countries where men have tended to outlive women, a result of high levels of death in childbirth (despite maternity facilities in hospitals), inadequate maternity care and the high work burdens of women, though by 1980 female life expectancies were lower than those of men in only four provinces (Gulf, Milne Bay, Simbu and North Solomons). Women are more vulnerable to ill-health because of their workload, level of education, nutritional status and domestic life, and are less likely than men to gain adequate access to health facilities.

It is neither possible to measure the extent of sickness in different parts of the country, nor the success of the health care system in improving the historic situation. At a national level there were substantial improvements in all mortality rates and in life expectancy in the post-war years, largely attributable to the activities of preventive and curative health services: malaria spraying, antibiotics and vaccinations. At a local level there were, and are, marked differences in IMR between villages with access to health services and those without; in one part of East Sepik, during this phase, IMRs were respectively 59 and 177 in villages that did and did not use health services (Sturt 1972). Since the 1980s the rate of decline in the IMR has slowed (and may even have reversed), as health services have become more inaccessible in remote areas and gains have not been consolidated through improved housing, sanitation and water supplies; greater mobility has increased the spread of infectious diseases, and epidemics occur intermittently. It has proved difficult to continue the slow improvement in health status and, at a national level, this may be worsening, despite its inadequate level relative to that in the rest of the Asia-Pacific region. (Child and maternal mortality rates are the highest in the region, malnutrition is more extensive than elsewhere in the Pacific and only five countries in the world have poorer access to safe water supplies.) Some tropical diseases have staged a resurgence and immunisation coverage has declined, so that measles, tuberculosis and tetanus remain virulent. Many of the classical tropical diseases remain and a variety of social changes has resulted in significant increases in the frequency and distribution of many diseases. 'Tuberculosis and sexually transmitted diseases, once potentially manageable urban problems, are now becoming much more common in rural and remote areas as well as taking on epidemic proportions in the cities' (Aitken 1991:33). Tribal warfare now incorporates guns; around Mount Hagen alone, gunshot wounds increased from none in 1984 to seventy-three in the first half of 1987, with much higher rates of trauma and mortality and at great cost to health care (Ollapallil 1987). The rise of non-communicable diseases and also of AIDS has emphasised urban health problems at the expense of continuing, serious – yet more preventable – rural health problems. Life expectancy is greater in urban areas, even if NCDs have sometimes affected the quality of that life.

The health system has begun to experience considerable problems, as the health budget has failed to increase relative to a growing population, and the solutions are more difficult to achieve. This is particularly so in rural areas; the Minister of Health has stated that the nation's health infrastructure has collapsed, up to 60 per cent of facilities in the provinces were closed, unmanned or not supplied with medicines or equipment (*TPNG* 24 February 1994). Though there is no urban bias in the distribution of ill-health, there is a growing urban bias in the distribution of curative services, as the health system moves away from PHC, which will not be reversed without greater political commitment (to provision of human resources, supplies, training and supervision) and improved access. A new 1996 National Health Plan thus sought to re-emphasize PHC and ensure the better delivery of services in rural areas. The nexus between health status, population growth and development is far from being realised.

EDUCATION

To an even greater extent than for the provision of health services, the relative recency of contact, the belated extension of services to remote parts of the country and the priority of economic growth, have all ensured that the education system is in places skeletal and cannot guarantee even universal primary education throughout the country. Moreover, in recent years, population growth has made access to primary, secondary and tertiary education no easier than it was in the past. This has been exacerbated by poor quality at all levels of the education system, with low rates of achievement and high drop-out rates (around 45 per cent at primary level and 33 per cent in secondary schools), so that the system has never been able to provide the skilled workforce for the country's employment needs.

At the start of the 1960s relatively few Papua New Guineans had access to education, and most of that was in mission primary schools. At independence just 56 per cent of those in the primary school age groups were in schools, while only 12 per cent of those in eligible age groups were in secondary schools. Few had benefited from any form of tertiary education though those few were the principal architects of independence. Post-independence governments have continued to aim for universal primary education but also initially sought to emphasise a more vocational education appropriate to a large rural population. Such an ideology conflicted with parental aspirations, which saw education in terms of potential social and economic mobility (M. Turner 1990:76–7). At all levels, curricula have been somewhat divorced from community activities, and from the probable life and employment outcomes of school-leavers.

During the 1980s the primary enrolment rate steadily increased, reaching 73 per cent at the end of the decade; the annual growth rate was 4 per cent, scarcely faster than the rate of population growth. If such rates are maintained, universal primary education will not be attained in the twentieth century. Moreover dropout rates have risen steadily from 1975 to 1991 (Gannicott and Avalos 1994), as a result of boredom, high opportunity costs, perceived lack of achievement and irrelevance. The supply of teachers is limited and there has also been a dropout rate of community school teachers of around 10 per cent per year. National policy has moved towards an extended universal education system of nine years, rather than the present-day six year primary system, to reduce the cost of education, since community school costs are lower than those in provincial high schools (partly because of boarding costs), land is more generally available, communities are more willing to mobilise finance and human resources to assist, and dropping out at the end of primary school will be less damaging to national development (*TPNG* 23 September 1993). The same issues of access, retention and cost of providing services also occur in secondary education. Although enrolment increased at 3.9 per cent per year during the 1980s, the same rate as for primary schools, there was an overall enrolment rate of only 16 per cent by

1992, because of the high dropout rate at the end of primary school. The high school system was still unable to take all eligible students, because of a shortage of places. Even to reach an enrolment rate of 50 per cent of the population would require 144 new provincial high schools and nearly 2,000 additional teachers (World Bank 1992:92–3). Currently the education system augments and reinforces imbalances between rich and poor, urban and rural, educated and illiterate and male and female.

Prior to independence the Australian administration rapidly constructed an infrastructure of modern institutions, including a university system modelled on the Australian one. The University of Papua New Guinea (UPNG) opened in 1967, and a second university, the University of Technology (Unitech), was established at Lae in 1973. The universities have not expanded since the mid-1980s, partly due to a lack of qualified high school graduates but primarily through a reduction in the real level of financial support, and have been unable to meet the demand for skilled professionals. The tertiary system has been extremely costly because of its fragmentation, including fifteen nursing schools and eight teachers' colleges (most run by church groups), and because of under-utilisation of facilities. Present policies, aimed at rationalisation of higher education, through amalgamation of institutions, the reduction of subsidies to students and the relative decline of support for universities rather than other elements of the education system, mirror those in tertiary education systems elsewhere.

Education outside the formal system has long been inadequate; 'Nonformal Education (NFE) has had a long and unfortunate history in PNG. Clear concise policy decisions on the location, management and administration and directions NFE should take are still missing' (World Bank 1992:91). Various initiatives have been tried, the responsibility has been shifted around within the bureaucracy, several major reviews have been conducted but little has been achieved. The quality of vocational training centres is low, because of a lack of resources and competent teachers and uncertainty over what is appropriate vocational education. Where it has been most successful, it has been undertaken by non-governmental organisations.

Despite investment in the expansion of the education system, the overall results have been limited. Of those in formal sector employment in 1982 some 47 per cent had not completed primary education, a clear indication of the low attainment levels of even the formal sector workforce. (Because of widespread skill shortages in the labour market, employers experience high mobility among skilled workers, which reduces both productivity and the return to investment in training.) The overall literacy rate at the start of the 1990s was around 45 per cent; for men the rate is around 62 per cent and for women 38 per cent, with the gap between male and female literacy rates actually increasing between 1970 and 1985. These are very high proportions compared with most other developing countries, and a legacy of earlier lack of investment. Local variations in literacy rates, where they can be measured, are much greater. It was not until 1992 that the first adult women in the

Porgera area became literate, after a special mine education programme; some areas have no literate adults. Achieving functional literacy or access to NFE is beyond the reach of many women who have never been to school; in many areas, as in more isolated areas of Madang province, 'women are discouraged from obtaining secondary or tertiary education because the location of the institutions requires them to leave the village. If a single woman leaves the protection of her family, it is considered by some village members that her reproductive capacity becomes vulnerable' (Fahey 1987:53). More generally parents fear the lack of security for migrant women, sexual problems, social changes (Gannicott 1993:144) and the greater probability of women not finding jobs commensurate with their education. Gender disparities have nonetheless declined in recent years, with females now accounting for 44 per cent of all primary school students, and provincial proportions varying from 40 to 48 per cent, though at secondary level this falls well below 40 per cent, as girls are less likely to stay on (World Bank 1992:90–2). Similarly relatively few go on to tertiary education.

There have been considerable variations in access to education because of the historical evolution of the agricultural system. Government and mission schools were first established in coastal areas of Papua and the islands, and reached the highlands relatively late. At the end of the 1970s a number of highland areas were still particular poorly served by the educational system – and thus had low enrolment rates and low levels of educational attainment (de Albuquerque and D'Sa 1986). In the mid-1980s some 86 per cent of children in the eligible age groups were enrolled in primary schools in New Ireland province; by contrast, the Western and Southern Highlands provinces got only 51 per cent of eligible children into school (Table 9.1), though the situation was improving more rapidly there. By the 1990s the Southern Highlands remained the poorest province, in educational facilities, but the enrolment rate had reached 64 per cent. Increased enrolment in the secondary sector has grown more slowly; by the 1990s Manus had passed the NCD to record 34 per cent whereas Enga had reached only 12 per cent (Gannicott 1993). Such differences, usually accentuated by variable quality of schools and teachers (alongside demands of home and family, school closures due to disturbances, poor health and nutritional status), substantially influence the life chances and career prospects of people in different parts of the country, with the Highlands and the Sepik provinces less well served than elsewhere.

The education system has been inefficient and expensive. Despite its still limited coverage, about 5 per cent of GNP is spent on education, a proportion that is higher than in most Asia-Pacific states. Most education is publicly financed. Despite minimal participation in tertiary education – with just 2 per cent of the population having experienced it – it absorbs 39 per cent of the public subsidy, compared with the primary school system, which receives 41 per cent of subsidies. This is an exceptionally uneven distribution of public spending, compared with that in most developing countries (Gannicott 1993:148). To provide free education, following World Bank recommendations, whilst seeking to increase enrolment rates at all levels, and achieve universal primary education, would demand PNG increasing its financial commitment to education to more than 12 per cent of GDP, a level higher than that of any developing country.

Education costs are high because of low teacher–pupil ratios, high salaries and accommodation costs of teachers, large numbers of boarders and a fragmented tertiary system. Salaries represent about 90 per cent of all recurrent costs at primary and secondary levels, and two-thirds of costs at the tertiary level. Quality may have declined, despite increased investment. 'The blackboards with bad grammar and incorrect spelling, shortages of writing materials, the lack of regular inspection, teacher absenteeism, threats of violence to persons and property are typical indicators of poor quality educational outcomes and are all too easy to find in rural Papua New Guinea' (M. Turner 1990:79–80). Teachers have moved away from, or been unwilling to go to, some parts of the country, especially the highlands, where schools have closed for lack of teachers, violence in classrooms and to teachers, and compensation claims. The immobility and unavailability of teachers have disadvantaged the poorer parts of the country and, in remote areas especially, teachers are often absent from the schools, abscond, are arrogant to the local population and feel neglected, ignored, isolated and unpaid (Weeks 1981:129–31). Education necessarily suffers, and there is little link between schools and communities. It is difficult for rural schools to obtain adequate supplies of appropriate materials from urban centres, in reasonable time. The teacher–pupil ratio has not improved since the start of the 1980s. The most crucial issue of quality is that the problems developed in primary schools become cumulative as they are transmitted upwards through the higher levels.

Poor households are not easily able to afford even small community school fees, let alone more demanding secondary school fees, especially where boarding is necessary, as it is for students from more impoverished, remote areas. Poor families, in rural and urban areas, may also be more likely to need the work of children. Urban schools invariably have the best teachers, equipment and standards, though access to education is most obviously uneven and inadequate for the poor in urban areas. Enrolments in the NCD are lower than the national average and, in one urban settlement (Nine Mile Quarry), some 78 per cent of school-age children were not in a school, since their parents could not get places for them (P.K. Townsend 1985:77). A wealthy urban elite send their children to the expensive international schools, initially designed for expatriate children, or even to Australian schools and colleges: a situation where 'the dominant classes are reproducing themselves' (M. Turner 1990: 80). Moreover the three international schools outside the national educational system have become increasingly popular: 'The Papua New Guinea elite is disenchanted with the state system. It has largely chosen to have its children educated, albeit expensively, in the international system or in Australia' (Callick *et al.* 1990:3.3). At the same time children from poorer households, in remote areas, struggle to find a school and all too quickly drop out of the system.

The tasks of developing the education system, from vernacular (*tokples*) primary schools to tertiary post-graduate courses, remain enormous. Significant components of the system are maintained by the missions. Their contribution remains crucial; the regional MP for Madang province has claimed that the province 'has the greatest number of bush material schools, aid posts (30 of which remain unmanned), and if it were not for the missions, 80 per cent of the population would not receive any services at all' (*PC* 17 January 1994). The overall contribution of the education system to national and personal development has been disappointing: 'Inadequate education has been one of the most significant constraints to economic and social development of Papua New Guinea and . . . has reduced international competitiveness and economic growth' (Gannicott 1993:138). From *tokples* schools through to universities, the education system has favoured those who were already in an advantageous social position and an accessible place (e.g. Montague 1982). Schools are simply inaccessible in remote areas, a situation true of other services; in one part of East Sepik, two days' walk from the nearest community school, those children who went to school had to live away from their parents but could find neither adequate food nor accommodation, missed their families and dropped out of school. Not one villager had gone beyond primary school (*TPNG* 15 April 1993). Absenteeism and dropout rates are highest in villages distant from schools – where access is difficult and the value of education may seem less obvious (Zelenietz and Grant 1986). By contrast, even at independence, the 'second generation of school students, whose parents may speak English at home and support the school objectives, are already beginning to replicate the middle class achievement patterns in countries like Australia' (Pettman 1984:139). Schools both allocate different futures and legitimate them, through the same meritocratic ideology present elsewhere; the spatial and social structure of the education system contributes to social stratification.

Despite the disappointments of the system, education continues to be keenly sought after, and the skills gained in schools are highly valued; English is prized for communication with government officials, and for gaining further knowledge. A widely shared belief is that school constitutes one of the main 'roads' to European knowledge and ways of life, encapsulated in the notion of *Delivering the Goods: Education as Cargo in Papua New Guinea* (Swatridge 1985). In places where few if any children have ever gone beyond primary school, their role is poorly understood, though the mystique of various forms of success via education remains. Pecuniary motives for education are combined with acute frustration at the task of achieving development through education.

The number of functionally illiterate and innumerate people is increasing. Quantity and quality of education are fundamental problems, and are likely to remain so, whilst education is perceived in ambiguous terms – a means of gaining success in the world but with some inter-generational conflict, a means of earning income beyond the village, but of limited use there (Zelenietz and Grant 1986). Despite the renaming of primary schools as community schools, not long after independence, their relationship to the community is often tenuous, especially in urban areas. 'Although the school may facilitate modernisation, it does so at considerable cost in individual frustration and social discontent' (ibid.:48) and thus has an ambiguous relationship to the wider process of development, especially in rural areas. Urban education, superior to its rural counterpart, has emphasised the structure of uneven development, apparent in the location of education services.

PRE-CAPITALISM, PROTO-CAPITALISM AND THE ADAPTABILITY OF HISTORIC FORMS

The establishment and consolidation of smallholder cash cropping and subsequently of 'medium-holders' (Chapter 4) alongside rural business development has had various social and economic ramifications. Cash cropping has failed to sustain the development of productive forces, in part because of its peripheral integration into the global economy (Howlett 1973b), though it has encouraged and contributed to social and economic differentiation throughout the country. The process of rural change has stimulated the emergence of rural elites, and the genesis of new – but sometimes transitory – forms of inequality. Incorporation into the world capitalist system has transformed existing social and economic relations. Traditional societies evolved in diverse ways out of pre-existing agricultural systems, principally under the impact of new markets, and the natural economy was altered and diversified following colonial penetration, even when that contact was seemingly remote or of minimal impact. Thus in Enga there was a 'boom' in local and regional trading as early as the 1880s, resulting from colonial 'pacification' along parts of the remote north coast (Lacey 1977:7, 35) though these colonial contacts were hundreds of kilometres away. The spatial differences inherent in the possession of resources and in exchange have been intensified and modified since colonisation in ways which have resulted in some structural differentiation. The country has moved from a large number of relatively classless, subsistence-based economies which existed prior to colonisation, towards a somewhat more unified, stratified and monetised society.

Most Melanesian societies seem to have been characterised historically by 'big-man' or 'great man' forms of political organisation (Chowning 1977:42–3). Areas where big-men existed had no permanently viable political units and almost always lacked centralised authority; moreover there was usually no concept of office. The authority of leaders was based on personal ability rather than on inheritance, descent or supernatural sanction; it was achieved rather than ascribed. Many other Melanesian societies were quite different. For example, in Buin (Bougainville) society was stratified; all Buins are said to be in one or other class, a membership ascribed at birth according to the class of the child's father (J.T. Keil 1975). In many coastal regions, most notably in Mekeo and the Trobriands, a formal office of headship was hereditary within a particular lineage or family (Hau'ofa 1981:291–2; cf. Morauta 1984). However, even in the highlands, where the ideology of achievement loomed large, there is a hereditary element in leadership; being the son of a leader, the eldest of a number of brothers, or having some other useful relationship confers certain advantages (e.g. A.J. Strathern 1975:371; Standish 1978b; Brown 1987). There are also a few societies where egalitarianism was so powerful that distinctive leaders were rare (Chowning 1979:68). A wide range of leadership structures has existed, and they have changed in different ways.

In describing how leaders have operated in colonial and post-colonial societies, the language of capitalism has often been invoked to suggest the modernity of development strategies. Big-men particularly have been compared with capitalist entrepreneurs, demanding much of their followers, and each acting 'like a capitalist financier, risking other people's wealth more than his own' (Modjeska 1982:93). In similar vein, highlands pig cycles 'have some of the features of capitalist business cycles' (ibid.:104; cf. Connell 1979b). Such perceptions are not universal. Feil's conclusion that highlands exchange constitutes 'an intricate economic situation involving credit, finance and repayment, often with interest', and with an 'increasing cognitive equivalence [with] business' (Feil 1984:38, 236) has been criticised both for the 'highly questionable use of the language of personal investment banking', and because the Enga (and others) were not engaging in 'any sort of primitive capitalism [since] pig exchange eventually evens out, no notion of accumulated profit obtains, and incremental return is based on sentiment rather than contract' (Lipset 1990:139). Social obligations, economic strategies, and the goods and media of exchange linked to them have become intricately entangled.

During pre-contact times, there was a substantial amount of trade and exchange between different cultural groups; in some areas trading routes extended more than a hundred kilometres. Exchanges had social, political and economic functions; in colonial Enga

> The participants are in effect buying and selling commodities and they haggle (frequently vigorously and at length) over the amounts asked or proposed. . . . This is a market situation albeit an imperfect one . . . rates of exchanges for many commodities varied among localities and through time, apparently in response to changes in supply and demand stemming from fluctuations in the weather, the fortunes of war, the incidence of sickness and the like . . . in the context of trade, the Enga and their neighbours operated under market conditions and were not significantly constrained by notions of traditionally defined, fixed values.
>
> (Meggitt 1971:195)

In places there was a clear distinction between ceremonial and commercial exchanges and even ceremonial exchange relations involved delayed returns with extended credit generating some kind of 'interest' (Meggitt 1971:197–8; cf. Harding 1994). Trade was assisted by the institutionalisation of certain aspects, including the acceptance of shell valuables as media of exchange. Shells effectively functioned as money, in a manner very close to if not exactly the same as contemporary currency, at least in parts of New Britain and Bougainville. They were a general means of exchange and a standard of value, analogous to that in a capitalist economy, and cannot simply be seen as metaphorical (Connell 1977a). However, throughout Melanesia, introduced money had overwhelming advantages over shell money, and the latter remains in use only for significant social exchanges. In a number of pre-contact economies there was nevertheless a more or less institutionalised financial structure which enabled the formal organisation of wealth acquisition and exchange and which was converted, rather than cancelled, in the post-colonial economy.

Metaphors of capitalism have become more real, as leaders have become involved in new business activities. Big-men were often the earliest to explore new economic ventures. Although many early commercial enterprises enhanced both the wealth and prestige of the big-man and his followers, there was invariably a movement away from large corporate (or even lineage) groups and associations towards smaller partnerships or individual owner-ship (e.g. Connell 1978). Traditional forms of organisation readily enabled a number of groups to adopt new ways, including many characteristics of a modern capitalist economy. T.S. Epstein's book on the Tolai, who reacted extremely quickly to the developmental changes of colonial society, was titled *Capitalism: Primitive and Modern* (1968). Though 'capital formation was at first facilitated by the traditional Tolai system of group ownership, capital formation has in turn undermined the very system which helped to create it' (T.S. Epstein 1964:68) particularly as individual entrepreneurs emerged. Elsewhere the flexibility and fluidity of Simbu society enabled the ready incorporation of substantial economic changes (Brown 1973), whilst the aggressive and competitive style of traditional Gorokan leadership was con-sidered to have provided the basic model for the emergence of contemporary businessmen (Finney 1973). Capitalism both conserved and dissolved various elements of traditional social and economic structures.

Many Melanesian societies were in some respects 'pre-adapted' to change by virtue of their traditional (pre-contact) values and institutions. Specifically the existence of the big-man system, based as it was on personal ambition and the achievement of status through accumulation and competitive exchange of wealth, ensured an environment that was conducive to the appearance of entrepreneurs. The introduction of the cash economy gave potential entrepreneurs a new means of acquiring wealth, in the form of cash, and therefore status of a different kind. The ability of such entrepre-neurs to innovate, by adapting new crops and technology to their own society, spurred involvement in the cash economy. In time other younger individuals were able to challenge the authority of big-men in the commercial arena through their superior understanding of business practices and technology. Those who had previously been supporters of big-men were often 'the first to head outwards into the actual capitalist system of wage labour', thus putting the support base of leaders under considerable pressure (A.J. Strathern 1987b:259) and enabling their own independent success. As a result in many places, especially on the coasts, the concept of 'big-man' status has faded. In Gapun (Sepik) no men 'show any interest in attaining the traditional big man status, which is hard work, and which involves devoting a great amount of energy and work to fostering a sense of community in the village, through skilful oratories and displays of generosity' (Kulick 1992:259). Status in small-scale village society has diminished meaning, where villages are no longer important loci of power and authority, relative to a wider economic and political realm. Differentiations in male prestige, influence and recognition have become less significant; though older men still exert influence, power and authority, in most places 'the more pronounced hierarchy of men by age and prestige has disintegrated' (Clay 1986:255; M.F. Smith 1994:80–1). In Pinikindu (New Ireland) the word *emasa*, the term of reference and address applied to the most influential big-men, has disappeared (Clay 1986:255); in Siwai (Bougainville), the equivalent term for a big-man, *mumi*, is rarely if ever used in contemporary times.

In some respects capitalism remains only a metaphor for the changes that have occurred, especially where rural societies have become part of the world capitalist system as petty commodity producers. Though there were distinct, historic inequalities in Melanesian societies, and these were sometimes accentuated through contemporary changes, such inequalities do not necessarily facilitate the establishment of a capitalist system of production. The separation of the producers from the means of production, in this case land, is essential to the emergence of capitalist social relations. Consequently most societies demonstrate the characteristics of an incipient peasant economy rather than a capitalist system. As in the case of the Kewa (Southern Highlands),

> Inequalities do exist, especially on gender lines. Yet this has not predisposed people to behave in a 'capitalistic' way. It has not encouraged 'good business sense', capitalist accumulation or investment in the area. This is because the indigenous gift economy remains the dominant mode of interaction.
>
> (Josephides 1985:91)

The balance between proto-capitalism or pre-adaptation, the structures of Melanesian societies, and the external penetration of an economic environment in which entrepreneurial activities might flourish, has been highly variable from place to place. In contrast to many other societies, Gorokans and Tolai were more fortunate in their initial experience with the outside world. Not all societies were so 'pre-adapted' to capitalism. For the Mekeo of Gulf Province: 'their system of hereditary leadership, the social condemnation of competitive behaviour, and the strong conservative force created by sorcery fears, operate against their own desire for progress' (Stephen 1974:xxii). Where external conditions (such as access) limited the establishment of capitalist forms, societies were more divided in their response to modernity.

Despite the rapid transformation of many societies, there was continuity in change. Traditional leaders were sought out by missionaries, plantation owners and *kiaps;* the pattern that emerged was for them to become the first 'modern' leaders and the first cash crop producers. The policy of encouraging larger producers was thus effectively a means of supporting the existing leadership structure. Big-men more quickly acquired contemporary resources of capital and land than others, became *luluais* (appointed village leaders), councillors and, later, national and provincial politicians (e.g. Lomas 1978), less frequently became church leaders but almost always sought to become businessmen. Post-colonial economic policy continued to favour 'progressive farmers' and 'big peasants' (e.g. MacWilliam 1990). By the 1970s the majority of politicians in areas of established commercial development were already the more successful agriculturalists and businessmen. Many were able to move between and manipulate both the modern world of commerce and established exchange systems in the gift economy, and could draw on supporters across a wide area (Donaldson and Good 1988:83–4), though as the experience of the Gorokan businessman, Joe Leahy, showed, this could be fraught with difficulties (Connolly and Anderson 1992). The uneven nature of commercial development was most apparent in the highlands, where rising coffee prices enabled wealth acquisition and accentuated conflict over scarce land resources. In the lowlands, usually lower population densities ensured that competition and conflict were less overt, though a similar evolution has occurred in some areas, as in Nagovisi (Bougainville) where there has been 'an inevitable swing towards institutionalised inequality of access to resources. It remains to be seen whether or not Nagovisi can overcome – or at least resist – these powerful forces pushing them to a class or class-like society' (D.D. Mitchell 1982:65). Social and economic inequalities have emerged on a scale that was not apparent in pre-colonial or early post-colonial societies. In the absence of structural transformation in any fundamental aspect of the local production system, indigenous society may however be caught in a state of permanent transition. Through the increased channelling of incomes into consumption of goods and services of external origin, together with inflation of the cash content of local payments, development has offered less and less in terms of a road to wealth, power and greater self-reliance. Rather more specifically, in the Goroka Valley of the Eastern Highlands,

> the constraints of the environment, indigenous socio-economic characteristics and development policies do not permit the achievement of a modern

society. On the contrary, the inevitable consequence will be the entrench-
ment of an economically unstable peasantry. . . . The Goroka Valley will be
for ever 'transitional'. The evidence suggests that this is a terminal stage,
modernisation arrested. In spite of themselves, the Gorokans will become
peasants. An infinite pause will settle on the valley of Goroka.

(Howlett 1973b:273)

In places as different as Goroka and Tanga (New Ireland), and elsewhere,
commodity relations have become increasingly intensified, characterised in
terms of a 'simple reproduction squeeze' where households experience greater
difficulty in maintaining or increasing the supply of commodities necessary
for the reproduction of existing levels of consumption and production, as a
result of a combination of factors including the exhaustion of land (or
labour), rural development schemes that encourage or impose more expensive
means of production and deteriorating terms of exchange, sometimes exacerbated by population growth (Foster 1995:61–2). Though society in Goroka,
and elsewhere, is far from static and fossilised, there are constraints to the
achievement of a more industrialised and 'modern' society in PNG. Change
has followed 'the disruption of . . . complementary relations of interdependence between village societies and the establishment of exploitative relations
of dependence with international capitalism that characterise an integral
phase of the process of dependency' (Boyd 1980:5). Even the most inaccessible rural areas are inextricably a part of the national and international
economy, and are significantly influenced by this.

At the local level, better access to land, capital (including credit), education
and other services has contributed to intra-village and inter-village socio-
economic differentiation. Clans or individuals who first gained access to the
commercial world were often able to build on this start at the expense of
those who sought to follow. One Wovan man, from the remote mountainous
uplands of Madang, has expressed the problem of new perceptions of
remoteness and relative deprivation quite clearly: 'Before we were better off
than they [the Wovan's lowland neighbours]. We had better finery. We made
better weapons. Now they think they are better than us' (Flanagan 1981:36).
In areas distant from urban centres, inequality has tended to be regional,
though also applying to lineages and individuals (e.g. Ploeg 1985:258),
whereas closer to urban centres, or where there are land shortages, inequalities within villages may be more pronounced. Inequalities appear to be
greatest where there is differential access to the potential of cash cropping,
a situation more true between villages rather than within them. In the
Maprik area

In 1971 and 1972 the highest per capita production of coffee was concentrated west of Maprik astride the Sepik Highway. Even then people in this
area were receiving incomes from coffee fifty times greater then those in the
areas of lowest production. In the ten years to 1981 this pattern of inequality intensified. Production increased three times in the highest-producing

villages, but fell in the lower-producing ones, so that in 1981 the former were receiving per capita incomes from coffee three hundred times larger than the later.

(B.J. Allen 1990:192)

In inaccessible Gapun all villagers are relatively poor, and annual income differences, though considerable, were given little local attention, since they led to no other salient differences, and money was used for social obligations and hence redistributed (Kulick 1992:45–47). Similarly, in the remote Gende area (Madang), where road access was non-existent and remittances the main source of income, 'income differences were extreme, with some village households having fifty times as much cash per individual member as other households' (Zimmer 1990a:213). Whether income differences are substantial or not, there remain considerable informal pressures at village level, to achieve a greater degree of equality, not least in Papua. In Roro/Paitana villages (Central Province), where income sources were quite diverse, there was very little social and economic differentiation.

Whatever levelling mechanisms exist they are effective – [a] range of informal sanctions prevented the establishment of enterprises on a family basis if it was felt that they might enable that family to profit at the expense of others. Some people do have capital accumulated but either invest it outside the village – in Port Moresby – or not at all rather than risk general criticism or non-cooperation if they use it within the village. Redistributive mechanisms are rife and very little cash within the village is not readily loaned . . . Individualisation of land ownership has not occurred and thus absent migrants relinquish land.

(D.A. Preston 1990:24; A. Turner 1984)

Where income sources are more diverse, inequality is more transient (depending on wages, cash crop prices, market access, demographic change and use of income) and perhaps more limited. Households that are relatively poor tend to be those at a particular phase of the development cycle (such as young households, old widows, single female parents) rather than those who are seemingly permanently disadvantaged, for one reason or another.

The processes contributing to uneven development and socio-economic differentiation have been most marked where land has been under pressure from cash cropping and growing populations, well documented in the Eastern Highlands (e.g. Donaldson and Good 1988; Stewart 1987). The general explanation for differentiation within localities has been the superior access to land of those who have been able to plant more cash crops, either because of historic inequality within landowning lineages or clans or because those individuals who first ventured into cash cropping were able to secure greater areas of land at the expense of those who followed. On the densely populated Nembi plateau (Southern Highlands), for example, individuals with capital secured more land by establishing smallholder cattle schemes, thus denying access to others (B.J. Allen *et al.* 1980; cf. Lea *et al.* 1988). Land-short and landless groups are more widespread than is generally recognised, but the extent is unknown. There is an absolute shortage of land suitable for the cultivation of both cash and subsistence crops in parts of Simbu, and this has contributed to out-migration and other problems (Chapter 7; G.T. Harris 1984; Trompf 1994:328–9). In a few areas, especially in East Sepik, Simbu and Eastern Highlands, there are a number of areas with very short or non-existent fallow periods which in some cases can be correlated with lowered nutritional status (Barnett 1977:144–5; Harvey and Heywood 1983). In different parts of the Tolai area of New Britain, where cash cropping had begun early, there was some degree of land shortage even by the mid-1960s (A.L. Epstein 1969:195–7; T.S. Epstein 1968:132). Where population densities are higher, inequalities seem to be greater (e.g. Zimmer 1990a) whereas where they are relatively low, or where cash cropping is in its infancy (e.g. Boyd 1990; White 1990), access to land remains of slight importance in socio-economic differentiation. The major land tenure problem remains uneven distribution rather than absolute shortage. Moreover

> unlike many other parts of the developing world, the bigger growers are not emerging at the expense of the smaller growers. Rather the larger growers are taking up more of the fallow and uncleared land to which their families have claim and are bringing it into production. So the larger growers have become bigger by bringing additional land into production.
>
> (B.J. Allen *et al.* 1991:10)

This process puts enormous pressure on swidden systems. Traditional inequalities in land tenure accentuate contemporary inequality since those with limited access to land cannot transform their rural economic status. Pressures on land have also contributed to the decline of an ethos of egalitarianism. In Wosera (East Sepik) landholding lineages have become increasingly reluctant to grant access to 'outsiders', that is to lineages which have settled within the host village within the past four generations. This change has occurred, not as a result of the transformation of indigenous exchange relations within the context of a market economy, but within the context of indigenous 'rules' of resource tenure and pre-capitalist exchange relations (Curry 1992), a situation that has led to some degree of impoverishment.

Land has remained crucial to society and identity in every way. Society is written on the ground. The flexibility and instability that were crucial elements of land tenure in Melanesia – though never perceived to be so in Melanesian perceptions – have given way to greater formality and rigidity. Land rights are more eagerly exerted than ever before, because of the increased necessity to ensure access, the possibility of the presence of mineral resources and the recognition that land tenure can be translated into capital gains, sometimes through claims for compensation. In Gapun (Sepik), 'villagers continue to maintain a strong identification with their land. What is changing, however, is what their land is good for. From being valued primarily for its link to the ancestors and the richness of its wildlife and the fertility of its soil . . . land is rapidly being revalued in terms of its market potential' (Kulick 1992:264; see also Chapter 4). Land has never previously been viewed so obviously as both identity and commodity.

There has been some tendency for individual ownership to replace communal ownership and for sales of land to occur, in those areas where agriculture is most commercialised and population pressures are greatest. In parts of the highlands, East New Britain, New Ireland and Bougainville, the sale of land between households is already substantial, though it is often covered by a veneer of tradition (MacWilliam 1988:79). Such sales alienate land even more permanently than does cash cropping, intensify conflict over land and have been one catalyst for a resurgence of tribal fighting in some highland areas. Rising population pressure on scarce land resources is a further contributory factor. On the Nembi plateau 'it is certainly not simply a land dispute that has prompted the Nembi to take up arms against each other. Rather it is an expression of their impatience and realisation that the commercial economy can only offer limited opportunities to gain wealth' (R. Crittenden, pers. comm., 1985). The availability of land underlies socio-economic differentiation.

Symptomatic of the growing importance of land, and of contemporary materialism and commercialism, are increased demands for compensation for changes of land use, even where that land has been used for the benefits of the local community, such as for a primary school or access road. Compensation requests have followed virtually every 'modern' development completed in the post-independence era. For example, before the upgrading of the Alotau–Gurney road (Milne Bay) in 1990, landowners demanded compensation, backdated their claims to 1952 and prevented surveying work, prompting the Minister of Works, Paul Wanjik, to comment

> It is regrettable that land problems or to be more specific compensation demands are fast becoming a growth industry of their own. People are now turning to land compensation demands as an easy way of making a fast buck. This behaviour is fast reaching epidemic proportions. I fear that if nothing positive is done to control and regulate this, we will experience some very serious problems in implementing capital works projects.
>
> (*TPNG* 27 December 1990; cf. Waiko 1993:45)

Other claims in the 1990s have sought K300,000 for the land occupied by Wapanemanda airstrip (Enga), K100,000 (and 200 pigs and many cassowaries) for the deaths of four people in road accidents near Mount Hagen (evidence that not all, or even most, compensation claims concerned land), K12 million for the land under Bogia township and K5 million for Tari township land, said to have been 'exchanged for axes and matches' in the 1950s (*PC* 23 November 1993). Whilst such demands are often ambit claims and are not always followed through, they have resulted in closed hospitals, schools and airstrips, disrupted road construction programmes and water supplies, stimulated violence and slowed the pace of social and economic development.

In rare instances, inequality has resulted in, and resulted from, situations where 'indigenous persons' have been expelled from rural communities by harassment, accusations of theft or sorcery, and through the emergence of 'a class of absentee landlords' (Zimmer 1990a:87). Despite all these changes, the process of transformation of land into a commodity has barely begun. However, land is likely to become 'a commodity in the long run. This transformation process will undoubtedly be the longest and most painful of all because it will be characterised by the emergence of strong class forces in the countryside and the development of poverty' (Gregory 1979:404). The continued significance of lineage or clan-owned land, alongside the efflorescence of gift exchange (Gregory 1982), are thus distinctive elements of contemporary PNG that have slowed the transition to capitalism. Land issues confront every development context.

The increased significance of capitalist relationships, and perhaps land shortages, is apparent in the growing significance of rural wage labour. In the highlands this emerged in the earliest years of coffee growing, and was a particular characteristic of the mode of operation of the more successful growers. A few years after the establishment of European coffee plantations in the Goroka valley, nearby villagers were employing labourers from the Fore region; by the late 1960s several Gorokan business leaders owned large coffee plantations and all hired labour (Finney 1973:85). In colonial times such leaders, who often hired labour at wages below the legal minimum, also opposed social change and independence, and aligned themselves with colonial interests. In coastal areas, where cash cropping started earlier, the local hiring of wage labour also began early; a form of wage labour by 'adoption' existed in the Tolai area in the first decade of the century (Salisbury 1970:156). In Siwai (Bougainville), the rapid extension of cocoa growing in the late 1950s resulted in some of the earliest planters hiring labourers from nearby Nagovisi; these remained in Siwai for periods of up to a year, being accommodated and paid in a similar manner to that of workers on European plantations. By the mid-1970s a number of cash crop producers in Bougainville and other coastal areas were hiring labour from the more remote and poorer parts of the New Guinea mainland and even from the nearby Solomon Islands (Connell 1978; McSwain 1977:106–7; Morauta 1974:55, 70), though falling cash crop prices have meant that these rural labour markets have rarely endured.

For a variety of reasons, inequalities have therefore increased between individuals and between groups, at various scales. In several places individuals organised themselves in opposition to such processes; in the Tolai area support for the Mataungan Association (Chapter 10) came principally from those with inferior access to resources, especially land, but also employment (Granger 1971:118). Elsewhere many communities turned to cult movements in disappointment over the benefits of participation in the commercial world (e.g. Burridge 1960; Counts 1971, 1972; Walter 1981b; Worsley 1957).

Although cargo cults may not be principally an economic phenomenon (see pp. 263–4), most have had a significant economic component and been one response to uneven development; in some cases, they were implicitly egalitarian, anti-elite and a threat to the position of local leaders (Gerritsen 1981:13). In the Madang hinterland, cult followers had significantly fewer cash crops than their fellows and cult membership was a function of 'deprivation' and an 'absence of alternatives' that had also led to conflict and growing social differentiation between cultists and non-cultists (Morauta 1972:440–1; cf. B.J. Allen 1990; Brunton 1971). Although this distinction did not exist everywhere, cult movements proved to be one refuge for those who perceived disadvantage. In Nagovisi (Bougainville) divisions emerged between local clans to the extent that there appeared to be

> the beginnings of a '"haves" versus "have nots" split' which would be the first of its kind in Nagovisi. Nagovisi have always had *momiako* and *bakilo* (big-men and destitutes), but this distinction has never rested on much more than hard work. Anyone could become a *momiako* through hard work and most *bakilo* were lazy and unskilful. But this is not the same as becoming a *momiako* because of a few hundred hectares of bush, or becoming *bakilo* because cash cropping froze the landholdings in a clan at a time when some had none.
>
> (D.D. Mitchell 1976:147–8)

Relatively poor clans in Nagovisi were then beginning to unite in a cargo-like organisation which was anti-modernist in ideology and socially factionalising in effect (Nash 1974:108–15). Such cults were capable of persisting for more than a quarter of a century; in the late 1980s, at Mosigetta on the fringes of Nagovisi, where economic development through cash cropping and migration had been substantial, an elaborate cargo cult, with strongly religious overtones, challenged the basis of incorporation into the capitalist economy. Other responses to inequality have taken the form of 'inchoate class action'; such action includes theft and violence on the Highlands Highway, 'tribal fighting' and coffee stealing, some of which activity 'resembles social banditry in its scale, persistence and opposition to property and property owners' (Donaldson and Good 1988:119). A corollary of the growth of rural elites in a situation of limited, increasingly sought after and scarce resources, is that other sectors of rural society have experienced relative disadvantage in access to both local resources and government attention. Many groups are strongly conscious of their new social and economic disadvantages, acutely aware that others fare better, but much less clear about how to overcome or ameliorate their disadvantaged position.

Despite the amplification of inequality there has been minimal recognition of the emergence of classes, though class is also a metaphor for capitalist transformation. 'Classes' have tended to be perceived in other forms: in terms of large (or rich) peasantries, small rural and urban working classes, and the emergence of a small educated petty bourgeoisie (Donaldson and Good

1988:1). The rich peasantry is politically active at local and national levels and sometimes organised into various farming, development, and marketing institutions. Cattle smallholders in many areas formed themselves into groups, as have agriculturalists of other kinds, with the aim of monopolising government extension advice and resources to maintain and expand their interests. By contrast, poorer rural workers are almost completely unorganised. In rural areas apparently new divisions replicated old ones: 'Traditional advantage plus an ability to seize the time enabled members of the old satrapy to take the opportunity to accumulate wealth and power created by an active and interventionist colonial state, and through the 1970s, to extend and entrench their position and privilege' (Donaldson and Good 1988:923). In most places even generalized notions of class have little bearing on social and economic changes. Elsewhere

> Inequality is still based on patterns of ranking that were present in traditional society, although economic factors have increased in importance as military ones have been eliminated . . . the changes caused by participation in a cash economy are too recent to have produced class divisions in villages. . . . Within the village, most inequality can be accounted for by either developmental processes of individual households or by the competition for rank in a traditional big man pattern.
>
> (Finch 1989:196–7)

In urban areas the temptation to recognise incipient class formation and the operation of class interests in a variety of contexts has been greater, yet classes, at best, are weak and embryonic, without efficacy in asserting and containing power and of limited durability. For the moment, in Goroka and elsewhere, 'the growing number of civil servants . . . form the most conspicuous new class' (Finney 1987:69), rather than those who have become rich through business development. There are material signs of economic stratification in rural areas, but social stratification '*remains* antithetical to the villagers' way of thinking. Although there is a growing concern among parents of educated children that their sons and daughters should not marry "down", rich and poor do continue to intermarry and interact on a daily basis with little sign of deference behaviour' (Warry 1987:118). Men were ranked more by their clan affiliation than by their wealth. Social distinctions remain more powerful than economic distinctions, though such distinctions are weaker and much less distinctive than in the past. Throughout PNG there are 'levelling mechanisms' and pressures for redistribution that encourage egalitarianism rather than differentiation. The extreme fragmentation and limited class solidarity of the French peasantry, that led Marx to characterise them as 'a sack of potatoes', is reflected in Howlett's comment that PNG peasants may prove to be no more than a 'sack of *kaukau* [sweet potatoes]' (1980:208). Examples of overt, self-conscious class action are few and ephemeral; for most people the world remains divided between moral kin and immoral outsiders, with whom cooperation is impossible or implausible.

Although there were significant elements of a proto-capitalist economy within a number of pre-contact Melanesian societies, to the extent that Finney's (1973) suggestion that some were 'pre-adapted' to capitalist business development has been eagerly elaborated upon, there was no easy transformation from pre-colonial times. Some societies have more easily incorporated a modern business ethic, and a number of individuals have become successful entrepreneurs; this is not unique to PNG and indicates no more than that there are always individuals in a good position to benefit from particular external changes. Nonetheless 'Papua New Guinea seems to have taken to capitalism like a duck to water' (Schwimmer 1991:155). However new 'material goods play complex symbolic roles and they [Papua New Guineans] find moral significance in prosperity' (M.F. Smith 1994:9), hence materialism must be qualified in that it has economic and cultural dimensions, and is not part of a new order. The notion that there has been any real process of class formation is implausible. Kinship – and wider relations of ethnicity – are much more crucial. Nevertheless, because of the unequal relationship between big-men and their followers, models of economic activity derived from class analyses of capitalist societies have some validity (A.J. Strathern 1975:374). Moreover the converse of big-men, the 'rubbish-men', sometimes without the ability to obtain wives and reproduce their own households, are all too numerous in various places (Panoff 1985; H. Thompson and MacWilliam 1992:91, 113); there are necessarily many others in between. Individuals who were initially successful entrepreneurs were often unable to maintain their position over time, whilst the economic importance of big-men and some other prominent individuals has been overemphasised, at the expense of the lineage (or other) group in whose ambit they operated. Group membership, for emerging entrepreneurs, politicians and the great bulk of men and women, remains of enormous importance, where land is crucial, and that is everywhere. New socioeconomic systems have embellished and elaborated upon their predecessors, in a wide range of contexts and with very diverse outcomes.

SOCIAL CHANGE AND CONTINUITY

Any attempt to generalise on socio-economic change in PNG is beset by three basic problems; firstly, there is a massive diversity of societies and geographical regions and variable colonial and post-colonial impacts. In some coastal and island areas, there has been complex colonisation, from the German plantation era to the introduction of large transnational, high technology mining enterprise; even a brief phase of Japanese wartime occupation had a substantial impact on mobility and employment, technological change, new scales of wealth, new role models and a new social order (sometimes involving cargoism), a demand for education and new perceptions of identity (e.g. Ogan 1996; Zelenietz and Saito 1989). Amongst the Hagahai of the remote inland, by contrast, the visible effects of 'modernity' may be slight, though not necessarily any less significant for change in ideologies and lifestyles. Key changes often pre-dated colonialism. Secondly, within Melanesian societies distinctions between economy, politics, religion or social organisation are weak, and unlike those in other regions, hence drawing conclusions about the extent and significance of change in particular spheres is fraught with uncertainty. In the Sepik region, for example, exchange practices have few European parallels as 'cult, ritual, marriage, relations between the generations, initiation and political competition are inseparably bound together in a cosmological web of complementarity' (Gardner and Weiner 1992:126). When cash enters Melanesian societies it does not do so as a purely monetary valuable, but takes a role that, in some contexts, is equivalent to that of traditional exchange valuables (Nihill 1989). Thirdly, those who have written about Melanesian societies have had very different perspectives and foci, have perceived alien institutions in different ways (or sometimes selectively ignored them) and thus have contributed accounts of particular places and societies, that provide minimal basis for generalisations.

The variations in the extent and significance of the changes that have resulted from greater incorporation into the world system 'are not easily explained, unless it be in such vague terms as cultural resilience' (Gardner and Weiner 1992:129) and all changes are certainly historically specific, a reflection of social organisation, the extent of contact with such influences as missions, government agencies, commerce (in various forms) and accessibility. The components of change are enormously variable; 'they range from what seem small details; like the use of matches, or the annoying new kinds of grass found on paths and in gardens, to things with diffuse extensive effects on their culture, like the stopping of warfare, the spread of cash or Pidgin English' (Lewis 1980:200). There are multiple layers of meanings, both syncretism and pluralism; moreover Melanesian societies 'were always open to *negotiate* relationships of social entailment and equality' (Gewertz and Errington 1991:172). Processes and practices influencing change and stability at local and national levels are quite different but operate simultaneously and are not easily distinguished. In any event local cultures and histories were never obliterated (e.g. Schieffelin 1995). Extensive debates over the distinction between 'big-men' and 'great-men' (Godelier and Strathern 1991), the validity of Margaret Mead's analyses of Manus and Arapesh (e.g. Foerstel and Gilliam 1992) or that of Rappaport on Maring ecology (e.g. Foin and Davis 1987; Rappaport 1984) and regional differentiation (Feil 1995) emphasise both the fluctuations of intellectual debate and temporal change but also the difficulties of comprehension. The task of comprehension has been magnified through ethnic and cultural interests becoming of increasing significance for political activity, evident in the emergence of landowner groups, secessionist aspirations and various expressions of difference and identity. In a number of areas, especially near the coast, elements of 'custom' have been revitalised, often as a political symbol in the rhetoric of nationalists and secessionists (Connell 1977b), as the incorporation of once remote societies into a global economy has drawn attention to unsatisfied needs.

Even in quite localised areas, some cultures have undergone rapid transformation, others have seemingly been remarkably resistant to change and still more have been adept at integrating the 'traditional' and 'modern', comprehensively or selectively. Most studies of social change have pointed to a limited range of undirectional changes, along the lines of greater individuality and conformity, the decline of the extended family, reciprocity and exchange relationships, the disappearance of cooperation, language shifts towards English and lingua francas, and so on, all of which are subsumed as evidence of westernisation, modernisation and the decline of tradition. However 'traditional' societies have not been static and have always been flexible and open to innovation. In some places there was extensive mobility, significant socio-economic and political change and no indication that pre-colonial society was egalitarian and communal (Connell 1982:508; Filer 1990:84–5; Watson 1985). Moreover socio-economic change has not been unilineal, simply embracing ideas of unending growth and greater rationality. Quite simply, 'there is no map, only endless kaleidoscopic permutations' (M. Strathern 1991:xvii). Variations have arisen because 'not all cultures are equally effective' (Forge 1990:169) at serving the diverse and changing needs of people over time, and because the various impacts of other worlds have ranged from overwhelming to trivial. Social change, and economic change, have been sporadic and unpredictable in their consequences. New bodies of knowledge, and new technologies, refined elsewhere, were of enormous consequence in a country long isolated from some of the most substantial changes in Western societies. 'Not only church and school, but trade store, plantation and administration all undermined indigenous definitions of reality and forms of social relations. The process was not uniform, nor regular, and many aspects of traditional society and many individuals, proved strongly resilient or adaptable. But the old truths were never to be safe or secure again' (Pettman 1984:134). For more than a century on the coasts, and for barely a decade in some isolated regions, societies have sought to incorporate, accommodate and resist alien ideologies, technologies and practices.

The most substantial impact of colonialism may well have been outside the economic sphere: 'the suppression of tribal fighting, the demarcation of colonial territories, and the incorporation of these spatial units into the structure of colonial administration had the effect of fixing and preserving a particular moment in the fluctuation of social fortunes' (Filer 1990:86). Tribes became externally perceived, rather than constructed, if at all, from within, and cultures were demarcated on the ground, their 'borders' defined by colonial mapping pens. Many well-known 'tribes', such as the Goilala, are the creations of patrol officers and missionaries with no equivalents in indigenous practice. The colonial order and the colonial gaze, through missions as much as through the administration, changed the whole trajectory of historical evolution into something supposedly more permanent. That permanence sometimes proved both elusive and threatening. The immediate post-contact phase appears to have been unusually harmonious in many areas, with new technologies and increased productivity. Disputes were passed to *kiaps* for resolution, health and longevity improved and neighbours were no longer so threatening. Though the harmony of early post-contact years may be over-stated, subsequent changes were more complex and less linear, hence development became more 'tense and frustrating' (Moylan 1981:65). More options have contributed to very different dynamics and impacts of change.

Pacification and its consequences, initially the development of a coastal plantation system, contributed to a massive increase in mobility, and with it a greater familiarity with different places and cultures, though no greater respect for different peoples. Pacification also stimulated short-term mobility. Villages relocated to more accessible, manageable locations away from hilltop defensive locations (e.g. Kulick 1992:37–9). Where once victors in tribal wars had literally risen above the losers, they subsequently found disadvantages in altitude and sought places on valley floors with land and road access. Mobility also influenced employment, education, health and marriage. Modern health and education services, and a legal system, followed pacifica-tion and missionisation. Health services have raised longevity and life expectations, improved the quality of life (particularly for women) and resulted in some syncretism of new and old health systems. By contrast intro-duced European legal systems, established through the imposition of a 'rule of law', were quite different from Melanesian dispute settlement procedures. There has however been a resurgence of customary law in many areas, and individuals may choose different strategies for legal redress. Village courts have been effective in contributing to the settlement of small-scale disputes, because of their link with local communities, though there has been a height-ened appetite for litigation, partly because of the manner in which economic change has provided new categories for dispute, such as unrepaid cash loans and contract disputes. At the same time litigation has become much more individualistic (Tuzin 1988). Education too has largely involved the imposi-tion of an external system. Whereas the health and legal systems have effectively been dual hierarchies of resort, the education system has largely stood apart from the transmission and legitimation of traditional know-ledge. There are two quite separate spheres, though 'modern' knowledge has tended to overwhelm 'traditional' knowledge, and its practitioners. The exclu-sion of traditional skills and knowledge from westernised school curricula amounts to a constant tacit assumption that such things are not worth learn-ing. Subservience and dependence, inculcated through the education system, may have wider ramifications; in one remote and then recently contacted Maring society,

> It is an irony that while the Bomagai-Angoiang still live in a relatively stable ecosystem they are becoming so impressed and intrigued by the arte-facts of the outside world's plundering economy that they feel they can only learn from the world, that they have nothing to teach it in return.
>
> (Clarke 1971:196)

The rewards to education have sometimes been disappointing and attitudes to it are ambivalent, in view of the limited benefits and the manner in which it distances children from parents and society (Zelenietz and Grant 1986; cf. Carrier 1984). Contemporary education emphasises and makes more familiar the values and expectations of distant societies, which conflict with more local values and expectations, and reduces the time available for socialisation in local cultures, and the legitimacy of those who undertake this.

Christianity has had as substantial an impact as pacification. Almost the whole national population are at least nominal Christians, and religious precepts are as widely involved in national political life as they are in local social contexts. Despite the significance of Christianity in terms of its public presence, and the rapid conversion of the bulk of the population, the content and details of Christian doctrine are rarely of interest. Christianity had some similarities with many traditional Melanesian belief systems, but emphasised individual accountability, rather than collective values which were often at the core of traditional belief systems. Christianity was accepted, even welcomed, in many areas, initially because of perceived material benefits and its role in pacification. In some areas rival social groups vied to obtain denominations different from those of their foes. The authority of the church to some extent derived from the manner in which local leaders were often the first to embrace Christianity; missions delegated considerable power to Melanesians, to village teachers and church leaders (catechists), and some of the few Melanesians who were able to distinguish themselves apart from village life between the wars were priests and pastors. Localisation came relatively early in the churches. By the time of independence around three-quarters of the population were nominally Christian; new, more fundamentalist, missions sought converts and revivalism was evident in some coastal areas. Christianity is, in some respects, more entrenched than in the home countries of the missions, with prayers opening meetings of social gatherings, religious leaders being elected to parliament and public actions considered in the light of Christian morality. The churches have also been prominent in the delivery of education, health and transport services, especially in rural areas, an important influence on the socialisation of Melanesians towards European lifestyles and widely supported for a host of reasons, not least their mediating role between Melanesians and the administration.

As Christianity has triumphed so old beliefs and practices have died out. The demise of certain forms of ritual, sometimes in dramatic irreversible and poignant form (Tuzin 1988), has ended particular forms of apprenticeship and initiation, and contributed to the erosion of traditional leadership. In some cases, 'evangelical intimidation' has resulted in 'the end of traditional music, dance and body decoration' (Schieffelin 1978). By contrast, the gravity and frequency of sorcery cases have accelerated since pacification; modernity has created 'new forms of violence and inequality that people must deal with and explain', and hence is conducive to sorcery (LiPuma 1994:147). A new epistemology has far from extinguished old ones.

Disappointment with development and progress, and recognition of uneven development and relative deprivation, have provoked anticipations of a new social order, with millenarian visions and often with a religious component, widely referred to as 'cargo cults'. Central to cargoism are comparisons that emphasise superior social and economic development elsewhere, and stress the crucial role of religious precepts and new forms of organisation and discipline in achieving the appropriate transformation. Development is thus perceived to have something of a religious meaning, and not to be a process but rather a sudden metamorphosis, a miraculous transmutation, with piety and faith producing factories, highways and modern goods (Brison 1991; Kulick 1992:60). Change is thus expressed within the idiom of Christianity, the need for faith and the guarantee of redemption, necessitating community harmony and sometimes communal work, to achieve the removal of inequalities, and potential prosperity. Cargo cults are both mystical millenarian events and a response 'to the crisis of indigenous society provoked by the disruptive effect of foreign capitalist penetration' (Barnett 1979:776). The terminology itself reflects one consistent theme: the desire for modern consumer goods. Many cult movements were associated with the potential return of ancestors, bearing cargo, and thus invoked the necessity to remove whatever was blocking their return. In some cases this involved the destruction of traditional cult items, the intensification of prayer and ritual, often in graveyards (the place of rest of the bones of ancestors), the imitation of perceived European ways (including village inspections, order and cleanliness) or even the construction of airstrips and aeroplanes. Cults have rarely diverged in their religious essence, merely seeking improved ways of finding the appropriate road to success and associated with new charismatic leaders: symbolic expressions of deep desires for radical social and cultural change, where the existing order holds out few possibilities. Regular cargo events have occurred since independence, mainly on the coasts and in the islands, where white colonial rule was more pervasive and restrictive.

Melanesians place a high value on materialism, and the possession of material goods was a prerequisite for social relationships: 'where there was no exchange of goods and services, there could be no sense of relationship, mutual obligation and value, but only suspicion, hostility and the risk of warfare' (Lawrence 1964:29). Material culture, apart from its immediate and obvious uses, is the symbol of all important relationships and social relationships. Materialism is not new, though it has become more visible and more individualistic. Ambitious men always accumulated, in order to redistribute, but redistribution has tended to give way to acquisition and consolidation. Increased expectations have emphasised the shift from production to consumption, the decline of exchange and an increase in social tensions. The spreading taste for commodities has influenced work habits. Co-operative work groups have lost importance, in the move towards individualism, the decline in reciprocity and the weakening of exchange relationships, more recently affecting house-building, marketing and road maintenance. Yet, in contrast to urban areas, the village largely remains 'a paradise of temporal freedom' (M.F. Smith 1980:514) where capitalist structures are far from entrenched. The consumption of imported goods of every kind has conferred status and prestige, not least in the perception of the consumers, and 'No one wishes even for a moment to return to a way of life without factory-produced clothing, metal tools, cash crops, outboard motors, knowledge of letters and access to medicine' (Kulick 1992:186). New social relations are partly based on the extent of acquisition. Those who have failed to obtain the trappings of modern development, whether once powerful or not, may now be branded as unacculturated *kanakas* (Jackson 1991b:20; Moylan 1981:64–5), by their neighbours and by distant others.

Material change is not always easy to achieve, leading to ideological shifts, including the response of cargoism. Kilenge villagers of West New Britain, 'at a subconscious level at least have managed to minimise their dependence by limiting their cash needs. Despite their verbal declarations of dedication to the idea of development via cash cropping and business, they find excuses to restrict their involvement in the global economy' (Grant 1980:17). Elsewhere there have also been partial withdrawals from the capitalist economy through unrealistic and naive expectations, and more exceptionally, because of the 'perceived unfairness of distribution of rewards' (D. Townsend 1980a:14–15). Withdrawal, disengagement and the revitalisation of tradition appear to have occurred principally in areas most remote from the centres of capitalism, such as Vanatinai (see p. 272), where attempts to engage in the cash economy have been of limited success. Such societies experienced frustrations as much with inadequate and insufficient capitalism as with capitalism itself. For the Hube of Morobe Province, after decades of incorporation, 'the people generally are groping around trying to find some autonomy and self-esteem, which were shattered by the capitalist system's forerunners about eighty years ago' (D. Townsend 1980b:293). Consequently 'some Papuans nowadays lament the relative lack of development in their region, and echo Kay's conclusion about inadequate capitalism' (D. Townsend 1980c:409), that is 'capital created underdevelopment not because it exploited the underdeveloped world but because it did not exploit it enough' (Kay 1975:x). External influences and internal conditions are extremely variable, yet some degree of opposition to colonialism and its social and economic consequences has been widespread, taking a variety of forms, violent and passive, sometimes creating something of a 'culture of resistance' directed against transformations that would destroy indigenous culture, the basis of survival and integrity. This opposition to some forms of development has been concentrated more obviously in coastal areas, a reflection of the greater emergence of post-colonial inequalities there (and the greater perception of differences between colonised and colonisers) rather than the more pervasive and continuous inequalities of parts of the highlands.

Societies and cultures have become more homogeneous and more internationalised; the 'exotic' in traditional life – clothes (or lack of them), polygamy, body adornment, shamanism, shell currency, cremations, cannibalism, etc. – has slowly disappeared as its presence is found to conflict with the norms of larger, more modernised societies and to suggest a no longer welcome situation of 'backwardness' that opposes 'progress'. Among the Bimin-Kuskusmin, for example, cannibalism has become an 'unpleasant duty' (Poole 1983). Other social phenomena, such as art and body decoration, have also declined as interests have shifted, different priorities have governed the allocation of time, and the elaborate cultural organisation, of which these were inextricably a part, has begun to disintegrate. Language changes emphasise the slight but significant shift towards homogeneity, and towards a minimal national identity. Most of the vast number of languages of PNG have survived; only a handful with a very small number of speakers appear to have disappeared completely in the twentieth century (Kulick 1992:5–6), but others will disappear in future: a parallel to the loss of biodiversity.

Sport has drawn PNG into a wider world, and also inculcated, via rugby league, some notion of nationhood. What was initially a colonial institutional transfer (Gissua and Hess 1993) has taken on major Melanesian overtones (e.g. O'Hanlon 1993:67) and is one of the principal visible symbols of PNG's international presence. Gambling has become widespread. Cardplaying is firmly entrenched in many areas, and especially the highlands. Gambling is both recreation and 'bisnis', an important means of redistributing wealth and a source of tension between villages, though it has tended to reduce gross income inequalities (Grossman 1984a; Healey 1986; Maclean 1984; Zimmer 1986). Nightclubs, at least in urban areas, are copies of those elsewhere, whilst in rural areas sometimes hastily erected 'discos' have become venues for overnight 'six-to-six' parties that have replaced courting (*tanim het*) ceremonies (N. Maclean, pers. comm, 1993; Read 1986:186–7). Commercial dance festivals (*singsing bisnis*) have transformed pig killing and distribution ceremonies, in parts of the highlands, through a commercialisation of ritual that enables both cultural resistance and renewal (Boyd 1985). In urban areas, birthdays, baptisms and entry to high school increasingly constitute the principal reasons for 'ceremonial' activity (Iamo and Ketan 1992). At these ceremonies, and at more 'traditional' gatherings, the consumption of alcohol, cigarettes, foods, clothes, and so on, is as integral to the success of ceremonies as rice was in some coastal areas even in the inter-war years; without a quantity of beer, a party cannot be successful. Patterns of commodity consumption are converging with those of other world regions. Though the direction of change has been towards increased linkages and homogeneity with the world beyond, continuity and stability are considerable – not least in some of the crucial elements of society: kinship, land tenure and the agricultural economy. Though modern commodities have been sought, and new international structures (legal, educational, medical, etc.) introduced, the lives of most Papua New Guineans are still very closely linked to ideologies and practices that existed before colonial times.

ENGENDERED INEQUALITY

Historically most women's lives were tied to household and domestic reproductive activities; their other roles were more limited, though often substantial in separate spheres. Gender stratification has been widely documented in ethnographic studies, especially in the highlands (Dickerson-Putman 1992, 1994; M. Strathern 1987); indeed 'the male domination of women is one of the greatest foregone conclusions of Melanesian ethnography' (Jorgensen 1991:257) though the nature of gender inequality and separation vary considerably. In most societies women and men generally perceived themselves and each other as living in some degree of autonomy, complementarity and interdependence, not in competition, in societies that lacked many of the sharp divisions, for example between public and private spheres, secular and sacred, that characterise more industrialised nations (Rohrlich-Leavitt 1975:625). The establishment of capitalism, and with it the emergence of cash cropping, wage labour, migration and greater individualism within nuclear families, tended to separate families from the community and brought women closer to men.

At least rhetorically successive governments have sought to integrate women into the development process. The seventh national aim was 'a rapid increase in the equal and active participation of women in all forms of economic and social activity'. No aim has so singularly failed, but no aim so conflicted with the existing organisation of society. The dead hand of government has changed little. Ultimately, in every modern sphere, those in power have simply not regarded women as important enough to waste time or money on. Though women were crucial to economic activity and the reproduction of society, often had their own sphere of ritual and exchange and were highly influential, even in the most apparently male-dominated societies (Feil 1984; M. Strathern 1987), they were very much part of a patriarchal society and rarely had power or influence of any kind beyond their own village or traditional social group. In the colonial era little changed. Missions emphasised western gender roles and thus women's domestic role, though they sought to improve their health and reduce the burden of work (MacIntyre 1989). It was however the men who travelled and experienced the wider world, gained education, acquired modern tools and who negotiated with, and worked for, the colonial administration. Only in the later years of the colonial era were women able to enjoy similar experiences, and take up employment in the 'modern' sector, and then primarily in the coastal and island districts. In some respects such 'modernity' was more easily available in the colonial era, when an alien administration was more concerned about equality and opportunity for women than were post-independence governments.

Most official attempts to incorporate women more fully into contemporary economy, politics and society have not gone beyond programmes and rhetoric, since greater equality for women was perceived as being opposed to national cultures and a threat to men's power and resources. This was well expressed by one West Sepik MP: 'As far as Papua New Guinea is concerned, women are always regarded as the lowest in the family. I do not want the concept of Western civilisation to give equal rights to women as are given to men. Men must get first priority in the society and not women' (quoted by M. Turner 1990:87). Thus, in Kove (New Britain), a woman who seeks to have children, receive the support (and demands) of her kin, and experience the prestige of being viewed as a 'good woman' must 'accept the restrictions, denigration and occasional physical abuse that reflect a value system subscribed to by all Kove' (Chowning 1987:148). Similar perspectives have recurred at all levels of society; they are most strongly held at village level hence the opportunities for girls to gain access to education (especially at secondary and tertiary level, where costly boarding is required) have been more limited than those for boys. Government programmes have generally failed to incorporate women, even in agriculture, where agricultural extension officers have been men (*didimen*) rather than women (*didimeri*), resulting in a focus on cash crops rather than food crops or, simply, little extension activity. Funding for women's programmes has declined both relatively and absolutely, a situation graphically described for Enga province (Baranay 1994). A combination of sexism, unequal opportunities (for education and employment), *wantokism* and women's fear of male retribution, if they venture too far into the public domain beyond local conceptions of appropriate behaviour, have weakened the ability of women to achieve new forms of success (Zimmer-Tamakoshi 1993).

Commercialism has contributed to new gender inequalities. The food production system has become even more obviously the arena of women, as men have entered the world of cash cropping. However women, and also children, have provided a large part of the labour, for food crops and such laborious tasks as picking and pulping coffee, pig-rearing and the production and reproduction of children. Women's position in pre-contact times was often difficult, women worked under the direction of men, and women's rights and responsibilities were limited to certain areas; though women were crucially important as primary producers, and as both intermediaries and instigators in ceremonial wealth exchanges (A.J. Strathern 1982) such roles were often denigrated, the fruits of their labour were appropriated and they were the victims of domestic and other forms of violence (e.g. Donaldson and Good 1988:21–5; Gelber 1986). In coastal societies, especially matrilineal societies, women were less likely to be perceived as simply supportive and secondary and more likely to control cultural resources and exert a degree of autonomy (e.g. Schwimmer 1991:147; A.B. Weiner 1976). Despite the denigration of the distinctive and critical roles of women in some areas, new tasks were allocated to them in the era of cash cropping. The more successful cash croppers were often those who were best able to mobilise the labour of their wife or wives; for Bena-Bena (Eastern Highlands) men, 'women are our tractors' (Langness 1967:172) whilst Kove men claimed that: 'Our women are like your [European] coconut plantations; they are the way we make money' (Chowning 1987:147). All too often, as in Baruya (Eastern Highlands), 'now that the production of coffee has taken its place alongside subsistence production, more use is made of the labor power of girls than before', even to the extent that they have been withdrawn from school (Godelier 1986: 212; Barnes 1981:281). More pressure was placed on women to feed their families and pigs and contribute to income generation. After a respite, following the introduction of steel technology, women's work loads may have again increased; certainly 'women continue to provide most of the labour in both the subsistence and cash economies, while receiving a disproportionately small share of cash income' (Warry 1987:151; see also Chapter 4).

In some areas women have organised groups, such as Kafaina in Simbu and *Wok Meri* (women's work) in the Eastern Highlands, that began as a diffuse plea for economic and political equality. Such groups, despite often substantial and widespread membership, have had relatively little wealth or power. They have planted their own coffee and vegetables, in attempts to generate independent economic power, assert the value of female labour and challenge some of the prevailing ideology of male domination, such as control and manipulation of money, gambling and beer-drinking, hence, unsurprisingly, there has been male hostility (Barnes 1981:282). As in Chuave, 'women protect wealth for years only to have men appropriate it, finally gaining in the process only tangential status and prestige within the development sector of the economy' (Warry 1987:178; Sexton 1986). Despite women's ability to maintain and establish business, the newly generated wealth is more likely to be produced by men and retained by them, so establishing new gender inequalities (Nash 1981), while the struggle for money provides a new and sharper focus to gender politics.

Women have come under pressure in different ways, not only to fulfil their 'traditional' tasks and duties as wives, mothers and food producers, but also to participate increasingly in modern professional life. Their efforts to do so have often been thwarted by men (and the exigencies of the contemporary political economy) and modernity has posed new problems for rural and urban women. Household incomes have been spent on alcohol rather than food, with worsened nutritional outcomes for women and there has been an increase in crime and domestic violence against women (Chapter 10) especially in urban areas. Much of this is a result of a perceived challenge to men's status and power in an era of change and uncertainty; on the one hand, women's access to employment and wages is perceived as particularly threatening and, on the other, women have moved away from indigenous cultures that gave them (and men) clear areas of influence. Because of colonial law, and mission influence, crimes of violence may now go before the courts, though courts are often biased against women (Warry 1987:148), police may take little action and women be unwilling to initiate procedures. Women are less likely to be fluent in Tok Pisin than men, and Tok Pisin itself is sometimes perceived as a primarily male language, learnt away from the villages where women reside. This gender difference 'permits the maintenance of a stereo-type in which all women can be portrayed as more or less incompetent in Tok Pisin' (Kulick 1992:91). This stereotype is strengthened because of the non-assertiveness of women in public forums, or in interactions with outsiders (in village contexts); women remain peripheral, emphasising the perception that they are less modern than men, more bound to tradition and to nature. Despite change, men continue to fear and mistrust women. Though 'each day sees its new share of occasions and examples of feminine resistance or indif-ference to the traditional practices and symbols of male domination' (Godelier 1986:198), challenges have not been without considerable costs. In practice men are not so much challenged by women, but threatened by the entire process of development that affects their autonomy and independence, resulting in 'dependence on the outside world, which now encapsulated them in a different social order. Money is emblematic of men's dependence on this world, and dependency is associated with femaleness' (Clark 1989:133). Men thus feel that they have become more like women, with limited control of their own lives. Gender relations have worsened and women have failed to secure development.

RELATIVE DEPRIVATION

Even in the 1990s there were several newspaper reports of the discovery of 'lost tribes' and 'first contact' with particular nomadic groups in remote areas of the country. Such stories – however valid – attest to the rugged terrain of many parts of the country, the inaccessibility of some areas, recency of con-tact and the lack of modern services. Attitudes to those in the periphery were encapsulated in one press report of possible first contact with the Liawep people of West Sepik province.

About 79 people of the nomadic Liawep tribe have been rounded up by a patrol of government officers in the Oksapmin district. The patrol set out in May after reports were received claiming that there were people living in the jungles of Oksapmin and Telefomin. The report said that the people were nomadic, they still roam around naked and have had no contact with the outside world. One of the people was caught by a hunting expedition early last year and he then revealed where other members of his tribe lived. The District Officer in-charge of the Oksapmin district, Peter Yasaro, said that though PNG has been independent for 18 years some of its own people still live in the stone age . . . Mr Yasaro said that he will help bring the services to the people and prevent them from living their nomadic life.

(*TPNG* 24 June 1993)

The task of extending service provision to remote areas is enormous and, in most regions, services have been withdrawn rather than extended. Political rhetoric favours rural development but because of lack of interest, negative attitudes and fear, inadequate finance, maladministration (and corruption) and the powerlessness of the remote, uneven development has been accentuated since independence. Indeed 'relative deprivation is an inevitable attendant of modernisation and economic development; Papua New Guinea's immature transport network and obstructive topography only intensify the country's developing spatial inequalities' (Clarke 1980:188). Simultaneously, increased mobility has contributed to a greater awareness of social and spatial inequalities.

There has been little to challenge the colonial legacy of centralisation and domination by the bureaucracy. It is in the cities that the word 'elite' has entered the national vocabulary (as 'class' has not done) with particular reference to politicians, businessmen and bureaucrats, and where inequalities are most visible and localised.

> The gap between the rich and the poor is getting wider and wider every year. . . . The rich, including politicians, dine in restaurants and drive the latest model cars with tinted glass while the poor try to make ends meet by selling empty bottles and betelnut. The rich live in apartments surrounded by three-metre tall fences crowned with razor wire. Their gates are remote-controlled and manned by 24-hour security personnel supported by large guard dogs. The poor live in crude sheds made of scrap metal, sawmill off-cuts and cardboard pieces.
>
> (A national journalist, quoted by National Research Institute 1992:v)

Migrants to the squatter settlements have often come from the more remote parts of provinces, where inadequate health, roads, education and other services have contributed to low life expectancies and incomes and poor nutrition. The greatest inequalities are between the towns and the remote borders of provinces, especially on the New Guinea mainland. Even at the rhetorical peak of decentralisation and egalitarian development, 'the ideology of decentralisation [was] mismatched with the practice of spatial concentration' (Jackson 1979:175); over time spatial concentration has been further emphasised.

PNG has largely failed to serve the needs of its poor, and to incorporate the bulk of the population, and especially women, into a process of development. It has the highest child mortality rate in the Pacific, around 38 per cent of children experience some malnutrition, school retention rates have declined since 1977 (and the promise of free education has been elusive), only five countries in the world (all in Africa) have poorer access to safe water and literacy rates are barely improving. In 1995 PNG was placed 126th of the 174 countries assessed through the United Nations Development Programme's Human Development Index. This composite index measured national income, life expectancy and educational attainment (adult literacy and mean years of schooling); though the data have limitations, PNG was ranked below all Asia-Pacific countries, other than Laos and Cambodia, and classified as exhibiting 'low human development' (UNDP 1995). A different attempt, using the same criteria, to construct a Pacific Human Development

Index ranked PNG below all other twelve countries for which data were available (UNDP 1994). There remains 'a large unfinished agenda of development: development that puts people at the centre, not the periphery' (National Research Institute 1992:vii). The legacy of the mining boom has been movement towards a situation where 'the central theme of development has been to imitate the Western nations as quickly as possible in terms of the form and content of their economic performance' (ibid.:12). Underlying these failures have been inadequate political will, limited concentration on human resource development and the failure to translate policies into practice. The fragility of coalition governments and the limited expertise of bureaucrats have hindered development (Chapter 10) whilst social policies have been conspicuously absent in election campaigns, in party platforms or individual promises, overshadowed by localism and economic policies and promises (R. Preston 1989). Decentralisation has reduced the effectiveness of service provision, in both quantity and quality, and failed to empower local communities.

Remoteness, isolation and the difficulties of participating in the 'modern' world have ensured continuity rather than change, and frustration rather than satisfaction with the direction and extent of development. Tribal affinities remain vastly more important than classes and the lives of most Melanesians are largely confined to land within visible horizons (though distant influences on that localised world are considerable). Disappointments of development have made those excluded resentful which, in turn, has engendered both a lack of self-confidence and spite towards those perceived to have been more fortunate (Keck 1993). In many circumstances, the impact of even heavy engagement in relatively new commercial and monetary transactions is similar to that in the Melpa area (Western Highlands).

> By preserving *moka* [ceremonial exchange] and certain associated key institutions, notably bridewealth payments, the Melpa have retained a sphere for their own continuous history, which acts as a filter in respect of the outside. It lets in enough to 'colour' the *moka* actions and enable the *moka* itself to play a role in contemporary adjustments, but not so much that the outside world would swamp or sweep away the internal world of meanings the Melpa themselves continue to construct.
>
> (A.J. Strathern 1991:211)

A complex of changes has brought societies into conditions of internal conflict and contradiction as new relationships have defeated both intention and convention. The incorporation of Melanesian societies into a global economy and participation in a modern society have enabled them to participate in 'a world of mistakes, frustrations, disappointments, anxiety and conflict' (Bailey 1966:409). The structures of modernisation that initially appear as alien, powerful and coercive have been slowly accommodated, but not without resistance and transformation.

Melanesian societies were never egalitarian; they were usually far from it.

There were significant gender inequalities (in workloads, access to power, control of resources, etc.) and seniority (and often ancestry) played an important role in leadership. Whilst leaders might not have owned more resources, they controlled the exchange and production of goods. Regional and local differences in access to resources became more crucial during the twentieth century. Whether new inequalities are worse than old inequalities, or merely different, will never be resolved, for so many places and scales. However it may generally be true that 'Villagers find themselves pondering their position as a group, the big men and their followers alike rendered small in comparison with new kinds and degrees of wealth and power' (M.F. Smith 1994:37). Contemporary inequalities have emerged from increasingly overt competition for more permanent access to resources, rather than from big-men seeking resources to redistribute, or power being accorded to men because of their seniority. Although incorporation into the new spatial order of the global economy has created some forms of uneven development, it has also opened up new alternatives for single or non-chiefly men and sometimes for women. Education and labour migration resulted in new skills and incomes, enabling the gaining of respect and a more fulfilling life away from or within the village (Newton 1985:202), and migration has almost always benefited the migrants.

There are enormous and critical variations in the manner in which local societies have become incorporated into the global economy, and hence equally great variations in response and reaction to that incorporation. Melanesian societies are not merely uniform and inert victims of international capitalism, but play a vital role in their own history. The existence of 'cultures of resistance' and the dialogue between disengagement and incorporation suggest that the structure of dependence is partly negotiated. Crude notions of dependency and underdevelopment are not helpful, nor are many of the metaphors of capitalism. Many societies are far removed from a situation where the repercussions of capitalism are the most important influences on social life. In some highlands societies, for example, commitments to the 'social production' of pigs may be the greatest source of inequality (Feil 1984; Modjeska 1982). Such inequalities are also quite different from the 'potentially permanent, large-scale and hidden forms of inequality which can be brought about by capitalist enterprise' (A.J. Strathern 1982:157). Though these are now more pervasive, they are often resisted. On Vanatinai island (Milne Bay), the islanders exhibit considerable and militant cultural conservatism and emphasise '"the way of the ancestors"'. Their decision not to give in to external economic, political and religious forces is quite conscious . . . deliberate resistance to coercive pressures' (Lepowsky 1991:219), involving a steadfast opposition to participation in the cash economy (cf. Pomponio 1992:xix; Battaglia 1990:3). By contrast, in Gapun, 'nothing the villagers seemed to do or say could legitimately be interpreted as constituting opposition to the western-derived discourses and economic forces that so fundamentally influence their lives, and that are unambiguously leading towards increasing disempowerment and loss of self respect' (Kulick

1993:12). If nothing else there are astonishing variations within PNG (and in the interpretation of these variations in terms of structure, autonomy and agency). Change has gone on in a climate of intellectual, political and economic uncertainty, ensuring that response is varied, the outcome uneven and that relativities dominate local structures of, and attitudes to, development.

10 The political economy of development

I will now turn to what I consider to be the greatest threat to our country, crime, and here I'm referring to both street crime and official corruption. Unless we can control it, it can destroy all the advances we have made in the last ten years. It must be controlled before it destroys us. The threat of crime has made life in our major towns difficult and tense. It has destroyed the quality of life and 'stolen' essential freedoms from our citizens. The challenge to the nation and the government is clear. We must take positive strong measures to combat it.

(Somare 1985:8)

In a country of such diversity, with substantial foreign investment, the role of politics is considerable in shaping national development, constructing a nation from a variety of islands, language groups and cultures, balancing provincial and regional interests, formulating policies and programmes and providing a social framework for development. Papua New Guinea is a 'soft state', with limited capacity to implement development policies and programmes, though with an ability to manipulate macro-economic policy and develop relations with transnational corporations. This weakness is to some extent a function of both the recent establishment of an imported, political system (alongside educational, health and industrial relations systems), and of the extent to which regional and local issues are of much greater importance, to the public and to politicians, than national issues. The structure of national development is, in many respects, the sum of development in the regions, and is weak because of the limited co-operation and integration between regions, and between the regions and the centre, and because of persistent factionalism and corruption at all levels of government. This political economy is far-reaching in its significance.

It is a truism that change has been rapid, and that this has been particularly important for the functioning of the state political system and the bureaucracy, alien structures grafted on to a fragmented society, where literacy levels were low, experience of the outside world slight, inaccurate and inadequate, and suspicion and hostility vastly more common than regional or national unity. In the circumstances there has been a remarkable degree of stability.

Many Papua New Guineans nonetheless exist only on the fringes of the modern state, purchasing and selling commodities, but paying little or no taxation and largely continuing to live in their areas of birth, where 'traditional' social organisation is more influential in their lives than most institutions – even schools and roads – of the contemporary state. Languages, cultures, races and, more recently, religions have divided Papua New Guineans in a country where the tasks of achieving physical communication are often considerable, and only rarely improving.

POLITICS: THE ART OF THE POSSIBLE AND IMPROBABLE

Before independence Australia had established a democratic political system in PNG, though with only a single chamber. After independence the Queen remained head of state and a Governor-General represented her in Port Moresby. There are eighty-nine 'open' constituencies but, in an attempt to reduce the extent of localism and encourage the election of educated individuals, each province and the National Capital District also elects a provincial member, who usually therefore represents a large number of different tribal groups. These provincial seats enabled a number of particularly prominent politicians, such as Sir Michael Somare, to retain power for a longer period of time than most of those elected for the smaller constituencies.

Democracy has proved highly effective in that most elections have seen the rejection of at least half the Members of Parliament by their dissatisfied electorates. It has also been unusually popular. Competition for seats is enormous, reflecting the pervasive view that the road to power, privilege and perks is through Parliament, with over forty candidates competing in some electorates at the last election. The number of candidates has increased over time, with 1,655 candidates for 109 seats in 1992, thus averaging more than 15 candidates per seat, with 48 in one Simbu constituency. The major reason for such large numbers is that 'the rewards of office are extremely attractive – power, status, high salary, big cars, better housing, company directorships, travel and business opportunities' (M. Turner 1990:105). Participating in elections is not about ideology, nor party loyalty, or even about ensuring and encouraging local development, although all candidates stress their local identity and goals, in a temporary surge of populism and egalitarianism, and many (sometimes more than one in a constituency) express an affiliation with a prominent political party. The high turnover of members, and the occasionally small number of votes required to win, encourages this kind of mass participation. In 1992 only seven MPs received a majority of the vote, and 52 of the 109 MPs won with less than 20 per cent of the total vote, in the first-past-the-post system. As the number of candidates has increased, so too has the localisation of their support. Fragmented social organisation means that there is no effective electoral accountability, because politicians need only cultivate a tiny sector of their electorate and can afford to ignore the majority and still 'survive' (Standish 1981:303). Convicted criminals remain as MPs in the same way. Though the bulk of the electorate are cynical about politics, and convinced that candidates merely secure personal advancement, turnout in elections is invariably high. For various reasons, including personal loyalty to candidates, opposition to the sitting member, financial inducement or the fear of not being seen to vote, turnouts have always been over 60 per cent, comparable to those in very different democracies elsewhere.

Politicians affiliate with parties; though these are of minimal ideological importance the major parties have remained in place since independence. These parties, notably Pangu Pati, long associated with Somare, are essentially personality parties identified with the charisma (and therefore power) and, to a much lesser extent, policies of the most important individual in that party. Fifteen political parties contested the 1992 election; five of them were new, formed only for those elections, and most disappeared without trace afterwards. None claimed to represent 'class' interests. Fragmentation of political parties has meant that most governments have been coalitions. Typically, the government that was formed by Paias Wingti after the 1992 elections consisted of three main parties and more than thirty nominal independents and defectors from other parties. After most elections, winning candidates have changed sides; 'many are for sale in the weeks after the polls are declared' (Moore 1992:34) and achieving power reflects what is financially possible. The 1992 contest was unusually close, with Wingti becoming Prime Minister only after an extended 'helicopter and hotels' period, when party leaders try to marshal their forces, isolate them from external blandishments and so retain or achieve government (op.cit.:36–7). Secure in office Wingti then attracted several more MPs to the victorious side, as the quest for individual power continued; one MP belatedly crossed the floor to join the government saying 'My people need me to be there to achieve power and money'. Such shifting allegiances and fractured factional alignments have plagued political stability. 'The shifting sands of parliament have tended to induce a form of policy paralysis or, at best, policy inconsistency, thereby considerably reducing the effectiveness of government' (Hegarty 1989:2). Parties exist only at election times, have no presence in the constituencies and no effective organisation inside or outside Parliament.

Politics is primarily a male preoccupation. Women rarely stand for election and few win. Since 1987 politics has been a wholly male preserve at the national level. Though eight women contested the 1992 elections, none came close to winning, in part because their ability to distribute largesse was perceived to be inferior, or less likely to be forthcoming, than that of men. At every level, politics is 'a masculine game of spoils and primordial rivalry, rather than of general good' (Lipset 1990:145). This is part of a wider context where women experience sexism and unequal opportunities (in education, the workplace and the home), regionalism, a double workday and fear of violence if they venture into the public domain, though there is also a disabling lack of unity amongst women's groups. Competition by women for economic and political power is strongly resented by men (Zimmer-Tamakoshi 1993), a situation very different from that espoused in the constitution.

Political longevity is rare. The insecurity of politics as a profession has contributed to strengthening many MPs' efforts to establish their own personal financial security whilst in office, and few leave Parliament in poverty. The lack of ideology, fission and fragmentation within political parties, the quest for power and privilege, and the brief tenure of most MPs have provided no continuity to the political system. Changes of government may not have been disruptive, but they have often been accompanied by purges of senior public servants which have disrupted continuity in the bureaucracy. Continuity has been further reduced by regular opposition attempts to achieve power, primarily through votes of no confidence, and successful votes have reduced the tenure of several governments. In 1991 the constitution was amended to ensure that there is at least an eighteen month post-election period that is free of such votes; ironically that legislation was passed only as a result of the Prime Minister's success with the widely criticised practice of paying for parliamentary support with all sorts of patronage: short stints in a ministerial office, overseas trips, or cash from the Prime Minister's discretionary funds (Saffu 1992:267). Coalitions are thus highly unstable though the notion of democracy has survived.

Parliamentarians are more educated and more affluent than the vast bulk of the population, but they constitute no ruling elite or class nor are they an 'indigenous bourgeoisie' for other than a limited time period. Elite conflict is over access to spoils and patronage, rather than over ideology, the bureaucracy is divided in the same way by the search for political and economic patrons, and cultural nationalism is not a cohesive force, resulting in problems of management of the economy. The absence of mobilised popular support for political parties has contributed to an increasing tendency to rely on expediency and patronage, as a means of conflict resolution and achieving political progress. Politics is both pragmatic and weak. At the constituency level, vote buying, bribery and even violence are not unusual, in the bid for power. In power politicians may become both recipients and distributors of illegal funds and goods. The concept of a social contract is limited with many politicians anticipating only one term in power, and uninterested in accountability during that period. The bureaucracy has been able to reduce and oppose the most blatant attempts at political chicanery, but has not always been averse to participation, for example in the forestry industry, as bureaucrats also seek to gain and redistribute resources.

In 1985 the PNG ombudsman reported that corruption was 'rampant and rife [and] the stability of the nation is threatened unless immediate action is taken to stop the rot' (quoted in M. Turner 1990:141). Since then it has increased. To some extent activities that might elsewhere be perceived as corrupt are seen differently. Politicians routinely distribute largesse and so 'buy votes' before elections. In the highlands especially there has been a 'commoditisation of votes' where politicians were perceived to be rich, had gained their riches through election to Parliament and thus had to outbid each other in offers of bribes to every elector (A.J. Strathern 1993:726). In the absence of trust between politicians and their electorates, this commoditisation represents one of the few direct gains that many individuals experience from the political process; contemporary politics has some similarities with cargo cults (Kaima 1991). Exchanges and gift giving are central to most PNG societies, to the extent that it could be perceived that 'failure to accept a gift is more improper than receiving one' (M. Turner 1990:142). The prominent highlands businessman and politician, Iambakey Okuk, renowned for showering goods from helicopters and buying several thousand cases of beer at the 1982 elections, argued that such behaviour was expected of a traditional leader, and thus of a modern leader. Violence, commoditisation of votes and wide-ranging corruption, at least in the highlands, have introduced a situation where 'warlords' have emerged. Politicians have been elected at least partly on the basis of their crude, and sometimes unprincipled power, supported by well-armed henchmen, and even with police collusion; bribery, intimidation and malpractice are increasingly common as political processes move 'towards gunpoint democracy' (Standish 1994, 1996; A.J. Strathern 1993). On the coasts, and in the islands, the electoral process bears a greater resemblance to that in democracies elsewhere.

At the constituency level opportunities for patronage and corruption have been built into the political system by the existence of generous 'slush funds' through which a proportion of the national budget is allocated directly to all MPs for use in their own constituencies. The term 'slush fund' originated with the Prime Minister's Discretionary Fund (later the Electoral Development Funds), which was already under criticism in 1980, with MPs accused of buying support and failing to fund projects. The underlying assumption was that MPs could identify good local projects and bypass inevitable bureaucratic red tape. In 1984 the Fund allocated all MPs an annual sum of K20,000 which, by 1990, had increased to K100,000. Cheques could be directly deposited in MPs' personal accounts, a situation which prevented any monitoring of how the money was spent. By 1994 the Electoral Development Fund had grown to K300,000 per member per year (more than K32.7 million in that year), supplemented by individual allocations from the Minor Roads Fund of K200,000 per year. Despite pressure for either the Fund to be abolished or proper accountability to be established, and promises by most governments of its abolition, it remained until the end of 1995, finally removed after World Bank and local student pressure. It did however ensure that many disgruntled constituents, with no access to the pork barrel, were eager to unseat their MPs in the next election.

A 1975 Leadership Code, that sought to prevent politicians and public servants from receiving loans or presents from individuals, companies and foreign enterprises, was ineffective. Political parties have received funds from overseas and, for substantial kickbacks, a number of Asian companies have gained leases and contracts, especially in the forestry and fishing industries. No prominent politicians have been above accusations of impropriety, much of which has been condoned at similarly high levels. The late Chief Justice, Sir Buri Kidu, commented: 'if we charged everyone who's corrupt, we'd probably have no-one left to run the place' (quoted in Standish 1993:219). The most prominent example of corruption in high places was the behaviour of the Minister of Forests, Ted Diro, set out in the Barnett Inquiry into malpractice in the industry (Chapter 5). The Inquiry recommended that charges be laid against Diro and others. Legal delays, the stabbing of Judge Barnett in a *raskal* attack at his home, the mysterious absence of crucial documents and the arson of the headquarters of the National Intelligence Office and the Anti-Corruption Squad, all slowed the process of justice. In 1991 Diro was eventually found guilty on eighty-one out of eighty-six charges laid against him, most of which involved the illegal receipt of goods and money, mainly from Asian entrepreneurs including Indonesia's Military Chief, General Benny Murdani. Diro was fined K3,300 and dismissed from Parliament and public office for three years. In this process, the Governor-General, from the same part of Papua as Diro, resigned, being unable to put political neutrality above extended kinship, patronage and, ultimately, friendship and loyalty, whilst Papuan MPs abandoned the government, which then lost power. The Prime Minister had opposed corruption and lost government. With enormous difficulty the legal and parliamentary systems have overcome various other attempts at corruption.

Patronage, especially within the bureaucracy, is normal and anticipated, in the sense that it too may be seen as pursuing traditional obligations and cementing expected relationships. The expectations that follow being both a *wantok* and a public official, who should be impartial, uphold the interests of the state and make meritocratic appointments, are sometimes in conflict; the granting of permits, leases and loans – sometimes illegally – and employment opportunities, are not uncommon in the public service system, at national and provincial level (M. Turner 1990:142). However the bureaucracy is more often criticised for inefficiency, irrelevance, complacency and waste. 'Unanswered letters, lost files, indifferent bureaucrats, "wantokism" and corruption are common experiences for anyone dealing with government agencies in PNG' (Hayes 1993a:174). The public service suffers from a deterioration in the sense of nationalism, envy and rivalry between departments at provincial and national levels, compartmentalisation and fragmentation of departments, a politicisation of the public service (undermining the responsibility of managers) and overlapping functions (Larmour 1995). At independence there were 50,000 public servants, 40 per cent of all formal sector employees; though that number grew only slowly, attempts to reduce numbers have been thwarted by the power of the Public Employees Association. Bureaucratic performance is therefore crucial but, especially in rural areas, workers and services have diminished or disappeared. Public servants do not want rural postings and have increasingly become urban-based, focused on forms rather than actual public service. Broadly 'the bureaucracy is gobbling up resources, but it is not using them in an efficient or effective manner' (M. Turner 1990:138). Accountability is minimal, the monitoring and evaluation of outcomes weak and restructuring has not improved public sector performance.

There is, in most regions, a hierarchy of problems. Corruption exists at provincial level and, at one time or another, more than half the provincial governments in PNG were suspended on the grounds of financial mismanagement (see p. 294). One of the more notorious was the Enga Provincial Government, deeply distrusted by the Engan people for stealing public funds and misusing vehicles. 'Mismanagement, waste and slipshod execution of jobs of all kinds were ever present, there was occasional peculation and much illicit use of public equipment and supplies, and the padding of project payrolls with friends and relatives was common' (Gordon and Meggitt 1985:133; see also Baranay 1994). These processes began in the late-colonial era. An Australian administration, for the first time with adequate capital, sought to build a social and economic system quickly, to be in place when PNG became independent. Building on the traditional order, the old leaders, the big-men, became recipients of financial largesse on an unprecedented scale. In turn they redistributed some wealth, cajoled and ordered, as they had always done, to put development projects in place. After independence the surfeit of cash declined, but the mechanisms remained in place, populations grew and the competition for resources increased. Politicians, often businessmen grown rich on investments in coffee plantations or trade stores, sought power through financial persuasion. The old big-man system became distorted through new forms of ostentatious wealth.

The return to prominence of many individuals convicted of corruption, and other crimes, supported by their kin and regional *wantoks* inside and outside Parliament, emphasises that malpractice is firmly established, recurrent and unlikely to disappear. It is nevertheless one of the achievements of postindependence PNG that so many 'leaders' have been brought to account, even if they later return. In no other country in the Asia-Pacific region has such a proportion of those occupying positions of power and privilege faced criminal courts. Various agencies have challenged unprincipled power, the press has retained its freedom to discuss abuses and the churches have played their part in stressing ethics; none has prevented corruption. Perceptions of the self-serving nature of politics have all contributed to the unwillingness of village people to be involved with, and bound by, contracts negotiated with governments, such as those involving mining concessions, and to the emergence and justification of crime. Maintaining the political and bureaucratic system, especially in rural areas, has become extraordinarily difficult. Almost all corruption is detrimental overall to the interests of the poor, in both rural and urban areas, and has reinforced or widened existing inequalities.

LAW AND DISORDER

Since independence public order has increasingly broken down in PNG, marked by a resurgence of tribal fighting (primarily in the highlands, but spilling over into other areas and, on occasion, into Lae and Port Moresby) and, more significantly, by the growth of violent crime, especially in large urban areas, associated with and organised by a number of gangs. Most crime is attributed to alienated youths, euphemistically referred to as *raskals*. Crime waves are of national concern, because of the instability, violence, cost of crime and crime prevention and the overseas media coverage of this, that has resulted in international (and domestic) perceptions that the country is moving towards anarchy and neither investment nor residence there is wise or safe. Somare stated in 1985 that crime was the most serious problem facing PNG and that 'If we do not control the situation now, questions relating to Papua New Guinea's direction in the next ten years would become truly academic' (1985:9). Crime has subsequently increased.

During the colonial period the administration devoted considerable energy and expenditure to preventing tribal fighting, especially in the Western Highlands, where contact had been relatively recent. The achievement of peace, the 'pax Australiana', was one of the great successes of colonialism, and was soon followed by the earliest phases of monetisation. However that period of peace and control was merely a short phase of temporary stability, that was again replaced by the resumption of tribal fighting, more or less where it had been interrupted (O'Hanlon 1993:53–4). As the greater authoritarianism of colonialism gave way to the somewhat superficial democratic processes of the independent state, old inequalities and grievances were resurrected or took on new forms. Disputes sometimes lasted decades, and were accentuated by population growth, land shortages, the decline in coffee prices in the late 1980s, the occupation of land (whose ownership was contested) and mobility towards more accessible village sites. Courts were usually unable to address the underlying issues in disputes, Christian missions did not fill the gap that followed the loss of sanctions associated with indigenous belief systems, there were new tensions following uneven development between rural and urban centres and 'between emergent social classes of people'; together this amounted to severe contradictions in social life brought about by various processes of change and a 'crisis of legitimacy' (A.J. Strathern 1993; Trompf 1994:328–31). Warfare took an 'economic' form in the sense that victors consistently burned down and destroyed the trade stores and cash crops of the vanquished to ensure the enhancement or emergence of inequality, and the weakening of power and competition (Connolly and Anderson 1992; W. Standish 1981). Warfare remained largely 'traditional', with fighting undertaken using spears and bows and arrows, enabling medical practitioners in recurrent fight zones to publish articles with such titles as 'Pierced by the arrows of this ghostly world' (P. Sharp 1981; cf. L. Fingleton 1987). By the mid-1980s, growing evidence of shotgun use marked an escalation in the amount of injury and death that could be caused. Politicians are often armed and among the most important suppliers of guns to their constituents because 'guns buy votes' (A.J. Strathern 1993:724). Improvement in transport and communications (resulting in the return migration of potential warriors), the greater use of alcohol and the 'retribalisation' of local disputes (A.J. Strathern 1992) have increased the scale of fighting, whilst the forces of law and order have been largely powerless to prevent the flare-up of traditional antagonisms or contain them when they occur. Since tribal fighting is a legacy of the pre-colonial era, not only are the police largely irrelevant to securing a peaceful outcome, but also reducing traditional enmities has escaped public policy formation. Tribal warfare is more akin to historical military operations than to contemporary urban violence. It has resulted in considerable costs in lost lives and injuries, the destruction of economic assets, loss of labour input into social and economic development, and disturbed harmony and welfare (as schools and aid posts have been destroyed, children receive less education, and teachers and health workers are unwilling to work in fight zones). The inability to solve tribal disputes produced police frustration, and the burning of village houses, shooting of pigs, and sometimes direct violence against participants and their kin. Police became perceived as another enemy, unpredictable and interfering. The continuation of tribal fighting, important though it is, has remained beyond solution.

Fewer lives have been lost in urban crime, but its impact and extent are considerable; its visibility is apparent in the fences and walls, behind which most formal housing is, hopefully, securely enclosed. However urban crime has affected the poor and the weak in towns, as much as it has affected the wealthy and powerful, and has affected the indigenous population much more than the expatriate population. Crime is not just a matter of 'blue-collar' (or tee-shirt) robbery, theft, violence and rape, but of white-collar bureaucratic crime and corruption. The Chief Ombudsman has commented on unwillingness by the police and public prosecutor to bring bribery or corruption charges under the criminal code: 'Such inaction breeds a corrupt mentality. You steal a tin of fish, you're in Bomana [Port Moresby] jail. Leaders misappropriate millions, they're still on the streets. In other countries this has led to revolutions and coups' (quoted in *AFR* 23 December 1992). The extent of crime is related to social disruption, accentuated by urbanisation, unemployment, boredom, the uneven distribution of incomes and wealth and a legacy of ethnic rivalry and discord. Alienation, poverty, limited education, inadequate policing, delayed and bureaucratic judicial systems and the erosion of community controls have all contributed to increased levels of urban crime. By contrast *raskalism* provides an identity, in opposition to the neo-colonial order, and has considerable social support:

> villagers see them as surrounded by an aura of adventure, education and power. Villagers believe that rascals are fighting a kind of protracted guerilla war against corrupt politicians, greedy businessmen and obstructionist missionaries, [which all villagers] can legitimately use to express their dissatisfaction with and even resistance to post-colonial, capitalist and Christian influences that are causing increasing disruption in their lives.
>
> (Kulick 1993:9–10)

Support is however often more ambivalent, with *raskals* perceived as disruptive elements and indicators of a generation gap (A.J. Strathern 1992). There is widespread dissatisfaction with the general socio-economic situation in many urban and rural areas. Violence and crime form one means of challenging the existing order, where few other means of resistance are possible.

While the forces of law and order have failed to reduce crime, the criminals have become better organised. Gangs occur in almost every town and, rather like the police, they have become, in some places, a 'pseudo-clan' (Trompf 1994:347). Most gangs are components of an urban gift economy, fed by theft and burglary, structured in a manner typical of pre-capitalist Melanesian societies. Criminal lifestyles represent not so much a response to alienation and unemployment, but a search for prestige, partly legitimised by the distribution of proceeds in a manner akin to that of traditional big-men (Dinnen 1995; Goddard 1995). In rural areas gangs have a more local, traditional basis, and are particularly prevalent alongside the Highlands Highway. Gangs now contain hardened criminals, as well as younger educated men, recruit members and have extensive and effective networks across the country. In 1986 when successful police action recovered stolen goods in Port Moresby, there was swift retaliation against police in Lae and Mount Hagen (May 1987:14). The scale of operations has increased to include armed holdups of coffee and cocoa buyers, and plantation owners (some of whom were forced to deliver wages by helicopter), bank robberies and pack rapes. Substantial volumes of coffee and cocoa were stolen, resulting in reduction of quality (MacWilliam 1996:61–2). Gangs took over the distribution and sale of stolen goods from middlemen, developed international links to Australia and the Philippines, organised marijuana marketing and set up protection rackets (B. Harris 1988) through what has been called 'vertically integrated criminal networks' (Hegarty 1989:8; Trompf 1994), which had some links with politicians and the police. Only the drastic use of 'states of emergency' and curfews has curbed the expansion of organised crime.

Early perceptions of theft suggested that there was an egalitarian 'Robin Hood' element to this, with goods stolen from the rich (expatriates, truck operators, big store proprietors, etc.) being given to or retained by the poor, hence such crimes were regarded with a certain degree of indulgence (May 1987). In reality criminals certainly gave away stolen goods, but usually to *wantoks* and friends, and not to the poor, whilst crimes were committed as often against the poor as the rich, and within the 'moral community' of fellow kin and *wantok* groups (Standish 1994). Crimes against the person, especially rapes and domestic violence, are even more likely to be made against and amongst the poor, and cannot conceivably have a more egalitarian outcome. Rapes and domestic violence against women have substantially increased since independence (though all crime statistics, especially in this area, are inadequate). Attacks against women are more common, with men defining their maleness, their poverty and their opposition to the state in this way (Schiltz 1985). In parts of the highlands rape is not only an adjunct to warfare but also a substitute for military operations which kill and injure men. Domestic violence is considerable, and regarded as 'normal' and acceptable in married life by many men and women (Counts 1990). It is more apparent in urban areas because of changes in the social role of women (including the absence of subsistence agricultural opportunities), conflicts over money, alcohol consumption and fewer social sanctions, but is probably just as prevalent in rural areas (UNDP/ILO-ARTEP 1993:246). It is more common in the highlands than in coastal regions, partly because of greater gender polarity, polygamy, limited marital choice for women, greater access to alcohol and fewer spiritual sanctions (W.E. Mitchell 1990). Increased violence is attributed to a number of other reasons, including sexual jealousy, the extreme expression of male dominance and beliefs in the subservience of wives and women generally.

There are no data on the regional distribution of criminal activity. Widespread assumptions are that it is principally an urban phenomenon, especially in the largest cities, notably Port Moresby and Lae; in part this is a function of better reporting (and greater paranoia) in those places. Highland provinces, headed by Enga, are assumed to be more violent than lowland and especially island provinces (Dinnen 1993). A single issue of the *Enga Nius* of August 1992, an official monthly publication of the Enga Provincial Government, recorded the following events there with disarming honesty. Firstly,

> police are alleged to have shot dead four men and wounded another three in what appears to be a 'payback' at Sirunki during a fight between two Kunaluni clans. . . . A fight broke out when a big *singsing* [traditional celebration] was disrupted by some rowdy youth. . . . A policeman received a stray arrow. It was not intended for police. But later police came in force and shot the men.

Secondly,

> four tribes are building a new road after intensive lawlessness on the existing road . . . after losing [General Election] candidate Frank Iki's people were holding up people on the road. The people don't care if they get paid or not. They are building . . . twenty kilometres of it, thick jungle they're cutting down . . . Iki's people have the wrong mentality [and] have dug a big ditch across the road cutting off over 15,000 people from receiving vital services. They have looted a Community High School and the Health Centre. The staff have fled.

Thirdly,

> over nine women are reported to have been pack-raped in different parts of the province but authorities could not confirm whether they were election related. Four rapes are reported to have taken place at gun-point. . . . In another incident three Kandep High School girls are reported to have been

pack-raped by Alitip youth in a hold-up near their school. In retaliation police moved in to make investigations, but catching no suspect are alleged to have burnt stores and destroyed other property. . . . The Provincial Police Commissioner [had] heard reports of armed bandits holding up people on the Kandep/Laiagam border and the Kompiam/Wabag border [district boundaries in Enga] but his men have not been able to catch one bandit yet.

An *Enga Nius* reporter was caught up in one armed hold-up:

I witnessed an armed hold-up in progress on the Laiagam–Kandep border. I was in the lead vehicle of a five vehicle convoy. We had driven up the mountainside for a few minutes and as we rounded a corner guns started firing and hooded men appeared from all sides. They probably had two high powered rifles and three home-made guns. Prior to the climb over the border we had all agreed to fight the rascals but the gunfire put out such thoughts. The rascals managed to scare the three vehicles in the front away and robbed the last two – the Kandep High School truck and Fr Lawrence, a priest at Moriant Catholic Mission in Kandep. Guns? Well every tribe seems to have at least one gun. But we knew that if we hurt one of the rascals or one of us got killed in retaliation the long-term implications appeared gruesome. Stunned from this experience I returned to Wabag. On the way I saw a singsing in progress, a new service station being built and people playing volleyball. These sights relieved me and gave me new hope that at least the bulk of Enga people are good citizens determined to develop their province.

A footnote revealed that this *singsing* was the one later disrupted by violence. Fourthly, Pausa high school was burnt down, after previous attacks on the school had destroyed other buildings, including a teacher's house, and a student was killed by a bush knife wielded by a villager. The Provincial Election Board had suspended up to twenty-one schools, including two high schools, for a variety of reasons; 'some of the reasons were that teachers' lives were threatened, their daughters raped, theft of school property and many more'. The Provincial Education Minister observed that 'the government can do little to help. Enough is enough. People should stop their stone-age attitudes. People should change together, work together and appreciate services.' In this sad, and brief, chronology of events the enormity of the problems of one province (different from other areas only in the extremes and regularity of crime) and the inability of the government and the police force to control or contain them is apparent. Indeed the *Nius* editorial called for alternative services for those cut off by violence, rather than for control of the violence, seemingly an impossible task.

Hitherto peaceful public demonstrations and strikes have also become more violent, often leading to riots. Violence between squatters and other urban residents in Lae resulted in deaths and the destruction of houses at the end of 1992. Striking mineworkers at Ok Tedi went on a rampage in 1988 during which machinery and buildings were destroyed and burned. The arson centred on the facilities of senior, often expatriate, staff, a result of perceptions of serious inequalities in the provision of recreational facilities. Riots have involved not only those who might be expected to be the most disaffected with life. Army personnel, and their supporters, marched on Parliament in 1989 to protest over poor pay and conditions; damage was caused to buildings and cars, including those of the police, as officers were unable to control their men (M. Turner 1990:172). Disillusionment, especially amongst young men, employed or unemployed, is widespread and has intermittently taken very violent forms.

The costs of criminality are considerable, both directly and indirectly. Property has been destroyed, business activities closed or curtailed, services, investment and infrastructure cut back, freedom of movement restricted and lives ended or ruined. In 1990 a group of villagers in the Western Highlands, cut off from access to health services, stores and basic government service by violence from an enemy tribe, between them and the Highlands Highway, had begun what was expected to be a two-year project to construct a bypass to the highway (*TPNG* 11 October 1990). It has become impossible to persuade public servants to work in the rural areas of some highland provinces, hence education and health have suffered, reinforcing existing relative deprivation. Overseas perceptions of lawlessness have discouraged the recruitment of skilled personnel in many areas (including business and education), prevented the development of a tourist industry, cut back foreign investment (especially in the service sector) and raised the cost (through security investments and insurance premiums) of existing investment. It has encouraged more mercenary attitudes amongst many expatriates, and others, rather than commitments to national development. The costs of dealing with crime, through recruiting and expanding the police, judiciary and prison systems, and undertaking preventive measures (reinforced fences, guard dogs, etc.) have been very high. Crime has hampered social and economic development to a greater extent than in most other countries.

The rise in crime is partly a result of the ineffectiveness of the police, who are no more efficient than other sections of the bureaucracy. They have been criticised for collusion with criminals, brutality, bad community relations, indiscipline, poor response to calls, woeful standards of crime investigation and low conviction rates. Instead of being a community based force they have long adopted para-military tactics in response to criminal activity (M. Turner 1990:177). Police excesses have been considerable, especially in parts of the highlands, a situation described by one PNG journalist as 'fear and loathing in the Highlands' (*PC* 15 November 1988), after one operation in which many houses were burnt to the ground and innocent people killed and injured. The morale of the police force has declined, especially after the police forces were withdrawn from Bougainville in 1990, having failed to overcome the rebels but having succeeded in alienating most of the local population. Antagonism between the police force and the defence forces has not been unusual, and has occasionally resulted in events akin to pitched battles. The military, in their domestic role, have scarcely contributed to peace and stability. At the time of independence the Papua New Guinea Defence Force (PNGDF) was regarded as a privileged elite and was one of the last entities over which Australia relinquished control. Increased crime and civil disturbances in Port Moresby resulted in the declaration of a state of emergency there in 1985, and the use of the defence forces in a domestic role, a move perceived as a threat to their elite status. A spontaneous military riot in 1989, with the army creating mayhem whilst marching on Parliament, emphasised its lack of discipline (and, to some extent, defused fears of a military coup) which was also apparent in premeditated attacks on civilians, and brutality and excessive force during joint military and police exercises in several provinces.

The collaboration of the police and the military in exercises to capture escaped criminals and suppress crime emphasised the growing domestic role of the military. This became particularly apparent in the Bougainville crisis when, for the first time, the military were formally opposed to other citizens of PNG (even if they perceived their role differently). Since 1982 the military have also been involved in eight formal states of emergency and curfews in Port Moresby, Lae, the highlands and north coast (Standish 1994). Both the police and the military have played a peace-keeping role at every mine site, except Misima, following the establishment of a Rapid Deployment Unit, that was particularly active at Mt Kare and Porgera, and accused of brutality there, with the Enga Premier seeking its withdrawal and accusing the government of having created a unique police unit beyond the control of the Royal Papua New Guinea Police Force (*TPNG* 1 October 1992). Not only were the military playing a more domestic role, but they were also playing a more political role. Various incidents have emphasised questions about the stability, resilience and legitimacy of civilian rule, in the face of a united defence force. There are elements of movement to a more controlled society in which the PNGDF, though still subject to civilian control, will play an important role; the distinction between the police and the army will become less sharp, and the security forces increasingly politicised (May 1993). The Internal Security Act of 1993 represented a move in that direction. After a particularly difficult month early in 1993 (when a former minister was killed in a street fight, two university students were murdered, resulting in ethnic riots in Port Moresby, a rampage by drunken soldiers led to one death and the arson of a social club, and the government offices in Enga were burnt down) the Minister for Provincial Affairs, John Nilkare, called for a national state of emergency. The annual report of the Asian Development Bank, released at the same time, stated of PNG: 'Failure to secure an improvement in peace and order will have a major adverse impact on the performance of the economy over the next few years' (quoted in *AFR* 21 April 1993). That failure has been extremely expensive, in a variety of ways, for more than a decade, a reflection of a weak state structure and a rapidly changing nation.

A NATIONAL IDEOLOGY?

Even in the best possible circumstances, weak states have considerable difficulty in constructing nations and national identities in post-colonial conditions. Circumstances have been very far from ideal in PNG, where all political borders are artificial colonial creations. Colonialism was effectively a thin veneer in most places, even if it had shaped the national political economy, and there was only localised opposition to it. Independence without struggle, against the wishes (or without the knowledge) of a substantial proportion of the population, especially in the highlands, meant there was no widespread support for it and little understanding of its implications. The transfer of power was a bureaucratic phenomenon rather than the establishment of a new ideological perspective. There was no economic or cultural shift at independence, no change in language use, education policy and development programmes, no new political system and few strands of unity across such a vast area. The task of taking over the reins of power, by the few skilled and experienced politicians and bureaucrats, largely precluded detailed debate on independence. Because power was effectively granted without mass pressure to an elite minority with limited contact with the people, the elite became isolated and only minimally and intermittently concerned with the construction of a national identity. The unity that existed was partly forged through the loosely radical, populist and socialist visions suggested in the Faber Report that preceded independence. However 'everyone in Papua New Guinea, it seems, had a different concept of self-reliance' (Stewart 1984:94), and few had any real sense of national goals.

The conventional categories through which national identity might be nurtured and kindled, as has occurred elsewhere – religion, language, history, race and land (place) – have all been inadequate, mainly because of the diversity of experiences. Late contact and development emphasised the task of shaping even the most basic elements of national identity. Efforts to agree upon a national flag, anthem and the name of the country (at least in the move towards independence) proved extremely difficult, and more subtle attempts to define cultural tradition have failed. The circumstances of early urban life – in small towns where Melanesians were intended to work temporarily – slowed the construction of any notion of a national identity; for Melanesians 'the texture of their urban existence must surely be one of the most important reasons for the slow development of nationalism among a people who were never allowed to mix freely together away from home, and to meet people from far-distant places' (Wolfers 1975:50). Intermittently, in the post-colonial era, there have been deliberate attempts to create a national identity, and even occasional desires to establish a national dress (*TPNG* 2 September 1993). The design of such national symbols as a new parliament house proved difficult, because of regionalism, and the final product was criticised for being both 'Sepik-centric' and 'internationalist' in using the indigenous architectural form most familiar to outsiders, and thus, in both respects, being unrepresentative of PNG as a whole (Rosi 1991). The symbols, let alone the spirit, of national identity have been difficult to achieve.

At both national and provincial level, cultural centres have been established, cultural revivals attempted and festivals organised to display traditional dance, dress and music. Simultaneously telecommunications have brought global images, brand names and styles to PNG. There is a syncretism of past and present, in every facet of social life (Connell and Lea 1993). In the era of late modernity, in impoverished states of the Third World periphery, such phenomena are emphasised through the increasing visibility of global reach. On a different scale, for a different audience, images of PNG 'tradition' are transmitted globally – through tourism, travelogues and the splendours of tropical nature – whilst global culture in diverse forms flows through the satellite dishes of the cities. 'Tradition' moves out as 'modernity' moves in. They combine uneasily, if at all, in the national political system.

Cultural change has been rapid but there has been relatively little consideration of how people define themselves and how identities are formed. Few question who they are or disavow a local identity (Gewertz and Errington 1991:116–17). Despite the acquisition of new lifestyles and 'modern' goods, the established linguistic and philosophical identity of Melanesians, even of such long-established urban residents as the Toaripi who remain 'tribesmen in town' (D. Ryan 1989), let alone attitudes to land tenure, where land is owned by the ancestors and held in trust by the living for those as yet unborn, are more important than the recent trappings of modernity. Modernisation and homogeneity, in a state where tribes are also recent inventions, have far from overwhelmed identity and difference. In almost every context tribal and regional affiliations are more important than national identity. Those who identify themselves as Papua New Guineans do so outside rather than inside the country.

The task of creating a modern state from a diversity of cultures that remain in many respects 'traditional' has ensured that the nation remains fragmented. The ingredients of national culture – flags, anthems, armies and so on – are at variance with minimal consensus on national history (time) and landscape (space), to the extent that models of collectivity are largely imported. Nationalism acquires its greatest legitimacy when ethnic boundaries do not cut across political ones but, in PNG, 'the great extent to which peoples' sense of self remains bound up in the gross actualities of blood, race, language, locality, religion or tradition' (Geertz 1973:258) limits the extent to which individuals might identify with a wider entity. This has been most obvious in Bougainville, where the greater ethnic consciousness, that followed more diverse contact with other parts of PNG, stimulated secessionism in defence of identity and wealth rather than any sense of shared national identity. Ethnicity is not merely a theoretical construct, but a practical phenomenon of enormous significance for identity, difference and conflicts of various kinds. It is apparent that, despite the familiar term 'nation-state', there can be no presumption that where there is a state there is necessarily a nation. Few if any nations are more imagined than PNG.

PROVINCES, REGIONS AND RESISTANCES

The historic structure of organisation and decision-making in PNG was as decentralised and divided as any in the world but 'a century of colonial rule established a highly centralized and specialized organisational structure which bore little or no relation to the traditional social organization' (Conyers 1976:3,9). PNG thus went from one extreme to another. By the 1970s, in the run-up to independence, it had become apparent that it was essential to counteract some trends towards centralisation, as serious social unrest began to appear in several regions, emphasising the problems of balancing national goals against regional and local goals.

The principal regional problems arose in Bougainville, the easternmost island of PNG, but geographically, historically and culturally more closely linked to the western Solomon Islands. Bougainvilleans have always claimed uniqueness. Only in the twentieth century, under colonialism, have traditional social and economic links become modernised and orientated westwards. Bougainvilleans are black, a characteristic that is shared in the Pacific by only a few peoples in the adjacent Solomon Islands and which enables them to refer disparagingly to Papua New Guineans as 'redskins'(Nash and Ogan 1990). Bougainville is the most distant part of the nation from Port Moresby, and was neglected for most of the colonial era. Between the two world wars, several maps and stamps of the colony did not even include it. Neglect quickly ended when copper and gold were confirmed. Villagers opposed exploration, the resumption of land – especially for the port – and eventual mining, emphasising their separateness and their view that the PNG administration had moved directly from neglect to exploitation. Once the mine was built, opposition gradually gave way to the view that Bougainvilleans should have all the royalties and taxes and that these should not be shared with other Papua New Guineans. This attitude was promoted by a newly formed Bougainville nationalistic society, Napidakoe Navitu, though there had been forerunners of village-based cultural nationalism, such as the Hahalis Welfare Society (Rimoldi and Rimoldi 1992). In 1973 the island was allowed to have the first provincial government in the country as a concession to emergent nationalism. Pressure for secession continued, paralleled by increasing profits from the mine (Mamak and Bedford 1974:12), although secessionists themselves discounted the economics of mining as an element in separatism. Loss of land to the copper mine was a critical issue. Almost all the prominent secessionists were Catholics, and religious principle and biblical precepts were constantly paraded in discourses; indeed 'the Catholic church was intimately bound up with the search for an independent cultural identity' (N. Sharp 1975:123). Christianity was much more a causative influence in sponsoring nationalism than a colonial intrusion to be opposed by nationalists.

After disappointing central government funding for the Bougainville Provincial Government's works programme, Dr Alexis Sarei, later to be the first President of the self-styled Republic of the North Solomons, claimed that 'Bougainville was a fat cow milked for the rest of Papua New Guinea' and the province declared its independence, on 1 September 1975, just two weeks before PNG became independent. The strength of the secessionist movement was that it combined traditional precepts of social and economic behaviour with distinctive ethnicity and a contemporary plea for a more appropriate distribution of the fruits of economic growth. Secession was sought both in defence of identity and in search of the material rewards of mining. The illegal Republic of the North Solomons was ignored both in the wider world, and by the new PNG government. After six months it effectively disintegrated, after it had been ignored nationally and internationally, and the province had been starved of funds. The PNG government dissolved the first Bougainville Interim Provincial Government but eventually agreed to reinstate provincial government, leaving the island with the only provincial government in the country, the right to fly its own flag alongside that of PNG and a more beneficial distribution of mining royalties. The two key issues that had contributed to secessionism nevertheless remained in place, though muted, as mining brought considerable wealth and rapid social change, and the province was largely tranquil for the first decade of independence.

On the island of New Britain there had long been tensions, again centring on the alienation of land. In German times a substantial proportion of the land around Rabaul was alienated, and most of it converted into plantations. Increasing population densities amongst the Tolai people led to acute land shortages, especially as the administration was encouraging the local expansion of cocoa cultivation, whilst some alienated land remained unused. In 1969 the Mataungan Association was formed to combat what the Tolai saw as foreign domination of their land and affairs. One immediate focal point was the newly proposed multi-racial Local Government Council. Councils were intended to have local people as well as expatriates, and be centres of grass roots political development. The Mataungan Association decided to oppose the council, announced it would refuse to pay council taxes and organised a boycott of the first elections, claiming that the council was yet another device to enable Europeans to control Tolai land and affairs. A council was elected but trouble continued and the army was placed on alert. Clashes between the Mataungan Association, supporters of the new council, and the police were almost continuous in 1971. The violence reached a climax later that year when the District Commissioner, the most senior official in the area, was murdered during a dispute involving landownership and squatting. The situation improved only after 1972 with the emergence of the first real national government, the resumption of some of the alienated land and the creation of strictly Tolai Local Government Councils.

The third area where significant regional problems were experienced, Papua, was larger and more diffuse since its identity was a colonial creation and it included the Southern Highlands, which had no affinity with the rest of Papua. In the core areas of Papua, around Port Moresby, grievances had built up over the direction of development. Although the national capital was in Papua, a significant part of post-war economic development had gone on in more densely populated and fertile New Guinea, and many Papuans felt they were being neglected, because of the limited agricultural potential and scarce natural resources (Dorney 1990:156). As in both Bougainville and East New Britain there was also some feeling that the administration was more interested in the concerns of foreign businessmen rather than the rights of Melanesians. The movement owed its origins in large part to fear and distrust of highlanders and concern over the influence they might wield, through their superior numbers, in an independent country. It was thus founded on a 'negative' basis rather than on appeals to popular Papuan sentiments, though distinctive ethnicity was an important element. In 1971 a group of Papuans in the House of Assembly formed a pressure group known as Papuan Action, and used the threat of secession to press for more economic development in Papua. While support for greater economic development was widespread in Papua, support for separation was largely restricted to Port Moresby. The Papua Besena secessionists made a unilateral and symbolic declaration of independence for Papua in early 1975; from then onwards the movement gradually lost support as the quest for secession died and the party adapted itself to securing greater political spoils for Papua, but above all for Central Province. Papuans largely remain convinced that they have been disadvantaged politically and economically since independence.

In each of these areas there were comparable structures of dissent, and similar sentiments were expressed, usually in more diffuse form, in many other parts of the country. In each case there were expressions of cultural difference, most evident in Bougainville, and of dissatisfaction with the pace and structure of economic development, through concern that national policy favoured other areas, particularly the highlands. Highlanders were regarded on the coast and in the islands with some degree of fear and contempt. Most local nationalist movements embraced a range of political, economic, social and cultural objectives; most operated outside the formal political system, some formally organised, others more akin to cult movements. In Bougainville and Papua, attempts at secession eventually collapsed, yet they posed severe problems for a nation nearing independence, and seeking some combination of economic growth, balanced economic and social development and the maintenance of national unity. Beyond that, at national and provincial level, there are few places where there has never been a threat of secession. For example, the Min people, who span the border between West Sepik and Western Provinces, have long sought their own province (Jorgensen

1996). In 1993, the people of Lumi (West Sepik) sought to break away and form a new province with the inland districts of East Sepik. Less than a year later the two Sepik provinces made a joint attempt to secede and set up a so-called Republic of New Melanesia. Micro-nationalism is quintessential to Papua New Guinea.

The most significant outcome of regional dissent around the time of independence was the establishment of a provincial government system, based on that introduced in Bougainville in 1973, and designed to give greater autonomy to the provinces and so weaken secessionist tendencies. Provincial government brought a new dimension to the process of decentralisation, the third of the Eight Aims. Although there was no provision for provincial government in the national constitution that came into place at independence, the government was ideologically and politically committed to it, despite concerns over loss of authority, financial costs, limited skilled human resources and administrative duplication. A Ministry for Provincial Government was established in 1976, as PNG embarked on the practice of decentralisation with national policy favouring self-reliance, equity and popular participation, and when other developing countries were recognising inherent problems in centralised planning (Axline 1986:1–2). By 1978 there were only two fully elected provincial governments – North Solomons and East New Britain – but all provincial governments had held elections by 1980. A complicated delivery process took some time to bring the new structure of government to most parts of the country, especially in a climate of widespread popular indifference (Standish 1979:14), where notions of democracy and participation were imperfectly understood.

In all but the island provinces of East New Britain and the North Solomons more than two-thirds of provincial finance came from direct national government funding allocations, though some provinces (especially the North Solomons) received considerable income through royalty payments and provincial taxes. The islands provinces (other than West New Britain) have been the most affluent with respect to the resources available to and controlled by them, whereas the highlands were the most economically disadvantaged region (Bonney 1986:40–2), and only the North Solomons and East New Britain have been even partly free of central government constraint. Relatively few powers were delegated to provincial governments, as the national government preferred to retain most responsibilities, other than in education, and there was strong bureaucratic resistance to decentralisation. Financial decentralisation was also limited and caution was exercised 'in allowing provinces to assume full financial autonomy – largely for fear of inexperience and incompetence in financial affairs by the new authorities' (op.cit.:26). Such concern was justified. Few provinces ever had adequate financial records, could not produce budgets, had inadequate capacity for financial planning and management, and corruption was rife. All provincial governments were interested in stimulating economic development in their provinces and most established some kind of 'business arm', such as the

North Solomons' Bougainville Development Corporation. The close nexus between politics and business was particularly apparent at provincial level. Conflicts developed between the provincial business arms and other private enterprises in the provinces, and the business arms experienced high failure rates. The financial affairs of both Simbu and Oro provinces had soon to be supported by the national government, and there were numerous cases of incompetence and malpractice. National government was slow to rectify these problems.

Opposition to the notion of provincial government on the part of some national politicians, as a challenge to their power base, and especially financial mismanagement and corruption, led to the suspension of many provincial governments. By the 1990s the evidence of mismanagement and corruption was enormous. Nine provincial governments had been suspended at one time or another: Enga and Simbu (1984), Western and Manus (1985), West Sepik (Sandaun) and Western Highlands (1987), Central (1988), Morobe (1989) and East Sepik (1991) whilst the North Solomons Provincial Government was also suspended after the renewed struggle for secession (see pp. 296–9). Some, like Enga, were suspended more than once. Four were suspended in 1992 – Southern Highlands, Milne Bay, Morobe and Western (Fly River) – on a range of grounds, involving corruption and mismanagement, including nepotism in business, massive purchases of new vehicles, special ministerial allowances, overseas trips, the use of government funds for electoral campaigns, provision of services to particular areas only, and so on. Hampered by limited devolution of power and finance, and plagued with mismanagement and corruption, the achievements of provincial governments were few. There was a lack of co-ordination among provincial divisions, partly a function of 'the exalted self-perception of provincial ministers' (Axline 1986:48), and highlands provinces such as Simbu, with a reputation for tribal fighting, occasional highway stonings and frequent urban burglaries, were usually unable to fill their quota of established posts and could not attract high quality staff (Standish 1981:277–8). Even so provincial governments also contributed to over-government. By the 1990s there were over 550 provincial politicians, and a substantial provincial government staff, that was absorbing a wage bill of K10 million in 1991. That bill was roughly three times the bill for governance in New Zealand, a country with a comparable population size.

The planning and policy-making carried out by provincial governments was mainly limited to the annual allocation of capital works expenditure. Most provincial governments never undertook any systematic consideration of their needs and priorities. Members, including ministers, acted as delegates rather than representatives, seeking to capture particular items – such as bridges or primary schools – for their constituencies, rather than contributing to cohesive decision-making (Saffu 1983). The delivery of services in most provinces failed to improve, conflict rather than co-operation occurred with other tiers of government, there was competition between provinces for the establishment of projects, and hence some duplication of responsibilities and facilities (and the inefficient location of others). The provinces were just as much colonial creations as the state, none was without border problems, they were 'too large' or 'too small' for varied activities, resources rarely reached beyond provincial capitals and there were secession moves within them (Larmour 1990:12–13). By the end of the 1980s, provincial governments had become costly, inefficient and often corrupt bureaucracies, constrained by national government and unable to develop effective policies. Nonetheless the existence of provincial governments had become virtually an article of faith, a central and key element in the structure of the nation and was widely perceived to be, if not beyond criticism, then beyond fundamental change or removal. Indeed it was long anticipated, even when the evidence suggested otherwise, that 'the experiment will succeed' (Axline 1986:47) because decentralisation of power was seen to be crucial to national development and government.

The provincial government system was reviewed at various times, as in 1992 when a Select Committee (the Hesingut Committee) on Provincial Government Review concluded that, despite the problems, provincial government was consistent with local traditions and the need for decentralisation, and should be retained. However, a year later, the Prime Minister, Paias Wingti, sought to remove provincial governments on the grounds that they had become too expensive, had produced a major imbalance in the distribution of scarce skilled human resources and were self-serving; they were also argued to contribute to diversity rather than national unity, being a result of historic Bougainvillean 'blackmail' (*PC* 8 October 1992). Fundamental changes followed, culminating in an Organic Law on Provincial Governments and Local-Level Governments (1995), which replaced the elected provincial assemblies with new assemblies consisting of local (community) government leaders, MPs from the province, up to three 'paramount chiefs' (where such a system was recognised), up to three appointed members and a nominated woman. The chairman of the provincial assembly, to be known as Governor, would be the provincial MP, and provincial ministers were abolished. The significance of the provincial governments was greatly reduced, with most financial powers reverting to central government, though the National Capital District and the North Solomons were exempted from the general recommendations. Whilst this reform potentially returned power and funds to the grassroots, it also strengthened the power of the national government and added to the tasks of the central bureaucracy. In the island provinces especially there was strong political opposition and concerted threats of secession.

The tier of government below provincial governments, local councils (or community governments), has had few responsibilities and limited finance (since finance was rarely allocated by the provincial governments and their revenue-raising capacity was minimal) whilst their administrative and planning skills were extremely weak. They were the principal losers in the establishment of provincial government, and never functioned adequately. Despite the collapse or dismantling of the historic local government councils 'and the clear understanding in Papua New Guinea that the real destination of the decentralization exercise is the level below the provincial level, nothing had been done by the provincial government [in West Sepik, as elsewhere] . . . to reform or even completely replace the local government system it inherited with community government' (Saffu 1983:31). Structures usually disintegrated. This administrative complexity posed particular problems for urban areas, such as Lae, that are without municipal government and depended on provincial governments (primarily composed of rural members) to allocate funds for urban management (Connell and Lea 1993). The revitalisation of local councils was proposed in 1993, with a Village Services Programme that would allocate K41 million in 1994 to the local councils – of which there were about 240 – for new programmes that might enable better coordination between provincial governments, the public service and the villages (*TPNG* 4 November 1993). The scheme was attacked as 'a move backwards to colonialism' by the Manus provincial premier (*TPNG* 10 February 1994). The revitalisation of a largely moribund and inefficient local government system will be difficult, after two decades of decay (Economic Insights 1996:57–9). Secessionism, and violence, have enhanced widespread perceptions that provinces and especially rural districts are not being adequately integrated into the nation in terms of access to services. The provincial government system, despite its aims of contributing to national unity by creating an intermediate level of government, failed and excluded rather than involved local people in decision-making. The lack of capacity within the public service has ensured that substantial problems of administration and regional development remain.

THE BOUGAINVILLE CRISIS

In Bougainville secessionist aspirations declined in the post-independence years, and there was considerable optimism over the development of the province; it was even possible to write 'Bougainville's successful economic future is assured. Ever increasing areas of cocoa, backed by copra, provide a solid, permanent base for economic development, and allow the benefits to reach almost every household . . . these assets can be developed adequately and the income invested to safeguard the future' (Connell 1976:654). Economic change, alongside social, political and environmental changes, proved such statements quite wrong. Despite affluence and access to services concern over the environmental damage caused by the mine increased and there was resentment over the distribution of mining profits, the immigration of a workforce from elsewhere in PNG, and various social problems (Chapter 6). Secessionist sentiments never disappeared, were rekindled on occasion (notably in Provincial Premiers Council Meetings, though they were usually conceived as threats rather than immediate demands) and resurfaced in dra-

Figure 10.1 Bougainville

matic form in 1989 when militant landowners closed the mine. Since then the struggle for Bougainvillean secession has provided the strongest challenge to the basis and stability of the Papua New Guinea state, and the most serious political and humanitarian issue in the South Pacific region since the war (Figure 10.1).

Mounting grievances over mining in 1989 evolved into a more general pressure for secession. The police force was unable to end the militancy, a national government Peace Package was rejected and the Bougainville Revolutionary Army (BRA) emerged, led by Sam Kauona. The presence of undisciplined PNG security forces on the island strengthened support for the BRA and opposition to PNG; both the police and the PNGDF were eventually withdrawn in March 1990. Subsequently the national government announced a total blockade of goods and services to the province, a decision quickly followed by the unilateral declaration of independence of the Republic of Bougainville. By this time the BRA was in apparent control of much of the island, though in distant Buka support for the rebellion was hesitant. An Interim Government was established on Bougainville, with Francis Ona as President and Joseph Kabui, the former Premier of the Province, as Minister of Justice. From then onwards an effective communications blackout restricted information from the island; health worsened, services collapsed and the economy disintegrated. PNG and Bougainville leaders held talks on board a New Zealand ship, the *Endeavour*, off Kieta in mid-1990, which resulted in the Endeavour Accord. The Endeavour Accord, which stated that services to Bougainville would be restored and that the long-term political status of Bougainville would be reconsidered, did not hold. PNG troops landed on Buka in September 1990 and restored some semblance of government control. Civil war was waged for several months and human rights abuses in various parts of the province occurred on both the PNG and BRA sides. The PNG blockade prevented the arrival of medical supplies and, despite international pressure and reports of preventable deaths in childbirth and from malaria, dysentery and other diseases, no supplies reached the island until early 1991. The PNGDF continued to play an important military role and extended its presence. There was fission and dissent within and between the Bougainville Interim Government and the BRA, some factions of which were out of control.

Towards the end of 1991 the PNG government proposed an Interim Legal Authority to administer Bougainville in four districts, in order to extend services further, and to divide and rule. Hostilities resumed in February 1992 after PNG government intervention between the BRA and pro-government groups on the east coast, but by the end of 1992 most of the north and centre of the island, and parts of south-western Bougainville, were under government control. The area around the Panguna mine remained under BRA control and there was sporadic violence in marginal areas. Government forces entered the town of Arawa in February 1993 and in 1994 temporarily gained control of Panguna. Further attempts were made to secure a political resolution of the crisis and services were restored to more areas of Bougainville. The change of government in 1994 led to Sir Julius Chan giving primacy to a peace initiative for Bougainville. A ceasefire was declared, a South Pacific Peacekeeping Force introduced and a peace conference organised at Arawa. Although the secessionist leaders were absent, a Bougainville Transitional Government was established in March 1995, but it excluded the areas where the BRA Bougainville Interim Government remained in control. More than 70,000 people remain in 'care centres' at various places in the province, violence (and deaths) continued during 1996, resulting in the lifting of the ceasefire, a further unsuccessful military attempt to defeat the BRA and the murder of the Premier of the Transitional Government, Theodore Miriung. Any end to violence and a peaceful solution for the whole of Bougainville remained distant.

Though the crisis did not fragment PNG, it resulted in massive devastation in Bougainville. The economy collapsed, hundreds of lives were lost, through violence and lack of medicine and medical services, children missed years of education, communities and families were torn apart, new divisions and hatreds emerged and old divisions were rekindled. A genuine peace, with the restoration of services and economic growth, will take years to accomplish. The development of factions within the BRA, including a *raskal* element, contributed to violence between Bougainvilleans, and, over time, between the BRA and the emerging local resistance forces that have opposed it. Reconciliation will not be easily achieved. For PNG the crisis had a multiple impact. The most obvious effect was economic, with a 5–6 per cent cumulative fall in the GDP in 1989 and 1990, though other mineral developments and cutbacks in government expenditure reduced the macro-economic impact and demonstrated that the PNG economy could withstand a major adverse effect without undue damage (Elek 1992). More serious has been the extent of human rights violations in Bougainville, whilst the extensive blockade of Bougainville, the refusal to allow the International Red Cross or medical supplies to enter for long periods of time, or give journalists access to the island, and the difficulties placed in the way of Amnesty International, led to considerable external criticism of the manner in which PNG was seeking to resolve the crisis, and damaged relations between PNG and both Australia and Solomon Islands. Though these costs were immediate and considerable, the crisis also demonstrated the extent of regional differences within PNG, and the ease with which political disharmony could plunge the nation into chaos. Ethnic and cultural identities were not quaint relics of traditional times but contributing elements to a powerful nationalist struggle that combined demands for control of the modern economy and local resources with elements of tradition. Decentralisation and the establishment of an effective provincial government were no guarantee of provincial satisfaction and stability. That there has been no national disintegration suggests that the PNG state will remain intact, but there may be difficulties in maintaining future unity.

THE STATE: BROKEN BACKED AND SOFT?

Somebody suggested 'Unity in Diversity' as the catchword and it stuck. Even today you hear some of us beating our chests and asserting on many occasions that the nation's strength is in its diverse cultures and traditions. The diversity is slowly strangling our nationhood.

(Paias Wingti, 8 October 1992)

Prior to independence there were fears that unity would be possible; one

African scholar pointed out that the Australian colonial administration had failed to stimulate in Papua New Guinea either any political infrastructure of nationhood, or the anti-colonialist nationalism which transcends ethnic and regional interests and binds the emergent state together (Mazrui 1970:56). Nevertheless even the most powerful secession movement, with multiple objectives and strong local support, has been unable to do more than achieve a limited number of objectives. Despite the fact that development is uneven and there is no national ideology, the central government has maintained – even enhanced – control over the nation. Yet a secessionist movement continues in Bougainville, and parts of the highlands, only effectively incorporated into the state in late-colonial times, have in some respects withdrawn from it. Crime, violence and corruption have all increased and there are relationships between these: *raskals* are sometimes perceived more positively than politicians. The bureaucracy has failed to maintain or extend the notion of public service whilst a fragmented and unstable parliamentary system has not risen to the challenge of long-term policy development. These trends epitomise Myrdal's characteristics of a 'soft state': some capacity for planning but little for implementation, difficulty in enforcing laws, populist rhetoric for reform (land, compensation, etc.), piecemeal policy action, a low level of social discipline and a tendency for corruption to increase as standards of probity amongst politicians and bureaucrats decline (Myrdal 1968; cf. Hegarty 1989:13). Politics is thus held together at the centre only by the fluctuating cohesion of rivalrous political elites.

Difficulties of national development have a very significant spatial component, apparent in the notion of a 'broken-backed' state (Tinker 1965) where a form of quasi-government exists, in the sense that the central government is weak, the regions contemplate or threaten secession and are intermittently rebellious but capable of co-operating with the centre when necessary (exemplified in tensions and disputes over mining issues). Despite violence, disorder and threats to national and provincial governments, the political system continues to muddle through, because opposition to the centre is fragmented and provinces divided. The political system has operated under considerable threat, has little perceived legitimacy in many areas – in parts of the highlands, amongst urban squatters and in the rural periphery – and has not delivered social and economic security or stemmed increased crime and violence. Difficulties in the political management of a fission-prone system, within a pluralist democracy, have resulted in a political process of trade-offs and bargaining, rather than of decisive action, immediate corrective measures or authoritarian solutions (Hegarty 1989:14). Fragmented, soft and broken-backed though this system might be, it has, so far, prevailed against secession and vague threats of military coup.

Perhaps more than in any other country in the world the influences on national integration are unusually weak. At all levels conceptions of others are invariably negative (e.g. Nash and Ogan 1990) and violence has become not just a reaction and response to different neighbours, but a generalised form of opposition to the state and its institutions, especially those that are perceived to create inequality. The extension of the commercial economy has not taken most Papua New Guineans away from their home area. An informed appreciation of national politics is restricted (Bonney 1986:57). Educational institutions are also weak, not all children go to school, and few proceed beyond regional high schools. Exposure to other national cultures, and problems, is minimal. The Bougainville crisis demonstrated that national security was more of a national than an international issue. Separatism, and regional dissent, has been a constant theme as independence removed much of the efficiency and all of the perceived neutrality of the colonial state (Kulick 1993:11; MacQueen 1993:148–9). The absence of an effective party system weakened the state when the assertion of political will was required. Though Bougainville is unusual in its combination of geographical separation, distinct ethnicity and resentment over perceived subsidies to 'another country', it is only a special case of regional distinctiveness.

Since independence there has been a growing perception that governments have failed to live up to the expectations vested in them. Many argue, as do Goilala, that 'colonial rule was better than this', more effective, progressive and less uneven (*PC* 28 June 1990). At Varia village (Gulf) the 'good old days' are similarly yearned for: a returning migrant observed that the administration presence had almost disappeared, and that 'The only change to Varia and surrounding villages has been the influx of political parties and ideologies, to which they refer as "the government game". Their hopes and dreams at the time of self-rule and decentralisation are slowly but surely dying. The word "development" has even become a slang term for "going backward"' (*PC* 2 March 1990). In being unable to ensure the delivery of projects and services, the government lost its legitimacy. Where the village is perceived to be the locus of national identity, and where 'grassroots' has become the most popular term for those who seek to distinguish themselves from urban elites (Lindstrom 1992), a process of 'disintegrative integration' (A.J. Strathern 1993) has occurred. A state has been created but with the most rudimentary symbols of national identity. Consequently there has been 'a pre-emptive resistance of people at local levels towards nationally planned development activities. Legitimacy is claimed at the bottom and only reluctantly delegated upwards. The national government does not have this legitimacy *ab initio*. It has to create it as best it can' (op.cit.:731). In the face of political opposition at every level, compensation claims for 'development', *raskals*, who have incorporated 'traditional' forms of organisation, and with a weak bureaucracy (and police force and army), governments have muddled through but failed to achieve economic growth and national development.

11 Conclusion
Neither growth nor development

Money makes me smile.
Money means beer.
I love money more than anything else.
When I lose even one toea [about one cent] I almost beat myself to a pulp.
Hey girls money can find you a lover, make you comfortable and bring harmony to your life.
Money is the dream of every teenager.
To hell with love. With money you can have refrigerators and stereos.
The age-old fairy-tale of love is fast being replaced by the hard reality of money.
If I'm a rich man I can get to marry the prettiest woman.
Somebody who doesn't have money cannot make love.
People work, people sweat, people suffer, people die, all for money.
(Essay by Tolai schoolboy, quoted by Errington and Gewertz 1993:1)

In its landscape, history, culture and economic development Papua New Guinea is one of the most diverse countries in the world, and has experienced late contact, late development and late independence. It became independent in 1975 with a largely agricultural economy; now the economy is primarily dependent on the export of gold, oil and other minerals, but subsistence agriculture, hunting and gathering remain important in most places. The first Foreign Minister, Sir Albert Maori Kiki, subtitled his autobiography *Ten Thousand Years in a Lifetime* (1963), a reflection of the rapidity of recent change. Despite the continued significance of subsistence economies throughout the country PNG is embedded in a global economic, cultural and political system, though there is debate on the extent and significance of globalisation. PNG is peripheral in the sense that foreign investment is concentrated in resource-based, export-oriented activities like mining and forestry. There is minimal internal economic hegemony and only rare attempts, many unsuccessful, to flex national muscles against transnational corporations. The dominance of this export economy is particularly striking where most people largely live with few of the benefits of modern technology but are greatly influenced by it.

Throughout the country modernity has resulted in a disjuncture between space and place. In pre-modern times these largely coincided, since the spatial dimensions of social life were dominated by localised activities. External links were tenuous and often highly dangerous, epitomised by the 'barter markets' where 'traders laid down their goods and withdrew to a safe distance while the exchange was made' (Gewertz 1978). Modernity and migration disrupted the relationship between space and place. Subsequently, economic relationships, notably commodity sales and trade store purchases, have influenced local life for almost every Melanesian society. However, the introduction into villages of the money acquired elsewhere frequently generated an expansion of the village-based gift economy (Gregory 1982; Carrier and Carrier 1989; Foster 1995), as people entangled, and made sense of, their relations with capitalism. More directly the village trade stores have become the final points of distribution in the world system; their goods, with their distant origins, are the symbols and substance of the diverse structure of incorporation and accommodation. Ineluctably 'cash was more of a necessity than people wanted it to be' (Finch 1989:272), as they absorbed the notions of progress and development. Place has become 'increasingly phastasmagoric' (Giddens 1992:19) as localities have become thoroughly penetrated and influenced by external economic and cultural influences, whose genesis and local ramifications are often beyond comprehension.

Global culture, economy and society are at least superficially entrenched in PNG, particularly in urban areas, yet intermittent cargo cults, whose terminology (and practice) mark the extent of dissonance with the newly received world, demonstrate the substantial differences that remain. Knowledge and technologies have been selectively incorporated, transformed and transcended, reinterpreted and imbued with particular significance for local social practice. The national economy, culture and identity are not direct products of new, increasingly global economic arrangements but are shaped by the everyday practices of ordinary people, and their feelings and understanding of their conditions of existence. The globalisation of social and economic life is far from complete; there are many people in PNG who are very distant both in space and impact from the institutional transformations of modernity. Such supposedly universal trends as the movement towards mass culture and the atomisation and privatisation of civil society are largely absent; even the emergence of a proletariat, a class system or a peasantry is scarcely apparent. Class may have become more important in some contexts but not at the expense of social organisation. Much more important there are reactions against, and responses to, modernity. The processes of development have mapped out a contested landscape of environmental, economic and cultural change, dramatically apparent around the Bougainville copper mine, but all cultures are products of a history of appropriation, resistance and accommodation.

The whole project of development has been simultaneously a process of both conservation and dissolution. From earliest colonial times to the present day, there have been seemingly contradictory policies that sought to keep village economy and society stable and viable whilst simultaneously seeking to engage workers in the commercial economy. Various elements of modernisation, such as education, have enabled individuals to participate in the modern sector, whilst also contributing to frustration and the alienation of others from it. Though this has not necessarily led to real challenges to the colonial and post-colonial order, other than in the violence of *raskalism*, it has meant that the processes of change must be understood in both economic and cultural terms, and, indeed, that there is no clear distinction between these. Most societies have not gone from pre-capitalism (or proto-capitalism) to capitalism but have incorporated both (Hayes 1993a). Thus three contemporary problems – urban violence, the resumption of tribal warfare in the highlands and the Bougainville crisis – can all be perceived as at least partly related to issues of male identity and the erosion of traditional authority, and, especially in the highlands, how this is linked to 'a move from male identity constructed out of marriage, ceremonial pig exchange systems, and clan warfare, to male identity constructed from syncretic, and often contradictory, components, with parts drawn simultaneously from pig exchange, crime and violence, business and the state' (Lipset 1990:146). Powerful social elements may be seen in other contemporary institutional structures, including money itself, unsurprising where so much change in so many places has been extremely recent. Economic development is inextricably linked to both social and political stability and change.

POLITICS AND PLACE

Though PNG inherited a Westminster-style parliamentary system, its recent history, and the lack of an ideological base to politics, means that it is an uneasy democracy. Leadership is weak and lacks power, in fragmented parties, to achieve the political will required for long-term policy formation and application. Nevertheless changes in power have come without disorder and, since independence, PNG has had only four Prime Ministers. Three of them – Sir Julius Chan, Paias Wingti and Rabbie Namaliu – first achieved power through votes of no-confidence rather than elections. Democracy was thinly established at the time of independence. Constitutional changes that elsewhere took decades were compressed into the two years between self-government and independence. Australia relinquished political power, bureaucratic authority and a legal system to Melanesians, few of whom had experience beyond their own rural areas.

Australia bequeathed a daunting list of tasks for the new country. Most related to building a nation, creating a national identity, and securing the development of the rich mineral resources that were increasingly being discovered. Not only was PNG politically ill prepared for independence, but social and economic development were limited. On the eve of self-government, about half of all children of primary school age had no school to go to. Those who could go had little chance of staying long enough to acquire skills for jobs that demanded functional literacy. Health services were similarly limited, life expectancies were lower than anywhere else in the Pacific region and there were virtually no Melanesian doctors. The decolonisation of PNG, in which Australians changed their nominal image from paternity to fraternity, did not enable the new state to become an effective nation-state. Colonial history had been a brief moment in Melanesian time. Even as the PNG flag was being raised throughout the country, Bougainville was declaring a short-lived, separate independence as the Republic of the North Solomons. With an 'atomised and parochial political culture, the nation-building enterprise remains to all practical effects suspended' (MacQueen 1993:150; see also Jacobsen 1995) while securing the continuity of the colonial borders is achievement enough. Fragmentation and political insecurity have ensured that politics has focused on domestic rather than international issues.

In early post-independence years PNG pursued a foreign policy described as 'universalism', friendship to all and hostility to none, a policy that began the slow process of distancing from the colonial power, despite retention of its 'special relationship' with Australia. In the 1980s universalism became a policy of 'active and selective engagement' designed to enable PNG to become more assertive and influential in the particular regions that concerned it. However most policy interests were primarily concerned with countries of historic significance: Australia, Japan, and the South Pacific island states. The European Community became more significant, as did Indonesia, which sometimes proved a difficult neighbour 'treated with great caution in public and often regarded with antagonism in private' (M. Turner 1990:149) or with covert fear. Foreign policy that went beyond specific economic interests was of limited concern in a nation struggling to achieve its priority of economic development.

When Wingti came to power in 1985 PNG entered a more active period of foreign policy, with greater detachment from Australia, a situation continued in Wingti's second phase of power after 1992, with the more assertive 'Look North' policy that favoured links with the Asian region (see pp. 41, 306–7). Relations with the colonial power remained relatively amicable, despite occasional exasperation over perceived Australian participation in wide-ranging commercial activity, obsession with law and order problems and paternalism over the nature of the aid relationship (see pp. 307–10). The 'special relationship' always involved substantial elements of neo-colonial 'big brother' domination, inevitable with Australia being the principal trading partner and source of investment, the main source of aid (including military aid), a source of cultural diffusion (through television, education systems, sport, music and so on) and sharing, eventually, the same language and similar religions. Unlike most other world regions, where former colonial powers were far distant from former colonies, Australia and PNG shared a common border (a source of later tension through illegal population movements and the smuggling of guns and marijuana), and were closely linked by transport and telecommunication systems. Such close ties emphasised the need for PNG to define and assert its own identity, and to seek a greater degree of self-reliance. Both universalism and selectivity stressed the establishment of new relationships, but not to the detriment of relations with Australia.

As PNG sought to distance itself from Australia, relations with Asia became more significant, and particularly complex and uneasy with neighbouring Indonesia. PNG inherited concerns over its much larger neighbour from Australia, but friction over border issues, and the movements of OPM (Organisasi Papua Merdeka) guerrillas, seeking an independent and Melanesian Irian Jaya, refugees and military across the poorly demarcated 800 kilometre long border ensured continued instability and uncertainty. There was considerable sympathy in PNG for Melanesian struggles for independence and, to a lesser extent, for the more than 12,000 refugees from Indonesia, who in 1984 had fled Indonesian military patrols, some of which crossed the border into PNG. Attempts to secure a more stable relationship with Indonesia were initially emphasised in treaties concerning the border in 1979 and 1980, but were extended in the ratification of a Treaty of Mutual Respect, Friendship and Cooperation in 1987 though this did little more than emphasise the need for good relations. The situation in Irian Jaya will continue to generate anxiety and tension in its Melanesian neighbour, a reflection of overall relations with Indonesia, which has been concerned with underpinning the security of PNG (Connell and van Langenberg 1988; MacQueen 1993) and converting it, as far as possible, into a client state. Since the signing of the 1987 Treaty, relations between PNG and Indonesia have been less concerned with political issues than with economic issues, which presented problems through accusations that Indonesian politicians were responsible for bribery in PNG, especially over access to timber resources, charges which led to the successful prosecution of Ted Diro. In an unusual way they demonstrated the growing economic links between PNG and Indonesia, and with other Asian states.

PNG has grown uneasily closer to the ASEAN states, as it has diversified its economic ties away from Australia; it has considered progressing from observer status to full membership and has acceded to ASEAN's Treaty of Amity and Cooperation (eleven years after the organisation had been founded). ASEAN refused to consider full PNG membership, primarily since it was perceived to be part of the South Pacific region with close ties to Australia (MacQueen 1993). Nevertheless Asian states have taken a growing interest in the South Pacific region, primarily for economic reasons but also for political reasons, in the search for international supporters. New Asian investors moved into forestry, commerce and manufacturing, and sought to enter the high-priority mining sector at Lihir. PNG also sought to recruit cheaper skilled labour from Asia (*PC* 22 September 1992) and became a full member of the Asia-Pacific Economic Cooperation forum in 1993. New investment ties have been at considerable environmental cost, and the ramifications of Asian investment in other sectors, including the media, are not yet clear. Their positive benefits for PNG may be limited. In one crucial sense

PNG has been wholly unable to look north: the model of Asian industrialisation has proved impossible to adopt. Asian culture, beyond ubiquitous Chinese restaurants, has had no impact. Trade, aid and investment have brought PNG only slightly closer to Asia, and the growing perception of few real gains from closer relationships resulted in a greater reluctance to look north, following the transition from Wingti to Chan in 1994.

A greater involvement in Asia did not preclude continued involvement in the South Pacific region, though there was greater selectivity there too. PNG, some five times greater in population than the largest Pacific state, Fiji, has intermittently sought political involvement in the region. Though PNG is inevitably bound up in South Pacific affairs, through its common and occasionally problematic boundary with Solomon Islands and its Melanesian identity, its frustrations in that region (especially over Bougainville), its lack of economic involvement and the apprehensiveness of the island micro-states to this much larger state, have resulted in greater involvement with Asia and Australia. Nonetheless PNG regards itself as a crucial intermediary between Asia and the South Pacific region, seeking, in 1996, to strengthen its relationships with ASEAN to 'make Papua New Guinea become a two-lane bridge linking a highway of practical cooperation between our two regions' (Jack Genia, Minister of Foreign Affairs and Trade, quoted in *The Independent*, 2 August 1996). That time is not imminent.

Relationships with the nearest neighbours, fraught with tension in the case of Indonesia, hampered with perceptions of neo-colonialism in the case of Australia and of limited consequence with Solomon Islands (other than in disputes over the Bougainville rebellion) have pragmatically dominated foreign policy. The great powers – the USA and the USSR – were always distant; though PNG belatedly agreed to a Soviet embassy in 1988 it was one of the first to be closed in the post-Soviet era. Despite concern over a greater Indonesia, PNG's greatest security threat is from inside rather than outside. 'Geographical neighbours they may be, but Indonesia and Papua New Guinea still look in opposite directions for their respective regional identities' (MacQueen 1993:152). Foreign policy has been dominated by conservatism and commercial interests, measured in the shift towards Asia. Much the most important nation for PNG – economically, culturally and politically – remains Australia, a situation that has contributed to PNG remaining a regional player, rather than being a presence in the Asian region or on a global stage.

AID

Aid, especially from Australia, remains extremely important and indicative of Australia's continued special relationship. At the start of the 1970s Australia contributed about half the PNG budget and this then represented more than two-thirds of all Australian overseas aid. Not only has Australia subsequently remained by far the most important aid donor – never contributing less than three-quarters of all bilateral aid – but it has continued to give much of its aid to PNG. A further element of the special relationship has been the manner in which, until recently, aid funds were transferred directly into the national budget, rather than being tied to particular development projects, as is otherwise typical of Australian aid and of most bilateral aid relationships. No other aid donor has provided budgetary support to a former colony to the extent that Australia has done for PNG.

After independence it was apparent that budget support was having both positive and negative effects. PNG governments did not have to take difficult decisions on revenue raising or allocation (because of the volume of aid) but aid inflows created a 'booming' government sector which grew faster than the economy, drawing more educated and entrepreneurial Papua New Guineans into the bureaucracy. Large aid flows may also have contributed to governments over-extending, spreading resources too thinly and undertaking inefficient and ineffective activities (Callick *et al.* 1990:8.1). The volume of aid led to the over-valuation of the kina, hence in the 1980s Australia sought a reduction in aid levels, by around 3 per cent per year, and a shift towards programme and project aid, that would dampen the growth of the bureaucracy. However economic growth in PNG was slight and there were few other aid donors. Pressure on Australia to increase aid revenues, and security problems in PNG, resulted in Australia accepting the principle of project aid but maintaining the practice of budgetary aid.

Australia and PNG concluded a Development Cooperation Treaty in 1989 under which Australia assured PNG of more than A$1 billion (about K750 million) aid over the following five years, with budget support being held constant (effectively declining by the rate of Australian inflation) and project aid increasing steadily from about A$20 million in 1989–90. This slight shift towards project aid heralded even stronger Australian opposition to budget aid and a determination to reduce its absolute domination of aid delivery, and so reduce criticism of the patron–client relationship. In 1992 the Development Cooperation Treaty was revised so that budgetary aid would be phased out by the end of the decade in favour of project aid. Between 1977 and 1993 Australian budgetary support declined from its contribution of 39 per cent of the budget to 12 per cent. Australia's shift towards project aid followed a growing consensus that budget aid was neither contributing directly to economic growth, nor was it stimulating the development of human resources, since the political system was oriented to its own short-term survival rather than long-term national development. Since other donors, including non-governmental organisations (NGOs), have been mainly committed to project aid, this has steadily become almost as important as budgetary aid.

The high level of Australian aid, and the broad perception of this special relationship, reduced the role and visibility of other aid donors. It was not until the late 1980s that such major multilateral donors as the International Monetary Fund, the World Bank and the Asian Development Bank had any significant financial presence, and NGOs are not substantially involved in PNG. Since 1985 Japan has been the second biggest aid donor; much of this aid has focused on human resource development (in education and health), and technical co-operation through the Japanese International Cooperation Agency (JICA). However JICA has also directly financed several Japanese logging companies, through low interest loans, and developed road and bridge projects that service them, emphasising a historic situation where Japanese aid imposed substantial costs on PNG and developed projects of greater priority to Japan (Conroy 1980:165; Shimizu 1992). Diversification of aid sources has not necessarily realised national development objectives, where donor self-interests are considerable and national priorities poorly articulated.

PNG also receives military aid – some A$28 million in 1992–3 – entirely from Australia, directed at improving PNG's defence capabilities. Under a Defence Cooperation Programme Australia has provided training for PNG military personnel (including, in earlier days, Sam Kauona, later to lead the BRA), military advisers, support for joint operations (mainly construction and surveying), military equipment (plus training and logistics support), patrol boats and surveillance flights. The growing domestic role of the Defence Force in Bougainville made Australian military aid more controversial, as Iroquois helicopters, intended for transport, surveillance and medical evacuations, were used as gun-ships and involved in human rights abuses, and patrol boats were used to blockade the island. Subsequently there was criticism of the increased Defence Force presence around highlands mine sites, where Australian investment was substantial. The shift to the militarisation of PNG has been enhanced by overseas aid.

The move towards project aid required closer collaboration between the two governments, and greater co-ordination with all other donors. In official quarters this was perceived as a 'maturing' of the aid relationship; elsewhere it was seen as demanding massive bureaucratic involvement in monitoring new projects (requiring a substantial new input of skilled labour) and a shift in the determination of priority programmes from PNG towards Australia, and hence the establishment of a new neo-colonial relationship (though this placed the PNG aid programme on a similar basis to that of other Australian country programmes). The Minister of Finance, Sir Julius Chan, criticised Australia's shift from 'philanthropy and openness' – and sought changes in direction – whilst the Minister of Foreign Affairs, John Kaputin, referred to the aid programme as 'thirty pieces of silver'. Project aid reduced PNG control over the aid programme and revealed the lack of national capacity to implement programmes; of K84 million allocated from concessional loans for infrastructure projects in 1993, PNG could implement only projects worth about K25 million (Callick 1993). To implement more projects would necessitate a larger bureaucracy and also a growing 'aid industry' of consultants, overseas investors and contractors, a situation that has begun to be put in place. The extent to which the shift from budget aid to project aid will influence the direction and success of development in PNG is yet to be seen. Aid remains as substantial as it has ever been, even if its format has changed as a result of one form of aid fatigue, but as a proportion of national income it has declined considerably since independence. Its positive impact has been, at best, uncertain and ambivalent.

ECONOMIC GROWTH AND DEVELOPMENT

With a low population density, a relative abundance of natural resources (especially minerals) and, in some respects, a light veneer of colonialism, PNG has had considerable opportunities for economic choice and change. However the extent to which late development has enabled a distinctive economic structure to be established has been minimal; PNG has largely failed to gain from the experiences, or learn from the failures, of other developing countries, and the basic economic system has not fundamentally changed since independence. At the time of independence PNG effectively lacked a national economy. The material basis of the state was primarily provided by small-scale commodity production and the state appeared only as a set of social relations at the national level, with no real links with production and no real base in society. PNG was primarily an agricultural country. Barely 10 per cent of the population lived in towns, and many were largely engaged in subsistence agriculture, but marketing some cash crops. The target of self-reliance, and greater economic independence, was enshrined in the Eight Aims, a radical series of goals directed to ensuring greater control of the economy, rather than its domination by overseas plantations and mining giants. Such perspectives pointed to directions of development different from those of many previously independent developing states. Other than rhetorically such directions were never sought. National politicians no longer subscribe to the historic goals that briefly dominated development ideology though they lasted many years in poster form or survived in the populism of the Melanesian Way (Narokobi 1980). Self-reliance, and other themes of the Eight Point Plan, became, as elsewhere, 'little more than a ritual for exorcising the devil of dependence' (Joseph 1978:228), as PNG firmly embarked on a capitalist road, a road that required long-term overseas investment in most sectors. Opposition to large-scale, capital-intensive projects (despite the evidence of Bougainville) has not led to any growing consciousness of a need to regulate either transnational corporations or collusive, complacent governments and politicians. Over time the conflict between a resources boom and stagnation in other sectors of the economy, and the neglect of service provision, redistribution and equity, may be greater challenges to the future of PNG than military coups or secessionist sentiments.

Though the Panguna copper mine dwarfed all subsequent mines, it was simply the first in a series of developments in remote areas, culminating in PNG becoming the first South Pacific oil exporter. In the excitement and affluence attached to mining, in dramatic and avaricious form at Mt Kare, other sectors of the economy were largely forgotten by politicians and the bureaucracy. None has suffered more than forestry, where corruption and plunder have been rife. Forests were removed without environmental safeguards, provisions for reforestation or 'downstream processing'. Environmental degradation was more widespread than in the mining industry, as rapacious politicians on the one hand and impoverished villagers on the other clamoured for 'development'. Just two economic activities operate by floodlight through the night – mining and forestry. A similar, but less devastating, situation was broadly true of the fisheries industry, where licences were allocated according to whim, a national fleet was never established, and where the only gains – in a nation of many islands and seas – have been from the lease payments of distant-water tuna-fishing nations. Sustainable development, a phrase in the constitution, has disappeared from sight. At independence the agricultural sector appeared exceptionally promising. Many rural areas evolved from subsistence to some degree of affluence as the prices of coffee and cocoa soared. Oil palm was being established in some lowland areas; temperate vegetables, like potatoes, were spreading through the highlands. A decade later the agricultural commodity boom went bust. Plantations were abandoned, producers turned to vegetables, betel nuts, or even marijuana, where they could, as local initiatives demonstrated the bankruptcy of state failures, whilst from more remote areas, they moved into towns in search of elusive wage employment. The rapid transition from agriculture to mining led to an imbalanced economy, with the negative effects primarily experienced in the rural sector.

The future of the mining industry, dependent externally on world prices and internally on compliant landowners, is fraught with uncertainty, yet other sectors display little promise. PNG demonstrates some of the classic symptoms associated with the 'resource-curse' thesis, where countries that are relatively well endowed with natural resources perform worse than less well-endowed countries – because of limited domestic linkages from this enclave sector, low revenue retention and the inability of the economy to deploy mineral rents effectively. This is manifest in the 'Dutch disease': the premature decline or stagnation of the agricultural economy and the underdevelopment of the manufacturing sector. Though PNG managed both the mineral booms of the 1970s and 1980s, and the downswing shocks, quite well, it was unable to avoid Dutch disease, so confirming that 'even a well-managed mineral economy will underperform if it neglects its non-mining tradeables' (Auty 1993:219) and fails to ensure necessary structural reforms to secure more broadly based development. The minerals boom of the late 1980s instigated a spate of construction and consumption; money and commodities circulated freely and snake-oil vendors from around the world competed for sales, business contracts and investment opportunities. Some were successful. As mining has risen to prominence so the whole structure of development has become highly politicised, and personalised, with politicians, bureaucrats and landowners seeking direct involvement in new projects. At every level economic activity is part of a political economy.

The minerals boom dampened lukewarm national interest in structural adjustment. The growth of the mining sector strengthened the fiscal basis of the state, enabling the expansion of the bureaucracy – perhaps even a bureaucratic class – but the state has been too weak to effectively manage the process of capital accumulation, notably its inability to stimulate an agricultural economy or regulate the forestry sector. Equally important the state has largely failed to serve the needs of the rural and urban poor, especially through service delivery. However rural neglect essentially reinforced and accelerated processes of differentiation and concentration that had begun in the colonial era. Fiscal gains were squandered and expansionist budgets depleted foreign reserves. Underlying structural problems remain: high urban wages and fringe benefits (for those in formal sector employment), a large bureaucracy of limited efficiency and effectiveness, an overvalued exchange rate and inadequate spending on infrastructure. However inflation has been low, economic policies flexible and capital flight largely avoided. Social problems have accompanied economic problems, but democracy remains, alongside a free media and judiciary. There is an almost continuous state of semi-emergency (natural hazard, epidemic, tribal fight, services or price collapse, etc.) in some part of the country. The state is constantly struggling to manage problems, is unable to set up the conditions for successful economic evolution, cannot achieve full control of its territory or guarantee the physical security of its citizens and never either completely vanquishes or incorporates a range of opponents, despite growing authoritarianism and militarisation (Cox 1993). The government has lost authority in many parts of the country and a weak, 'broken-backed' and divided state has become rather more like the collection of fragmented places of precolonial times.

If development has necessarily been dependent it has, in large part, been a negotiated dependence. Though Papua New Guinea is small and poor, even with high levels of foreign trade, investment and aid, it has had substantial scope for policy choice (Garnaut 1981). The most significant early example of that choice was the renegotiation of the BCL agreement, where the state bargained effectively with a major transnational corporation. Subsequently the state has set priorities in economic development but has usually chosen not to radically confront the existing international political economy. In the 1990s it intermittently challenged international mining companies (but not forestry companies), but in a disorganised, pragmatic (and rhetorical) manner, rather than out of any genuine attempt to redirect national development by choosing a new long-term relationship with the international economic system. Simultaneously it sought to become an investment partner in mining. The openness of the economy, rather than any new market liberalisation or privatisation, has contributed to elements of cronyism (especially in the forestry sector) and more extensive foreign investment. Both these phenomena have weakened the national economy. Even an Australian government review of relations with PNG concluded that 'the lack of Australian non-mining investment in Papua New Guinea is disturbing' (Australia 1991:118), an acute reflection on the narrow focus of economic development. State confrontation of mineral companies contributed to loss of investor confidence, and problems within the mining sector, rather than a new political economy that broadened the base of national development.

THROUGH A GLASS DARKLY: TOWARDS THE FUTURE

PNG has essentially chosen a 'big push' development strategy which involves rapid development of natural resources and hence the importation of foreign capital (alongside technology and labour). This strategy, alongside a continued heavy dependence on Australian budgetary aid, has to some extent reduced the ability of the state to manage the national economy. For a decade after independence, the rate of economic growth was low, even negative, averaging a miserly 0.5 per cent (below even the steady population growth rate) until a mineral-led spurt in the 1990s. Because of the focus on mineral development, emphasised by the decline of agricultural commodity prices, few new employment opportunities have been generated since independence. In urban areas the rate of job creation slowed after early post-independence expansion and, in a relatively small economy, it is improbable that formal sector employment can be generated at a rate equivalent to that of population increase. Population growth has contributed to problems of development, including unmanageable urbanisation, pollution and environmental degradation. However shantytowns and malnutrition are currently of limited extent, and excessive population growth is certainly not the principal cause of poverty and uneven development.

Natural resource led development, whilst creating substantial increases in the national income, has been disappointing because of its creation of relatively few new jobs, limited positive effects on the rest of the economy and the absence of sustainable development. It has also resulted in highly unequal incomes, at various scales, which have led to frustration and resentment. Resource projects have also resulted in costs in infrastructure provision and the management of an inflated bureaucracy, which have diverted attention from the consideration of human resource and rural development issues. In 1978 the World Bank concluded that, 'the underlying picture remains one of a natural resource base sufficiently rich and well proven so that eventually PNG should become fully self-reliant in its external accounts . . . enough evidence is at hand so that predicting self-reliance is a reasonable act of faith (1978:133). Financial self-reliance is scarcely closer now, despite the establishment of more mines than could then have been predicted. The problems of regional economic inequalities and the divergence between a rural sector, characterised by small semi-subsistence farmers with low and perhaps falling incomes, and an urban sector, where those in formal sector employment are likely to remain relatively well-off, is unlikely to decline in the immediate future.

Uneven development is exacerbated by the social and geographical fragmentation of the country. The recency of contact (and hence communications of all kinds) has emphasised broad regional differences, which inadequate service delivery and provincial governments were unable to resolve. Historic patterns of spatial inequality have barely changed in the post-independence years; it is very much an understatement that 'differences have not succumbed entirely to the homogenising influence of "modernisation" nor have they disappeared before the "underdeveloping" pressures of international capitalism' (Fahey 1988:3). Other than through the 'accidents' of mineral resource exploitation and development, inter-provincial inequalities have been maintained and even exacerbated. To some extent, 'PNG may come to be much like many other newly independent nations with a hinterland where people are economically dissatisfied . . . and politically repressed. . . . Highlanders and other less developed people have become an underclass in the present nation' (Brown 1982:18). Regional friction may increase, the legitimacy of the national government be further eroded and secessionist sentiments strengthen.

The economy will remain essentially rural and agricultural (in terms of the distribution of the labour force) for many years to come and agricultural development must absorb the bulk of an expanding labour force. Rural development is problematic since the most appropriate development strategies take the long view and incorporate non-economic issues. Rural development is a slow process, yet in PNG speed has become the essence of all development projects. However the disintegration of rural roads and services, for many rural people, 'confirmed their suspicions and deepened their cynicism and they began refusing to cooperate in projects unless frequently unrealistically high returns were guaranteed to them' (B.J. Allen 1983:235). Not only was the bureaucracy incapable of the implementation of rural projects but 'it proved to be entrenched, urban orientated and as inefficient, uncoordinated and immune to political pressure as the colonial administration before it' (ibid.). In many provinces the prospects for future economic development are particularly bleak; in Enga, for example,

the gap between expectations and reality, for the young at least, can only be expected to widen. As more of the young are educated they will find their paths to participation in the modern world in Enga effectively blocked by lack of wage employment, intransigent male attitudes to women's progress and lack of access to arable land, which is already in short supply . . . the young in Enga, who already have less opportunities than enjoyed by their counterparts in many parts of PNG, can expect only a bleak future . . . Outside agriculture, employment prospects are even poorer, offering only a limited number of alternatives (such as PMVs, trade stores and garages), the 'niches' . . . that only a few can occupy.

(Carrad 1982:177)

Even this depressing scenario depends on internal peace, alongside greater national government assistance and response to Enga initiatives, yet the government's capacity to respond is slight, at any scale. Cutbacks in expenditure on the public service and problems of social and economic infrastructure provision are likely to impose a greater degree of self-reliance on many regions and districts, result in the re-emergence or strengthening of old inequalities and enmities between and within provinces and increase local frustrations and tensions, encouraging a downward spiral in development. In a country of fragmented loyalties and divisive tendencies, the chances of finding long-term solutions are poor.

Public finance has been oriented to consumption rather than investment and governments have spent small proportions of budgets on running and maintaining, rather than constructing, the country's hospitals, schools and roads. Women play a restricted and marginalised role in contemporary development. Human resource development has constantly played second best to economic growth. Within most rural areas the combination of low incomes, limited social development and inadequate infrastructure provision has emphasised the seeming permanence of present inequalities. In the post-independence years almost all development institutions and activities, including mines, forestry projects, small business, aid posts and schools, provincial government and even Christianity, either failed to deliver the anticipated services and rewards, or became less promising vehicles of change, through corruption, mis-use, disuse (or inadequate funding) or simply incomprehension.

There are several stabilising factors, most obviously the continued viability of the semi-subsistence sector; land is available to almost all people and landlords have not emerged, though mobilising land for any development has proved inordinately difficult. Whatever government has been in power there has been virtually no change in the financial structure, and little evidence of any breakdown in the basis of democracy, despite constitutional crises. Other stabilising factors include the diversity and extent of the resource base, and considerable overseas financial support. Slow urban growth has been beneficial in the absence of industrialisation, but towns are coming under stress, through violence, the collapse of infrastructure, mismanagement and disruptive compensation claims.

Human rights issues, principally linked to the problems of secession and violence in Bougainville, and their legacy into the future, are serious problems for national unity. Although Bougainville is a special case, the national and international ramifications of disturbance there have been vast. It is the most serious conflict in the South Pacific since the war, and has lasted longer. Elsewhere, social conflicts are sure to persist and regional tensions remain undiminished. Cultural complexity, extending into other spheres, does however reduce the risk of both military coups and regional secessionism, whilst ensuring that a variety of 'incidents' receive unfavourable media coverage. PNG is experiencing similar problems to those of other developing countries in the post-independence era, but in an unparalleled array that matches the diversity of the country and the recent establishment of modern institutions and development trends. In an island state of largely artificial unity, it has its own very distinct historical specificity.

Crime and violence have increased substantially to constitute a widespread problem, mainly in the larger urban areas, reducing overseas interest in foreign investment and leading to the Leader of the Opposition, Jack Genia, stating, 'the daily pattern of our lives has been shattered at the hands of mindless criminals, with a multitude of assaults, mob violence, ethnic clashes, gang rapes, student murders and the continuing harassment of our women' (quoted in *SMH* 4 May 1993). Soon afterwards the Prime Minister gave his support for the erection of boom gates on the three highways into Port Moresby as 'a major deterrent to car thefts, drug and arms smuggling and other criminal activities in and out of Port Moresby' (*SMH* 11 May 1993). Whilst violence and *raskalism* may represent inchoate resistance to the trajectory of development, they also inhibit more broadly based development, and the emergence of brutalised young males reflects the weakened power of traditional leaders, older people, educated people and the churches as moral authorities. This is the contemporary legacy of authoritarian traditions alongside a new consciousness of ethnicity and relative deprivation. Corruption – described by Sir Mekere Morauta as 'systemic and systematic Bribe-onomics' – has also become a part of the normal political process, both nationally and in the provinces. Parliamentarians rarely stay in opposition for long, preferring the economic rewards that come from power. This has not prevented persistent votes of no-confidence, short-lived governments, and difficulties in long-range development planning. Corruption and incompetence have been more endemic in the provinces. For a country where monetisation is largely a post-war phenomenon, and the advanced capitalism of finance and investment a product of the post-independence years, the pursuit of money plays an extraordinary role in the practice of politics. Money has become the oil of social relations, crucial for greasing the wheels of political and bureaucratic machines.

Critical economic linkages are outwards, as PNG remains dependent on investment, aid, technological assistance and preferential trading agreements for national development, whilst there is still only the slightest semblance of an integrated national economy. Though some PNG politicians have stated that PNG will be an aid donor within the South Pacific by the end of the century, the reality may be quite different. Near the end of the 1980s the Finance and Planning Minister, Paul Pora, stated that by the 1990s PNG would no longer depend on Australian aid: 'By that time we will be donors and not receivers; we will be mainly looking at assisting the smaller Pacific Island nations'. Sir Julius Chan made similar statements in 1994, yet PNG is the largest aid recipient in the Pacific. Aid has emphasised the uneasy special relationship with Australia (which is the main trading partner and also remains the largest source of investment, imports and technical skills, and the main destination for education, capital transfer and private overseas investment).

No other country has a fraction of the significance of the former colonial power, though the relationship is vastly different from that of early post-colonial times.

No country in the Pacific, and few in Asia, has more diverse and abundant resources. Exploiting these resources has created constant and increasing dissent. There remains enormous potential for economic growth; in 1976 for example it was proclaimed that in the not too distant future PNG would be 'one of the richest countries in the world' (*Australian* 16 September 1976; cited by Sundhaussen 1977:309). Similar, if more subtle, claims have continued. At the same time a vast number of reports have concluded along the lines of, 'PNG can still gain a very high return from its timber industry if . . . ' (Daniel and Sims 1986b:81), on the assumption that the right policies, political will, stability and a beneficial international climate will engender both growth and development. As the case of the timber industry well demonstrates, such conditions have rarely been met, and growth has been unmatched by development; 'it may not be too late' in such reports has tended to become 'it may now be too late'. Basic needs, notably health and education, are no longer improving. In a country where some components of change have gone through ten thousand years in a lifetime, and the pace of change has scarcely slowed, the days of post-independence euphoria have ended. In this fragmented state, neither consistent growth nor sustainable development have been achieved.

Bibliography

Ahlburg, D. (1992) Fertility and family planning in Papua New Guinea, Minneapolis: unpub. mimeo.

Aitken, K. (1991) The health services of Papua New Guinea, in J.A. Thomason *et al.* (eds) *Decentralisation in a Developing Country*, Canberra: ANU NCDS Pacific Research Monograph No. 25, 23–35.

Allan, B. and Hinchliffe, K. (1982) *Planning Policy Analysis and Public Spending: Theory and the Papua New Guinea Practice*, Aldershot: Gower.

Allen, B.J. (1983) Paradise lost? Rural development in an export led economy: the case of Papua New Guinea, in D.A.M. Lea and D.P. Chaudhri (eds) *Rural Development and the State: Contradictions and Dilemmas in Developing Countries*, London: Methuen, 215–40.

Allen, B.J. (1990) The importance of being equal: the colonial and post-colonial experience in the Torricelli foothills, in N. Lutkehaus (ed.) *Sepik Heritage*, Durham, NC: Carolina Academic Press, 185–96.

Allen, B.J. (1992) The geography of Papua New Guinea, in R. Attenborough and M. Alpers (eds) *Human Biology in Papua New Guinea*, Oxford: Clarendon Press, 36–66.

Allen, B.J. and Bourke, M. (1988) Some observations on expenditure and consumption patterns in rural Papua New Guinea, *Pacific Economic Bulletin*, 3(1), 26–9.

Allen, B.J. and Crittenden, R. (1987) Degradation and a pre-capitalist political economy, in P. Blaikie and H.C. Brookfield (eds) *Land Degradation and Society*, London: Methuen, 145–56.

Allen, B.J., Bourke, R.M., Clarke, L.J., Coghill, B., Pain, C.F. and Wood, A.W. (1980) Child malnutrition and agriculture on the Nembi Plateau, Southern Highlands, Papua New Guinea, *Social Science and Medicine*, 14D, 127–32.

Allen, J., Gosden C. and White, J.P. (1989) Human Pleistocene adaptations in the tropical island Pacific: recent evidence from New Ireland, a Greater Australian Outlier, *Antiquity*, 63, 548–61.

Allen, B.J., Collett, G. and Yarbro, S. (1991) Beware the pitfalls in smallholder surveys, *Tok Bilong SPFF* 36, July, 6–10.

Allen, B.J., Bourke, R.M. and Hide, R. (1995) The sustainability of Papua New Guinea agricultural systems: the conceptual background, *Global Environmental Change*, 5, 297–312.

Amarshi, A., Good, K. and Mortimer, R. (1979) *Development and Dependency: The Political Economy of Papua New Guinea*, Melbourne: Oxford University Press.

Anere, R. (1985) Economic issues: 1975–1985, *Yagl-Ambu*, 12, 27–42.

Aruga, W. (1992) An overview of urban infrastructure services in Papua New Guinea, Beijing: unpub. paper to United Nations Seminar on Urban Information Systems.

Asia-Pacific Action Group (1990) *The Barnett Report*, Hobart: Asia-Pacific Action Group.

Asian Development Bank (1992) *Papua New Guinea: Urban Sector Profile*, Manila.

Australia (1991) *Australia's Relations with Papua New Guinea*, Canberra: Parliament of the Commonwealth of Australia, Joint Committee on Foreign Affairs, Defence and Trade.

Auty, R.M. (1991) Managing mineral dependence: Papua New Guinea 1972–89, *Natural Resources Forum*, 15, 90–9.

Auty, R.M. (1993) *Sustaining Development in Mineral Economies: The Resource Curse Thesis*, London: Routledge.

Axline, W.A. (1986) *Decentralisation and Development Policy: Provincial Government and the Planning Process in Papua New Guinea*, Port Moresby: IASER Monograph No. 26.

Bailey, F. (1966) The peasant view of the bad life, *Advancement of Science*, 23, 399–409.

Bakker, M. (1986) *The Mortality Situation in Papua New Guinea*, Port Moresby: National Statistical Office, Research Monograph No. 4.

Baldwin, G.B. (1978) *Papua New Guinea: Its Economic Situation and Prospects for Development*, Washington, DC: The World Bank.

Banks, G. (1993) Mining multinationals and developing countries: theory and practice in Papua New Guinea, *Applied Geography*, 13, 313–27.

Banks, G. (1996) Company, compensation and community at the Porgera Gold Mine, Papua New Guinea, in R. Howitt, J. Connell and P. Hirsch (eds) *Resources, Nations and Indigenous Peoples*, Melbourne: Oxford University Press, 223–35.

Baranay, I. (1994) *Rascal Rain: A Year in Papua New Guinea*, Sydney: Angus and Robertson.

Barnes, H. (1981) Women in highlands agricultural production, in D. Denoon and C. Snowden (eds) *A Time to Plant and a Time to Uproot*, Port Moresby: Institute of Papua New Guinea Studies, 265–84.

Barnes, H. (1982) Population growth and status of women, in South Pacific Commission, *Population of Papua New Guinea*, Noumea: South Pacific Commission, 255–63.

Barnett, T. (1977) A note on the man–land relationship in Papua New Guinea, *Oceania*, 48, 141–45.

Barnett, T. (1979) Politics and planning rhetoric in Papua New Guinea, *Economic Development and Cultural Change*, 27, 769–84.

Barnett, T. (1990) *Report of the Commission of Inquiry into Aspects of the Forest Industry*, Port Moresby.

Barnett, T. (1992) Legal and administrative problems of forestry in Papua New Guinea, in S. Henningham and R.J. May (eds) *Resources, Development and Politics in the Pacific Islands*, Bathurst: Crawford House, 90–118.

Barss, P. and Blackford, C. (1983) Medical emergency flights in remote areas: experience in Milne Bay province, Papua New Guinea, *Papua New Guinea Medical Journal*, 26, 198–202.

Bartelmus, P., Lutz, E. and Schweinfest, S. (1992) *Integrated Environmental and Economic Accounting: A Case Study for Papua New Guinea*, Washington, DC: World Bank Environment Working Paper No. 54.

Battaglia, D. (1990) *On the Bones of the Serpent: Person, Memory and Mortality in Sabarl Island Society*, Chicago: University of Chicago Press.

Battaglia, D. (1991) Punishing the yams: leadership and gender ambivalence on Sabarl Island, in M. Godelier and M. Strathern (eds) *Big Men and Great Men: Personifications of Power in Melanesia*, Cambridge: Cambridge University Press, 83–96.

Bayliss-Smith, T. (1977) Energy use and economic development in Pacific communities, in T. Bayliss-Smith and R. Feachem (eds) *Subsistence and Survival: Rural Ecology in the Pacific*, London: Academic Press, 317–59.

Bayliss-Smith, T. (1991) Food security and agricultural sustainability in the New Guinea Highlands: vulnerable people, vulnerable places, *IDS Bulletin*, 22, 5–11.

Bedford, R.D. (1980) *Perceptions of a Future for Melanesia*, Christchurch: University of Canterbury Press.

Berry, R. (1977) Some observations on the political economy of development in Papua New Guinea: recent performance and future prospects, *Yagl-Ambu*, 4, 147–61.

Berry, R. (1978) *Recent Economic Performance in Papua New Guinea in Relation to the Eight Aims*, Port Moresby: UPNG Economics Department Discussion Paper No. 38.

Berry, R. and Jackson, R.T. (1981) Inter-provincial inequalities and decentralization in Papua New Guinea, *Third World Planning Review*, 3, 57–76.

Bonney, N. (1986) *The Politics and Finance of Provincial Government in Papua New Guinea*, Canberra: ANU Centre for Research on Federal Financial Relations Monograph No. 43.

Bourke, R.M. (1986) Periodic markets in Papua New Guinea, *Pacific Viewpoint*, 27, 69–76.

Bourke, R.M. (1988) Food shortages in the Papua New Guinea Highlands: national policy and villagers, in J. Hirst *et al.* (eds) *Small-Scale Agriculture*, Canberra: Commonwealth Geographical Bureau and ANU Department of Human Geography, 11–22.

Bourke, R.M. (1990) Subsistence Food Production Systems in Papua New Guinea: old changes and new changes, in D. Yen and J. Mummery (eds) *Pacific Production Systems: Approaches to Economic Prehistory*, Canberra: ANU Occasional Papers in Prehistory No. 18, 148–60.

Bowers, N. (1971) Demographic problems in Montane New Guinea, in S. Polgar (ed.) *Culture and Population*, Cambridge: Schenkman, 11–31.

Boyd, D.J. (1980) The development of dependency in a Papua New Guinea village, Galveston: unpub. paper to ASAO Conference.

Boyd, D.J. (1981) Village agriculture and labor migration: inter-related production activities among the Ilakia Awa of Papua New Guinea, *American Ethnologist*, 8, 74–93.

Boyd, D.J. (1984) Awa women in Papua New Guinea, *Cultural Survival Quarterly*, 8(2), 36–7.

Boyd, D.J. (1985) The commercialisation of ritual in the Eastern Highlands of Papua New Guinea, *Man*, 20, 325–40.

Boyd, D.J. (1990) New wealth and old power: circulation, remittances and the control of inequality in an Eastern Highlands community, Papua New Guinea, in J. Connell (ed.) *Migration and Development in the South Pacific*, Canberra: NCDS Monograph No. 24, 97–106.

Brison, K. (1991) Community and prosperity: social movements among the Kwanga of Papua New Guinea, *The Contemporary Pacific*, 3, 325–55.

Brookfield, H.C. (1968) The money that grows on trees, *Australian Geographical Studies*, 6, 97–119.

Brookfield, H.C. (1973) Full circle in Chimbu: a study of trends and cycles, in H.C. Brookfield (ed.) *The Pacific in Transition*, London: Edward Arnold, 127–62.

Brookfield, H.C. with Hart, D. (1971) *Melanesia: A Geographical Interpretation of an Island World*, London: Methuen.

Brown, P. (1973) *The Chimbu: A Study of Change in the New Guinea Highlands*, London: Routledge and Kegan Paul.

Brown, P. (1978) *Highland Peoples of New Guinea*, Cambridge: Cambridge University Press.

Brown, P. (1982) Chimbu disorder: tribal fighting in newly independent Papua New Guinea, *Pacific Viewpoint*, 32, 1–21.

Brown, P. (1987) New men and big men: emerging social stratification in the Third World; a case study from the New Guinea Highlands, *Ethnology*, 26, 87–106.

Brown, P. and Podolefsky, A. (1976) Population density, agricultural intensity, land tenure and group size in the New Guinea Highlands, *Ethnology*, 15, 211–18.

Brown, P., Brookfield, H.C. and Grau, R. (1990) Land tenure and transfer in Chimbu, Papua New Guinea: 1958–1984 – a study in continuity and change, accommodation and opportunism, *Human Ecology*, 18, 21–49.

Brunton, R. (1971) Cargo cults and systems of exchange in Melanesia, *Mankind*, 8, 115–28.

Bryant, J. (1977) Urbanization in Papua New Guinea: problems of access to housing and services, *Pacific Viewpoint*, 18, 43–57.

Buchbinder, G. (1977) Nutritional stress and post-contact population decline among the Maring of New Guinea, in L.S. Greene (ed.) *Malnutrition: Behavior and Social Organization*, New York: Academic Press, 109–41.

Bukenya, G. (1993) Sanitation and health in urban settlements of Papua New Guinea, in T. Taufa and C. Bass (eds) *Population, Family Health and Development*, Port Moresby: UPNG Press, 232–37.

Bulmer, R.N.H. (1971) Traditional forms of family limitation in Papua New Guinea, in *Population Growth and Socioeconomic Change*, Canberra and Port Moresby: New Guinea Research Bulletin No. 42, 137–62.

Burridge, K. (1960) *Mambu: A Study of Melanesian Cargo Movements and their Social and Ideological Background*, New York: Harper.

Callan, V.J. and Wilks, J. (1984) Perceptions about the value and cost of children: Australian and Papua New Guinea High School youth, *Journal of Biosocial Science*, 16, 35–44.

Callick, R. (1988) PNG's coming of golden age, *Australian Financial Review*, 14 July, 13.

Callick, R. (1993) The new aid game, *Australian Financial Review*, 1 December, 17.

Callick, R., Hughes, H., Vincent, D. and Weisman, E. (1990) *The Papua New Guinea Handbook*, Canberra: NCDS.

Campbell, H.F., Menz, K.M. and Owen, A.D. (1994) Economic issues in tuna management and development in Papua New Guinea, in H.F. Campbell and A.D. Owen (eds) *The Economics of Papua New Guinea's Tuna Fisheries*, Canberra: ACIAR, 3–11.

Carrad, B. (1982) The economy, in B. Carrad, D. Lea and K. Talyaga (eds) *Enga: Foundations for Development*, Armidale: University of New England, Department of Geography, 146–78.

Carrad, B., Bourke, R.M. and Heywood, P. (1979) *Papua New Guinea's Food Problems*, Port Moresby: UPNG History of Agriculture Discussion Paper No. 34.

Carrier, J.G. (1981) Labour migration and labour export on Ponam Island, *Oceania*, 237–55.

Carrier, J.G. (1984) *Education and Society in a Manus Village*, Port Moresby: Education Research Unit Report No. 47, UPNG.

Carrier, J.G. (1988) *The Ponam Fish Freezer*, Port Moresby: UPNG Department of Anthropology and Sociology Occasional Paper No. 4.

Carrier, J.G. and Carrier, A.H. (1989) *Wage, Trade and Exchange in Melanesia*, Berkeley: University of California Press.

Centurion, D. and Philpott, M. (1994) Transferring rhetoric into reality: Papua New Guinea's new communication policy, *Media Information Australia*, 71, 89–94.

Chan, J. (1992a) *Economic and Development Policies*, Port Moresby: Government of PNG.

Chan, J. (1992b) Keynote address, Sydney: PNG Mining and Petroleum Seminar, mimeo.

Chao, M.I.P. (1985) Life in a squatter settlement, *Catalyst*, 15, 168–207.

Chowning, A. (1977) *An Introduction to the Peoples and Cultures of Melanesia*, 2nd edn, Menlo Park, CA: Cummings.

Chowning, A. (1979) Leadership in Melanesia, *Journal of Pacific History*, 14, 66–84.

Chowning, A. (1980) Culture and biology among the Sengseng, *Journal of the Polynesian Society*, 89, 7–31.

Chowning, A. (1987) 'Women are our business': women, exchange and prestige in Kove, in M. Strathern (ed.) *Dealing with Inequality*, Cambridge: Cambridge University Press, 130–49.

Christie, M. (1980) *Changing Consumer Behaviour in Papua New Guinea: Its Social and Ecological Implications*, Canberra: CRES Report No. 3.

Cilento, R.W. (1928) *The Causes of the Depopulation of the Western Islands of the Territory of New Guinea*, Canberra: Government Printer.

Clark, J. (1989) The incredible shrinking men: male ideology and development in a Southern Highlands society, *Canberra Anthropology*, 12, 120–43.

Clark, J. (1993) Gold, sex and pollution: male illness and myth at Mt. Kare, Papua New Guinea, *American Ethnologist*, 20, 742–57.

Clarke, W.C. (1971) *Place and People: An Ecology of a New Guinean Community*, Berkeley: University of California Press.

Clarke, W.C. (1976) Maintenance of agriculture and human habitats within the tropical forest ecosystem, *Human Ecology*, 4, 247–59.

Clarke, W.C. (1980) At the tail of the snake, in J.N. Jennings and G.J.R. Linge (eds) *Of Time and Place*, Canberra: ANU Press, 173–92.

Clay, B.J. (1986) *Mandak Realities: Person and Power in Central New Ireland*, New Brunswick, NJ: Rutgers University Press.

Clunies-Ross, A. (1984) *Migrants from Fifty Villages*, Port Moresby: IASER Monograph No. 21.

Coiffier, C. (1991) 'Cannibal Tours', l'envers du décor: Mani bilong waitman, *Journal de la Société des Océanistes*, 92–3, 181–7.

Colebatch, H. (1977) Rural development: does it mean anything?, *Administration for Development*, 8, January, 3–21.

Connell, J. (1976) Bougainville is legitimate again, *Geographical Magazine*, 48, 650–54.

Connell, J. (1977a) The Bougainville connection: changes in the economic context of shell money production in Malaita, *Oceania*, 48, 81–101.

Connell, J. (1977b) *Local Government Councils in Bougainville*, Christchurch: Bougainville Special Publications No. 3.

Connell, J. (1978) *Taim Bilong Mani: The Evolution of Agriculture in a Solomon Island Society*, Canberra: ANU Development Studies Centre Monograph No. 12.

Connell, J. (1979a) A kind of development? Spatial and structural changes in the beef cattle industry of Papua New Guinea, *Geojournal*, 3, 587–98.

Connell, J. (1979b) The emergence of a peasantry in Papua New Guinea, *Peasant Studies*, 8, Spring, 103–38.

Connell, J. (1980) Development deprivation: the potential for agricultural change in Bogia, in M.A.H.B. Walter (ed.) *Cattle Ranches are About People*, Port Moresby: IASER Monograph No. 14, 99–140.

Connell, J. (1982) Development and dependency: divergent approaches to the political economy of Papua New Guinea, in R. May and H. Nelson (eds) *Melanesia: Beyond Diversity*, Canberra: ANU Press, 501–27.

Connell, J. (1984a) Betel mania in PNG, *Islands Business*, 10(9), October, 57–8.

Connell, J. (1984b) Status or subjugation? Women, migration and development in the South Pacific, *International Migration Review*, 18, 964–83.

Connell, J. (1985a) *Migration, Employment and Development in the South Pacific: Country Report No. 14, Papua New Guinea*, Noumea: SPC and ILO.

Connell, J. (1985b) Copper, cocoa and cash: terminal, temporary and circular mobility in Siwai, North Solomons, in M. Chapman and R. Prothero (eds) *Circulation in Population Movement: Substance and Concepts from the Melanesian Case*, London: Routledge, 119–48.

Connell, J. (1988a) Temporary townsfolk? Siwai migrants in urban Papua New Guinea, *Pacific Studies*, 11, 77–100.

Connell, J. (1988b) Mining the rim of fire, *Pacific Islands Monthly*, 59(3), March, 20–3.

Connell, J. (1990) The Carteret Islands: precedents of the greenhouse effect, *Geography*, 75, 152–4.

Connell, J. (1991) Compensation and conflict: the Bougainville Copper Mine, Papua New Guinea, in J. Connell and R. Howitt (eds) *Mining and Indigenous Peoples in Australasia*, Melbourne: Oxford University Press, 54–75.

Connell, J. (1992) 'Logic is a capitalist cover-up': compensation and crisis in Bougainville, Papua New Guinea, in S. Henningham and R. May (eds) *Resources, Development and Politics in the Pacific Islands*, Bathurst: Crawford House, 30–54.

Connell, J. and Curtain, R. (1982) Urbanisation and inequality in Melanesia, in R.J. May and H. Nelson (eds) *Melanesia: Beyond Diversity*, Canberra: ANU Press, 461–500.

Connell, J. and Hamnett, M. (1978) Famine or feast: sago production in Bougainville, *Journal of the Polynesian Society*, 87, 231–41.

Connell, J. and Lea, J.P. (1993) *Planning the Future: Melanesian Cities in 2010*, Canberra: NCDS Pacific Policy Paper No. 11.

Connell, J. and van Langenberg, M. (1988) Indonesia: a giant awakens, *Pacific Islands Monthly*, 59(3), March, 26–8.

Connolly, R. and Anderson, R. (1987) *First Contact*, New York: Viking.

Connolly, R. and Anderson, R. (1989) *Joe Leahy's Neighbours*, Sydney: Film Australia.

Connolly, R. and Anderson, R. (1992) *Black Harvest*, Sydney: Film Australia.

Conroy, J.D. (1980) Aid from the recipient's viewpoint: disturbing possibilities for Papua New Guinea, *Australian Outlook*, 34, 159–68.

Conroy, J.D. (1982) *Essays on the Development Experience*, Port Moresby: IASER Monograph No. 17.

Conyers, D. (1976) *The Provincial Government Debate*, Port Moresby: IASER Monograph No. 2.

Copes, P. (1990) *Fisheries Policy and Fisheries Development in Papua New Guinea*, Port Moresby: Institute of National Affairs Discussion Paper No. 44.

Counts, D. (1971) Cargo or council: two approaches to development in North West New Britain, *Oceania*, 41, 288–97.

Counts, D. (1972) The Kaliai and the story: development and frustration in New Britain, *Human Organization*, 31, 373–83.

Counts, D. (1990) Domestic violence in Oceania: conclusion, *Pacific Studies*, 13, 225–54.

Cox, E. (1979) Gavien and Bagi: rubber/profit vs. people/community, in C.A. Valentine and B.L. Valentine (eds) *Going through Changes: Villagers, Settlers and Development in Papua New Guinea*, Port Moresby: Institute of Papua New Guinea Studies, 15–32.

Cox, E. (1993) The trend towards militarisation in PNG, in R. Nowak and J. Atkinson (eds) *Development in Papua New Guinea*, Melbourne: Community Aid Abroad, 32–4.

Crittenden, R. (1987) Aspects of economic development on the Nembi Plateau, Papua New Guinea, *Journal of the Polynesian Society*, 96, 335–59.

Crittenden, R. and Baines, J. (1986) The seasonal factors influencing child malnutrition in the Nembi Plateau, Papua New Guinea, *Human Ecology*, 14, 191–224.

Crittenden, R. and Lea, D. (1989) Whose wants in 'needs-based planning'? Some examples of unwritten agendas from the provincial integrated rural development programmes of Papua New Guinea, *Public Administration and Development*, 9, 471–86.

Crittenden, R. and Lea, D. (1990a) Evaluating the impact of integrated rural development programmes in the less developed areas of Papua New Guinea, *Yagl-Ambu*, 15(4), 18–31.

Crittenden, R. and Lea, D. (1990b) Linking research to extension in the Southern Highlands of Papua New Guinea: the problems of a modified farming systems approach, *Agricultural Systems*, 34, 151–67.

Crittenden, R. and Lea, D.A.M. (1991) Geography and 'logical' development practice: the smallholder market access and food supply programme in Papua New Guinea, *Applied Geography*, 12, 47–64.

Crittenden, R., Eveno, J., Kimbu, R., Wane, T., Betitis, T. and Takahu, T. (1988) *Gavien and Kaupena: Assessing the Impacts of Development Projects in the East Sepik and Southern Highlands Provinces*, Port Moresby: UPNG Department of Geography Occasional Paper No. 8.

Crocombe, R.G. (1971) Economic development and social change in Fiji, *Journal of the Polynesian Society*, 80, 505–20.

CSIRO (1992) *A Blueprint for Sustainable Use of PNG's Forests*, Canberra: CSIRO.

Curry, G. (1992) Kin and Kina: a study of emerging inequalities in a rural lowland society in Papua New Guinea, Armidale: unpub. Ph.D. thesis, University of New England.

Curtain, R. (1980) The structure of internal migration in Papua New Guinea, *Pacific Viewpoint*, 21, 42–61.

Dahanayake, P. (1991) *Housing Market Anomalies in Papua New Guinea*, Canberra: NCDS Islands/Australia Working Paper No. 91/6.

Dahanayake, P. and Mannur, H.G. (1989) *Prospects of Industrialisation as a Strategy for Economic Development in Papua New Guinea*, Port Moresby: National Research Institute Discussion Paper No. 59.

Dakeyne, R. (1967) Labour migration in New Guinea: a case study from Northern Papua, *Pacific Viewpoint*, 8, 152–8.

Dalton, K.J. (1979) *Chimbu People under Pressure: The Social Impact of Urbanization*, Canberra: Centre for Resource and Environmental Studies Report No. 2.

Dalzell, P. (1993) Developments in pelagic fisheries in Papua New Guinea, *SPC Fisheries Newsletter*, 65, 37–42.

Daniel, P. (1985) *Minerals in Independent Papua New Guinea: Policy and Performance in the Large-scale Mining Sector*, Canberra: NCDS Working Paper No. 85/10.

Daniel, P. and Sims, R. (1986a) *Swings, Shocks and Leaks: The Making of Economic Policy in Papua New Guinea, 1980–82*, Brighton: Institute of Development Studies Discussion Paper No. 211.

Daniel, P. and Sims, R. (1986b) *Foreign Investment in Papua New Guinea: Policies and Practices*, Canberra: NCDS Pacific Research Monograph No. 12.

Das, D.K. (1982) Marketing costs and margins of fruit and vegetables in Papua New Guinea, *Proceedings of the Second Papua New Guinea Food Crops Conference*, Port Moresby: Department of Primary Industry, 500–5.

de Albuquerque, K. and D'Sa, E. (1986) *Spatial Inequalities in Papua New Guinea*, Port Moresby: IASER Discussion Paper No. 49.

De'ath, C. (1980) *The Throwaway People: Social Impact of the Gogol Timber Project, Madang Province*, Port Moresby: IASER Monograph No. 13.

De'ath, C. (1983) Forest exploitation in the South Pacific: the Manus experience, *Bikmaus*, 4, 69–72.

Deklin, F. (1992) Papua New Guinea forest policy and local interest groups, in S. Henningham and R. May (eds) *Resources, Development and Politics in the Pacific Islands*, Bathurst: Crawford House, 119–28.

Dennett, G. and Connell, J. (1988) Acculturation and health in the Highlands of Papua New Guinea: dissent on diversity, diets and development, *Current Anthropology*, 29, 273–99.

Denoon, D. (1985) Capitalism in Papua New Guinea: development or underdevelopment, *Journal of Pacific History*, 20, 119–34.

Denoon, D. (1989) *Public Health in Papua New Guinea*, Cambridge: Cambridge University Press.

Densley, D. (1979) *Fisheries*, Port Moresby: Department of Primary Industry.

Densley, D. (1981) Rural policies: planning and programmes, 1945–1977, in D. Denoon and C. Snowden (eds) *A Time to Plant and a Time to Uproot*, Port Moresby: Institute of Papua New Guinea Studies, 285–92.

Dickerson-Putman, J. (1988) Women's contribution to the domestic and national economy of Papua New Guinea, *Research in Economic Anthropology*, 10, 201–22.

Dickerson-Putman, J. (1992) Age and gender stratification in the Highlands of Papua New Guinea: implications for participation in economic development, *Human Organization*, 51, 109–21.

Dickerson-Putman, J. (1994) Women, development and stratification in the Eastern Highlands Province of Papua New Guinea, *Urban Anthropology*, 23, 13–38.

Dinnen, S. (1993) Urbanisation, inequality and crime, *Catalyst*, 23, 79–90.

Dinnen, S. (1995) Praise the Lord and pass the ammunition – criminal group surrender in Papua New Guinea, *Oceania*, 66, 103–18.

Donaldson, M. and Good, K. (1981) The Eastern Highlands: coffee and class, in D. Denoon and C. Snowden (eds) *A Time to Plant and a Time to Uproot*, Port Moresby: Institute of Papua New Guinea Studies, 143–69.

Donaldson, M. and Good, K. (1988) *Articulated Agricultural Development: Traditional and Capitalist Agricultures in Papua New Guinea*, Aldershot: Avebury.

Dorney, S. (1990) *Papua New Guinea*, Sydney: Random House.

Dornstreich, M.D. (1973) An ecological study of Gadio Enga (New Guinea) subsistence, New York: unpub. Ph.D. thesis, Columbia University.

Dove, J., Miriung, T. and Togolo, M. (1974) Mining bitterness, in P. Sack (ed.) *Problems of Choice: Land in Papua New Guinea's Future*, Canberra: ANU Press, 181–9.

Downs, I. (1980) *The Australian Trusteeship: Papua New Guinea 1945–75*, Canberra: Australian Government Publishing Service.

Driscoll, D. and Winyard, G. (1979) Patterns of use of Madang Hospital, *Papua New Guinea Medical Journal*, 22, 85–9.

D'sa, E.R. (1987) Provincial inequalities in Papua New Guinea, *Yagl-Ambu*, 14, 53–68.

Duncan, R. (1994) *Melanesian Forestry Sector Study*, Canberra: AIDAB International Development Issues No. 36.

Dwyer, P.D. (1985) The contribution of non-domesticated animals to the diet of Etolo, Southern Highlands Province, Papua New Guinea, *Ecology of Food and Nutrition*, 17, 101–15.

Dyke, T. (1993) The environment strikes back: injury in Papua New Guinea, *TPNG*, 30 December, 21–2.

Eagle, A.M., Brown, C.M. and Uiari, K. (1992) Copper mining and the environment in Papua New Guinea: the Ok Tedi case study, Sydney: unpub. paper.

Economic Insights Pty Ltd (1994) *Papua New Guinea: The Role of Government in Economic Development*, Canberra: AIDAB International Development Issues No. 33.

Economic Insights Pty Ltd (1996) *The Economy of Papua New Guinea*, Canberra: AusAID International Development Issues No. 46.

Elek, A. (1992) Economic adjustment to the Bougainville crisis, in M. Spriggs and D. Denoon (eds) *The Bougainville Crisis 1991 Update*, Canberra: ANU Political and Social Change Monograph No. 6, 62–82.

Epstein, A.L. (1969) *Matupit. Land, Politics and Change among the Tolai of New Britain*, Canberra: ANU Press.

Epstein, A.L. (1988) Matupit revisited: social change, local organization and the sense of place, *Journal de la Société des Océanistes*, 86, 21–40.

Epstein, T.S. (1964) Personal capital formation among the Tolai of New Britain, in R. Firth and B.S. Yamey (eds) *Capital, Savings and Credit in Peasant Societies*, Chicago: Allen and Unwin, 53–68.

Epstein, T.S. (1968) *Capitalism: Primitive and Modern*, Canberra: ANU Press.

Errington, F. and Gewertz, D. (1989) Tourism and anthropology in a post-modern world, *Oceania*, 60, 37–54.

Errington, F. and Gewertz, D. (1993) The triumph of capitalism in East New Britain: a contemporary Papua New Guinean rhetoric of motives, *Oceania*, 64, 1–17.

Errington, F. and Gewertz, D. (1995) *Articulating Change in the 'Last Unknown'*, Boulder, CO: Westview Press.

Etherington, D. and Carrad, B. (1983) The appropriate scale for South Pacific agriculture: some evidence from Papua New Guinea and the Solomon Islands, in D. Gupta and S. Polume (eds) *Economic Policy Issues and Options in Papua New Guinea*, Canberra: Development Studies Centre Working Paper No. 41, 85–102.

Faber, M. (1974) Bougainville re-negotiated: an analysis of the new fiscal terms, *Mining Magazine*, 131, December, 446–9.

Fahey, S. (1987) Development, labour relations and gender in Papua New Guinea, in M. Pinches and S. Lakha (eds) *Wage Labour and Social Change*, Melbourne: Monash Papers in Southeast Asia No. 16, 45–66.

Fahey, S. (1988) Class, capital and spatial differentiation in Papua New Guinea, Canberra: unpub. Ph.D. thesis, Australian National University.

Fairbairn, I. (1992) *The Role of Small-Scale Industry in Pacific Island Countries with Observations on Papua New Guinea's Recent Experience in Industrial Promotion*, Sydney: University of New South Wales Pacific Studies Monograph No. 4.

Fairbairn, I. (1994) *Minerals Boom in Papua New Guinea: Key Management Issues*, Sydney: University of New South Wales Pacific Studies Monograph No. 12.

Feil, D.K. (1984) *Ways of Exchange*, Brisbane: University of Queensland Press.

Feil, D.K. (1987) *The Evolution of Highland Papua New Guinea Societies*, Cambridge: Cambridge University Press.

Feil, D.K. (1990) New Guinea: paradise found, *Australian Gourmet Traveller*, 90(2), February, 28–37.

Feil, D.K. (1995) The evolution of highland Papua New Guinea societies: a reappraisal, *Bijdragen tot de Taal*, 151, 23–43.

Fernando, N.A. (1990a) *Formal Agricultural Credit in Papua New Guinea: an analysis of supply and demand*, Canberra: NCDS Islands/Australia Working Paper No. 90/14.

Fernando, N.A. (1990b) Forestry in Papua New Guinea: an overview, in N. Fernando and T. Nen (eds) *Towards a National Forest Plan*, Port Moresby: IASER, 1–9.

Fernando, N.A. (1992) *Provincial Human Development in Papua New Guinea: Its Level and Inequality 1972 and 1980*, Port Moresby: UNDP and National Research Institute.

Filer, C. (1990) The Bougainville Rebellion, the mining industry and the process of social disintegration in Papua New Guinea, in R.J. May and M. Spriggs (eds) *The Bougainville Crisis*, Bathurst: Crawford House Press, 73–112.

Filer, C. (1991) Two shots in the dark: the first year of the task force on environmental planning in priority forest areas, *Research in Melanesia*, 15, 1–48.

Finch, J. (1989) Coffee, development and inequality in the Papua New Guinea Highlands, New York: unpub. Ph.D. thesis, City University of New York.

Fingleton, J. (1992) Papua New Guinea's line in resource development and environmental protection, *Development Bulletin*, 23, April, 9–11.

Fingleton, J. (1994) Forest resource management in the South Pacific: logging your way to development, *Development Bulletin*, 31, 19–22.

Fingleton, L. (1987) Arrow wounds to the heart and mediastinum, *British Journal of Surgery*, 74, 126–8.

Finney, B.R. (1973) *Big Men and Business: Entrepreneurship and Economic Growth in the New Guinea Highlands*, Canberra: ANU Press.

Finney, B.R. (1987) *Business Development in the Highlands of Papua New Guinea*, Honolulu: Pacific Islands Development Program, Research Report No. 6.

Fisk, E.K. (1975) The response of non-monetary production units to contact with the exchange economy, in L.G. Reynolds (ed.) *Agriculture in Development Theory*, New Haven, CT: Yale University Press, 53–83.

Fitzpatrick, P. (1978) Really rather like slavery: law and labour in the colonial economy of Papua New Guinea, in E.W. Wheelwright and K. Buckley, *Essays in the Political Economy of Australian Capitalism*, vol. 3, Sydney: Australia and New Zealand Book Company, 102–18.

Fitzpatrick, P. (1985) The making and the unmaking of the Eight Aims, in P. King, W. Lee and V. Warakai (eds) *From Rhetoric to Reality? Papua New Guinea's Eight Point Plan and National Goals After a Decade*, Port Moresby: UPNG Press, 22–31.

Flanagan, J.G. (1981) To be the same but different: a Wovan dilemma, in R. Gordon (ed.) *The Plight of Peripheral People in Papua New Guinea*, Cambridge: Cultural Survival Inc, 23–36.

Flanagan, J.G. (1983) Migration in Papua New Guinea, *Cultural Survival Quarterly*, 7, 45–6.

Fleming, E. (1988) Short-run supply responsiveness for long-run crops in the South Pacific: a review of recent studies and policy implications of their findings, *Economic Bulletin for Asia and the Pacific*, 39(2), December, 21–30.

Flores, A.S. and Harris, G.T. (1982) The marketing of fresh fruit and vegetables in Port Moresby, *Pacific Viewpoint*, 23, 147–60.

Foerstel, L. and Gilliam, A. (eds) (1992) *Confronting the Margaret Mead Legacy*, Philadelphia, PA: Temple University Press.

Foin, T.C. and Davis, W.G. (1987) Equilibrium and non-equilibrium models in ecological anthropology: an evaluation of 'stability' in Maring ecosystems of New Guinea, *American Anthropologist*, 89, 9–31.

Forge, A. (1990) The power of culture and the culture of power, in N. Lutkehaus (ed.) *Sepik Heritage*, Durham, NC: Carolina Academic Press, 160–70.

Foster, R. (1992) Commoditization and the emergence of *Kastam* as a cultural category, *Oceania*, 62, 284–94.

Foster, R. (1995) *Social Reproduction and History in Melanesia*, Cambridge: Cambridge University Press.

Fox, F. (1927) *Australia*, 2nd edn, London: A & C Black.

Gaigo, B. (1977) Present day fishing practices in Tatana Village, in J.H. Winslow (ed.) *The Melanesian Environment*, Canberra: ANU Press, 176–81.

Gannicott, K. (1993) Human resource development, in AIDAB, *The Papua New Guinea Economy*, Canberra: AIDAB International Development Studies No. 30, 138–58.

Gannicott, K. and Avalos, B. (1994) *Women's Education and Economic Development in Melanesia*, Canberra: NCDS Pacific Policy Paper No. 12.

Gardner, D. and Weiner, J. (1992) Social anthropology in Papua New Guinea, in R. Attenborough and M. Alpers (eds) *Human Biology in Papua New Guinea*, Oxford: Clarendon Press, 119–35.

Garnaut, R. (1977) Urban growth: an interpretation of trends and choices, in R.J. May (ed.) *Change and Movement*, Canberra: ANU Press, 71–95.

Garnaut, R. (1981) The framework of economic policy-making, in J.A. Ballard (ed.) *Policy-Making in a New State: Papua New Guinea 1972–77*, Brisbane: University of Queensland Press, 157–211.

Garnaut, R., Wright, M. and Curtain, R. (1977) *Employment, Incomes and Migration in Papua New Guinea Towns*, Port Moresby: IASER Monograph No. 6.

Garner, P., Talwat, E., Hill, G., Reid, M. and Garner, M. (1986) Yaws reappears, *Papua New Guinea Medical Journal*, 29, 247–52.

Geertz, C. (1973) *The Interpretation of Cultures*, New York: Hutchinson.

Gelber, M.G. (1986) *Gender and Society in the New Guinea Highlands*, Boulder, CO: Westview Press.

Gerritsen, R. (1981) Aspects of the political evolution of rural Papua New Guinea: towards a political economy of the terminal peasantry, in R. Gerritsen *et al.*, *Road Belong Development*, Canberra: ANU Department of Political and Social Change Working Paper No. 3, 1–60.

Gerritsen, R. and MacIntyre, M. (1991) Dilemmas of distribution: the Misima Gold Mine, Papua New Guinea, in J. Connell and R. Howitt (eds) *Mining and Indigenous Peoples in Australasia*, Melbourne: Oxford University Press, 34–53.

Gewertz, D. (1978) Tit for tat: barter markets in the Middle Sepik, *Anthropological Quarterly*, 51, 37–44.

Gewertz, D. and Errington, F. (1991) *Twisted Histories, Altered Contexts: Representing the Chambri in a World System*, Cambridge: Cambridge University Press.

Gibson, J. (1993) Rice self-sufficiency and the terms of trade: why rice is a good thing to import, Canberra: National Centre for Development Studies Economics Division Working Paper No. 93/6.

Gibson, J. (1995) *Food Consumption and Food Policy in Papua New Guinea*, INA Discussion Paper No. 65, Port Moresby.

Giddens, A. (1992) *The Consequences of Modernity*, Cambridge: Polity Press.

Gillett, J. (1990) *The Health of Women in Papua New Guinea*, Goroka: PNG Institute of Medical Research Monograph No. 9.

Gillison, G. (1980) Images of nature in Gimi thought, in C. MacCormack and M. Strathern (eds) *Nature, Culture and Gender*, Cambridge: Cambridge University Press, 53–62.

Gissua, J. and Hess, M. (1993) Icing on the cake? Colonialism, institutional transfer and sport in Papua New Guinea, *Sporting Traditions*, 10, 78–91.

Goddard, M. (1992) Big man, thief: the social organization of gangs in Port Moresby, *Canberra Anthropology*, 15, 20–34.

Goddard, M. (1995) The rascal road: crime, prestige and development in Papua New Guinea, *The Contemporary Pacific*, 7, 55–80.

Godelier, M. (1986) *The Making of Great Men: Male Domination and Power among the New Guinea Baruya*, Cambridge: Cambridge University Press.

Godelier, M. and Strathern, M. (eds) (1991) *Big Men and Great Men*, Cambridge: Cambridge University Press.

Goodman, R., Lepani, C. and Morawetz, D. (1985) *The Economy of Papua New Guinea: An Independent Review*, Canberra: ANU Development Studies Centre.

Gordon, A. (1977) The future of plantation systems after independence, in B. Enyi and T. Varghese (eds) *Agriculture in The Tropics*, Port Moresby: UPNG, 192–7.

Gordon, R.J. and Meggitt, M.J. (1985) *Law and Order in the New Guinea Highlands: Encounters with Enga*, Hanover: University Press of New England.

Gorlin, P. (1977) The inter-relationships of disease and culture in a primitive New Guinea community, *Human Ecology*, 5, 39–47.

Granger, K.J. (1971) Population and land in the Gazelle Peninsula, in M.W. Ward (ed.) *Population Growth and Socioeconomic Changes*, Canberra: New Guinea Research Bulletin No. 42, 108–21.

Grant, J. (1980) Struggles with dependency: Melanesian struggles for self-reliance, Galveston: unpub. paper to ASAO Conference.

Grant, J. (1987) The impacts of dependent development on community and resources in Kilenge, Papua New Guinea, *Human Ecology*, 15, 243–60.

Grant, J. (1988) The effects of new land use patterns on resources and food production in Kilenge, West New Britain, *Food and Foodways*, 3, 99–117.

Grant, J., Saito, H. and Zelenietz, M. (1986) Where development never comes: business activities in Kilenge, Papua New Guinea, *Journal of the Polynesian Society*, 95, 195–219.

Gregory, C. (1979) The emergence of commodity production in Papua New Guinea, *Journal of Contemporary Asia*, 9, 389–409.

Gregory, C. (1982) *Gifts and Commodities*, London: Academic Press.

Grey, M. (1993) Agriculture: problems and prospects, in AIDAB, *The Papua New Guinea Economy*, Canberra: AIDAB International Development Studies No. 30, 85–123.

Grieve, R. (1986) The oil palm industry of Papua New Guinea, *Australian Geographer*, 17, 72–6.

Griffin, J., Nelson, H. and Firth, S. (1979) *Papua New Guinea: A Political History*, Melbourne: Heinemann.

Grossman, L.S. (1980) *From Subsistence Affluence to Subsistence Malaise: Cash Cropping and the Subsistence System in the Highlands of Papua New Guinea*, Port Moresby: UPNG History of Agriculture Working Paper No. 46.

Grossman, L.S. (1984a) *Peasants, Subsistence Ecology and Development in the Highlands of Papua New Guinea*, Princeton, NJ: Princeton University Press.

Grossman, L.S. (1984b) Sheep, coffee prices, and ceremonial exchange in Papua New Guinea, *Geographical Review*, 74, 315–30.

Grossman, L.S. (1991) Diet, income and subsistence in an Eastern Highlands Village, Papua New Guinea, *Ecology of Food and Nutrition*, 26, 235–53.

Gupta, D. and Vickerman, A. (1983) Some recent economic policy developments in Papua New Guinea, *Yagl-Ambu*, 10, 16–31.

Halliday, J. (1975) *A Political History of Japanese Capitalism*, New York: Pantheon.

Hallpike, C.R. (1977) *Bloodshed and Vengeance in the Papuan Mountains*, Oxford: Clarendon Press.

Hammar, L. (1992) Sexual transactions in Daru, *Research in Melanesia*, 16, 21–54.

Hamnett, M.P. and Connell, J. (1981) Diagnosis and cure: the resort to traditional and modern medical practitioners in the North Solomons, Papua New Guinea, *Social Science and Medicine*, 15B, 489–98.

Hannett, L. (1975) The case for Bougainville secession, *Meanjin Quarterly*, 34, 286–93.

Harding, T.G. (1967) *Voyagers of the Vitiaz Strait*, Seattle: University of Washington Press.

Harding, T.G. (1985) *Kunai Men: Horticultural Systems of a Papua New Guinea Society*, Berkeley: University of California Press.

Harding, T.G. (1994) Precolonial New Guinea trade, *Ethnology*, 33, 101–25.

Harris, B. (1988) *The Rise of Rascalism*, Port Moresby: IASER Discussion Paper No. 54.

Harris, G.T. (1979) Current issues in agricultural policy in Papua New Guinea, *Yagl-Ambu*, 1, 21–40.

Harris, G.T. (1982) *Subsistence Agriculture and Nutrition in Papua New Guinea: A Research Review*, Port Moresby: IASER Discussion Paper No. 42.

Harris, G.T. (1984) Perceptions of land shortages in six Simbu villages, *Yagl-Ambu*, 11(2), 54–62.

Harris, G.T. (1985) Motives for migration and land pressure in Simbu Province, Papua New Guinea, *Pacific Studies*, 9, 1–12.

Hart, K. (1974) A model of development to avoid, *Yagl-Ambu*, 1(1), 8–15.

Harvey, P. and Heywood, P. (1983) Twenty-five years of dietary change in Simbu Province, Papua New Guinea, *Ecology of Food and Nutrition*, 13, 27–35.

Hasluck, P. (1976) *A Time for Building: Australian Administration in Papua and New Guinea 1951–1963*, Melbourne: Melbourne University Press.

Hau'ofa, E. (1981) *Mekeo: Inequality and Ambivalence in a Village Society*, Canberra: ANU Press.

Hayano, D.M. (1979) Male migrant labour and changing sex roles in a Papua New Guinea highlands society, *Oceania*, 50, 37–50.

Hayano, D.M. (1990) *Road Through the Rain Forest*, Prospect Heights, NJ: Waveland Press.

Hayes, G. (1993a) 'Mirab' processes and development on small Pacific islands: a case study from the Southern Massim, Papua New Guinea, *Pacific Viewpoint*, 34, 153–78.

Hayes, G. (1993b) Demographic change and population policy responses in Papua New Guinea: a critical perspective, *Yagl-Ambu*, 17(1), 11–53.

Healey, C. (1986) Dependence and development in the Jimi Valley: a report on research, *Research in Melanesia*, 10, 12–36.

Heaney, W.H. (1989) Circular labour migration and entrepreneurship in the Wahgi Valley. Papua New Guinea, New York: unpub. Ph.D. thesis, Columbia University.

Hegarty, D. (1989) *Papua New Guinea: At the Political Crossroads*, Canberra: ANU Strategic and Defence Studies Centre, Working Paper No. 177.

Henderson, M. (1994) *Forest Issues in Papua New Guinea*, Rabaul: Pacific Heritage Foundation.

Herlihy, J. (1976) Government as development inhibitor: two case studies of administration and planning in the West Sepik, Canberra, ANU Research School of Pacific Studies, unpub. mimeo.

Heywood, P. and Jenkins, C. (1992) Nutrition in Papua New Guinea, in R.D. Attenborough and M. Alpers (eds) *Human Biology in Papua New Guinea*, Oxford: Clarendon Press, 249–67.

Hirsch, E. (1994) Between mission and market: events and images in a Melanesian society, *Man*, 29, 689–711.

Hogbin, I. (1958) *Social Change*, London: Watts.

Holzknecht, H. (1994) Managing Papua New Guinea's forest resources, *Development Bulletin*, 31, 27–31.

Holzknecht, H. and Kalit, K. (1995) Forest reserves: what hope for the future?, *Pacific Economic Bulletin*, 10, 95–100.

Howlett, D.R. (1965) *The European Land Settlement Scheme at Popondetta*, Canberra: New Guinea Research Bulletin No. 6.

Howlett, D.R. (1973a) *Papua New Guinea: Geography and Change*, Melbourne: Nelson.

Howlett, D.R. (1973b) Terminal development: from tribalism to peasantry, in H.C. Brookfield (ed.) *The Pacific in Transition*, London: Edward Arnold, 249–73.

Howlett, D.R. (1980) When is a peasant not a peasant: rural proletarianization in Papua New Guinea, in J.N. Jennings and G.J.R. Linge (eds) *Of Time and Place*, Canberra: ANU Press, 193–210.

Howlett, D.R., Hide, R. and Young, E. (1976) *Chimbu: Issues in Development*, Canberra: ANU Development Studies Centre Monograph No. 4.

Huber, P.B. (1978) Organising production and producing organisations: the sociology of traditional agriculture, in E.K. Fisk (ed.) *The Adaptation of Traditional Agriculture*, Canberra: ANU Development Studies Centre Monograph No. 11, 158–79.

Hughes, I. (1977) *New Guinea Stone Age Trade*, Canberra: Terra Australia No. 3.

Hughes, P. and Sullivan, M. (1989) Environmental impact assessments in Papua New Guinea: lessons for the wider Pacific region, *Pacific Viewpoint*, 30, 34–55.

Hulme, D. (1982) Land settlement schemes in Papua New Guinea: an overview, *Land Reform*, 1, 21–42.

Hyndman, D. (1991) Zipping down the Fly on the Ok Tedi Project, in J. Connell and R. Howitt (eds) *Mining and Indigenous People in Australasia*, Melbourne: Oxford University Press, 76–90.

Hyndman, D. (1993) Sea tenure and the management of living marine resources in Papua New Guinea, *Pacific Studies*, 16, 99–114.

Iamo, W. and Ketan, J. (1992) *How Far under the Influence? Alcohol Related Law and Order Problems in the Highlands of Papua New Guinea*, Port Moresby: National Research Institute.

Ilave, H.S. and Cox, E. (1988) Planned rural development or institutionalised gender bias? – Resettlement schemes and women in Papua New Guinea, in I.P. Getubig and A.J. Ledesma (eds) *Voices from the Culture of Silence*, Kuala Lumpur: Asia-Pacific Development Centre, 267–307.

Imbun, B. (1995) Enga social life and identity in a Papua New Guinea mining town, *Oceania*, 66, 51–61.

Inglis, A. (1974) *Not a White Woman Safe: Sexual Anxiety and Politics in Port Moresby, 1920–1934*, Canberra: ANU Press.

International Bank for Reconstruction and Development (1965) *The Economic Development of the Territory of Papua and New Guinea*, Baltimore, MD: Johns Hopkins Press.

Jackson, D. (1981) *The Distribution of Incomes in Papua New Guinea*, Port Moresby: National Planning Office.

Jackson, R.T. (ed.) (1976) *An Introduction to the Urban Geography of Papua New Guinea*, Port Moresby: UPNG Department of Geography, Occasional Paper No. 13.

Jackson, R.T. (1977) The growth, nature and future prospects of informal settlements in Papua New Guinea, *Pacific Viewpoint*, 18, 22–42.

Jackson, R.T. (1979) Running down the up-escalator: regional inequality in Papua New Guinea, *Australian Geographer*, 14, 175–84.

Jackson, R.T. (1982a) *Ok Tedi: The Pot of Gold*, Port Moresby: World Press.

Jackson, R.T. (1982b) The trend towards large-scale agriculture in Papua New Guinea, *Singapore Journal of Tropical Geography*, 3, 44–52.

Jackson, R.T. (1983) Ok Tedi revisited, *SMH*, 6 August, 29–32.

Jackson, R.T. (1989) New policies in sharing mining benefits in Papua New Guinea – a note, *Pacific Viewpoint*, 30, 86–93.

Jackson, R.T. (1991a) Hydrocarbon development and customary land users in Papua New Guinea, *Geography*, 76, 263–5.

Jackson, R.T. (1991b) Not without influence: villages, mining companies and governments in Papua New Guinea, in J. Connell and R. Howitt (eds) *Mining and Indigenous Peoples in Australasia*, Melbourne: Oxford University Press, 18–33.

Jackson, R.T. (1993) *Cracked Pot or Copper Bottomed Investment? The Development of the Ok Tedi Project 1982–1991, A Personal View*, Townsville: James Cook University Melanesian Studies Centre.

Jackson, R.T., Emerson, C.A. and Welsch, R. (1980) *The Impact of the Ok Tedi Project*, Port Moresby: Department of Minerals and Energy.

Jacobsen, M. (1995) Vanishing nations and the infiltration of nationalism: the case of Papua New Guinea, in R.J. Foster (ed.) *Nation Making: Emergent Identities in Postcolonial Melanesia*, Ann Arbor: University of Michigan Press, 227–49.

Jarrett, F. (1991) Set in concrete? The proposed cement clinker plant in Papua New Guinea, *Pacific Economic Bulletin*, 6(2), 20–4.

Jarrett, F.G. and Anderson, K. (1989) *Growth, Structural Change and Economic Policy in Papua New Guinea: Implications for Agriculture*, Canberra: NCDS Pacific Policy Paper No. 5.

Jenkins, C. (1987) Medical Anthropology in the Western Schrader Range, Papua New Guinea, *National Geographic Research*, 3, 412–30.

Jenkins, C. (1988) Health in the early contact period: a contemporary example from Papua New Guinea, *Social Science and Medicine*, 26, 997–1006.

Jenkins, C. (1992) Medical anthropology in Papua New Guinea: a challenge, in R. Attenborough and M. Alpers (eds) *Human Biology in Papua New Guinea*, Oxford: Clarendon Press, 387–97.

Jenkins, C., Dimitrakakis, M., Cook, I., Sanders, R. and Stallman, N. (1989) Culture change and epidemiological patterns among the Hagahai, Papua New Guinea, *Human Ecology*, 17, 27–59.

Johnson, J. (1984) Labour in the Papua New Guinea plantation economy: a Mount Hagen case study, Sydney: unpub. B.A. (Hons) thesis, University of Sydney.

Johnson, P.L. (1981) When dying is better than living: female suicide among the Gainj of Papua New Guinea, *Ethnology*, 20, 325–34.

Johnson, P.L. (1990) Changing household composition, labor patterns and fertility in a Highland New Guinea population, *Human Ecology*, 18, 403–16.

Jonas, W. (1985) The commercial timber industry in colonial Papua New Guinea, *Pacific Studies*, 8, 45–60.

Jorgensen, D. (1991) Big men, great men and women: alternative logics of gender difference, in M. Godelier and M. Strathern (eds) *Big Men and Great Men*, Cambridge: Cambridge University Press, 256–71.

Jorgensen, D. (1996) Regional history and ethnic identity in the hub of New Guinea: the emergence of the Min, *Oceania*, 66, 189–210.

Joseph, R.A. (1978) Affluence and underdevelopment: the Nigerian experience, *Journal of Modern African Studies*, 16, 221–9.

Josephides, L. (1985) *The Production of Inequality: Gender and Exchange among the Kewa*, London: Tavistock.

Josephides, L. and Schiltz, M. (1982) Beer and other luxuries: abstinence in village and plantation by Sugu Kewas, Southern Highlands, in M. Marshall (ed.) *Through a Glass Darkly: Beer and Modernization in Papua New Guinea*, Port Moresby: IASER Monograph No. 18, 73–82.

Joughlin, J. (1986) Rice in PNG: an economic evaluation, *Harvest*, 12(1), 10–15.

Kahn, M. (1986) *Always Hungry, Never Greedy: Food and the Expression of Gender in a Melanesian Society*, Cambridge: Cambridge University Press.

Kaima, S. (1991) The evolution of cargo cults and the emergence of political parties in Melanesia, *Journal de la Société des Océanistes*, 92–3, 173–80.

Kaitilla, S. (1993) Urban land release and development in Papua New Guinea, *Journal of Asian and African Studies*, 28, 253–8.

Kaitilla, S. (1994) Urban residence and housing improvement in a Lae squatter settlement, Papua New Guinea, *Environment and Behavior*, 26, 640–68.

Kaitilla, S. and Sarpong-Oti, W. (1994) A study report on urban home-ownership in Papua New Guinea, *TPNG*, 24 February: 4.

Kavanamur, D. (1993) The Papua New Guinea official view of development, *Catalyst*, 23, 57–78.

Kay, G. (1975) *Development and Underdevelopment: A Marxist Analysis*, London: Macmillan.

Kearney, R.E. (1977) The expansion of fisheries in Papua New Guinea: prospects and problems, in B. Enyi and T. Varghese (eds) *Agriculture in the Tropics*, Port Moresby: UPNG, 110–28.

Keck, V. (1993) Talk about a changing world: young Yupno men in Papua New Guinea debate their future, *Canberra Anthropology*, 16, 67–96.

Keil, D.E. (1977) Markets in Melanesia? A comparison of traditional economic transactions in New Guinea with African markets, *Journal of Anthropological Research*, 33, 258–76.

Keil, J.T. (1975) Local group composition and leadership in Buin, Harvard: unpub. Ph.D. thesis.

Kekedo, R. (1983) Wages, employment and localisation policies, in D. Gupta and S. Polume (eds) *Economic Policy Issues and Options in Papua New Guinea*, Canberra: ANU Development Studies Centre Working Paper No. 41, 141–52.

Kelleher, G. (1991) Sustainable development for traditional inhabitants of the Torres Strait Region, in D. Lawrence and T. Cansfield-Smith (eds) *Sustainable*

Development for Traditional Inhabitants of the Torres Strait Region, Canberra: Great Barrier Reef Marine Park Authority, 15–21.

Kelleher, M.K. (1984) Control of transfer pricing in the fishing industry, in A. Sawyerr (ed.) *Economic Development and Trade in Papua New Guinea*, Port Moresby: UPNG Press, 204–9.

Kennedy, D. (1994) Development is not sustainability: a case study of the Kutubu Petroleum Development Project, Papua New Guinea, Sydney: unpub. B.Sc. Hons. thesis, Macquarie University.

Kennedy, D. (1996) Development or sustainability at Kutubu, PNG, in R. Howitt, J. Connell and P. Hirsch (eds) *Resources, Nations and Indigenous Peoples*, Melbourne: Oxford University Press, 236–50.

Kiki, A.M. (1963) *Kiki: Ten Thousand Years in a Lifetime*, Melbourne: Cheshire.

King, D. (1992a) Socio-economic differences between residential categories in Port Moresby, *Yagl-Ambu*, 16(3), 1–16.

King, D. (1992b) The demise of the small towns and outstations of Papua New Guinea, *Yagl-Ambu*, 16(3), 17–33.

Kirk, M.S. (1969) Journey into Stone Age New Guinea, *National Geographic*, 135, 568–92.

Knauft, B. (1993) Like money you see in a dream: petroleum and patrols in South New Guinea, *Oceania*, 64, 187–90.

Kreye, O. and Castell, L. (1991) Development and the environment: economic-ecological development in Papua New Guinea (Starnberg Institute Study), *Catalyst*, 21, 1–117.

Kulick, D. (1992) *Language Shift and Cultural Reproduction: Socialization, Self and Syncretism in a Papua New Guinean Village*, Cambridge: Cambridge University Press.

Kulick, D. (1993) Heroes from Hell: representations of 'rascals' in a Papua New Guinean village, *Anthropology Today*, 9, 9–14.

Kulick, D. and Willson, M.E. (1992) Echoing images: the construction of savagery among Papua New Guinean villagers, *Visual Anthropology*, 5, 143–52.

Lacey, R. (1977) Dynamics of precolonial agriculture: an exploratory essay, Port Moresby: UPNG History of Agriculture Discussion Paper No. 8.

Lamb, D. (1990) *Exploiting the Tropical Rain Forest: An Account of Pulpwood Logging in Papua New Guinea*, Paris: UNESCO.

Lambert, J.N. (1979) The relationship between cash crop production and nutritional status in PNG, Port Moresby: UPNG History of Agriculture Working Paper No. 33.

Langness, L. (1967) Sexual antagonism in the New Guinea Highlands: a Bena Bena example, *Oceania*, 37, 161–77.

Larmour, P. (1990) Ethnicity and decentralisation in Melanesia: a review of the 1980s, *Pacific Viewpoint*, 31, 10–27.

Larmour, P. (1995) State and society, *Pacific Economic Bulletin*, 19(1), 40–7.

Lawrence, P. (1964) *Road Belong Cargo*, Melbourne: Melbourne University Press.

Lea, D.A.M. (1969) Some non-nutritive functions of food in New Guinea, in F. Gale and G. Lawton (eds) *Settlement and Encounter*, Melbourne: Oxford University Press, 173–84.

Lea, D.A.M. (1972) Indigenous horticulture in Melanesia: some recent changes in Eastern New Guinea, the Solomon Islands and the New Hebrides, in R.G. Ward (ed.) *Man in the Pacific Islands*, London: Oxford UP, 252–79.

Lea, D.A.M. (1980) Tourism in Papua New Guinea: the last resort, in J. Jennings and G. Linge (eds) *Of Time and Place*, Canberra: ANU Press, 211–31.

Lea, D. and Gray, N. (1982) Enga demography, in B. Carrad, D. Lea and K. Talyaga (eds) *Enga: Foundations for Development*, Armidale: University of New England, 41–58.

Lea, D., Joel, N. and Curry, G. (1988) A Maprik journey: backwards or forwards in time? Cash cropping among the Abelam, in J. Hirst, J. Overton, B. Allen and Y. Byron (eds) *Small-Scale Agriculture*, Canberra: Commonwealth Geographical Bureau and ANU Department of Human Geography, 23–31.

Lepowsky, M. (1991) The way of the ancestors: custom, innovation and resistance, *Ethnology*, 30, 217–35.

Levett, M.P. (1992) A comparative study of gardening systems in two mountainous census divisions of Kaintiba District, Gulf Province, *Yagl-Ambu*, 16(4), 71–85.

Lewis, G. (1980) *Day of Shining Red*, Cambridge: Cambridge University Press.

Lifu, K. and Nakikus, M. (1982) Papua New Guinea, Noumea: unpub. paper to SPC/ILO Conference on Migration, Employment and Development in the South Pacific.

Lindstrom, L. (1992) Pasin Tumbuna: Cultural Traditions and National Identity in Papua New Guinea, Honolulu: East West Center Institute of Culture and Communication Working Paper.

Lipset, D. (1990) A double tragedy: political authority and male identity in the New Guinea Highlands, *Reviews in Anthropology*, 15, 137–48.

LiPuma, E. (1994) Sorcery and evidence of change in Maring justice, *Ethnology*, 33, 147–163.

Lodewijks, J. (1988) Employment and wages policy in Papua New Guinea, *Journal of Industrial Relations*, 30, 381–411.

Lodewijks, J., Enahoro, D. and Argyrous, G. (1991) Stabilising developing economies: challenging the IMF in PNG, *Pacific Viewpoint*, 32, 43–65.

Lomas, P. (1978) Copra and councillors: village enterprise in Northern New Ireland, *Ethnos*, 4, 30–50.

Lombange, C. (1984) Trends in sexually transmitted disease incidence in Papua New Guinea, *Papua New Guinea Medical Journal*, 27, 145–57.

Lombange, C., Lakipane, M. and Papak, J. (1987) A study of the health status of the Wapi People in Enga Province, Papua New Guinea, *Papua New Guinea Medical Journal*, 30, 229–37.

McCoy, C. (1992) Disputes hit Papua New Guinea project, *Asian Wall Street Journal*, 10 June.

McDowell, N. (ed.) (1988) *Reproductive Decision Making and the Value of Children in Rural Papua New Guinea*, Port Moresby: IASER Monograph No. 27.

McGavin, P.A. (1991) *Wages, Incomes and Productivity in Papua New Guinea*, Port Moresby: Institute of National Affairs Discussion Paper No. 48.

McGavin, P.A. (1993) The 1992 minimum wages board determination: implications for employment and growth, in AIDAB, *The Papua New Guinea Economy*, Canberra: AIDAB International Development Issue No. 30, 52–84.

McGavin, P.A. and Millett, J. (1992) *Industrialization in Papua New Guinea: Unrealized Potential?*, Port Moresby: Institute of National Affairs Discussion Paper No. 52.

McGee, T.G. (1975) *Food Dependency in the Pacific*, Canberra: ANU Development Studies Centre Occasional Paper No. 2.

McGee, W.A. and Henning, G.R. (1990) Investment in lode mining, Papua 1878–1920, *Journal of Pacific History*, 25, 244–59.

MacIntyre, M. (1987) Nurturance and nutrition: change and continuity in concepts of food and feasting in a Southern Massim community, *Journal de la Société des Océanistes*, 84, 51–9.

MacIntyre, M. (1988) Moving mountains on Misima, *Australian Society*, October, 28–9.

MacIntyre, M. (1989) Better homes and gardens, in M. Jolly and M. MacIntyre (eds) *Family and Gender in the Pacific*, Cambridge: Cambridge University Press, 156–69.

Mackay, P.D. (1976) *New Guinea*, Amsterdam: Time-Life.

McKillop, B. (1981) Managing plantations in Papua New Guinea today: who wants to be the labourer?, in M. Walter (ed.) *What Do We Do About Plantations?*, Port Moresby: IASER Monograph No. 15, 25–32.

McLaren, L. and Owen, C. (1991) *Cowboy and Maria in Town*, Sydney: Australian Film Commission.

Maclean, N. (1981) Politics of development in an underdeveloped area: a case from the Jimi Valley, in R. Gordon (ed.) *The Plight of Peripheral People in Papua New Guinea*, Cambridge, MA: Cultural Survival Inc., 37–49.

Maclean, N. (1984) Is gambling 'bisnis'? The economic and political functions of gambling in the Jimi Valley, *Social Analysis*, 16, 44–59.

McMurray, C. (1985) *Recent Demography of Papua New Guinea*, Canberra: ANU Development Studies Centre Working Paper No. 85/5.

McMurray, C. (1992) Issues in population planning: the case of Papua New Guinea, *Development Bulletin*, 24 July, 13–6.

McPherson, N. (1994) Modern obstetrics in a rural setting: women and reproduction in Northwest New Britain, *Urban Anthropology*, 23, 39–72.

Macpherson, S. (1981) Basic health services in Papua New Guinea: a study of aid post orderlies, *Development News Digest*, 5, 58–64.

MacQueen, N. (1993) An infinite capacity to muddle through? A security audit for Papua New Guinea, *Journal of Commonwealth and Comparative Politics*, 31, 133–54.

McSwain, R. (1977) *The Past and Future People: Tradition and Change on a New Guinea Island*, Melbourne: Oxford University Press.

MacWilliam, S. (1986) International capital, indigenous accumulation and the state in Papua New Guinea: the case of the Development Bank, *Capital and Class*, 29, 150–81.

MacWilliam, S. (1988) Smallholdings, land law and the politics of land tenure in Papua New Guinea, *Journal of Peasant Studies*, 16, 77–109.

MacWilliam, S. (1990) The politics of an agricultural disease in Papua New Guinea, *Journal of Contemporary Asia*, 20, 291–311.

MacWilliam, S. (1995) Unemployment, order and commodity stabilisation funds, *Pacific Economic Bulletin*, 10, 24–30.

MacWilliam, S. (1996) 'Just like working for the dole': rural households, export crops and state subsidies in Papua New Guinea, *Journal of Peasant Studies*, 23, 40–78.

Mamak, A. and Bedford, R. (1974) *Bougainvillean Nationalism. Aspects of Unity and Discord*, Canterbury: Bougainville Special Publication No. 1.

Manning, M. (1983) Towards an agricultural policy, in D. Gupta and S. Polume (eds) *Economic Policy Issues and Options in Papua New Guinea*, Canberra: ANU Development Studies Centre Working Paper No. 41, 103–10.

Manning, M. (1991) *Development and Performance of Management Agencies in Papua New Guinea Agriculture*, Port Moresby: Institute of National Affairs Discussion Paper No. 45.

Marshall, L., Rojas, P. and Heaney, B. (1988) Who attends antenatal clinics in the National Capital District?, *Papua New Guinea Medical Journal*, 31, 269–76.

Matwijiw, P. (1982) Urban land problems in Port Moresby, Papua New Guinea, *Tijdschrift voor Economische en Sociale Geografie*, 73, 286–94.

May, R.J. (1987) PNG, Moresby and the Bush, *Current Affairs Bulletin*, 63(8), January, 4–15.

May, R.J. (1993) *The Changing Role of the Military in Papua New Guinea*, Canberra: ANU Strategic and Defence Studies Centre.

May, R.J. and Skeldon, R. (1977) Internal migration in Papua New Guinea: an introduction to its description and analysis, in R.J. May (ed.) *Change and Movement: Readings on Internal Migration in Papua New Guinea*, Canberra: ANU Press, 1–26.

Mazrui, A. (1970) An African's New Guinea, *New Guinea*, 5, 45–56.

Meggitt, M. (1965) *The Lineage System of the Mae-Enga of New Guinea*, New York: Barnes and Noble.

Meggitt, M. (1971) From tribesmen to peasants: the case of the Mae Enga of New Guinea, in L.R. Hiatt and C. Jayawardena (eds) *Anthropology in Oceania*, Sydney: Angus and Robertson, 191–209.

Meigs, A.S. (1984) *Food, Sex and Pollution: A New Guinea Religion*, New Brunswick, NJ: Rutgers University Press.

Milne, S. (1991) Tourism development in Papua New Guinea, *Annals of Tourism Research*, 18, 508–11.

Mitchell, D.D. (1976) *Land and Agriculture in Nagovisi*, Port Moresby: IASER Monograph No. 3.

Mitchell, D.D. (1982) Frozen assets in Nagovisi, *Oceania*, 53, 56–66.

Mitchell, W.E. (1990) Why Wape men don't beat their wives, *Pacific Studies*, 13, 141–50.

Modjeska, N. (1982) Production and inequality: perspectives from central New Guinea, in A. Strathern (ed.) *Inequality in New Guinea Highlands Societies*, Cambridge: Cambridge University Press, 50–108.

Modjeska, N. (1991) Post-Ipomoean modernism: the Duna example, in M. Godelier and M. Strathern (eds) *Big Men and Great Men*, Cambridge: Cambridge University Press, 234–55.

Monsell-Davis, M. (1993) Urban exchange: safety-net or disincentive? *Wantoks* and relatives in the urban Pacific, *Canberra Anthropology*, 16, 45–66.

Montague, S. (1982) Kaduwagan attitudes towards formal and non-formal education: a Trobriand Island perspective, *Papua New Guinea Journal of Education*, 18, 1–21.

Moore, C. (1992) The PNG General Election of 1992: its implications for Australia, *World Review*, 31(4), 26–44.

Morauta, L. (1972) The politics of cargo cults in the Madang area, *Man*, 7, 430–47.

Morauta, L. (1974) *Beyond the Village: Local Politics in Madang, Papua New Guinea*, London: University of London Press.

Morauta, L. (1981) Mobility patterns in Papua New Guinea: social factors as explanatory variables, in G.W. Jones and H.V. Richter (eds) *Population Mobility and Development: Southeast Asia and the Pacific*, Canberra: ANU Development Studies Centre Monograph No. 27, 205–28.

Morauta, L. (1984) Social stratification in lowland Papua New Guinea: issues and questions, in R.J. May (ed.) *Social Stratification in Papua New Guinea*, Canberra: ANU Department of Political and Social Change Working Paper No. 5, 3–28.

Morauta, L. and Hasu, M, (1979) *Rural–Urban Relationships in Papua New Guinea: Case Material from the Gulf Province on Net Flows*, Port Moresby: IASER Discussion Paper No. 25.

Morauta, L. and Olela, C. (1980) *Expenditure on Alcohol in Port Moresby Households*, Port Moresby: IASER Discussion Paper No. 30.

Morauta, L. and Ryan, D. (1982) From temporary to permanent townsmen: migrants from the Malalaua District, Papua New Guinea, *Oceania*, 53(1) September, 39–55.

Morren, G.E.B. (1986) *The Miyanmin: Human Ecology of a Papua New Guinea Society*, Ann Arbor, MI: UMI Research Press.

Mosko, M. (1985) *Quadripartite Structures: Categories, Relations and Homologies in Bush Mekeo Culture*, Cambridge: Cambridge University Press.

Moylan, T. (1981) Some notes on change, in S. Weeks (ed.) *Oksapmin: Development and Change*, Port Moresby: UPNG Education Research Unit Occasional Paper No. 7, 61–8.

Mullins, M. and Flaherty, M. (1995) Customary landowner involvement in the Kumil Timber Project, Papua New Guinea, *Geoforum*, 26, 89–105.

Murphy, K. (1988) The modern Stone Age goldrush, *The Bulletin*, 9 August, 50–2.

Mylius, L. and Wigley, S. (1971) The squatter settlements of Port Moresby and tuberculosis, *Papua New Guinea Medical Journal*, 14, 87–93.

Myrdal, G. (1968) *Asian Drama*, New York: Random House.

Nadarajah, T. (1994) *The Sustainability of Papua New Guinea's Forest Resource*, Port Moresby: National Research Institute Discussion Paper No. 76.

Narokobi, B. (1980) *The Melanesian Way*, Port Moresby: Institute of Papua New Guinea Studies.

Nash, J. (1974) *Matriliny and Modernisation: The Nagovisi of South Bougainville*, Canberra and Port Moresby: New Guinea Research Bulletin No. 55.

Nash, J. (1981) Sex, money and the status of women in south Bougainville, *American Ethnologist*, 8, 107–26.

Nash, J. and Ogan, E. (1990) The Red and the Black: Bougainvillean perceptions of other Papua New Guineans, *Pacific Studies*, 13, 1–17.

National Planning Office (1981) *The National Public Expenditure Plan 1982–85*, Port Moresby.

National Research Institute (1992) *First Things First: Towards People-Centred Development*, Port Moresby: National Research Institute.

National Statistical Office (1991) *Population Trends in Papua New Guinea*, Port Moresby: National Statistical Office.

Naylor, R., Dewdney, J. and Mylius, R. (1993) The health system, in AIDAB, *The Papua New Guinea Economy*, Canberra: AIDAB, 159–89.

Nelson, H. (1976) *Black, White and Gold: Goldmining in Papua New Guinea 1878–1930*, Canberra: ANU Press.

Nelson, H. (1992) Gully-rakers, mining companies and parallels of war, in S. Henningham and R.J. May (eds) *Resources, Development and Politics in the Pacific Islands*, Bathurst: Crawford House, 11–29.

Newton, J. (1985) *Orokaiva Production and Change*, ANU Development Studies Centre, Canberra: Pacific Research Monograph No. 11.

Nibbrig, N. (1992) Rascals in paradise: urban gangs in Papua New Guinea, *Pacific Studies*, 15, 115–34.

Nihill, M. (1989) The new pearlshells: aspects of money and meaning in Anganen exchange, *Canberra Anthropology*, 12, 144–60.

Norwood, H. (1981) The Goilalas: Mafia or maligned? *Pacific Viewpoint*, 22, 81–8.

O'Collins, M. (1980) Family planning programmes in Papua New Guinea and Solomon Islands, *Yagl-Ambu*, 7(4), 31–44.

O'Faircheallaigh, C. (1982) *Mining in the Papua New Guinea Economy, 1880–1980*, Port Moresby: UPNG Department of History, Occasional Paper in Economic History No. 1.

O'Faircheallaigh, C. (1983) Economic policy in historical perspective, *Yagl-Ambu*, 10, 1–15.

O'Faircheallaigh, C. (1984) *Mining and Development*, London: Croom Helm.

Ogan, E. (1986) 'Taim bilong Sipak': Nasioi alcohol use, 1962–1978, *Ethnology*, 25, 21–33.

Ogan, E. (1996) Copra came before copper: the Nasioi of Bougainville and plantation colonialism, 1902–1964, *Pacific Studies*, 19, 31–51.

O'Hanlon, M. (1993) *Paradise: Portraying the New Guinea Highlands*, London: British Museum Press.

Ohtsuka, R., Inaoka, T., Umezaki, M., Nakada, N. and Abe, T. (1995) Long-term subsistence adaptation to the diversified Papua New Guinea environment, *Global Environmental Change*, 5, 347–53.

Ollapallil, J. (1987) The changing tribal warfare, in P. Heywood and B. Hudson (eds) *Rural Health Services in Papua New Guinea*, Boroko, NCD: PNG Dept of Health, 125–7.

Oram, N. (1976) *Colonial Town to Melanesian City: Port Moresby 1884–1974*, Canberra: ANU Press.

O'Rourke, D. (1987) *Cannibal Tours*, Canberra: O'Rourke and Associates.

Overfield, D. (1995) The economics of social subordination: gender relations and market failure in the Highlands of Papua New Guinea, Leeds: unpub. Ph.D. thesis, University of Leeds.

Overseas Development Group, University of East Anglia (1973) *A Report on Development Strategies for Papua New Guinea*, Port Moresby: Office of Planning and Coordination.

Paijmans, K. (1976) *New Guinea Vegetation*, Canberra: ANU Press.

Panoff, M. (1985) Une Figure de l'abjection en Nouvelle-Bretagne: le *rubbish man*, *L'Homme*, 94, 57–71.

Papua New Guinea (1978) *The National Public Expenditure Plan 1978–1981*, Port Moresby: National Planning Office.

Papua New Guinea (1991) *An Integrated National Population Policy for Progress and Development*, Port Moresby: Department of Finance and Planning.

Papua New Guinea Central Planning Office (1976) *The Post-Independence National Development Strategy*, Port Moresby: Central Planning Office.

Papua New Guinea Department of Forests (1991) *National Forestry Policy*, Port Moresby.

Papua New Guinea Department of Lands and Physical Planning (1988) *Land Mobilisation Programme*, Port Moresby.

Papua New Guinea National Planning Office (1977) *Managing Urbanisation in Papua New Guinea*, Port Moresby.

Pernetta, J. (1988) The Ok Tedi Mine: environment, development and pollution problems, in J. Pernetta (ed.) *Potential Impacts of Mining on the Fly River*, Noumea: UNEP Regional Seas Reports and Studies No. 99, 1–8.

Pernetta, J. and Hill, L. (1983) A review of marine resource use in coastal Papua, *Journal de la Société des Océanistes*, 37, 175–91.

Pérusse, Y. (1993) *Bushwalking in Papua New Guinea*, Melbourne: Lonely Planet.

Pettman, J. (1984) Schooling, stratification and resocialization in Papua New Guinea, in R.J. May (ed.) *Social Stratification in Papua New Guinea*, Canberra: ANU Department of Political and Social Change Working Paper No. 5, 133–51.

Pintz, W.S. (1984) *Ok Tedi: Evolution of a Third World Mining Project*, London: Mining Journal Books.

Placer Pacific (1992) *Annual Report 1991*, Melbourne.

Ploeg, A. (1971) *The Situm and Gobari Ex-Servicemen's Settlements*, Canberra and Port Moresby: New Guinea Research Bulletin No. 39.

Ploeg, A. (1985) Dependency among the Kovai, Siassi, Morobe Province, Papua New Guinea, *Oceania*, 55, 252–71.

Plowman, D. (1979) Some aspects of trade union development in Papua New Guinea, *Australian Outlook*, 33, 326–38.

Polier, N. (1996) Of mines and Min: modernity and its malcontents in Papua New Guinea, *Ethnology*, 35, 1–16.

Pomponio, A. (1992) *Seagulls Don't Fly into the Bush: Cultural Identity and Development in Melanesia*, Belmont, CA: Wadsworth.

Poole, F. (1983) Cannibals, tricksters and witches: anthropophagic images among Bimin-Kuskusmin, in P. Brown and D. Tuzin (eds) *The Ethnography of Cannibalism*, Washington, DC: Society for Psychological Anthropology, 6–32.

Preston, D.A. (1990) People and land: resource use in household livelihood strategies in Roro and Paitana villages in Papua New Guinea, Leeds: University of Leeds School of Geography Working Paper No. 535.

Preston, R. (1989) Hidden and open agendas: social policy issues, in M. Oliver (ed.) *Eleksin: The 1987 National Election in Papua New Guinea*, Port Moresby: UPNG Printery, 69–80.

Quodling, P. (1991) *Bougainville: The Mine and the People*, Sydney: Centre for Independent Studies Pacific Papers No. 3.

Radford, A. (1980) The inverse care law in Papua New Guinea, in N.F. Stanley and R.A. Junke (eds) *Man and the Evolution of Health*, London: Academic Press, 323–43.

Ranck, S. (1982) New dimensions emerging in Port Moresby's informal retail sector, *Australian Geographer*, 15, 180–2.

Ranck, S. (1984) Telecommunications in Papua New Guinea, in C. Kissling, *Transport and Communications for Pacific Microstates*, Suva: Institute for Pacific Studies, 49–60.

Ranck, S. (1987) An attempt at autonomous development: the case of the Tufi Guest Houses, Papua New Guinea, in S. Britton and W. Clarke (eds) *Ambiguous Alternatives: Tourism in Small Developing Countries*, Suva: University of the South Pacific, 154–66.

Ranck, S. and Tapari, B. (1984) At the bottom of the ladder: a focus on villagers' perceptions of deer farming in the Bensbach area of Western Province, in A. Sawyerr (ed.) *Economy and Trade in Papua New Guinea*, Port Moresby: UPNG, 164–73.

Rappaport, R.A. (1984) *Pigs for the Ancestors. Ritual in the Ecology of a New Guinea People*, 2nd edn, New Haven, CT: Yale University Press.

Read, K.E. (1986) *Return to the High Valley: Coming Full Circle*, Berkeley: University of California Press.

Renner, D. (1990) *The People in Between: A Case Study on the Kumil Timber Project, Madang Province, Papua New Guinea*, Copenhagen: International Workgroup for Indigenous Affairs Document No. 65.

Richardson, J. (1987) Health and health care in Papua New Guinea: problems and solutions, in C. Throsby (ed.) *Human Resources Development in the Pacific*, Canberra: NCDS Pacific Policy Paper No. 3, 25–53.

Riley, I. (1983) Population change and distribution in Papua New Guinea: an epidemiological approach, *Journal of Human Evolution*, 12, 125–32.

Riley, I. and Davies, J. (1982) Population and Health Development, in ESCAP, *Population of Papua New Guinea*, Noumea: United Nations and South Pacific Commission, 159–83.

Rimoldi, M. and Rimoldi, E. (1992) *Hahalis and the Labour of Love*, Oxford: Berg.

Robbins, R.G. (1972) Vegetation and man in the South-West Pacific and New Guinea, in R.G. Ward (ed.) *Man in the Pacific Islands*, Oxford: Clarendon Press, 74–90.

Rohrlich-Leavitt, R. (1975) Conclusions, in R. Rohrlich-Leavitt (ed.) *Women Cross-Culturally: Challenge and Change*, The Hague: Mouton, 619–41.

Rosenbaum, H. and Krockenberger, M. (1993) *Report on the Impacts of the Ok Tedi Mine in Papua New Guinea*, Melbourne: Australian Conservation Foundation.

Rosi, P.C. (1991) Papua New Guinea's New Parliament House: A Contested National Symbol, *The Contemporary Pacific*, 3, 289–323.

Ross, C.W. (1991) Staged Development and Environmental Management of the Porgera Gold Mine in Papua New Guinea, in D. Lawrence and T. Cansfield-Smith (eds) *Sustainable Development for Traditional Inhabitants of the Torres Strait Region*, Canberra: Great Barrier Reef Marine Park Authority, 119–32.

Rowley, C.D. (1965) *The Australians in German New Guinea, 1914–1921*, Melbourne: Melbourne University Press.

Ryan, D. (1989) Home ties in town: Toaripi in Port Moresby, *Canberra Anthropology*, 12, 19–27.

Ryan, P. (1991) *Black Bonanza: A Landslide of Gold*, Melbourne: Hyland House.

Saffu, Y. (1983) Decentralization in Papua New Guinea: the West Sepik Provincial Government, *Australian Journal of Politics and History*, 29, 26–37.

Saffu, Y. (1992) Papua New Guinea January–December 1991, *Australian Journal of Politics and History*, 38, 262–9.

Salisbury, R.F. (1964) Changes in land use and land tenure among the Siane of the New Guinea Highlands (1952–1961), *Pacific Viewpoint*, 5, 1–10.

Salisbury, R.F. (1970) *Vunamami: Economic Transformation in a Traditional Society*, Berkeley and Los Angeles: University of California Press.

Salisbury, R.F. and Salisbury, M.E. (1972) The rural oriented strategy of urban adaptation: Siane migrants in Port Moresby, in T. Weaver and D. White (eds) *The Anthropology of Urban Environments*, Washington, DC: Society for Applied Anthropology, 49–68.

Samana, U. (1988) *Papua New Guinea: Which Way?*, Melbourne: Arena Publications.

Samaranayake, H. (1992) *PNG Visitor Survey 1991*, Suva: Tourism Council of the South Pacific Survey Report No. 11.

Sargent, S. (1985) *The Foodmakers*, Melbourne: Penguin.

Schaffer, B. (1965) Advising about development: the example of the World Bank Report on Papua and New Guinea, *Journal of Commonwealth Political Studies*, 4, 30–46.

Schieffelin, E.L. (1978) *The End of Traditional Music, Dance and Body Decoration in Bosavi, Papua New Guinea*, Port Moresby: Institute of Papua New Guinea Studies Discussion Paper Nos. 30–2.

Schieffelin, E.L. (1995) Early contact as drama and manipulation in the highlands of Papua New Guinea, *Comparative Studies in Society and History*, 37, 555–80.

Schieffelin, E.L. and Crittenden, R. (1991) *Like People You See In A Dream*, Stanford, CA: Stanford University Press.

Schiltz, M. (1985) Rascalism, tradition and the state in Papua New Guinea, in S. Toft (ed.) *Domestic Violence in Papua New Guinea*, Port Moresby: Law Reform Commission Monograph No. 3, 141–60.

Schiltz, M. and Josephides, L. (1981) Current problems and prospects: view from the Sugu Valley, Southern Highlands Province, in M.A.H.B. Walter (ed.) *What Do We Do About Plantations?*, Port Moresby: IASER Monograph No. 15, 136–42.

Schmid, C.K. (1991) *Of People and Plants: A Botanical Ethnography of Nokopo Village*, Basel: Basler Beitrage zur Ethnologie No. 33.

Schmid, J. (1990) The response to tourism in Yensan, in N. Lutkehaus (ed.) *Sepik Heritage. Tradition and Change in Papua New Guinea*, Durham, NC: Carolina Academic Press, 241–4.

Schwartz, L. (1969) The hierarchy of resort in curative practices: the Admiralty Islands, Melanesia, *Journal of Health and Social Behavior*, 10, 201–9.

Schwartz, T. (1982) Alcohol use in Manus villages, in M. Marshall (ed.) *Through a Glass Darkly: Beer and Modernization in Papua New Guinea*, Port Moresby: IASER Monograph No. 18, 319–403.

Schwimmer, E. (1979) The self and the product: concepts of work in comparative perspective, in S. Wallman (ed.) *Social Anthropology of Work*, London: Academic Press, 287–315.

Schwimmer, E. (1991) How Oro Province societies fit Godelier's model, in M. Godelier and M. Strathern (eds) *Big Men and Great Men*, Cambridge: Cambridge University Press, 142–55.

Scragg, R.F.R. (1954) *Depopulation in New Ireland: A Study of Demography and Fertility*, Port Moresby: Minister for Territories.

Sexton, L. (1986) *Mothers of Money, Daughters of Coffee: the Wok Meri Movement*, Ann Arbor, MI: UMI Research Press.

Sexton, L. (1988) 'Eating' Money in Highland Papua New Guinea, *Food and Foodways*, 3, 119–42.

Shack, K., Dewey, K. and Grivetti, L. (1990a) Effects of resettlement on the dietary intakes of mothers and children in lowland Papua New Guinea, *Ecology of Food and Nutrition*, 24, 55–70.

Shack, K.W., Grivetti, L. and Dewey, K. (1990b) Cash cropping, subsistence agriculture and nutritional status among mothers and children in lowland Papua New Guinea, *Social Science and Medicine*, 31, 61–8.

Sharp, N. (1975) The Republic of the Northern Solomons, *Arena*, 40, 119–27.

Sharp, P. (1981) Pierced by the arrows of this ghostly world: a review of arrow wounds in Enga province, *Papua New Guinea Medical Journal*, 24, 150–63.

Sharpless, J.B. (1992) The troubled history of population policy initiatives in Papua New Guinea, 1968–1988, *Yagl-Ambu*, 16(4), 1–16.

Shaw, D., Bourke, R.M., Bell, S. and Shaw, B. (1986) *Implications of the 1986 Outbreak of Coffee Rust in Papua New Guinea*, Canberra: Islands/Australia Working Paper No. 86/15, NCDS.

Sheen, A. (1984) Papuan canoes, *IFDA Dossier*, 40, 39–46.

Shimizu, Y. (1992) Papua New Guinea, the last paradise of tropical rain forests and Japanese timber companies, *Catalyst*, 22, 80–95.

Sillitoe, P. (1993a) A ritual response to climatic perturbations in the Highlands of Papua New Guinea, *Ethnology*, 32, 169–85.

Sillitoe, P. (1993b) Losing ground? Soil loss and erosion in the highlands of Papua New Guinea, *Land Degradation and Rehabilitation*, 4, 143–66.

Sillitoe, P. (1994) *The Bogaia of the Muller Ranges, Papua New Guinea*, Sydney: Oceania Monograph No. 44.

Sinnett, P., Kevau, I. and Tyson, D. (1992) Social change and the emergence of degenerative cardiovascular disease in Papua New Guinea, in R. Attenborough and M. Alpers (eds) *Human Biology in Papua New Guinea*, Oxford: Clarendon Press, 373–86.

Skeldon, R. (1979) Internal migration, in R. Skeldon (ed.) *The Demography of Papua New Guinea*, Port Moresby: IASER Monograph No. 11, 77–145.

Skeldon, R. (1980) Recent urban growth in Papua New Guinea, *Australian Geographer*, 14, 267–77.

Smith, D.G.V. (1992) Coffee marketing margins in Papua New Guinea, in E. Fleming and H. Coulter (eds) *Agricultural Export Marketing in the South Pacific*, Canberra: NCDS Pacific Policy Paper No. 8, 148–60.

Smith, M.F. (1980) Bloody time and bloody scarcity: capitalism, authority and the transformation of temporal experience in a Papua New Guinea village, *American Ethnologist*, 9, 503–18.

Smith, M.F. (1982) The Catholic ethic and the spirit of alcohol use in an East Sepik Province village, in M. Marshall (ed.) *Through a Glass Darkly: Beer and Modernization in Papua New Guinea*, Port Moresby: IASER Monograph No. 18, 271–88.

Smith, M.F. (1990) Business and the romance of community cooperation on Kairiru Island, in N. Lutkehaus (ed.) *Sepik Heritage*, Durham, NC: Carolina Academic Press, 212–20.

Smith, M.F. (1994) *Hard Times on Kairiru Island: Poverty, Development and Morality in a Papua New Guinea Village*, Honolulu: University of Hawaii Press.

Smith, R. (1991) Biological investigations into the impact of the Ok Tedi Copper Mine, in D. Lawrence and T. Cansfield-Smith (eds) *Sustainable Development for Traditional Inhabitants of the Torres Strait Region*, Canberra: Great Barrier Reef Marine Park Authority, 261–82.

Smith, T., Earland, J., Bhatia, K., Heywood, P. and Singleton, N. (1993) Linear growth of children in Papua New Guinea in relation to dietary, environmental and genetic factors, *Ecology of Food and Nutrition*, 31, 1–25.

Somare, M. (1973) New goals for New Guinea, *Pacific Perspectives*, 2, 1–4.

Somare, M. (1975) *Sana: An Autobiography of Michael Somare*, Port Moresby: Niugini Press.

Somare, M. (1977) Foreword, in J.H. Winslow (ed.) *The Melanesian Environment*, Canberra: ANU Press, ix–xii.

Somare, M. (1985) The past ten years of independence, *Yagl-Ambu*, 12(1), March, 5–10.

Sorenson, E.R. (1972) Socio-ecological change among the Fore of New Guinea, *Current Anthropology*, 13, 349–83.

Sorenson, E.R. (1976) *The Edge of the Forest: Land Childhood and Change in a New Guinea Protoagricultural Society*, Washington, DC: Smithsonian Institution Press.

Souter, G. (1963) *New Guinea: The Last Unknown*, Sydney: Angus and Robertson.

Southern, R.J. (1973) *Road Transport in the New Guinea Highlands*, Port Moresby: UPNG Department of Geography Occasional Paper No. 6.

Standish, B. (1993) Papua New Guinea in 1992: Challenges for the State, *Asian Survey*, 33, 211–17.

Standish, B. (1994) Papua New Guinea: the search for security in a weak state, in A. Thompson (ed.) *Papua New Guinea: Issues for Australian Security Planners*, Canberra: Australian Defence Studies Centre, 51–97.

Standish, B. (1996) Elections in Simbu: towards gunpoint democracy?, in Y. Saffu (ed.) *The 1992 PNG Election: Change and Continuity in Electoral Politics*, Canberra: ANU Political and Social Change Monograph No. 23, 277–322.

Standish, W. (1978a) Pork, talk and beer: colonial and post-colonial electioneering in Chimbu, Papua New Guinea Highlands, Canberra: unpub. mimeo, ANU.

Standish, W. (1978b) *The 'Big-man' Model Reconsidered: Power and Stratification in Chimbu*, Port Moresby: IASER Discussion Paper No. 22.

Standish, W. (1979) *Provincial Government in Papua New Guinea: Early Lessons from Chimbu*, Port Moresby: IASER Monograph No. 7.

Standish, W. (1981) Maunten na barat: policy-making in Chimbu Province, in J.A. Ballard (ed.) *Policy Making in a New State: Papua New Guinea 1972–77*, Brisbane: University of Queensland Press, 280–305.

Standish, W. (1983) Power to the people? Decentralization in Papua New Guinea, *Public Administration and Development*, 3, 223–38.

Stanner, W.E.H. (1951) The economic development of Pacific peasant peoples against their social background, Canberra: unpub. mimeo.

Stein, L. (1991) *Papua New Guinea: Economic Situation and Outlook*, Canberra: AIDAB International Development Issues No. 16.

Stein, L. (1992) Structural adjustment in Papua New Guinea, *Pacific Economic Bulletin*, 7(2), 25–30.

Stent, W.R. (1984) *The Development of a Market Economy in the Abelam*, Port Moresby: IASER Monograph No. 20.

Stephen, M. (1974) Continuity and change in Mekeo society, 1890–1971, Canberra: unpub. Ph.D. thesis, ANU.

Stevenson, M. (1987) Wage labour and intercultural relations, in M. Pinches and S. Lakha (eds) *Wage Labour and Social Change*, Melbourne: Monash Papers on Southeast Asia No. 16, 31–44.

Stewart, R.G. (1984) Autonomy, dependency and the state in Papua New Guinea, in R. May (ed.) *Social Stratification in Papua New Guinea*, Canberra: ANU Department of Political and Social Change Working Paper No. 5, 82–118.

Stewart, R.G. (1987) Coffee, development and class struggle in Papua New Guinea, in C. Jennett and R. Stewart (eds) *Three Worlds of Inequality: Race, Class and Gender*, Melbourne: Macmillan, 202–42.

Stewart, R.G. (1992) *Coffee: The Political Economy of an Export Industry in Papua New Guinea*, Boulder, CO: Westview Press.

Story, D. (1989) The 'non-growth state' within the internationalisation of capital: economic policy in PNG in the 1980s, *Yagl-Ambu*, 15, 50–65.

Story, D. (1990) Households in change in rural PNG, *Yagl-Ambu*, 15, 50–102.

Strathern, A.J. (1975) By toil or by guile? The use of coils and crescents by Tolai and Hagen big men, *Journal de la Société des Océanistes*, 49, 363–78.

Strathern, A.J. (1982) Tribesmen or peasants?, in A. Strathern (ed.) *Inequality in New Guinea Highlands Societies*, Cambridge: Cambridge University Press, 137–57.

Strathern, A.J. (1987a) Problems of health and development strategy in the Western Highlands, Papua New Guinea, in T. Suzuki and R. Ohtsuka (eds) *Human Ecology of Health and Survival in Asia and the South Pacific*, Tokyo: University of Tokyo Press, 133–47.

Strathern, A.J. (1987b) Social classes in Mount Hagen? The early evidence, *Ethnology*, 26, 245–60.

Strathern, A.J. (1989) Health care and medical pluralism: cases from Mount Hagen, in S. Frankel and G. Lewis (eds) *A Continuing Trial of Treatment: Health Care and Medical Pluralism in Papua New Guinea*, Dordrecht: Kluwer, 141–54.

Strathern, A.J. (1991) Struggles for meaning, in A. Biersack (ed.) *Clio in Oceania: toward a historical anthropology*, Washington, DC: Smithsonian Institute Press. 205–30.

Strathern, A.J. (1992) Let the bow go down, in R. Ferguson and N. Whitehead (eds) *War in the Tribal Zone*, Santa Fe: School of American Research Press, 229–50.

Strathern, A.J. (1993) Violence and political change in Papua New Guinea, *Bijdragen tot de Taal*, 149, 718–36.

Strathern, M. (1972) Absentee businessmen: the reaction at home to Hageners migrating to Port Moresby, *Oceania*, 43, 19–39.

Strathern, M. (1975) *No Money On Our Skins: Hagen Migrants in Port Moresby*, Port Moresby: New Guinea Research Bulletin No. 61.

Strathern, M. (1977) The disconcerting tie: attitudes of Hagen migrants towards home, in R.J May (ed.) *Change and Movement*, Canberra: ANU Press, 247–66.

Strathern, M., ed. (1987) *Dealing with Inequality*, Cambridge: Cambridge University Press.

Strathern, M. (1991) *Partial Connections*, Savage: Rowman and Littlefield.

Sturt, R. (1972) Infant and toddler mortality in the Sepik, *Papua New Guinea Medical Journal*, 15, 215–20.

Sullivan, N. (1993) Film and television production in Papua New Guinea: how media became the message, *Public Culture*, 5, 533–55.

Sundhaussen, U. (1977) Ideology and nation-building in Papua New Guinea, *Australian Outlook*, 31, 308–318.

Swatridge, C. (1985) *Delivering the Goods: Education as Cargo in Papua New Guinea*, Manchester: Manchester University Press.

Tapari, B. (1988) *Problems of Rural Development in the Western Papuan Fringe: A Case Study of the Morehead District, Western Province*, Port Moresby: UPNG Department of Geography Occasional Paper No. 9.

Taylor, R. (1992) Sustained yield forest management in Papua New Guinea: can it survive the demands of landowners and politicians?, in S. Henningham and R. May (eds) *Resources, Development and Politics in the Pacific Islands*, Bathurst: Crawford House, 129–44.

Tefuarani, N. and Smiley, M. (1989) A study of compliance of paediatric patients attending for tuberculosis treatment in the National Capital District, *Papua New Guinea Medical Journal*, 32, 177–80.

Temu, I. (1993) Export processing zone policy in Papua New Guinea, *Pacific Economic Bulletin*, 8, 35–9.

Territory of Papua and New Guinea (1948) *Report of the Economic Development Committee*, Port Moresby.

Territory of Papua New Guinea (1968) *Programmes and Policies for the Economic Development of Papua and New Guinea*, Port Moresby.

Thomason, J. and Edwards, K. (1991) Using indicators to assess quality of hospital service in Papua New Guinea, *International Journal of Health Planning and Management*, 6, 309–24.

Thomason, J. and Newbrander, W. (1991) A survey of Papua New Guinea's health sector financing and expenditure, *Papua New Guinea Medical Journal*, 34, 129–43.

Thomason, J., Newbrander, W.C. and Kolehmainen-Aitken, R. (eds) (1991) *Decentralization in a Developing Country: The Experience of Papua New Guinea and its Health Service*, Canberra: ANU NCDS Pacific Research Monograph No. 25.

Thompson, H. (1985) The rural economy of Papua New Guinea: blissful ignorance, *Yagl-Ambu*, 12(3), September, 4–18.

Thompson, H. (1986) Subsistence agriculture in Papua New Guinea, *Journal of Rural Studies*, 2, 233–43.

Thompson, H. (1990) *Mining and the Environment in Papua New Guinea*, Perth: Murdoch University Economics Programme Working Paper No. 39.

Thompson, H. and MacWilliam, S. (1992) *The Political Economy of Papua New Guinea*, Manila: Journal of Contemporary Asia Publishers.

Thompson, L. (1996) Porgera's pollution, *Pacific Islands Monthly*, 66(3), March, 44–5.

Tilbury, F.E. and Tilbury, R.N. (1993) Urban migration from the Mount Brown area of the Inland Rigo District of Central Province, Papua New Guinea, in T. Taufa and C. Bass (eds) *Population, Family Health and Development*, Port Moresby: UPNG Press, 105–24.

Tilton, J., Millett, J. and Ward, R. (1986) *Minerals and Mining Policy in Papua New Guinea*, Port Moresby: Institute of National Affairs.

Tinker, H. (1965) *Reorientations: Studies on Asia in Transition*, London: Pall Mall.

Townsend, B. (1988) Giving away the river: environmental issues in the construction of the Ok Tedi mine, 1981–84, in J. Pernetta (ed.) *Potential Impacts of Mining on the Fly River*, Noumea: United Nations Environment Programme, 107–19.

Townsend, D. (1977) The 1976 coffee boom in Papua New Guinea, *Australian Geographer*, 13, 419–22.

Townsend, D. (1980a) Disengagement and incorporation – the post-colonial reaction in the rural villages of Papua New Guinea, *Pacific Viewpoint*, 21, 1–25.

Townsend, D. (1980b) Articulation, dissolution and migration: the partial integration of the Hube area, Papua New Guinea, *Tijdschrift voor Economische en Sociale Geografie*, 71, 285–94.

Townsend, D. (1980c) Spread effects among food producers in Port Moresby's hinterland, Newcastle: unpub. paper to Institute of Australian Geographers Conference.

Townsend, P.K. (1985) *The Situation of Children in Papua New Guinea*, Port Moresby: IASER.

Treadgold, M.L. (1978a) Regional inequality in Papua New Guinea: some new evidence, *Pacific Viewpoint*, 19, 129–48.

Treadgold, M.L. (1978b) *The Regional Economy of Bougainville: Growth and Structural Change*, Canberra: ANU Development Studies Centre Occasional Paper No. 10.

Treadgold, M.L. (1987) *Inter-Provincial Income Inequality in Papua New Guinea 1966 to 1983*, Canberra: NCDS Islands/Australia Working Paper No. 87/10.

Tree, I. (1996) *Islands in the Clouds: Travels in the Highlands of New Guinea*, Melbourne: Lonely Planet.

Trompf, G. (1994) *Payback: The Logic of Retribution in Melanesian Religions*, Cambridge: Cambridge University Press.

Turner, A. (1984) Labour migration and rural development: the cases of Ayuan and Ajoa, Honolulu: unpub. MA thesis, University of Hawaii.

Turner, M. (1986a) Economic development in Papua New Guinea: the new orthodoxy, *Pacific Affairs*, 59, 476–83.

Turner, M. (1986b) Plantations, politics and policy-making in Papua New Guinea, 1965–1986, *Journal de la Société des Océanistes*, 82–3, 129–38.

Turner, M. (1986c) *The Framework of Rural Development in Papua New Guinea*, Port Moresby: UPNG Land Studies Centre Occasional Paper 86/3.

Turner, M. (1990) *Papua New Guinea: The Challenge of Independence*, Melbourne: Penguin.

Tuzin, D.F. (1972) Yam symbolism in the Sepik: an interpretative account, *Southwestern Journal of Anthropology*, 28, 230–54.

Tuzin, D.F. (1976) *The Ilahita Arapesh: Dimensions of Unity*, Berkeley: University of California Press.

Tuzin, D.F. (1988) Prospects of village death in Ilahita, *Oceania*, 59, 81–104.

UNDP (1994) *Pacific Human Development Report*, Suva: UNDP.

UNDP (1995) *Human Development Report*, Oxford: Oxford University Press.

UNDP/ILO-ARTEP (1993) *Papua New Guinea: Challenges for Employment and Human Resources Development*, New Delhi: ILO-ARTEP.

UNFPA (1984) *Population Perspectives: Statements by World Leaders*, New York: UNFPA.

Vail, J. (1993) The impact of the Mt Kare goldrush on the people of the Tari District, in T. Taufa and C. Bass (eds) *Population, Family Health and Development*, Port Moresby: UPNG Press, 256–66.

Vallance, P., Anderson, H. and Alpers, M. (1987) Smoking habits in a rural community in the Highlands of Papua New Guinea in 1970 and 1984, *Papua New Guinea Medical Journal*, 30, 277–80.

Varpiam, T., Turner, M. and Hulme, D. (1984) Problems and prospects for import substitution: the experience of fresh fish marketing in Port Moresby, *Australian Geographer*, 16, 58–60.

Vavine, P.W. (1984) Ivane Settlement – a case study of first generation migrants to Port Moresby, Papua New Guinea, *Ambio*, 13, 309.

Voutas, A.C. (1981) Policy initiative and the pursuit of control, 1972–74, in J. Ballard (ed.) *Policy-Making in a New State: Papua New Guinea 1972–77*, Brisbane: University of Queensland Press, 33–47.

Waddell, E. (1972) *The Mound Builders: Agricultural Practices, Environment and Society in the Central Highlands of New Guinea*, Seattle: University of Washington Press.

Waddell, E. (1973) Raiapu Enga adaptive strategies: structure and general implications, in H. Brookfield (ed.) *The Pacific in Transition*, London: Arnold, 25–54.

Waiko, J. (1993) *A Short History of Papua New Guinea*, Melbourne: Oxford University Press.

Walsh, A.C. (1982) *Street Vending in Port Moresby, 1982*, Port Moresby: UPNG Department of Geography.

Walsh, A.C. (1983a) The Papua New Guinea informal sector: illusion, dream or nightmare? *Australian Geographer*, 15, 414–17.

Walsh, A.C. (1983b) Up and down the Papua New Guinea urban hierarchy, *Yagl-Ambu*, 10(3), September, 28–46.

Walsh, A.C. (1985) *Inter-Provincial Migration in Papua New Guinea*, Port Moresby: 1980 National Population Census Research Monograph No. 3.

Walter, M.A.H.B. (1981a) Put yourself in the villager's position, in M. Walter (ed.) *What Do We Do About Plantations*, Port Moresby: IASER Monograph No. 15, 102–6.

Walter, M.A.H.B. (1981b) Cult movements and community development associations: revolution and evolution in the Papua New Guinea countryside, in R. Gerritsen *et al.*, *Road Belong Development*, Canberra: ANU Department of Political and Social Change Working Paper No. 3, 81–116.

Ward, R.G. (1971) Internal migration and urbanisation in Papua New Guinea, in M.W. Ward (ed.) *Population Growth and Socio-economic Change: Papers from the Second Demography Seminar*, Canberra: New Guinea Research Bulletin No. 42, 81–107.

Ward, R.G. (1973) Urbanisation in the Pacific – facts and policies, in R.J. May (ed.) *Priorities in Melanesian Development*, UPNG and ANU, 362–72.

Ward, R.G. (1980) Migration, myth and magic in Papua New Guinea, *Australian Geographical Studies*, 18, 119–34.

Ward, R.G. (1982) Changes in subsistence cropping, in R.J. May and H. Nelson (eds) *Melanesia: Beyond Diversity*, Canberra: ANU, 327–38.

Ward, R.G. and Ballard, J. (1976) In their own image: Australia's impact on Papua New Guinea and lessons for future aid, *Australian Outlook*, 30, 439–58.

Ward, R.G. and Proctor, A. (1980) *South Pacific Agriculture: Choices and Constraints*, Canberra: ANU Press.

Ward, R.G., Howlett, D., Kissling, C.C. and Weinand, H.C. (1978) *Maket Raun:* the introduction of periodic markets to Papua New Guinea, in R.H.T. Smith (ed.) *Market-Place Trade: Periodic Markets, Hawkers and Traders in Africa, Asia and Latin America*, Vancouver: Centre for Transportation Studies, 99–111.

Warry, W. (1987) *Chuave Polities: Changing Patterns of Leadership in the Papua New Guinea Highlands*, Canberra: ANU Political and Social Change Monograph No. 4.

Watson, J.B. (1985) The precontact northern Tairora: high mobility in a crowded field, in M. Chapman and R. Prothero (eds) *Circulation in Population Movement: Substance and Concepts from the Melanesian Case*, London: Routledge and Kegan Paul, 15–38.

Weeks, S. (1981) Education, in S. Weeks (ed.) *Oksapmin: Development and Change*, Port Moresby: UPNG Education Research Unit Occasional Paper No. 7, 95–134.

Weinand, H.C. and Ward, R.G. (1979) Area preferences in Papua New Guinea, *Australian Geographical Studies*, 17, 64–75.

Weiner, A.B. (1976) *Women of Value, Men of Renown: New Perspectives in Trobriand Exchange*, Austin: University of Texas Press.

Weiner, A.B. (1988) *The Trobrianders of Papua New Guinea*, New York: Holt, Rinehart and Winston.

Weiner, J.F. (1986) The social organisation of Foi Silk production: the anthropology of marginal development, *Journal of the Polynesian Society*, 94, 421–39.

Welsch, R. (1986) Primary health care and local self-determination: policy implications from rural Papua New Guinea, *Human Organization*, 45, 103–112.

Wesche, D. (1987) The incorporation and development of traditional medicine with western scientific medicine: some ethical considerations, in S. Stratigos and P. Hughes (eds) *The Ethics of Development: Justice and the Distribution of Health Care*, Port Moresby: UPNG Press, 71–8.

Wesley-Smith, T. (1993) Papua New Guinea, *The Contemporary Pacific*, 5, 411–21.

White, J. (1990) Education, inequality and social change in the Rai Coast district of Papua New Guinea, in J. Connell (ed.) *Migration and Development in the South Pacific*, Canberra: NCDS Pacific Research Monograph No. 24, 120–35.

Whitworth, A. (1989) *Public Enterprise Policy in Papua New Guinea*, Canberra: NCDS Islands/Australia Working Paper No. 89/1.

Williamson, P. (1977) Is there an urban informal sector or just poverty?, *Yagl-Ambu*, 4(1): 5–24.

Wilson, R.K. (1975) Socioeconomic indicators applied to sub-districts of Papua New Guinea, *Yagl-Ambu*, 2, 71–87.

Wolfers, E.P. (1975) *Race Relations and Colonial Rule in Papua New Guinea*, Sydney: Australian and New Zealand Book Company.

Wolfers, E.P. (1981) Papua New Guinea in 1980: a change of government, aid and foreign relations, *Asian Survey*, 21, 274–84.

Wood, A. and Humphreys, G. (1982) Traditional soil conservation in Papua New Guinea, in L. Morauta, J. Pernetta and W. Heaney (eds) *Traditional Conservation in Papua New Guinea*, Port Moresby: IASER, 93–114.

Wood-Bradley, R., Flint, D.M. and Wahlquist, M.L. (1980) Food and nutrition in an independent Papua New Guinea, *Search*, 11(3), March, 73–7.

World Bank (1965) *The Economic Development of the Territory of Papua and New Guinea: Report of a Mission Organized by the IBRD*, Baltimore, MD: Johns Hopkins University Press.

World Bank (1978) *Papua New Guinea: Its Economic Situation and Prospects for Development*, Washington, DC: International Bank for Reconstruction and Development.

World Bank (1990) *Papua New Guinea: The Forestry Sector: A Tropical Forestry Action Plan Review*, Washington, DC: International Bank for Reconstruction and Development.

World Bank (1992) *Papua New Guinea: Competitiveness, Growth and Structural Adjustment*, Washington, DC: International Bank for Reconstruction and Development.

Wormsley, W. (1978) Imbonggu culture and change: traditional society, labour migration and change in the Southern Highlands Province, Papua New Guinea, Pittsburgh: unpub. Ph.D. thesis, University of Pittsburgh.

Worsley, P. (1957) *The Trumpet Shall Sound: A Study of 'Cargo' Cults in Melanesia*, New York: Schocken.

Wright, A. (1985) Marine resource use in Papua New Guinea: can traditional concepts and contemporary development be integrated?, in K. Ruddle and R. Johannes (eds) *The Traditional Knowledge and Management of Coastal Systems in Asia and the Pacific*, Jakarta: UNESCO, 82–99.

Wylie, J. and Sims, R. (1981) Commercial agriculture production in Papua New Guinea, in M. Walter (ed.) *What Do We Do About Plantations?*, Port Moresby: IASER Monograph No. 15, 200–4.

Young, M.W. (1971) *Fighting with Food: Leadership, Values and Social Control in a Massim Society*, Cambridge: Cambridge University Press.

Young, M.W. (1983) The best workmen in Papua: Goodenough Islanders and the labour trade, 1900–1960, *Journal of Pacific History*, 18, 74–95.

Zelenietz, M. and Grant, J. (1986) The ambiguities of education in Kilenge, Papua New Guinea, *Pacific Studies*, 9, 33–52.

Zelenietz, M. and Saito, H. (1989) The Kilenge and the war, in G. White and L. Lindstrom (eds) *The Pacific Theater: Island Representations of World War II*, Honolulu: University of Hawaii Press, 167–84.

Zimmer, L. (1986) Card playing among the Gende: a system for keeping money and social relationships alive, *Oceania*, 56, 245–63.

Zimmer, L. (1990a) When tomorrow comes: future opportunities and current investment patterns in an area of high out-migration, in J. Connell (ed.) *Migration and Development in the South Pacific*, Canberra: NCDS Pacific Monograph No. 24, 82–96.

Zimmer, L. (1990b) Conflict and violence in Gende Society: older persons as victims, troublemakers and perpetrators, *Pacific Studies*, 13, 205–24.

Zimmer-Tamakoshi, L. (1993) Nationalism and sexuality in Papua New Guinea, *Pacific Studies*, 16, 61–97.

Zimmerman, L. (1973) Migration and urbanization amongst the Buang of Papua New Guinea, Detroit: unpub. Ph.D. thesis, Wayne State University.

Index